Ted Kaminski

Polish Publicists and Prussian Politics (1890–1894)

Band 38

Studien zur modernen Geschichte

Herausgegeben von
Fritz Fischer
Klaus-Detlev Grothusen
Günter Moltmann
Bernd-Jürgen Wendt

Universität Hamburg

Franz Steiner Verlag Wiesbaden GmbH
Stuttgart 1988

Ted Kaminski

Polish Publicists and Prussian Politics

The Polish Press in Poznan during the Neue Kurs of Chancellor Leo von Caprivi 1890–1894

Franz Steiner Verlag Wiesbaden GmbH
Stuttgart 1988

Gedruckt mit Unterstützung
der Universität Hamburg

CIP-Titelaufnahme der Deutschen Bibliothek

Kaminski, Ted:
Polish publicists and Prussian politics : the Polish press in Poznań during the chancellorship of Leo von Caprivi 1890 – 1894 / Ted Kaminski. – Stuttgart : Steiner-Verl. Wiesbaden, 1988
(Studien zur modernen Geschichte ; Bd. 38)
ISBN 3-515-04948-7
NE: GT

Printed in the Fed. Rep. of Germany

TABLE OF CONTENTS

PREFACE

This study was accepted by the Fachbereich Geschichtswissenschaft of the Universitaet Hamburg in July 1986 as a Ph.D. thesis. At this time the author would like to thank all those who made its compilation and publication possible.

I should like to extend my appreciation to the employees and administrators of the archives and libraries where the research was conducted. In particular, Dr. J. Dębski and Mgr. J. Wiśniewski facilitated my research of the Polish newspapers at the Raczyński Library in Poznań. I should also like to thank the Universitaet Hamburg for the financial support without which publication of this work would not have been possible.

I should like to extend special thanks to my supervisor, Professor Dr. Klaus-Detlev Grothusen for the advice and expertise offered me during my research. His guidance was particularly helpful in the choice of the theme and its deliniation. His patience and support were instrumental in helping me, a non-German student, to understand the specifics of a dissertation to be submitted to a German university. Each phase of my thesis was met on his part by conscientious study and instructive recommendations. I should like to thank him and all the editors of the "Studien zur modernen Geschichte" as well as the publishing house for the publication of this work in the series. Prof. Dr. Frank Golczewski of the Universitaet der Bundeswehr consented to act as the second reviewer of the work and made many meritorical comments on the text, for which I am indebted. I should like to thank also Prof. Dr. Karl-Heinz Schlarp, who, on short notice, acted as the second examiner and offered useful advice on several points. Finally, I should like to thank Prof. Lech Trzeciakowski of the Adam Mickiewicz University in Poznań for expert advise given me while I was conducting research in Poznań.

No amount of editing work by the author will ever eradicate all the errors encountered in his thesis. At this point, I should like to thank Karen Duehring, Violetta Borucki, Lutz Haefner and Nicholas Mildenhall for their work on the English and German texts.

In our modern times no academic undertaking is possible without the understanding and support of those closest to the author. This is particularly true for authors with a family, where the normal parental division of labour is upset by endless hours poring over notes and the computer. This is why I am dedicating this book to my wife, Barbara, without whose extra labours I would still be writing.

Hamburg, December, 1986

Ted Kaminski

ABBREVIATIONS

Akta PKW	= Akta Komitetu Prowincjonalnego Wyborczego na Wielkie Księstwo Poznańskie
B. Racz.	= Biblioteka Raczyńskich w Poznaniu
BK.	= Biblioteka PAN w Kórniku
Berichte Abg.H.	= Stenographische Berichte ueber die Verhandlungen des Preussischen Hauses des Abgeordneten
Berichte Herrenhaus	= Stenographische Berichte ueber die Verhandlungen des Preussischen Herrenhauses
Berichte Rtg.	= Stenographische Berichte ueber die Verhandlungen des Reichstages
GW.	= Otto von Bismarck, Die gesammelten Werke
PSB.	= Polski Słownik Biograficzny
PP-Posen	= Polizeipraesidium zu Posen
WSB.	= Wielkopolski Słownik Biograficzny

Note about place-names: Wherever a recognized English term does not exist for place-names, the Polish or German names have been used according to the majority of inhabitants. Thus Bromberg (predominantly) German), but Września (predominatly Polish).

Gedruckt mit Unterstuetzung der Universitaet Hamburg

Chapter One: Introduction

1.1 Definition and Deliniation of Theme

The present study will concern itself with the Polish-language press in the city of Poznań during the Caprivi era (1890-1894). It hopes to offer the reader a view of the Polish community during the "Neue Kurs" through its own press; a study of Polish society under Prussian rule in a turbulent and eventful period that witnessed a wide range of political opinion and unprecedented domestic polemic. Although the bulk of the study concerns the Caprivi years, the author has also consulted the press for the critical year 1888, when the Polish loyalists linked so many hopes to the short rule of Friedrich III. The work has tried to concentrate on the theme of public opinion; the thoughts of the Polish community, as represented through the various Polish newspapers, in regard to the many important events of the Caprivi era. Simultaneously, the study will attempt to exploit this hitherto little-used primary source to examine Polish political life under Prussian rule: the organizational structures, the principal orientations, and the 'political education' of Prussian Poles through the medium of the newspaper in their Polish national duties. Confronted by a suspicious and vigilant Prussian bureaucracy and police ever on the lookout for manifestations of 'grosspolnische nationale Agitation', the newspapers played a leading role in the self-expression of Polish society.

In Prussian Poland literacy was near universal by mid-century, in contrast to Galicia and Russian Poland where large pockets of illiteracy existed to 1918. The growth of the political press was a key aspect of the modernization process which by 1900 had undermined the gentry's domination of Polish political life. Several monographs exist which examine the Polish press from various points of view, but to date the crucial transition period of the Neue Kurs has not been specifically dealt with. Recent works by Wiktor Molik and Wojciech Wrzesiński on the Polish press in Poznania (1), and Tadeusz Cieślak in West Prussia (2), have begun to approach the press as a theme worth studying in itself. None of these authors, however, has devoted any significant attention to the Caprivi era. Wrzesiński's essay covered the views of the Dziennik Poznański from 1859 (the year of its founding) to 1914, and barely touched on the Caprivi years. Molik's essay on the Przegląd Poznański offers useful information about the origins of this liberal intelligentsia cultural and political weekly but concerns itself rather with the Hohenlohe years before its collapse in 1896. Of great importance is Molik's essay on the profession of journalism in Prussian Poland from 1890-1914. but this study did not address the dominant political issues of the day. The work of Tadeusz Cieślak in West Prussia has been more intensive, but this province was generally recognised as having a secondary importance in relation to Poznania. For the province of Poznania, a discernible gap exists which the present study will try and fill. Lech Trzeciakowski, professor of history at the Adam Mickiewicz University in Poznań, chose the theme of Polish politics during the Caprivi years as his dissertation thesis in 1959.(3) Trzeciakowski's work was based on a wide range of primary sources, including the all-important archives in Merseburg and Potsdam, and used the Polish press frequently in his thesis. Trzeciakowski has also written two biographies of Roman Szymański, editor and owner of the Orędownik, the only newspaperman in Prussian Poland to have received any biographical attention to date.(4)

German scholarship has shown a greater interest in press studies in general and works by Walter Guenzel, Fritz Prause, Leonhard Mueller and Berthold Wiegand recognized the importance of the Polish press.(5) German scholars felt that the Polish newspapers represented a tremendous weapon in the nationality conflict in the Prussian East. It was stressed that the press mobilized Polish sentiment against Germany and spread the conflict to the previously quiet province of Upper Silesia. Guenzel's study, as the title suggests, concentrated on the era of Bernhard von Buelow (1900-1909), where the Polish press engaged in a continuous war against Chancellor Buelow's determined Germanization campaign. Mueller's work concentrated on ecclesiastical disputes and clerical newspapers largely in Silesia, at a time when the Polish-German rivalry over this province was at its height. Prause's short book discussed the interwar period. Berthold Wiegand came closest to the theme of the present study as he did cover the Caprivi years briefly, but both his and Prause's study were written during the Nazi occupation of Poland and their scholarly value is diminished by their severely tendential tone. In 1936 Wilhelm Muenstermann wrote a very interesting and substantive study of the German press and German public opinion on the Polish question during the Caprivi years.(6) The present work may be seen as a similar effort from the Polish side of the coin.

The importance of the Polish press and public opinion had been noted by many German contemporaries. Leading German newspapers employed writers fluent in Polish to translate and comment upon articles in the Polish press. Some, like the Catholic Germania, regularly reprinted Polish articles while the leading Polish newspapers reprinted much from it. Newspapers like the Hamburger Nachrichten also translated and printed articles from the Polish press, but with a different view in mind from the Germania: they wanted to discredit the Polish community by publishing incriminating articles. The Schulthess' Europaeischer Geschichtskalender quoted the Polish press from time to time, in particular the Dziennik Poznański. The first organisation, apart from the Prussian police, to concern itself systematically with the Polish newspapers was the Ostmarkenverein, which made a point of translating and mailing copies of Polish articles to sensitive receptors of German public opinion. Between 1898 and 1908 the Ostmarkenverein published three volumes of translations of Polish articles,(7) with the clear determination to alarm German society of the 'Polish danger'. The selection of articles, all chosen from the period 1897-1908, reflected the intensity of antagonism which followed the aborted reconciliation attempt under Caprivi.

Two German scholars of the Imperial Period paid a good deal of attention to the Polish press: Ludwig Bernhard and Wilhelm von Massow.(10) Massow, editor-in-chief of the Berliner Neueste Nachrichten, was stationed in Poznań as an army officer from 1889-1893, and could comment on the activities of the Polish community from firsthand knowledge. In his book on the Polish danger to the German east he devoted 40 pages to the anti-German functioning of the Polish press.(9) Professor Bernhard, a member of the Ostmarkenverein, was the first German scholar to make an exhaustive study of Polish organizational life and placed great emphasis upon the Polish press as a factor in the growth of political pluralism within Prussia. Other scholars, including the often-quoted Manfred Laubert and Friedrich Schinkel, contented themselves with pointing out the dangerous anti-German influence of the Polish newspapers.(10)

Most recently, two American authors, Richard Blanke at the University of Maine and Harry K. Rosenthal of Southern California have used the Polish press extensively in books and articles on Prussian Poland.(11) Blanke's book, which is the most detailed study of Prussian Poland in the English language, devotes a good deal of attention to the Caprivi era and emphasizes the importance of

The Polish newspapers as a power to be reckoned with. Rosenthal's articles similarly stress the leading role of the Polish newspapers in both promoting and combating the loyalist initiative.

The Caprivi years have been chosen as the time period under consideration for several reasons. Firstly, the years 1890-1894 represented the last time Germans and Poles could talk about "reconciliation" with any seriousness; after 1894 the nationality conflict deteriorated to what Bogdan von Hutten-Czapski called "ein regelrechter deutsch-polnischer Kleinkrieg".(12) Both before and after the Caprivi interlude, the German-Polish relationship was characterized by mutual suspicion, hostility and social isolation. While the Caprivi years saw enough of these darker feelings, there also existed a conscious attempt by leading Poles and Germans to overcome mutual resentment and open a new phase in Prussia's Polenpolitik. For the Polish community, the "era ugodowa" constituted a abortive attempt to duplicate the pro-monarchical stance of the Galician nobility in order to secure a greater amount of social and cultural autonomy. Political autonomy was out of the question in Prussia, but Polish loyalists hoped that consistent support for Caprivi in the Reichstag would lead to a dismantling of Bismarck's oppressive legislation passed by the Prussian Landtag. For the first time since Bismarck's accession to power in 1862 there was reason to believe that the Prussian government would retreat from a 'hardline' Germanization policy towards a more relaxed, humane assimilation that would recognize the "special status" of Poles within Prussia. They felt that their very survival as a distinct people was dependent on better treatment at the hands of the state. What few concessions Caprivi permitted while Ministerpraesident of Prussia gave everyone, both friend and critic, the impression that he was genuinely interested in changing course. The debate within German public opinion was furious and far out of proportion to the limited concessions that the Poles received. Indeed, Harry Rosenthal has gone so far as to say that Caprivi had no real Polish policy at all and was only reacting in a very uneven manner to a Polish initiative.(13) Nevertheless, the Caprivi Polenpolitik aroused German nationalists and the 'Bismarckfronde' to great anger, and played no small roll in bringing about his fall.

The years 1890-1894 also are significant in a more general way for the development of Polish society under Prussian rule. For the first time the sacrosanct principle of 'national solidarity' was violated and a form of political pluralism introduced. The hegemony of the Polish szlachta, in particular the wealthy magnate families who had dominated Polish political life in Prussia since the partitions, suffered a serious setback and was to fall into full eclipse within a decade after the collapse of the loyalist initiative. The Polish press played a great role in these transformations, both reporting on and manipulating events in the interests of owners and readers.

The present study will concern itself with the following political dailies: The Dziennik Poznański, Kuryer Poznański, Goniec Wielkopolski, Orędownik, Postęp and Wielkopolanin. For 1894 it will also take into consideration the Przegląd Poznański, which appeared weekly and was in fact a political paper despite its claim to be a cultural review. This list represents all the political newspapers that appeared in Poznań during the Caprivi era. The Gazeta Robotnicza, the voice of the Polish Social Democrats, has been excluded because it was published in Berlin and not Poznań, and because it could boast of a circulation of only 174 copies in the whole province of Poznania by 1895.(14) In addition to political newspapers, Poznań published a number of trade, agricultural and economic newspapers, but these will not be examined here. The present study will also exclude the Polish press in West Prussia, for two reasons: West Prussia's population was predominantly German and the province was clearly subordinate to Poznań as the social and political capital of Prussian Poland. The Gazeta Grudziądzka, a West Prussian Polish paper whose circulation reached the remarkable level of 128,000 in 1914, was founded only in 1894, and had no influence on the events of that year.(15) Poznań contained the largest Polish community in Prussia and remained so until 1918.

1.2 Structure of the Study and Problem Areas

The present study consists of seven chapters of which the first is the introduction; thus, there are six chapters that deal with the body of material itself. The principal thought in deciding upon the organization of the chapters has been chronological with the exception of chapter two which looks at the press from many aspects and surpasses at times the chronological bounds implied in the title.

It was thought essential to include an in-depth study of the origins of newspapers, circulation figures, ownership and business organization, press laws and censorship, editorial leadership and policy. Without such a section, citing various newspapers would leave the reader unclear as to the relevance of the source: who stood behind the various newspapers and how important were their statements? It is hoped that this section will familiarize the reader with each of the seven newspapers and their role in Poznań's Polish press constellation. In doing so a wide range of questions are addressed which serve to define their socio-political positions: the relationship to the Prussian government; the attitudes toward the war question and Russia; the hostility towards "godless international Social Democracy; and press alliances and disputes. It is interesting that despite the sharp invective levelled at each other, the Polish newspapers held similar viewpoints on a wide range of social and political problems of the day.

The Dziennik Poznański is examined first because it was without doubt the leading voice of the Polish landed gentry, and is followed by its client paper, the mass-circulation Wielkopolanin. The next two papers account for the minority groups within the Polish gentry class; the voice of the ultramontanes (Kuryer Poznański), and the irreconcilable nationalists (Goniec Wielkopolski). These four gentry newspapers are followed by the 'populist' or middle-class press: the radical Orędownik, which led the struggle against the domination of the landed gentry, the anti-Semetic Postęp, and the cultural weekly Przegląd Poznański, which later observers saw as the first evidence of the National Democratic movement in Prussian Poland. In cases where more information is available about the editors-in-chief, such as Franciszek Dobrowolski (Dziennik Poznański), the Kantecki brothers (Kuryer Poznański) and Roman Szymański (Orędownik), their roles in the social and political life of Poznań are examined. The final section of this chapter looks at the links of the Polish newspapers to the Komitet Prowincjonalny Wyborczy na Wielkie Księstwo Poznańskie, the Central Electoral Committee of the Grand Duchy of Poznań (hereafter Central Committee), the Polish political machine in Prussia.

The remainder of the work (chapters three through seven) examines the Caprivi era in a chronological manner and the work of the Polish newspapers towards the formation of public opinion and policy. The author has felt it necessary to go back briefly to the beginnings of the Polish loyalist movement around 1884 and the very important events of 1888, to understand better Polish political thought during the Neue Kurs of Caprivi. The remainder of chapter three looks at the early disputes over the loyalist initiative in 1890: the Polish votes on the "small" Army Bill of 1890; the silence of the Polish press over the passage of the first part of the Rentengutsgesetz of 1890; and the first phase of the process leading up to the appointment of Florian Stablewski to the Archbishopric of Gniezno-Poznań. This last theme has been divided into two phases: the first contained in chapter three which covers the events from the death of Archbishop Dinder (May 1890) to the end of 1890; while the second contained in chapter four looks at the events from September 1891 to the appointment in December, 1891. It was felt desirable to divide the Stablewski question into two phases to remain loyal to the guiding principle of chronological methodology.

Chapter four examines the era of relative Polish "successes" in 1891: limited concessions in the fields of emigrant-expulsion policy; private language teaching; and the very important appointment of Stablewski. It also looks at the significance of the appointment of Graf Robert von Zedlitz-Truetzschler as Kultusminister and the Polish reaction to the possibility of German-Polish co-operation in combating the growing strength of Social Democracy in the Prussian East. The year of the greatest Polish successes also featured an open quarrel among the Polish powerbrokers over the policy of loyalism when the priest Ludwik Jażdżewski and the aristocrat Józef Kościelski attacked each other in public, thus breaking a long-standing tradition of public silence when the politicians could not agree.

Chapter five is entitled "The Period of Transition", and examines the events from the spring of 1892 to the spring of 1893, when the Neue Kurs towards the Poles shifted slowly away from the promising concessions of 1891. Attention here is given to the collapse of the Prussian School Reform Bill of March 1892 and the ensuing personnel changes in the Prussian cabinet, Bismarck's sharp attacks on Chancellor Caprivi's Polish policy, and the Polish attitudes towards an impending Russo- German war. This chapter is of great importance because the events described therein signalled to all clear-headed observers the limitations of the reconciliation process. It was the failure of the loyalists in the Polish political apparatus to recognize this fact that led to the strife in 1893 and 1894.

Chapter six is devoted to the domestic struggle within the Polish community between populists and the gentry-dominated political apparatus over the Great Army Bill votes, the Reichstag election of 1893 and the aftermath in Poznania's principal towns. The events of 1893 constituted what may be called a "take-off" phase in the development of the Polish middle class and its progress towards political maturity. There is a particular wealth of documentary evidence in the records of the Raczyński Library pertaining to the election of 1893 and it is useful to compare them with newspaper and police accounts. The chapter covers the period from spring to autumn, 1893, from the first clashes within the Polish press over how to vote on the Great Army Bill to the Prussian Landtag election of October.

Chapter seven begins with the controversy over Chancellor Caprivi's trade treaties in 1894. It then looks at the the new language bill of March; the pilgrimages to Bismarck in Varzin that gave rise the the formation of the Deutsche Ostmarkenverein; the anti-Polish speech of Kaiser Wilhelm II at Thorn and finally the resignation of Caprivi and the end of the Neue Kurs. Chapter seven also concerns internal political developments within the Polish community: the campaign to select a replacement for the seat of Józef Kościelski in Inowrocław; and the futile attempts to resolve the Poznań secession that had plagued the Polish community from the previous year.

A chronological methodology has resulted in frequent changes of theme and location, from concessions to ministerial changes, from Poznań to Berlin, and from issues as seemingly unrelated as the anti-Polish attacks of the 'Bismarckpresse' to quarrels among Polish politicians in Poznań. Yet to deal with the Caprivi reconciliation era on a thematic basis would result in the loss of continuity in the formation of Polish public opinion. Public opinion is formed by an interplay of various factors all active at a given time. It is easier to study it through a chronological approach rather than a thematic one, although there is room for debate on this subject.

1.3 Primary Sources

The principal primary source for this study is, logically enough, the Polish language press printed in Poznań between 1890 and 1894. All the material is found exclusively in the public libraries of Poznań, with the notable exception of the Goniec Wielkopolski, which has not survived in its entirety. The author has been forced to re-create the views of the Goniec Wielkopolski until January 1893 from the other Polish newspapers, which often cited it in their press quarrels. From January, 1893 to September, 1894, the author has relied on the records of the Poznań police, who translated and compiled a number of important editorials from the Goniec in the "Gesamtueberblick ueber die polnische Tagesliteratur".(16) The issues of the last quarter of 1894 have been preserved. Although the author is aware of the shortcomings arising from the incomplete stock of the Goniec Wielkopolski, he has found the contributions of the Goniec essential to the development of the domestic Polish debate and could not exclude it.

There are several reasons why this source has been chosen for concentration. Firstly, other primary sources have largely been appraised and used previously. The principal archival sources - the papers of the Ministerium des Innern and the Ministerium der Geistlichen, Unterrichts- und Medizinalangelegenheiten in Merseburg, or the Reichskanzlei in Potsdam - have been widely explored by the many scholars, both Polish and German, who have had access to them. The Polish language press remains one of the few substantial bodies of primary material yet to be studied systematically.

Secondly, the press offers the scholar a rich source of information on the social and political life of the Polish community in Prussia which cannot be reproduced from Prussian archives. The Prussian bureaucrats compiled the archival materials on the Poles from the perspective of "rebellion", "treason" and "internal subversion". They related to Prussian state security rather than the social, economic and political development of the Polish community. This difference is illustrated nowhere better than in the Polish newspapers. The social inter-actions covered in the press relate to the local economy, the Polish- German friction, social, cultural and political life, religious instruction, agricultural innovations, and the 'Polish view' of every modern question from a European war to the introduction of the telephone. The area of political life was especially well-covered by the newspapers, either 'officially' in the formal declarations issued by the Polish political apparatus or in the 'gossip' spread about by opposition papers. In the words of Witold Jakóbczyk, the leading scholar of the Polish press in Prussia, "All these newspapers provide the historian with a rich source of information in the area of the formation of political orientations, the position of different groups vis-à-vis the partitioning power and the Polish question in general. Newspapers offer more to the historian than other sources." (17)

Thirdly, the Polish newspapers constitute the principal Polish-language source for the period. Unlike Germans, very few Poles kept journals and alternative sources are sparce indeed. The Polish archival materials relating to the functioning of the Central Committee and the local committees are often dull superficial documents which were written in a very formal style usually by committee secretaries devoted to preserving the image of 'national solidarity'. Thanks to the existence of the opposition populist newspapers, the Polish community takes on a much more animated appearance. Without the newspapers, remaining Polish-language primary sources would be insufficient for a serious study.

Keeping in mind the benefits of using the Polish newspapers as a primary source it would be fruitful to consider some of the possible pitfalls. The principal reservation facing the scholar is the question of credibility. The Polish newspapers throughout the period of Prussian rule were regarded as 'staatsfeindlich' and hence subject to great scrutiny by the Prussian police. Articles which too-strongly criticized Prussian officials or called for greater 'national awareness' ('nationale Agitation' in the eyes of the police) were in danger of being confiscated and the editors fined. To avoid penalties and to preserve certain images of the Polish community within Prussia, the papers exercised self-censorship. The Polish press lords considered it their duty to convey a positive picture of the Polish community to the outside world, especially to the policy-makers in Berlin, and did not think twice about omitting information which reflected negatively upon it.

It cannot be stressed enough that the purpose of publicism was not to disseminate accurate information, but to promote the ends of interest groups and owners. The modern reader is astonished at the often brutal manner in which dissenting views were crushed, in which quarrels were covered up, and in which the public was told what it should believe. What is considered today 'objective and investigative reporting' was unknown to the Polish press lords of the 1890s, and each newspaper fiercely promoted a specific political philosophy which often manipulated the facts to suit its case. In particular the gentry press manipulated events to match the political imperatives of its shareholders. Although the populist press disclosed more of the behind-the-scenes dealings its muckraking was intended to discredit the political establishment and it often engaged in outrageous falsifications when it suited its purposes. The anti-Semitic Postęp, which viewed all events as machinations of world Jewry, is a case all by itself. Only by comparing various press accounts with other source materials is a reliable view possible. Any scholar who based his research solely on the Polish newspapers would receive a distorted picture indeed.

Because of the shortcomings stated above, the author has gone to other available source materials for back-up and verification. In the Polish language, two archival source materials are of inestimable value: the records of the Polish political apparatus in Poznania found in the Manuscript Section of the Raczyński Library (18), and the minutes of the Polish Party in the Landtag, found in the Polish state archives at Kórnik.(19) The records of the provincial political apparatus contain the minutes of all political meetings held in the principal towns of the 38 "powiaty" (districts), as well as the records of the Central Committee and the General Assemblies held before every Reichstag or Landtag election to confirm candidates and plot strategy. The most useful files cover the districts of Poznań-miasto (city), Bydgoszcz-miasto (Bromberg-city) Inowrocław and the Central Committee itself. Contained in the files are also protest letters signed by dissident voters and addressed to Franciszek Dobrowolski, secretary of the Central Committee and responsible for correspondence. The chief drawback of these records is that they were written by local district secretaries often more interested in preserving images of social peace and unity than in reflecting accuracy. Bad news and dissenting views were suppressed. Opponents were invariably described as "troublemakers" in the official minutes, agents of the Germans out to destroy "national solidarity.

The minutes of the Landtag Party found in Kórnik are of great value in recreating the thoughts and strategy of the Polish caucus in Berlin to acquire concessions in the sensitive areas of religion, language and land purchases. Unfortunately, the corresponding minutes of the Reichstag Party have been lost.(20) The internal proceedings of the caucus just before important issues came up for debate were never intended for publication and were thus free from the scrutiny of the press. They offer a dispassionate account of disputes, political ploys and often sharp criticisms of deputies who ignored the image of "national solidarity".

Other Polish language primary works used include: the chronicle kept by the Reichstag deputy Roman Komierowski published in 1906 (21), the unpublished letters of the Landtag deputy Henryk Szuman (22), the unpublished biography of the Landtag deputy Piotr Wawrzyniak by J. Kusztelan (23), and the memoirs of one of the founders of the Przegląd Poznański, Bernard Chrzanowski (24).

In the area of German language primary sources, the principal material used has been the stenographic records of the German Reichstag and both houses of the Prussian Landtag. Without any representation in the Prussian cabinet and lacking influential voices promoting the Polish cause in Berlin, the two German parliamentary bodies represented the major medium for Polish political activity. In the view of the Prussian monarch and German Kaiser the Polish question was solely an internal Prussian affair, and most of the parliamentary debates on it took place in the lower Prussian chamber in the spring of each year during the budget reviews of the ministries of the Interior (the Ansiedlungsgesetz review) and Education (the language and educational questions). This was unfortunate, because the Poles could not benefit from the extra leverage they enjoyed thanks to consistent Centrum and SPD support in the Reichstag. Whenever the anti-Kartell parties raised the ill-treatment of the Poles they were sharply reminded that they were interfering in an internal Prussian affair. However, the Polish role in the Reichstag during the Caprivi years was of great significance, since it was here that the divisive issues of the military bills and trade treaties were voted on. The Prussian Landtag also acted as a forum for the Conservative, Centrum, National Liberal and Progressive standpoints represented during the annual 'Polendebatte'. The Polish hopes for a better future under Caprivi's chancellorship were born out of the Reichstag election of February, 1890; they collapsed in the statements by Kultusminister Bosse and Ministerpraesident zu Eulenburg in the Prussian Abgeordnetenhaus.

A second primary source of great value has been the Poznań police archives. (25) The Prussian police kept a keen eye on Polish natonal activity, monitoring almost every aspect of political life. They read, translated and summarized the newspapers, attended and took notes at the political rallies, kept files on leading Polish politicians, newspapermen and priests, and were always interested in visiting Poles from Galicia or the Congress Kingdom. The key files used in this study concern the Polish press: personal files of editors Roman Szymański, Józef Siemianowski, Karol Rzepecki (26); politicians Ferdynand Radziwiłł, Stefan Cegielski, Leon Czarliński (27); newspaper files of the Kuryer Poznański and the Goniec Wielkopolski (28); and other files on a number of aspects of publishing (29). The most valuable files were the "Gesamtueberblick ueber die polnische Tagesliteratur" (files no. 4806a and 4806b) which contained important translated articles from the Polish press, weekly summaries of the Polish mood and reports on the chief political rallies held in Poznań. The last is of utmost importance in that the Prussian police very often acted as the most objective observers of the heated rallies, and it is instructive to compare their dispassionate accounts with the crusading editorials of the Polish newspapers.

The present study has also made use of a number of personal diaries and published letters of leading German contemporaries. While they represent a more selective type of "public opinion" and are strictly speaking not the theme of this study, it is important to keep in mind their views because of their influence on the fortunes of the Neue Kurs. Ludwig Raschdau and Bogdan von Hutten-Czapski were both very interested in the outcome of Caprivi's Polish policy, though from different positions.(30) Raschdau, a self-appointed expert on Polish affairs, wrote numerous memoranda to Caprivi decrying the concessions to the Poles, which the chancellor never answered. Raschdau also spent a lot of time in the company of Prussian ministers, such as Gustav von Gossler, Johannes von Miquel and Robert Bosse, and undoubtedly tried his best to discredit Caprivi in their eyes. Hutten-Czapski, a scion of a Polish family and a Prussian officer and envoy on familiar terms with Wilhelm II, was torn throughout his life between his Polish origins and his Prussian loyalties. After World War One he decided he was a Pole after all and was granted citizenship in the new republic. Hutten-Czapski's observations are particularly relevant in regard to the appointment of Stablewski as Archbishop of Gniezno-Poznań, the reaction of Galicians and Russian Poles to the loyalist initiative of the Prussian Poles, and the renewed antagonism between Poles and Germans under the chancellorship of Hohenlohe.

Although officially in retirement, the figure of Otto von Bismarck continued to cast a long shadow over Prussia's Polish policy. Beginning in 1891, Bismarck engaged in a fierce campaign to topple Caprivi, and used his 'soft' Polish policy as one of the principal weapons against him. Hence it has been necessary to analyze Bismarck's many speeches during the period that touched on the Polish question.(31) In addition, the works of Johann Penzler (32), Heinrich von Poschinger (33) and Hermann Hofmann (34), all acquaintances of Bismarck who were instrumental in the development of his cult, contain many relevant remarks of the former Chancellor on the Polish question. Penzler's work comprises seven volumes, and includes the bulk of important newspaper articles emanating from the so-called 'Bismarckpresse' aimed at the Polish community.

The author has also examined the memoirs of leading German statesmen at the time to determine Caprivi's standing among his subordinates. Critical comments were found in the memoirs of: Lothar von Schweinitz (35), the German ambassador in St. Petersburg who was concerned about the negative impact of Caprivi's Polish policy on German-Russian relations; Carl Graf von Wedel (36); Alfred Graf von Waldersee (37), Chief of Staff until 1891 and the champion of the pre-emptive strike concept against Russia; and Friedrich von Holstein (38), the 'grey eminence' in the foreign office who disagreed with Caprivi's Polish policy but supported him in general. Otto Hammann, Caprivi's press chief, defended his superior's policies but stayed clear of the Polish question.(39) In addition a number of published letters have been consulted.(40)

A collection of documents relating to Church and langauge affairs in Poznania has been compiled by Edwin Gatz.(41) Gatz includes many documents relevant to the nomination of Stablewski in 1890-1891. A contemporary who concerned himself greatly with the Polish question was Hans Delbrueck, editor of the Preussische Jahrbuecher and the Schulthess' Europaeischer Geschichtskalender. Delbrueck's comments on the Polish-German relationship were published in the Preussische Jahrbuecher under the title 'Die Polenfrage' in 1894 (42) and earned him the goodwill of many Polish publicists.

1.4 Secondary Literature

Although the direct theme of this study has not received much attention to date in historical study, the author has consulted a wide range of secondary sources to examine it against a wider historical background. This literature can be divided thematically into four groups: a) studies of the development of newspapers and publishing in the German Reich and in particular the Polish provinces; b) the growth and development of the Polish community under Prussian rule; c) Prussia's Polenpolitik; and d) histories and evaluations of the Neue Kurs.

Statistical information on the growth of German language and Polish language newspapers is found in the works of Isolde Rieger (43) and Gerd Muser (44). Of particular interest are the studies of Guenther Eichhorn (45) and Fritz Schultz (46), both of whom concerned themselves with the growth of newspapers east of the Oder river during the Imperial Period. The basic information about the Polish newspapers has come from the works of Witold Jakóbczyk (47), Teresa Tyszkiewicz (48) and Tadeusz Cieślak (49). A good deal of biographical information about editors, patrons and journalists has come from the Polski Słownik Biograficzny.(50) Lech Trzeciakowski has written two biographies of the Orędownik's editor Roman Szymański (51), and has frequently dwelt upon the Polish press in his other studies of Poznania under Prussian rule. Wiktor Molik has published two long essays about the profession of journalism in Prussian Poland (52) and about the short-lived existence of the Przegląd Poznański (53). Wojciech Wrzesiński has examined the principal editorial viewpoints of the Dziennik Poznański over a 55 year period from 1859 to 1914 (54), but has said little about the Caprivi period. From the German side the works of Fritz Prause (55), Leonhard Mueller (56), Walter Guenzel (57) and Berthold Wiegand (58) all concern of hostile Polish publicism in Prussia and have helped the author in developing a wider perspective of the problem. Questions of censorship and repression against Polish newspapers are answered in the studies of Wolfgang Wetzel (59), Władysław Chojnacki (60) and Adam Galos (61).

The principal sources for the Polish community in Prussia mostly stem from the 'Poznań school' of the post-war era: Witold Jakóbczyk (62), Lech Trzeciakowski (63) and Zdzisław Grot. (64) The massive 'Dzieje Wielkopolski' (The History of Wielkopolska), comprising two volumes of roughly 900 pages each covers most areas of social, political and economic life and includes an exhaustive bibliography of over 60 pages.(65) Antoni Czubiński has edited two collections of essays on various aspects of life in Prussian Poland.(66) Of special interest has been the studies dedicated to economic life: wages, living standards, working conditions, etc. Information about the successes and failures of Social Democracy in the Polish provinces and the growth of the 'PPS-zaboru pruskiego' are found in the works of Boleslaw Danilczuk (67), Czesław Łuczak (68) and Stefan Kowal (69). In the German language, the study of the Polish 'Vereinswesen' by Ludwig Bernhard remains a classic despite its date of publication.(70) The economic life of Poznania and the German-Polish commercial rivalry are covered in the studies of Leo Wegener (71), Waldemar Mitscherlich (72), and Wilhelm von Massow (73).

The body of scholarship concerning Prussia's Polenpolitik is immense and attests to the stature of the problem within the set of domestic Prussian issues in the last decades of the 19th century. The classic works which have helped the author place the problem of Caprivi's short administration in its historical perspective are those by Manfred Laubert (74), Friedrich Schinkel (75), Richard Witting (76), Albert Brackmann (77) and Albert von Bogusławski (78). With few exceptions, the tone of German scholarship until the end of the Second World War was more in the spirit of Bismarck than Caprivi, and the Caprivi interlude was seen as a serious reversal to the German element in the Prussian East. With the end of the Second World War, however, German scholarship began to view both Caprivi and the Polish question in a different perspective, recognizing earlier mistakes and excesses. Of particular significance here are the works of Martin Broszat (79), Hans-Ulrich Wehler (80) Roland Baier (81) and Maria Lammich (82). Historians from the German Democratic Republic like Joachim Mai (83), Felix-Heinrich Gentzen (84) and Edgar Hartwig (85) are extremely critical of Prussia's Polish policy and argue the "Polish cause" often more vociferously than the Poles themselves. In regard to specific periods and problem areas, the works of Hanne-Lore Land on the Polish question among the German Conservative Party is of great value (86); Hans-Ulrich Wehler has dealt with the nationality policy of the SPD (87); Rudolf Korth (88) and Helmut Glueck (89) have studied the language problems during the imperial area; Lotte Kaminski covered the transition period under Chancellor Hohenlohe to a more confrontational relationship (90); and Wilhelm Muenstermann in a very valuable work has looked at the discussion about Caprivi's Polish policy among German political parties and interest groups. (91) Polish works devoted to Prussia's Polish policy are fewer in number but no less animated in spirit; the polemical tone which has dominated Polish-German relations since the partitions is very evident in Polish scholarship. The works of Józef Feldman were very valuable to the author in setting the perspective for Caprivi's chancellorship (92), and that of his father, Wilhelm Feldman, surveyed Polish political thought during the era of the partitions (93). Józef Bużek, a professor in Lwów, wrote a highly critical study of Prussia's Polish policy in 1907 that is still often cited today.(94) Stanisław Karwowski, a young man at the time of the Caprivi administration, wrote a history of the province of Poznania in chronicle form directly after independence in 1919 that offers a great deal of information if little analysis.(95) Recent works by Lech Trzeciakowski (96), Bolesław Grześ (97), Adam Galos (98) and Janusz Pajewski (99) have also been consulted to appreciate the reception of Prussian policy in Poznania on various aspects of Polish national life. The study by Joachim Benyskiewicz on Polish parliamentary activity from 1866-1890 has been very useful in the research on the beginnings of loyalism in Prussia.(100)

With regards to the Neue Kurs and Caprivi's administration, Polish scholarship has three directly relevant studies which the author has consulted: Lech Trzeciakowski's Ph.D. thesis on the politics of the Polish loyalists (101); Alfred Kucner's essay on the politics of the Reichstag Party (102) and Adam Galos's essay about Archbishop Stablewski and the tragedy of reconciliation (103). In English, the author has consulted the works of J. Alden Nichols (104) and J.G.C. Roehl (105) for a general survey of the Caprivi era in all its facets, and the works of Richard Blanke (106) and Harry K. Rosenthal (107) for Caprivi's Polish policy. The latter are of great importance because of their frequent references to the Polish press of the time. In German, there are a number of studies on Caprivi that deserve mention: above all the biography by Heinrich-Otto Meisner which attempts to defend the Neue Kurs against its sharp critics.(108) In the inter-war years, Caprivi's military bills were studied by Johann Werdermann (109) and Heinz Goebel (110); his trade treaties by Georg Gothein (111); his quarrel with Bismarck by Robert Geis (112) and Walter Held

(113); and his sharp dispute with the Conservatives by Karl-Heinz Kroeger (114). The Polish question under Caprivi has received a good deal of sympathetic coverage in the Ph.D. theses of Hans-Christian Sievers (115) and Peter Leibenguth (116), while Horst Oehlmann's study of Caprivi's domestic policies did not cover the Polish question at all (117). The significance of Caprivi's trade policies on Germany's economy has been studied recently by Rolf Weitowitz (118), and the difficulties he had in replacing Bismarck in the eyes of German public opinion has formed the subject of study of Juergen W. Schaefer (119).

NOTES TO INTRODUCTION

1. Wiktor Molik, "Wokół 'Przeglądu Poznańskiego'. Próby politycznego usamodzielnienia się inteligencji polskiej w Poznańskim w końcu XIX w.", in: Inteligencja Polska, ed. Ryszard Czepulis-Rastensis. Study no. 2 (Warszawa, 1981); by the same author, "Dziennikarze polscy pod panowaniem pruskim 1890-1914", in: Inteligencja Polska...Study no. 3 (Warszawa, 1983); Wojciech Wrzesiński, "Oblicze polityczne 'Dziennika Poznańskiego' w latach 1859-1914", in: Na warsztatach historyków polskiej myśli politycznej, ed. Henryk Zieliński, (Wrocław, 1980).

2. Tadeusz Cieślak, Z dziejów prasy polskiej w Pomorzu gdańskim w okresie zaboru pruskiego (Gdańsk, 1964); "Prasa polska na Pomorzu w II połowie XIX wieku i początkach XX wieku", in: Szkice z dziejów Pomorza, vol.3. (Warszawa, 1961); "Gazeta Grudziądzka 1894-1918. Fenomen wydawniczy", in: Studia i materiały do dziejów Wielkopolski i Pomorza 2 (1956).

3. Lech Trzeciakowski, Polityka polskich klas posiadających w Wielkopolsce w erze Capriviego 1890-1894 (Poznań, 1960).

4. Lech Trzeciakowski, "Roman Szymański", in: Wielkopolanie XIX wieku, ed. Witold Jakóbczyk, vol. 2 (Poznań, 1969); idem., "Roman Szymański. Poglądy i praktyka polityczna", in: Acta Universitatis Wratislaviensis 36 (1981).

5. Walter Guenzel, Die nationale Arbeit der polnischen Presse in Westpreussen und Posen zur Zeit der Kanzlerschaft Buelows 1900-1909 (Lodz, 1933); Fritz Prause, Die polnische Presse im Kampf gegen die deutsche Volksgruppe in Posen und Westpreussen (Wuerzburg-Aumuehle, 1940); Leonhard Mueller, National-polnische Presse, Katholizismus und katholischer Klerus (Breslau, 1931); Berthold Wiegand, Die anti-deutsche Propaganda der Polen von 1890-1914 (Danzig, 1940).

6. Wilhelm Muenstermann, Die preussisch-deutsche Polenpolitik der Caprivizeit und die deutsche oeffentliche Meinung (Muenster, 1936).

7. Franz Wagner, Fritz Vosberg, Der Polenring (1899); idem., Polenstimmen (1902); idem., Polenspiegel (1908). All three volumes were printed by the Deutsche Ostmarkenverein in Berlin.

8. Ludwig Bernhard, Das polnische Gemeinwesen im preussischen Staat. Die Polenfrage (Leipzig, 1907); Wilhelm von Massow, Die Polen-Not im deutschen Osten (Berlin, 1903).

9. Massow, Die Polen-Not..., pp. 76-117.

10. for example, M. Spatz, Die Kampfsorganisationen Neu-Polens (Muenchen, 1910), p. 24; E. Herr, Neue Bahnen der Polenpolitik (Berlin, 1903), pp. 44-49; Wilhelm Ohnesseit, "Der Kampf um die Ostmark und der deutsche Ostmarkenverein", in: Preussische Jahrbuecher 213 (1928); Richard Witting, Das Ostmarken-Problem (Berlin, 1907), p. 19.

11. Richard Blanke, Prussian Poland in the German Empire (New York, 1981); idem., "The Development of Loyalism in Prussian Poland, 1886-1890", in: Slavonic and East European Review 52 (1974); idem., "An Era of Reconciliation in German-Polish Relations (1890-1894)", in: Slavic Review 36 (1977); Harry K. Rosenthal, German and Pole. National Conflict and Modern Myth (Gainsville, 1976); idem., "Germans and Poles in 1890. Possibilities for a New Course", in: East European Quarterly 5 (1971); idem., "The Problem of Caprivi's Polish Policy", in: European Studies Review 2 (1972); idem., "Rivalry between 'Notables' and 'Townspeople' in Prussian Poland: The First Round", in: Slavonic and East European Review 49 (1971).

12. Bogdan von Hutten-Czapski, Sechzig Jahre Politik und Gesellschaft (Berlin, 1936), vol. 1, p. 442.

13. Rosenthal, "The Problems of Caprivi's Polish Policy"..., p. 264.

14. Lech Trzeciakowski, Walka o polskość miast poznańskiego na przełomie XIX i XX wieku (Poznań, 1964), p. 180.

15. Oskar Michel, Handbuch deutscher Zeitungen (Berlin, 1917), p. 280.

16. Archiwum Panstwowe Miasta Poznania i Województwa Poznańskiego, Poznań. Polizeipraesidium zu Posen (hereafter PP-Posen), file no. 4806a (1893) and no. 4806b (1894)

17. Witold Jakóbczyk, "Prasa", in: Dzieje Wielkopolski, ed. Witold Jakóbczyk, (Poznań, 1973), vol. 2, p. 875.

18. Biblioteka Raczyńskich w Poznaniu. Akta Komitetu Prowincjonalnego Wyborczego na Wielkie Księstwo Poznańskie (hereafter Akta PKW)

19. Biblioteka PAN w Kórniku. Protokoły posiedzień Koła Polskiego w sejmie pruskim, manuscript no. 1456/1457.

20. Lech Trzeciakowski in a personal interview with author, 5 August, 1984.

21. Roman Komierowski, Koło polskie w Berlinie 1875-1900 (Poznań, 1906).

22. Biblioteka Raczynskich w Poznaniu. Korespondencja Henryka Szumana. Manuscript no. 1636.

23. Ibid., J. Kusztelan, Piotr Wawrzyniak (unpublished manuscript). Manuscript no. 1527.

24. Ibid., Autobiography of Bernard Chrzanowski (unpublished manuscript). Manuscript no. 1375.

25. See note 16.

26. File no. 3740 (Szymanski), no. 3696 (Siemianowski), no. 3682 (Rzepecki).

27. File no. 3660 (Radziwiłł), no. 3515 (Cegielski), no. 3525 (Czarliński).

28. File no. 4912 (Kuryer Poznański), no. 4914 (Goniec Wielkopolski).

29. File no. 4149 (Aufsicht von oeffentlichen Gesellschaften), no. 4759 (Ueberwachung und Beschlagnahme 1864-1891), no. 4869 (Sammlungen von Subskriptionen),no. 4876 (Haltung der polnischen Presse gegenueber der kaiserlichen Russischen Regierung), no. 4877 (Acta betr. die polnische Tagespresse, ihre Haltung und Verbreitung 1886-1890).

30. Ludwig Raschdau, Unter Bismarck und Caprivi. Erinnerungen eines deutschen Diplomaten aus den Jahren 1885-1894 (Berlin, 1939); Bogdan von Hutten-Czapski, Sechzig Jahre Politik und Gesellschaft (Berlin, 1936), 2 vols.

31. Otto von Bismarck, Die gesammelten Werke (Berlin, 1924-1932), 15 vols.

32. Fuerst Bismarck nach seiner Entlassung, ed. Johann Penzler (Leipzig, 1897) 7 vols.

33. Heinrich von Poschinger, Fuerst Bismarck. Neue Tischgespraeche und Interviews (Stuttgart, 1895), 2 vols.

34. Hermann Hofmann, Fuerst Bismarck 1890-1898 (Stuttgart, 1913), 3 vols.

35. Lothar von Schweinitz, Denkwuerdigkeiten des Botschafters General von Schweinitz (Berlin, 1927), 2 vols.

36. Carl Graf von Wedel, Zwischen Kaiser und Kanzler. Aufzeichnungen des Generaladjutanten Grafen Carl von Wedel aus den Jahren 1890-1894, ed. Erhard Graf von Wedel, (Leipzig, 1943).

37. Alfred Graf von Waldersee, Denkwuerdigkeiten des Alfred Grafen von Waldersee, ed. Heinrich Otto Meisner, (Osnabrueck, 1967, reprint from 1922), 3 vols.

38. Friedrich von Holstein, The Holstein Papers, ed. Norman Rich (Cambridge, 1955).

39. Otto Hammann, Der Neue Kurs (Berlin, 1918).

40. Holstein und Hohenlohe, ed. Helmut Rogge, (Stuttgart, 1957); Letters of the Empress Frederick, ed. Frederick Ponsonby (London, 1928); Lothar von Schweinitz, Briefwechsel des Botschafters General von Schweinitz (Berlin, 1928); Marie Radziwill, Briefe vom deutschen Kaiserhof 1889-1915 (Berlin, 1936).

41. Akten zur preussischen Kirchenpolitik in den Bistumern Gnesen-Posen, Kulm und Ermland 1885-1914, ed. Edwin Gatz, (Mainz, 1977).

42. Hans Delbrueck, "Die Polenfrage" Preussische Jahrbuecher 78 (Oct.-Dec. 1894).

43. Isolde Rieger, Die wilhelmische Presse in Ueberblick 1888-1918 (Muenchen, 1957).

44. Gerd Muser, Statistische Untersuchungen ueber die Zeitungen Deutschlands 1885-1914 (Leipzig, 1918).

45. Guenther Eichhorn, Geschichte des Zeitungswesen im deutschen Ostraum zwischen Frankfurt a. Oder und Danzig (Dresden, 1939).

46. Fritz Schultz, Die politische Tagespresse Westpreussens (Deutsch-Krone, 1913).

47. Witold Jakóbczyk, "Wielkopolska 1859-1918" in: Prasa Polska, ed. Jerzy Łojek, vol. 2, 1864-1918 (Warszawa, 1976).

48. Teresa Tyszkiewicz, Sobótka 1869-1871 (Poznań, 1961).

49. See note 2.

50. The Polski Słownik Biograficzny was begun in 1936, interrupted by the war and Stalinism until 1956, and is now at the letter "P".(hereafter PSB)

51. See note 4.

52. See note 1.

53. Ibid.

54. Ibid.

55. See note 5.

56. Ibid.

57. Ibid.

58. Ibid.

59. Wolfgang Wetzel, Presseinnenpolitik im Bismarckreich 1874-1890. Das Problem der Repression oppositioneller Zeitungen (Bern, 1975).

60. Władysław Chojnacki, "Niemieckie tłumaczenia z prasy polskiej", in: Przegląd Zachodni 14 (1958).

61. Adam Galos, "Antypolska działalność policji pruskiej", in: Polska Niemcy Europa, ed. Antoni Czubiński (Poznań, 1977).

62. Dzieje Wielkopolski, ed. Witold Jakóbczyk (Poznań, 1973), 2 vols.; Witold Jakóbczyk, Studia nad dziejami Wielkopolski w XIX wieku (Poznań, 1959) 2 vols.; Wybitni Wielkopolani XIX wieku, ed. Witold Jakóbczyk, (Poznań, vol. 1, 1959; vol. 2, 1969).

63. Lech Trzeciakowski, Pod pruskim zaborem 1850-1914 (Warszawa, 1973); Walka o polskość miast poznańskiego na przełomie XIX i XX wieku (Poznań, 1964); Zygmunt Boras, Lech Trzeciakowski, W dawnym Poznaniu (Poznań, 1969); Maria and Lech Trzeciakowski, W dziewiętnastowiecznym Poznaniu (Poznań, 1982).

64. Zdzisław Grot, Hipolit Cegielski 1813-1868 (Poznań, 1980); idem., Dezydery Chłapowski 1788-1879 (Poznań, 1983); idem., "Koło polskie w Berlinie", in: Wiek XIX. Festschrift Stefan Kieniewicz (Warszawa, 1967).

65. Dzieje Wielkopolski, ed. Witold Jakóbczyk (Poznań, 1973), 2 vols.

66. Studia z dziejów Polski, Niemiec i NRD XVI-XX w., ed. Antoni Czubiński (Poznań, 1974); Polska Niemcy Europa, ed. Antoni Czubiński (Poznań, 1977).

67. Bolesław Danilczuk, Działalność SPD i PPS zaboru pruskiego w Poznańskim w latach 1891-1914 (Toruń, 1962).

68. Czesław Łuczak, Życie gospodarczo-społeczne w Poznaniu 1815-1918 (Poznań, 1965).

69. Stefan Kowal, Społeczeństwo Wielkopolski i Pomorza Nadwiślańskiego w latach 1871-1914 (Poznań, 1982).

70. Ludwig Bernhard, Das polnische Gemeinwesen im preussischen Staat. Die Polenfrage (Leipzig, 1907).

71. Leo Wegener, Der wirtschaftliche Kampf der Deutschen mit den Polen um die Provinz Posen (Posen, 1903).

72. Waldemar Mitscherlich, Die Ausbreitung der Polen in Preussen (Leipzig, 1913).

73. Wilhelm von Massow, Die Polen-Not im deutschen Osten (Berlin, 1903).

74. Manfred Laubert, Die preussische Polenpolitik von 1772 bis 1914 (Krakau, 1944).

75. Friedrich Schinkel, Polen, Preussen und Deutschland (Breslau, 1931).

76. Richard Witting, Das Ostmarken-Problem (Berlin, 1907).

77. Deutschland und Polen, ed. Albert Brackmann, (Berlin, 1933).

78. Albert von Boguslawski, 85 Jahre preussische Regierungspolitik in Posen und Westpreussen von 1815 bis 1900 (Berlin, 1901).

79. Martin Broszat, Zweihundert Jahre deutschen Polenpolitik (Muenchen, 1963).

80. Hans-Ulrich Wehler, "Die Polenpolitik im deutschen Kaiserreich 1871-1914", in: Politische Ideologien und nationalstaatliche Ordnung. Festschrift fuer Theodor Schieder. Ed. W. Mommsen and K. Kluxen, (Muenchen, 1968).

81. Roland Baier, Der deutsche Osten als soziale Frage (Koeln, 1980).

82. Maria Lammich, Das deutsche Osteuropabild in der Zeit der Reichsgruendung (Boppard am Rhein, 1978).

83. Joachim Mai, Die preussisch-deutsche Polenpolitik 1885-1887 (Berlin-Ost, 1962).

84. Felix-Heinrich Gentzen, "Die Hakatisten 1914-1934" in: Die Hakatisten Der Deutsche Ostmarkenverein 1894-1934, ed. Janusz Pajewski (Berlin-Ost, 1966). Adam Galos and Witold Jakóbczyk were co-authors.

85. Edgar Hartwig, "Der Alldeutsche Verband und Polen", in: Wissenschaftliche Zeitschrift der Friedrich Schiller Universitaet Jena 19 (1970-1972).

86. Hanne-Lore Land, Die Konservativen und die preussische Polenpolitik 1886-1912 (Berlin, 1963).

87. Hans-Ulrich Wehler, Sozialdemokratie und Nationalstaat (Wuerzburg, 1962).

88. Rudolf Korth, Die preussische Schulpolitik und die polnischen Schulstreiks (Wuerzburg, 1963).

89. Helmut Glueck, Die preussisch-polnische Sprachenpolitik (Hamburg, 1979).

90. Lotte Kaminski, Die Auseindersetzung um die polnische Frage zur Zeit der Reichskanzlerschaft des Fuersten Hohenlohe (Hamburg, 1938).

91. Wilhelm Muenstermann, Die preussisch-deutsche Polenpolitik der Caprivizeit und die deutsche oeffentliche Meinung (Muenster, 1936).

92. Józef Feldman, Problem polsko-niemiecki w dziejach (Katowice, 1946); idem., Bismarck a Polska (Kraków, 1947).

93. Wilhelm Feldman, Geschichte der politischen Ideen in Polen seit dessen Teilungen 1795-1914 (Muenchen, Berlin, 1917).

94. Józef Bużek, Historya polityki narodowościowej rządu pruskiego wobec Polaków od traktatów wiedeńskich do ustaw wyjątkowych z r. 1908 (Lwów, 1909)

95. Stanisław Karwowski, Historya Wielkiego Księstwa Poznańskiego (Poznań, 1919), 3 vols.

96. Lech Trzeciakowski, Pod zaborem pruskim 1850-1914 (Warszawa, 1973); idem., "Wpływ zaboru pruskiego na świadomość społeczenstwa polskiego", in: Dziedzictwo zaborów, ed. Janusz Ośica (Warszawa, 1983).

97. Bolesław Grześ, "Rola naczelnych prezesów poznańskiego w kształtowaniu i realizacji germanizacyjnej polityki rządu pruskiego w II połowie XIX w. in: Studia z dziejów Polski, Niemiec i NRD XVI-XX w., ed. Antoni Czubiński; idem., "Teoretyczno-propagandowe aspekty dyskryminacji Polaków poznańskiego na przelomie XIX i XX wieku" in: Polska Niemcy Europa, ed. Antoni Czubiński (Warszawa, 1977).

98. Adam Galos, "Antypolska działalność policji pruskiej" in: Polska Niemcy Europa, ed. Antoni Czubiński (Poznań, 1977); idem., "Obraz Polaka w Niemczech w XIX w." Śląski Kwartalnik Historyczny Sobótka 33 (1978).

99. Janusz Pajewski, "Niemcy a kwestia polska 1871-1914" Studia Historica Slavo-Germanica 1 (1972).

100. Joachim Benyskiewicz, Posłowie polscy w Berlinie w latach 1866-1890 (Zielona Góra, 1976).

101. Lech Trzeciakowski, Polityka polskich klas posiadających w Wielkopolsce w erze Capriviego 1890-1894 (Poznań, 1960).

102. Alfred Kucner, "Polityka Koła Polskiego w Berlinie w erze kanzlerza Capriviego" in: Nauka i Sztuka 5 (1947).

103. Adam Galos, "Tragizm ugody. Władze pruskie a arcybiskup Stablewski" in: Przegląd Zachodni 31 (1975).

104. J. Alden Nichols, Germany after Bismarck. The Caprivi Era (Boston, 1958).

105. J.C.G. Roehl, Germany without Bismarck (London, 1967).

106. See note 11.

107. Ibid.

108. Heinrich Otto Meisner, "Der Reichskanzler Caprivi", in: Zeitschrift fuer die gesamte Staatswissenschaft 111 (1955).

109. Johann Werdermann, Die Heeresreform unter Caprivi (Greifswald, 1928).

110. Heinz Goebel, Die Militaervorlage 1892-1893 (Leipzig, 1935).

111. Georg Gothein, "Die Wirkung des Handelsvertraege", in: Volkswirtschaftliche Zeitfragen 17 (1896); idem., "Reichskanzler Graf Caprivi", in: Fehler und Forderungen 5 (1918).

112. Robert Geis, Der Sturz des Reichskanzlers Caprivi (Berlin, 1930) Historischen Studien no. 192.

113. Walter Held, Caprivi und Bismarck (Leipzig, 1931).

114. Karl-Heinz Kroeger, Die Konservativen und die Politik Caprivis (Rostock, 1937).

115. Hans-Christian Sievers, Die Innenpolitik des Reichskanzlers Caprivi (Kiel, 1953), 2 vols.

116. Peter Liebenguth, Modernisierungskrisis des Kaiserreichs an der Schwelle zum wilhelmischen Imperialismus: politische Probleme der Aera Caprivi 1890-1894 (Koeln, 1975).

117. Horst Oehlmann, Studien zur Innenpolitik des Reichskanzlers Leo von Caprivi (Freiburg, 1953).

118. Rolf Weitowitz, Deutsche Politik und Handelspolitik unter Reichskanzler Leo von Caprivi 1890-1894 (Duesseldorf, 1978).

119. Juergen W. Schaefer, Kanzlerbild und Kanzlermythos in der Zeit des Neuen Kursus (Paderborn, 1973).

Chapter Two: A General Survey of the Polish Press in Poznań (1848-1890)

2.1 Origins of the Leading Papers to 1890

The history of the Polish press in Poznań during the second half of the 19th century was closely connected to the province's political life. From their inception, newspapers became the spokesmen for several orientations and philosophies, and engaged in lively debate and rivalry with each other. With rising circulation and social recognition the press assumed an ever greater political significance. This is in keeping with the growth of political newspapers all over the German Reich.(1)

By the time of Otto von Bismarck's (Fuerst from 1871) dismissal and the onset of Leo von Caprivi's (Graf from 1891) Neue Kurs there were four clearly identifiable political orientations evident within Poznań's Polish press: the 'national-liberal' (Dziennik Poznański and Wielkopolanin), the 'ultramontane' (Kuryer Poznański), the 'irreconcilable nationalist' (Goniec Wielkopolski) and the middle-class 'populist' (Orędownik and, from 1890, Postęp). Relations among these four groups were invariably hostile, though, their political ideas were to a large degree compatible. They were all firmly opposed to Germanization, to Social Democracy, to the Prussian bureaucracy and to any conspiratorial activity on behalf of a resurrected Poland. Given this broad area of agreement, the scholar is surprised at the intense feuds that permeated the newspapers, particularly in view of the need to preserve "national solidarity".

The national-liberal press had its beginnings in the events in Prussia of March 1848. With the abolition of censorship over the press Walenty Stefański, Hipolit Cegielski and Marcelli Motty founded the Gazeta Polska (first issue on 22 March, 1848). The Gazeta Polska was recognised as the voice of the Liga Polska, a committee of conservative landowners formed during the turbulent Spring of Nations in 1848 to take charge of Polish political affairs. It propagated organic work, class solidarity, social conservatism and exclusively legal resistance to the violations of Polish rights by the Prussian government. From the outset, the Gazeta Polska opposed the growth of revolutionary tendencies and stressed the need to reach a peaceful accomodation with Prussia.(2)

Dissatisfaction with the timidity and strict legalism of the Liga Polska and its paper gave birth to a rival, the Dziennik Polski, founded and edited by the philosopher and politician Karol Libelt.(3) The first issue came out in June, 1849 after the enthusiasm of the Spring of Nations had subsided, and it remained in print until June, 1850. Libelt had been sent to the Frankfurt parliament by the Liga Polska to argue the cause of Polish freedom and had arrived full of optimism that a constitutional Prussian government would grant the Poles their just rights. However, he left disillusioned after it became apparent that the Poles were not going to be accorded any significant degree of autonomy.(4) Libelt later served as chairman of the Polish Party in the Prussian Abgeordnetenhaus from 1859-1870 and became well-known for his philosophical tracts. His assertive defence of Polish rights and his courage in voicing opposition to the moderate policies of the more conservative landowners inspired the founders and adherents of the Goniec Wielkopolski, though Libelt himself was not a radical and later co-operated closely with the national-liberal camp.

Both Libelt's Dziennik and the Liga Polska's Gazeta fell victim to the post-1848 reaction and were forced to give up publication in June, 1850.(5) For nine years the only Polish paper that appeared regularly in Poznań was the clerical Przegląd Poznański, edited by Jan Koźmian. It survived till 1865 and set the pattern for the ultramontane press.(6) With the end of the Manteuffel era in 1858, the national-liberals under the leadership of a much wealthier Hipolit Cegielski founded the Dziennik Poznański. The Dziennik began publication in 1859 and survived until 1939. Cegielski had made a fortune through his farm-tools factory and together with Mieczysław Kwilecki and other wealthy landowners invested the necessary funds to start the paper. Much of the staff was still available from the former Gazeta Polska, including two leading editors, Władysław Bentkowski and Ludwik Jagielski. The Dziennik's philosophy resembled closely that of the former Gazeta: 'liberalism', which then meant largely anti-clericalism, legal opposition to Germanization and the need to maintain national solidarity under the leadership of the 'szlachta' (gentry class).(7) The Dziennik's liberalism was designed to counter the predominant influence of the Catholic clergy on national life and it argued for an end to Papal temporal power.

Two newspapers founded during the great era of literary expansion of the early 1870s survived into the Caprivi years: the Kuryer Poznański and the Orędownik. The Church had suffered a blow when the Przegląd Poznański failed in 1865, and it was determined to challenge the national-liberals for supremacy in Prussian Poland. Together with sympathizing landowners it founded the Kuryer Poznański, which first appeared on 1 January, 1872 and remained in print until 1905.(8) Its first managing editor was Ludwik Merzbach, a bookseller and printer who was rumoured to be of Jewish origin, (9) and its first editor-in-chief was Teodor Żychliński, who had been editor of the Dziennik Poznański until the arrival of Franciszek Dobrowolski there in January 1871.(10) The Kuryer started with a small circulation of 750, whose readers were almost exclusively the clergy and ultramontane landowners. It had been planned as a counterweight to the liberal Dziennik Poznański, but was soon thrust fully into the storm over the Kulturkampf.(11) Its most illustrious period was the 1870s, when the popularity generated through resistance to the Kulturkampf was augmented by the ultramontane teachings of the Vatican Council. During the height of Bismarck's struggle against the Catholic Church the Kuryer Poznański and Dziennik Poznański joined hands, and afterwards remained in a loose alliance as the key spokesmen for the landowner establishment. During the 1870s and 1880s no Polish newspaper was so severely prosecuted by the Prussian authorities. (12) Its most famous editor-in-chief, Father Antoni Kantecki, who directed the paper from 1876 to 1887, became something of a regional hero through his resolute defence of the Church hierarchy and his frequent periods of imprisonment. (13)

With the ever-increasing pace of social change in Prussian Poland the national-liberals tried to found a newspaper that would educate and mould the rising middle class in their spirit. In early 1871 the landowner Maksymilian Jackowski, later to become famous as the Patron of Poznania's well-developed rural societies (kółko rolniczy), raised 2250 talers to found the Orędownik. That he felt strongly about the project is evidenced by the fact that 1500 talers came from his own pocket.(14) As its first editor Jackowski engaged Roman Szymański, a former seminarian and conspirator who had gained editorial experience at the Sobótka and the Gazeta Toruńska. The Orędownik first appeared on 1 April, 1871. Circulation was set at from 700-800 and it initially appeared three times weekly.(15)

Jackowski's relationship with his young and dynamic editor began to deteriorate within months of the Orędownik's inception. Their quarrel centred around editorial policy. Jackowski wanted a tame paper that would faithfully echo the views of the landowner class while Szymański called upon the middle class to assert itself in demanding a share of power in social and political affairs. Throughout 1872 animosity between owner and editor deepened and after a few warnings Jackowski decided to break with Szymański, complaining to the other shareholders that he was irresponsibly attacking the established order.(16) Rather than give up the Orędownik, Szymański borrowed from friends and took out long-term loans to buy the paper, and managed to keep it running despite continual harassment from both the Polish landowners and the Prussian police.

Although positivism dominated social and political thought among Poles after the collapse of the 1863 Uprising, a certain group of lower gentry never lost their allegiance to the cause of Polish independence. The tradition begun by Karol Libelt in 1849 with the outspoken Dziennik Polski was continued in 1877 with the birth of Poznań's most radical nationalist daily, the Goniec Wielkopolski. The Goniec was founded by Ludwik Rzepecki, a teacher of mathematics, linguist and man of letters.(17) Its leading spokesman to 1885, however, was Władysław Niegolewski, who was Poznań's representative to the Reichstag until 1884 and chairman of the Polish Reichstag Party from 1871-1876. (18) The Goniec enjoyed an early rise in popularity among the lower ranks of the Polish gentry, but its circulation was deeply cut by the emergence of the Wielkopolanin in 1883.

The four political orientations all had their press spokesmen by the end of the 1870s. The national-liberals, representing the bulk of the wealthy landowners and upper bourgeoisie, owned and operated the Dziennik Poznański. The ultramontanes managed the Kuryer Poznański while the irreconcilable Polish nationalists read the Goniec Wielkopolski. Finally, middle-class urban residents supported Roman Szymański's Orędownik. Two other newspapers appeared in Poznań before the onset of the Caprivi era. In 1883 the Dziennik Poznański's shareholders decided to found a newspaper that was to present their conservative views in a simple voice to the urban and rural poor. The Dziennik's rivals all felt that the new paper, which was called the Wielkopolanin, was directed against them; the Goniec Wielkopolski thought it was intended to prevent the lower classes from demanding national independence, while the Orędownik charged that its purpose was to keep the urban classes ignorant and pliant. Its first patron and chief investor was the wealthy banker Mieczysław Łyskowski and its editor-in-chief was Julian Bukowiecki.(19) The initial plan called for the printing of 5000 copies, but landowners found it so much to their liking that circulation soon reached 9000-10,000, a very large number for the time.(20) Both its critics and the Prussian police noticed that issues were always bought up by the landowners and the clergy and distributed free among the rural poor.(21) Having few other links to the printed word, many of the poor treated it with special reverence.

Finally, on 1 January, 1890, Stanisław Knapowski, a printer and clothes salesman, founded the Postęp, an anti-Semitic paper whose surprising expansion underlined the latent hostility that existed against Jews in Prussian Poland. The origins of the Postęp are obscure. There is some evidence that Knapowski received large cash donations from Stefan Cegielski, son of the Dziennik Poznański's founder Hipolit, and Reichstag representative for Poznan, until the summer of 1893.(22) Cegielski was a confirmed anti-Semite who once tried to induce the Polish Landtag Party to introduce a resolution "against the Jews", though he withdrew it when it became apparent he really did not know how to articulate his grievances. (23) As a newspaperman and publicist Knapowski felt it to be his duty to sound the alarm against the 'worldwide Jewish conspiracy'.

2.2 Circulation, Financing and Organization

There is some confusion about the circulation of Polish political papers in Poznania and other provinces of the Reich during the later phase of the Imperial Period. There are few authoritative figures and estimates vary widely. The most common way to determine circulation is to examine post office records that listed subscribers. Subscription rates were quoted per quarter and via post, though it was possible to drop by the printshop and purchase individual copies. The newspapers themselves are of little help because their statements on circulation were fragmentary and very ambiguous.

The scholar will encounter several difficulties when trying to determine the circulation figures of Polish papers. The German press law distinguished between 'political' newspapers and those of a cultural, agricultural or commercial nature. Contemporaries often did not make this distinction and thus figures they presented seem highly exaggerated. For example, the Goniec Wielkopolski proudly claimed in 1894, "Ten years ago we had only ten political papers in Poznania with 10,000 readers, now we have thirty and a readership of 50,000." (24) How is the scholar to interpret this figure? There most certainly were not thirty political papers in Poznania in 1894; the Goniec must have counted all literary, agricultural and trades magazines as well. Similarly, the Dziennik Poznański in 1896 reported that ,"30,000 (Polish) papers are being printed in Poznania and 67,000 in the whole Reich".(25) Again one asks the significance of this figure; does it refer to all papers or only 'political' ones, dailies or weeklies?

An additional difficulty is determining how many papers were sold in addition to regular subscriptions. No records exist for over-the-counter sales. It is also not known how many copies found their way into other provinces of the Reich or Polish lands in Russia and Austria-Hungary. The Prussian police seemed to feel that Poznań was a kind of press capital from which inflammatory newspapers were destined for West Prussia, East Prussia, Berlin and Upper Silesia. Perhaps the papers themselves kept quiet about their own circulation to mislead the Prussian authorities and deflect the attention of overly-enthusiastic police observation.

After consulting the corresponding police files and other available materials the following table has been reconstructed as a rough guideline for circulation figures of Poznań's leading dailies that form the subject matter of this study.(26)

		Price Mk.		Circulation	
Paper	Founded	(quarter)		1890	1902
Dziennik Poznański	1859	4.5	1400(1886)	1650	3500
Orędownik	1871	2.	900(1872)	750	3500
Kuryer Poznański	1872	4.5	750(1886)	1000	1500
Goniec Wielkopolski	1877	2.5	2500(1882)	1000	2000
Wielkopolanin	1883	1.	5000(1883)	9000	12,000
Postęp	1890	1.		350	5500

The above table reveals that press circulation serves to indicate the pace of social change that was occurring in Prussian Poland. The Kuryer Poznański experienced the slowest growth of any Polish paper between 1890 and 1902 (50%). This was linked to the loss of stature caused by the failure of its loyalty program under Caprivi and its inability to make inroads into the middle classes. The dynamic growth of the two populist newspapers, the Orędownik and the Postęp, reflect the steady rise of the urban population and its growing political consciousness. In 1890 the landowner and clergy press (excluding the maverick Goniec Wielkopolski) printed about 12,700 papers daily against only about 1200 populist papers. This represented a ratio of ten to one. By 1902 the relationship was about 17,000 to 10,000, or about five to three. Circulation in the towns was limited by the widespread poverty encountered in the urban areas of the Prussian East. The average Polish workingman's annual wage has been estimated at 500 Mk., about 30-40% less than in other areas of the Reich.(27) About 750 Mk. was necessary to maintain a family of six. The 8 Mk. annual subscription rate to the Orędownik, for example, was simply too great for a number of townspeople who may well have shared the same viewpoints and wished the paper success.

The middle-class papers largely remained inside the provincial capital, though a few copies must have been sent to smaller towns throughout Poznania. The landowner press, however, was mostly sent out to the estates in the countryside. Of the 1400 copies printed by the Dziennik in 1886, 1200 were sold outside Poznań. Corresponding figures for the Kuryer Poznański and Goniec Wielkopolski were 625 of 750 and 841 of 950, respectively.(28)

As revealed in the table, the greatest circulation was credited to the Wielkopolanin. Its owners, wealthy landowners who also controlled the Dziennik Poznański, could decide to print as many copies as they saw fit, increasing the number at critical moments, such as elections, and reducing it when little of interest was happening. The great number of copies printed should not, however, lead to the conclusion that the Wielkopolanin was in such great demand, since it was by and large distributed free of charge by the landowners to the rural poor working on their estates. Not even the Prussian police took the Wielkopolanin very seriously.(29)

The Dziennik Poznański and Goniec Wielkopolski both doubled circulation during the 1890s, but the greatest rise came in the middle-class populist papers. After fighting off the landowner-led boycott during the critical years 1893-94 circulation expanded at an incredible rate. The most phenomenal growth was witnessed by the Postęp, the only Polish paper to regularly disclose its circulation. In early 1890 the Prussian police noted that the Postęp printed about 350 copies.(30) By the end of the year it was rumoured to have over 500 subscribers in the city of Poznań alone.(31) Knapowski claimed to print over 4000 copies in late 1892, likely an exaggeration, and insisted that he had another 800 readers by late 1893.(32) Even allowing for some degree of inaccuracy on the part of its editor, the Postęp's popularity reveals that its anti-Semitism had struck a responsive chord in Prussian Poland.

Knapowski was one of the few newspapermen who was able to make money in his chosen profession. A major reason why he remained solvent despite the hostility of the landowner class was his success in avoiding costly encounters with the Prussian state. Apparently, anti-Semitism was not considered subversive or a manifestation of 'Polish agitation'. Other Polish papers were not so fortunate. The financial burdens that confronted Polish publishers were awesome, and without regular subsidies and a vigorous campaign to bring in advertising most papers would probably been forced to shut dowm.

Apart from the enormous costs of press violations and court costs, Polish newspapers took it upon themselves to raise money and make donations to a number of national causes both inside and outside Prussian Poland. This was done ber of national causes both inside and outside Prussian Poland. This was done as much to enhance their reputation as leaders of the community as from the patriotism of the owners. The press regularly donated to the upkeep of Polish public libraries, to private instruction in the Polish language, and, in 1890, launched a massive fundraising drive to aid the victims of the Galician famine.(33) Furthermore the Poznanian press lords felt themselves morally obligated to come to the rescue of other press initiatives in West Prussia, East Prussia and Upper Silesia, ventures that demanded substantial capital outlays.(34) The Prussian police often accused Poznań's press of financing Polish papers in Upper Silesia and East Prussia, areas outside the Polish kingdom of 1772 and hence unquestionably Prussian territory.

Publishing newspapers was by no means a lucrative proposition. At times the police persecution was so great that financial assistance had to come from wealthy Poles outside Prussia.(35) The average cost of a press conviction was about 500 Mk., and at least a half dozen cases could be expected per year during periods of heightened national antagonism like the Kulturkampf. Wiktor Molik has calculated that a paper at a quarterly subscription rate of 1-1.5 Mk. would have needed a circulation of about 4500 to exist without subsidies.(36). Only the Wielkopolanin had such a high number during the Caprivi years, leading one to conclude that newspapers either operated at a loss or benefitted from public contributions.

In regard to business organization, the Polish newspapers can be divided into joint-stock companies and the personal property of owners. To the first category belong the Dziennik Poznański and the Kuryer Poznański, owned jointly by wealthy landowners and the Church. The owners appointed a "Rada Nadzorcza", or executive board, which in turn appointed the managing editor and editor-in-chief. Szymański's Orędownik, Knapowski's Postęp and the Rzepecki family's Goniec Wielkopolski constituted personal property.

The Dziennik Poznański commanded perhaps the greatest financial support; its shareholders in the 1870s included the wealthy landowners Kwilecki, Potocki and Mielżyński.(37) Later on, Stefan Cegielski, one of the wealthiest Poles in Poznań joined the board. The Kuryer Poznański was heavily subsidised by the Catholic Church and several landowner families, like the Chłapowskis, Mycielskis and the Żółtowskis.(38) Józef Kościelski, the leader of the loyalist initiative which the Kuryer so strongly supported during the Caprivi era, was arguably the wealthiest Pole in Prussia and could have easily financed the paper himself.(39) Less fortunate was the Goniec Wielkopolski, which was constantly in financial crisis as it lacked wealthy benefactors and ran afoul of the Prussian authorities so often. It likely received funds from gentry sympathizers from time to time to keep it alive. Szymański's Orędownik regularly operated on a shoestring budget and seemed destined to cease publication at some critical juncture, but it enjoyed the firm commitment of several Poznań residents of moderate wealth, such as the real-estate owner Stanisław Offierski and the physician Tomasz Drobnik.(40)

All the newspapers strove as best they could to acquire advertising. The Dziennik Poznański enjoyed the greatest advertising revenue because it's readers tended to be wealthy, a fact recognised by both Polish and German businessmen. Its first issue in 1893, for example, contained the standard four pages of news and editorials, followed by six full pages of advertisements.(41) Other papers could charge substsantially less for advertising space. The Dziennik advertised the latest in women's fashions from London and Paris, expensive furniture, perfumes and other luxuries within the reach of the propertied classes, while the Orędownik had to settle for workmen's clothing and inexpensive home utensils.

Finally, it should be noted that many of the newspaper publishers engaged in other forms of social and political work that either detracted or added to their modest incomes. Dobrowolski, editor-in-chief of the Dziennik Poznański from 1871 to 1896, was also director of Poznań's Polish theatre; Szymański, in addition to the Orędownik, directed the Society of Catholic Craftsmen and was often asked to give lectures at the Association of Young Industrialists. The Kantecki brothers at the Kuryer Poznański sold a wide variety of religious artifacts in a shop linked to the newspaper, and Knapowski was the owner of a clothes shop when he founded the Postęp in 1890.

One can conclude that publishing newspapers was very much a patriotic obligation on the part of socially committed Poles that often required hard and dangerous work. Keeping the press alive was one of the few defensive weapons available to the Poles in their legal resistance to Germanization.

2.3 The Polish Press and the Prussian Press Authorities

The difficulties experienced by the Poles with Prussian press laws began in 1850 with the closure of both Hipolit Cegielski's Gazeta Polska and Karol Libelt's Dziennik Polski. Rather than ban the publications, the Prussian authorities simply imposed a mandatory deposit of 5000 talers which exceeded the financial resources of the papers' owners.(42) The repressive atmosphere generated during the Manteuffel era led to the creation of the first systematic monitoring of the Polish press in 1858. Under the direction of Edmund Baerensprung, the chief of police in Poznań, analyses of Polish newspapers and trends in Polish national and social thought were compiled and sent to policy-makers in Berlin. These analyses were of particular interest to the Ministers of Interior and Education, the two officials most directly concerned with Polish affairs, and of course to the Prussian Ministerpraesident.(43)

Under Bismarck's rule the Polish press was obliged to operate under rigid restrictions. Bismarck was convinced that Poles all over Europe constituted a danger to peace and stability and was particularly sensitive to the Polish influence in the Russian press.(44) Closer to home, Bismarck felt that the papers dominated by the landowners and clergy were a means of spreading Polish national agitation and hence ordered his ministers to prosecute at the slightest provocation.

In 1874 a new press law was enacted in the Reich that represented an important step forward in increasing the freedom of speech available to the Polish community. It was based on repression after the fact rather than outright censorship before publication.(45) The law called for a mandatory "Pflichtexemplar" to be submitted to the responsible monitoring authority and the naming of a responsible editor who was liable to prosecution if objectionable material were printed. Because this editor spent so much time in prison, German newspapermen called the job "Sitzredakteur". The result of the 1874 law was that papers could print what they wanted, but at their own risk. A total of 4924 cases arose in which questionable articles were confiscated and editors fined between 1874 and 1890. 3287 cases came to court and 80% of these ended in convictions.(46)

The Polish newspapers were severely prosecuted and at times the existence of several were imperilled. During the years 1874-1890, for example, the Catholic daily Germania was taken to court by the government 120 times. Enjoying the support of Catholics all over Germany and having a circulation of 4000 in Berlin alone, it possessed the resources necessary to overcome the long list of convictions.(47) Yet during the same time the Kuryer Poznański, which had a total circulation of only 800-1000 was taken to court 87 times.(48) Clearly, the financial losses incurred by the Polish papers were more deeply felt and could never be met by the meagre revenues brought in by sales. At such times the owners were forced to seek extra donations to survive.

The peak years of government action against the Polish newspapers were from 1873-1877, the height of the Kulturkampf. The Kuryer Poznański was forced to retract 44 articles in 1875 alone, mostly in protest against the arrest and imprisonment of Archbishop Ledóchowski.(49) In the 1880s, when pressure against German opposition papers was relaxed somewhat, the Polish press continued to be rigorously monitored and fined. At one point almost every major Polish paper had at least one responsible editor in prison(50), with sentences ranging from three months to three years. During the renewed anti-Polish campaign of 1885-1887, centering around the expulsions and the establishment of the Ansiedlungsgesetz, a total of 18 charges were laid in court against the Polish papers, averaging a conviction every month.(51) Needless to say, if found guilty the paper had to pay not only the fine but also the court costs. The two most common charges were slander and 'activities against the state'.

As circulation of Polish papers grew, inspection and analyses of their contents intensified. The Prussian bureaucracy began to pay increasingly greater attention to the newspapers as the voice of the Polish community with the rising respectability of journalism. Two officials who worked with the Polish press were Raimund Zacher, a Poznań police officer, and Christoph von Tiedemann, regent of Bromberg.(52) Tiedemann regularly cited the Polish press in his reports to Bismarck that stressed the need to combat Polonism. Zacher monitored the Polish newspapers daily and sent out weekly handwritten reports to responsible officials in Berlin. These reports were systematized in 1893 when a new file was created, "Gesamtueberblick ueber die polnische Tagesliteratur", a very influential source for policy-makers within the government. The bulky material was edited and printed in 150 copies for official use, and Zacher attached insightful analyses week by week. The practice continued until 1918.(53)

During the Caprivi years pressure against the Polish papers declined noticeably and very few court cases were brought against them. The much needed respite convinced many Poles that Caprivi indeed intended to initiate a new era in Polish Prussian realtions.(54) Held back for over 20 years by Chancellor Bismarck's quick temper and watchful eye, the Polish papers delighted in the greater leeway permitted under Caprivi.

It is important to note that the Poles were fully aware that their newspapers were being scrutinised daily and that their statements formed an important source for the reports sent to policy-makers in Berlin. They knew about Zacher and the printed version of the "Gesamtueberblick".(55) Because of this most newspapers practised self-censorship, not only to avoid fines and court cases but also to create the right impression vis-a-vis the Prussian government. The moderate newspapers carried on a constant campaign to restrain the outspoken Goniec Wielkopolski, which refused to tone down its demands for greater autonomy and eventual independence despite the knowledge that this would be used as ammunition in the hands of German nationalists.(56) Every word written by Polish journalists was not only for domestic consumption but also for the watchful eye of the Prussian government and German public opinion.

2.4 The Polish Newspapers as Representatives of Political and Economic Interest Groups. Editorial Policy

2.4.1 The Dziennik Poznański

The most professional Polish newspaper in Poznań characterized by the highest journalistic standards was the Dziennik Poznański. It was well-managed, well-edited and never short of money thanks to the firm commitment of the national-liberal group of landowners and wealthy burghers. Its circulation of 1700-2000 during the Caprivi era was second only to that of the Wielkopolanin, which was owned by the Dziennik's shareholders. The Dziennik viewed itself in a category above the other newspapers and made a policy of keeping away from the heated quarrels that pervaded the whole of the Polish press in Poznań.

The readership consisted of educated middle and upper-class landowners and the wealthiest townspeople. Its conservative social and political viewpoints were geared to the interests of its patrician readers, and its self-proclaimed 'liberalism' should in no way be understood as socially progressive. The Dziennik also had the best relationship of any Polish paper to the Polish parliamentarians and was often regarded as the party organ, an assumption it staunchly denied. Its shareholders always included a few Reichstag or Landtag deputies and many deputies wrote articles for it.(57)

If not necessarily the voice of the Polish parliamentarians in Berlin, the Dziennik Poznański was without doubt the official voice of the Provincial Central Committee for the Grand Duchy of Poznania, the only recognized Polish political organization in the province. Franciszek Dobrowolski, the Committee's secretary, ran the Dziennik from January, 1871 to his death in 1896. Born in Russian Poland in 1830 he studied law in Moscow and took part in the 1863 Uprising as a key conspirator and minor official in the Provisional National Government. Imprisoned for a year in central Russia, he was pardoned and left Russian Poland forever, settling first in Dresden, where he formed a life-long friendship with Józef Ignacy Kraszewski.(58) While in Dresden he acquired Saxon citizenship, a smart move in view of the inability of the Prussian police to expel him later on as a 'foreigner', and wrote articles to the Dziennik and the literary Sobotka about his role in the ill-fated Uprising. (59)

As editor-in-chief, Dobrowolski transformed the Dziennik into a top-quality newspaper. He recruited a professional staff, paid top wages, opened up offices abroad and used his influence masterfully to promote the national and political cause championed by his employers.(60) But editing the Dziennik was only one of his many activities. He was also director of the Polish theatre in Poznań and belonged to almost every social organization of any importance.(61) After a term as member of Poznań's municipal electoral committee, he became its chairman in 1888, and was appointed secretary of the Central Committee in October of that year.(62)

Dobrowolski's social and political philosophy is almost impossible to distinguish from that of the Dziennik. He was regarded as one of Poznan's leading 'liberals', which in the vocabulary of Prussian Poland meant that he did not attend Mass and rejected the ultramontane creed.(63) Nevertheless, when the Catholic Church was assaulted during the Kulturkampf, Dobrowolski placed the Dziennik in the forefront of its defense because he recognized the importance of the Catholic faith in preserving the Polish identity within Prussia. A splendid organizer and smooth and persuasive public speaker, Dobrowolski was one of

Poznań's most influential residents and enjoyed a great amount of personal prestige.

Following the Kulturkampf the Dziennik's main tasks were to resist Germanization and maintain the hegemony of the gentry. It pursued a course of strict adherence to Prussian law but simultaneously demanded that the special status accorded the Poles in the treaties of Vienna and in royal proclamations be respected.(64) It was ready to forsake an independent Polish state for the right to live as free and equal citizens in Prussia, a statement that many Germans found difficult to believe. Although many of its staff were veterans of the 1863 Uprising (e.g. Dobrowolski, Edmund Callier) the Dziennik repudiated insurrections on behalf of Polish independence. It was thoroughly positivist in this respect and echoed the statements of the leading conservative newspapers in Galicia and Russian Poland. The Dziennik showed no sympathy for revolutionary activity. When a young Pole was arrested in Russia on charges of conspiracy it commented glibly, "(He) does not know what is good for his country".(65)

Of great significance was the Dziennik Poznański's editorial policy on the possibility of a future armed conflict against Russia. While many German publicists felt that the Poles eagerly awaited the outbreak of a European conflagration in order to rebuild an independent Polish state, the organ of the Polish national-liberal gentry went to great lengths to show its abhorence at the very thought of war. In 1893, in response to charges that the aristocracy was in league with Austrian Pole to have war declared against Russia, it wrote, "The fact is that no one in all Poland, not even our hot-blooded youth, is thinking of such a course of action or working to promote it. All of us know very well that we must stay out of all, we repeat a l l (emphasis in the original) international quarrels and intrigues. (Instead) we must work diligently and calmly to preserve our nationality."(66) Independence, if at all, would result from, "the will of Providence and the logical mechanics of history."(67) The Polish community had to maintain a passive and disinterested posture.

The Dziennik was opposed to both national and international revolutionary movements. It detested the radical social views of Social Democracy but was slow to engage in a large-scale press campaign against it. As usual it left such unpleasant tasks to its surrogate paper, the Wielkopolanin. The Dziennik had a very high opinion of itself; its duty was to speak for the Polish community to statesmen and ministers, not to debase itself by refuting "anarchists and socialists".

Of all the Polish newspapers the Dziennik Poznański most frequently made use the term 'national solidarity'. Throughout the 19th century, the landed gentry was able to convince the middle and lower classes that any challenge to their total control over political affairs constituted a form of "treason", arguing that criticism would harm the Polish community in its struggle against Germanization. During the election campaign in 1890 it wrote, "If our Reichstag candidates are asked: what is your program? They can have but one answer - we are Poles and Catholics who will promote and defend everything that is sacred through the power of words and the strength of arguments."(68) Of course, it was the landed gentry who determined what was "Polish and Catholic", and upheld an otherwise anachronistic social structure by unfurling the sacred banner of 'national solidarity'. For the Dziennik the decisions of the Central Committee and the local district committees subject to its supervision were equivalent to the national will and not a theme open to discussion. This is an important point, for under Caprivi the Dziennik was by and large opposed to the loyalist initiative, but stood by the Reichstag Party in its hour of crisis in order to save whatever prestige the gentry still possessed and maintain the fiction of a united Polish front. It refused to print any scandals or disagreements concerning Party affairs, but also refused to glorify the efforts of the deputies, refraining from showing any admiration for the Party leaders.(69) Whether the challenge came from extreme gentry nationalists linked to the Goniec Wielkopolski or from below in the form of the populist urban challenge, the chief argument behind censure was "disrupting national solidarity".(70)

Another important feature of the Dziennik Poznański was its key role in interacting with the German-language press in Poznań. It conducted a running battle with the local German papers, the Posener Zeitung and Posener Tageblatt, and crossed swords with the leading organs of the "Kartellpresse", such as the Koelnische Zeitung, voice of the National Liberals, Hamburger Nachrichten, Bismarck's semi-official organ, and the Kreuzzeitung, voice of the Conservatives. It subscribed to major German newspapers and systematically translated all articles even remotely related to Polish affairs, whether friendly or critical. Its regular contact with German public opinion through the press inclined it to be very pessimistic about the prospects for a permanent Polish-German peaceful co-existence in the eastern provinces. The Poles were victims of a monstrous injustice, as much their own fault as the fault of their partitioners. Having lost their independence it was now their sad fate to obey the laws and relentlessly work to assure the authorities that they were not disloyal or dangerous citizens. "Let the Kreuzzeitung and all Germans rid themselves of suspicions that we are harbouring secret hostile designs (upon Prussian territorial integrity T.K.). We have no need of these and they would bring us nothing...We do not need to be Germanized (to be loyal) for we shall never turn against you or against Germany."(71)

2.4.2 The Wielkopolanin

It is fitting to treat the Dziennik Poznański and the Wielkopolanin in the same breath because they were owned and managed by the same shareholders. It was common knowledge in Poznań that the Wielkopolanin was the Dziennik's "sonny boy" and wrote everything the Dziennik's editors told it to.(72) During the 1880s the Wielkopolanin's chief target was the nationalist Goniec Wielkopolski and it was successful in reducing the Goniec's circulation by over half. During the Caprivi era, however, its attention was turned to combating the middle-class challenge led by the Orędownik.

The Wielkopolanin was printed primarily for the rural poor. As such it was concerned largely with local news that its editors wanted the poor to know. It informed the rural community about the obligation to attend Catholic rallies, to observe religious feastdays and to invest in new agricultural implements. It warned about the pitfalls of emigration to Brazil or America and admonished its readers to remain true to their Polish identity by staying at home despite the hardships of life in Prussian Poland. Discouraging emigration was an important aim of the paper's gentry sponsors, for it kept the rural labour supply constant and, consequently, wages low. Equally important, the Wielkopolanin was the loyal organ of the Polish political machine at election times.

Its style was simple and geared to the minimally educated. Statements were roughly phrased and dogmatic in tone. The Wielkopolanin did not argue with its readers; it lectured them on how they should behave. In 1889, for example, it wrote, "Whoever does not vote for our candidate Zdzisław Czartoryski in the 29 March by-election is not o u r s but a J u d a s, or a wolf in sheep's clothing, or has a cabbage head for a brain."(73) Never mixing their words, the writers at the Wielkopolanin could be effusive in their praise or scathing in their criticism. They saved their strongest invective for the Orędownik's editor Roman Szymański. In June, 1893 they called him a "moral corpse"; in August an "ally of the socialists"; and by October a "traitor and heretic".(74)

Throughout the Caprivi years the Wielkopolanin refrained from criticising the loyalists and hardly mentioned the political differences that split the power brokers at all. This suggests that the gentry had reached a silent deal over the editorial policy of the Wielkopolanin, hiding their divisions from their rural workers. The dispute was one among gentlemen; the poor had no need to be kept informed. When the Polish community was thrown into crisis over the failure of loyalism in 1893-94 the Wielkopolanin rallied around the Reichstag deputies and the existing political apparatus.

The Wielkopolanin reacted in blunt language and dogmatic formulas to the growth of Social Democracy. The slogans of the socialists were answered with slogans just as simple. When the announcement was made that a socialist newspaper would be printed in the Polish language in Berlin, the Wielkopolanin ordered its readers to hunt down the copies and burn them. "We shall have no dealings with blasphemers! Only the dregs of society, faithless and dishonourable people, can give support to the socialist band... The workers are no more than sacrificial lambs and will be squeezed dry like a lemon by the socialist leaders and then thrown to the four winds. Let German socialists play these games if they like but let us make it very clear that whoever among us who donates even a penny to their coffers is betraying his Faith and his nationality." (emphasis in the original) (75)

Like the Dziennik Poznański, the Wielkopolanin deplored the sufferings of Poles in Russia but was far removed from advocating a policy of war to liberate them. Descriptions of Russian rule were written in the language of the rural poor. The Muscovites were described as "wild" people with a "Tatar-Mongol character",(76) and , "The Russian government has declared war upon us in the Polish Kingdom and the annexed lands, a war to the death."(77)

The paper was written and edited by a combination of laymen and clergy initially under the direction of Julian Bukowiecki, then Father Jeżewski. Its enemies charged that Jeżewski had hired bands of troublemakers and loudmouths to attend political rallies and shout down the populist speakers.(78) If true, this may have been masterminded by the shrewd Dobrowolski of the Dziennik, who, as chairman of Poznań's municipal committee was determined to crush the populist challenge. Costing only 1 Mk. per quarter and usually available for free to all who wanted it, the Wielkopolanin was a strong weapon in the hands of the landowner class in their struggle to swim against the current of social change.

2.4.3 The Kuryer Poznański

Few aspects of life were as important to Poles in Prussia as their religious upbringing and their allegiance to the Catholic Church. That the Church should take an active part in social and political affairs during Poland's era of partitions was a fact of life that no one, apart from the rising populist movement, seemed to challenge. One important manifestation of the Church's social and political work was its press. The Kuryer Poznański was started in 1872 to offset the failures of the Przegląd Poznański and the Tygodnik Katolicki. The Church needed a counterweight to the 'liberalism' being espoused by Dobrowolski and Callier at the Dziennik Poznański. Its readership consisted of the clergy and like-minded landowners, and it had great difficulty in reaching other social groups. From 1876, the Kuryer was run by the Kantecki brothers, Antoni until 1887 and then Maksymilian until 1899. Like the Dziennik, the Kuryer ran a foreign news column and maintained correspondents in other European cities but unlike the Dziennik it was never successful in attracting a lot of advertising. Not surprisingly it needed regular injections of capital to keep it solvent.(79)

Antoni Kantecki studied theology in Muenster and was ordained in 1871 as a Catholic priest. During the Kulturkampf years he was imprisoned several times and became something of a local hero for his stubborn resistance to Bismarck's policies. The Prussian police seemed intent on making a martyr of the elder Kantecki. Wolfgang Wetzel has written, "Gegen kein anderes polnisches Blatt sind die preussischen Behoerden in so offenkundig tendenzioeser Weise vorgegangen wie gegen den Kuryer Poznański und seinen verantwortlichen Redakteur Dr. Kantecki." (80) On 1 August, 1875, the Kuryer's owners appointed him co-editor, then editor in chief in 1876. That same year he became head of Poznań's municipal committee and later served on the Central Committee until his death in 1893.(81)

Antoni Kantecki managed to combine a political career with journalism and his priestly duties. He used the Kuryer to promote a philosophy that was slowly coming to the fore among Catholic social thinkers, a Christianization of modern life and the setting up of workingmen's organizations directed by the clergy to counter the influence of Social Democracy. As an extra service to the poor workingmen, his printshop put out translations of various labour laws and social services offered by the government.(82)

A. Kantecki's political career took a turn for the worse under the administration of Julius Dinder as Archbishop of Gniezno-Poznań. In 1887 he was imprisoned twice for writing inflammatory articles on the expulsions of non-Prussian Poles. The highest levels of authority in Berlin put pressure on Dinder to remove Kantecki from his newspaper. The Archbishop acceded and Kantecki was "promoted" to the position of penitentiary at the Gniezno Cathedral.(83) Hoping to use his oratorical skills to counter the decision of the Kultusministry which banned the teaching of Polish in public schools, the Central Committee placed his name in the running for the Prussian Landtag election of 1888. Once again, pressure from Berlin forced Dinder to forbid Kantecki from becoming a candidate.

After A. Kantecki's removal as editor-in-chief in 1887, the Kuryer was entrusted to his younger brother Maksymilian.(84) M. Kantecki guided the paper until his death and took much of the blame for the failure of the loyalist initiative under Caprivi. He studied in Breslau from 1876-1880 and became a teacher in Poznań in 1882, then in Srem in 1884. Like all Polish schoolteachers he was faced with the likelihood of being transferred to the western provinces of Prussia, and this may have influenced him to give up teaching and undertake a journalistic career. His promotion to the position of editor-in-chief at the age of 30 attests both to his intelligence and to the faith placed in him by the Kuryer's shareholders.

In addition to his press duties M. Kantecki was also elected secretary of Poznań's municipal committee in 1888, but for some unexplained reason gave this up in early 1891, perhaps due to disagreements over the policy of loyalism with the committee's chairman, Dobrowolski.(85) He remained on the committee, however, as a normal member until it resigned in a body in 1893. Like his elder brother, M. Kantecki promoted the formation of Catholic workingmen's organisations and placed great emphasis upon the social and economic teachings contained in the Rerum Novarum of 1891. Alone among Poznań's Polish publicists the younger Kantecki confronted the problems of abject poverty and freely criticized the excesses of liberal capitalism.

M. Kantecki suffered from poor health throughout his life and his condition deteriorated noticeably after his brother's death in 1893. He died in 1899 at the age of 42. The Kuryer Poznański, badly shaken by the total failure of loyalism, ceased publication in 1905.

Scholars have tended to identify the Kuryer exclusively with a narrow program of ultramontanism and blind loyalty to Prussia. A closer analysis of the paper's editorial creed, however, reveals a broader and more compassionate view of the surrounding world and a willingness to address social problems that other newspapers generally neglected. The Kuryer was frequently able to rise above the narrow confines of the nationality conflict and offer its readers a Catholic answer to the manifold economic and social problems that had accompanied rapid industrialization and urbanization. It deplored the hardships encountered by the poor in Poznań and ridiculed the complacency of the well-to-do. In 1892 it wrote "Those of us privileged who throw stones at the mass of poor and unemployed, the morally and materially destitute living on the borderlines of existence, have no heart or conscience. Let him not speak of "humanitarianism" because he does not understand life and the vagaries of fortune. None of us riding in horse-drawn carriages today can be sure that in a year or in a decade we, or our children, will not be homeless or living in a flophouse, forced to confront poverty and desperation from day to day."(86) 'Liberalism', was portrayed as unchecked speculation, greed, and a crude form of Social Darwinism. The root cause of cruelty towards one's fellow men was the phenomenon of vulgar materialism and the corresponding decline in religious values. What was needed was a process of Christianization in the workplace, in the towns and inside the family, a mixture of modernization and Catholic ethics.

Along with its concern over living standards and working conditions, the Kuryer was inordinately sensitive to the growth of Social Democracy in Germany and its relatively small inroads within the Polish community. Social Democracy was "the symptom of a disease that has affected all national life, a disease which our educated classes have promoted through their blindness."(87) This 'disease' was clearly liberal capitalism and the dire poverty of the mass of underpaid and often unemployed workers. It was accompanied by a decline in spirituality and a gross pursuit of materialistic wealth. "The times are very serious", wrote the Kuryer in 1890 just before the May Day demonstrations. "A lot of explosive material has accumulated among our lower classes. A single spark could set it off."(88)

The answer to the challenge of godless Social Democracy seemed obvious enough. Catholic, or at least Christian, education and ethics had to be re-introduced into public life, and a united front had to be formed not only against socialism but also against atheistical liberals and free-thinkers. This notion was postulated in 1890 as a coalition of Conservatives, Catholics and Poles working together to save the moral character of Germany and reverse the dangerous slide to socialism. This coalition by definition rejected two of the Poles' most faithful parliamentary allies, The Progressive Party and the SPD, both of whom had consistently opposed Bismarck's anti-Polish policies. As equals in the struggle for monarchy, order and Christianity, the coalition was supposed to help Chancellor Caprivi do battle with the dark forces of anarchy, godlessness, socialism and national hatreds. The Kuryer hoped that Germans would see the need for this coalition and reject Bismarck's hardline anti-Polish policy. The determining factor in the Polish-German relationship should not be nationality but rather a conservative, Christian consensus. In 1891, the Kuryer wrote, "We want to live and work together with you (Germans T.K.). We consider ourselves Prussian citizens; we are against the cancerous growth of socialism that is infecting our whole society and we oppose all anarchistic tendencies. We always obey the law... are we not, then, a peaceful element? Let the government do away with its hated policies against us and it will see that, just as Poles in Galicia have become a bastion of support for the throne once they were treated justly, so also will we sincerely support all moves to strengthen the nation both in domestic and in foreign affairs."(89)

Both German and Polish critics felt that the Kuryer needlessly stressed the Russian war factor in attempting to win over the Prussian government to the abolition of Bismarck's legislation.(90) The Kuryer brushed off the charge that loyalists were looking to war against Russia as a "big lie". In April, 1890, it wrote, "We do not want to pull anyone's chestnuts out of the fire. We have been burnt too often in the past."(91) Its position was identical to that of the Reichstag Polish Party - Poles did not seek war but would march if called upon by their sovereign.(92)

In addition to taking aim at the German-language dailies, the Kuryer was obliged to defend loyalty in the face of an increasingly dubious Polish public. Undaunted, it rose to the challenge and spared no degree of invective and ingenuity against its principal enemies, the Orędownik and the Goniec Wielkopolski. The feud with the Goniec was very old and reached unprecedented levels of recrimination during the Caprivi era. The Kuryer charged that the unrestricted rhetoric of the Goniec was material evidence used by the Bismarck press network to sabotage the Polish-German reconciliation process. After reading the wildly romantic Goniec, who would not believe that all Poles were 'agitators'? In early 1893, the Kuryer asked, "Who is inspiring (Kultusminister) Bosse's unfriendly statements? Someone must be because he knows nothing about local conditions here. The information he has received was based on Polish chauvinism, which we consider far more dangerous than German chauvinism."(93) By the end of 1893, it was so frustrated by the determined resistance of the Goniec that it thundered, "Whenever Polish chauvinism threatens the state and society it should be punished!"(94), indirectly denouncing a Polish newspaper before the Prussian bureaucracy. The tendency of Polish newspapers during the Caprivi years to ruthlessly denounce each other in the face of Prussian monitoring undoubtedly represented one of the saddest chapters in the history of national solidarity in Prussian Poland.

The charges against the Orędownik were linked to its direct challenge to Poznania's Polish political apparatus. Although the Kuryer initially allowed that Polish politics in Poznania was in need of a basic democratization (95), it was nonetheless dedicated to the hegemony of the landowners and upper Catholic clergy. Szymański was treated as an unscrupulous demagogue, sometimes as a dangerous element and sometimes as a harmless fool intent on inspiring public ridicule. "The handful of Orędownik's adherents are not the representatives of the people, but rather an unhealthy wart on our social body. It has been caused by personal ambitions and is being fed by the sinful alliance of weak, shallow people and the common guttersnipes."(96) The Orędownik's headlines were called "criminal slogans" and its editor a "pseudo-tribune of the upstart middle class" whose destructive crusade against the established order only worked in favour of German chauvinists. This feud got completely out of hand in 1893 when both papers sued each other for libel and the Kuryer's owners were obliged to pay Roman Szymański 150Mk. for accusing him of aiding the Social Democratic movement.(97)

2.4.4 The Goniec Wielkopolski

Less is known about the functioning and the policies of the Goniec Wielkopolski than other papers because relatively little of it has survived to the present day. Characterizations of the Goniec vary widely; Richard Blanke has described it as the "organ of the chauvinistic intelligentsia" while the Polish " historian Jerzy Marczewski has called it the organ of the "progressive landed gentry."(98) The present author sees it as the voice of the irreconcilable landed gentry, a relatively small but vocal group that never accepted the finality of the Polish partitions. They went as far as the law permitted to remind Poles of their ancient heritage and the certainty of their national resurrection. The Goniec Wielkopolski's intellectual roots went back to the tradition of insurrection and revolution that dominated Polish thought until 1863. It had never made the full conversion to Positivism evidenced by the other newspapers. Anger, bitterness and cruel irony filled its pages. In early 1895, it wrote on the hundreth anniversary of the third partition, "Wir sind die eingeborenen Kinder dieses Landes. Wenn es nicht genuegend Brot fuer beide Nationalitaeten gibt, so moegen sie (die Deutschen) in ihre Heimatgehenden zurueckgehen, uns aber in Ruhe lassen. Es hat sie ueberhaupt niemand bei uns zu Gast geladen, sie brauchen sich bei uns nicht ruinieren, da so viel Platz im grossen 'Vaterlande' haben." (99)

Founded in 1877 by the team of Ludwik Rzepecki and Władysław Niegolewski, the Goniec enjoyed a rapid rise in popularity and was able to print about 2500 copies in 1883. Its circulation dropped to about a thousand with the appearance of the Wielkopolanin, but was able to expand slowly to about 2,000 by 1900. Under the dynamic leadership of Ludwik Rzepecki's son, Karol, it became the first National Democratic newspaper in Prussian Poland in 1901.(100)

Its readers were primarily middle-income and poor landowners, the sons and grandsons of those who had fallen in 1848 and 1863. The Goniec Wielkopolski had no wealthy patrons that scholarship is aware of, and the Rzepecki family undoubtedly had chronic shortages of funds and materials, particularly in view of the frequency of court cases brought against it. The Prussian police succinctly described it as "extremely chauvinistic".(101) Articles such as that of 1 January, 1893, infuriated the Prussian officials, "What can we wish ourselves this New Year? Our people can have only one wish: Freedom for the Fatherland! (emphasis in the original)...We wish this New Year's Day to hear no more of reconciliation where a Polish Party is working for the greatness of Prussia and Germany".(102) The only national policy that was compatible with Polish patriotism and self-respect was the reversal of the partitions and a reunion of the three sections. Since another armed uprising was out of the question the Poles had to prepare themselves for the day of national liberation and not integrate themselves any deeper into the societies of their partitioners. In 1893, the Goniec wrote, "From day to day our numbers and our strength are growing. No minister's decree can stop this force. It is the force that will lead to the reconstruction of a free Poland!"(103) The greatest danger facing the Polish community was 'de-nationalization', giving up one's Polish identity in the name of material comfort or short-term advantages.

In keeping with the policies of the other Polish newspapers, the Goniec Wielkopolski stayed far away from war speculation. National resurrection could come about through a general European war, but it was not in the interest of the Polish nation to take part. In 1893 it wrote, "The Polish people should not take the side of either Germany or Russia. Our role in such a war would be to suffer, for if a war finally broke out it would be on Polish lands that blood is split. Europe will come to realize that Poland's restoration is necessary for its own security, not because of any humanitarian feelings."(104) Although sharply critical of the way that Poles were being mistreated in Russian Poland, it opposed the Polish participation in Germany's military build-up as a national disgrace.

The Goniec Wielkopolski styled itself as a newspaper for all classes, and indeed its nationalism overrode social class and economic barriers. It welcomed the urbanization and modernization that was taking the Polish community by storm and, unlike the other gentry papers, was aware that these trends constituted the wave of the future that had to be utilized in furthering the aims of Polish independence. The Goniec showed no signs of resentment towards either the peasantry, the middle class or the working class so long as these groups served the national cause. True to its intellectual roots, it promoted democratization as the means to strengthen the nation, as the radical patriots in 1831, 1848 and 1863 had done. The only group that attracted its full invective was the wealthy landowners who sought a reconciliation with the Prussian government and, thus, betrayal of the national cause. It vehemently opposed the loyalist initiative of the Kuryer Poznański and often accused the Polish Party leaders of treason. Its reaction to the Polish vote in favour of the 1893 Great Army Bill is indicative, "What shame and vileness! At least those who were forced to sign the act recognising the second partition could say that they were surrounded by Russian bayonets. But on 6 May (the day of the first vote on the Great Army Bill T.K.) there was no force used in the Reichstag."(105)

The greatest hostility was reserved for the Reichstag Party's leader, Józef Kościelski. The Goniec Wielkopolski was the first and most consistent in calling for his removal from the Party. In April 1893 it wrote, "We declare ourselves firmly against the election of Kościelski. Whoever votes for him is no more than a 'Polish-speaking Prussian'. He wants to ostentatiously wash away our national character and have us disappear within Prussia and the German Reich". (106) Three days later it wrote, "Many deputies are ashamed of themselves and of Kościelski. Against the wishes of his peers he has been pursuing a policy centred around his own person. No Pole is permitted to say that he places the interests of Germany above those of Poland. Whoever votes for Kościelski after having committed such a list of national crimes is as much a renagade as he is."(107)

The Kuryer charged that the Goniec was being unrealistic and unpatriotic.Its obstinance was wrecking any chance the Party in Berlin had of overcoming the legal barriers that limited the full expression of the Polish language and religion. The Goniec simply did not believe that a reconciliation with Prussia was possible. One was either a Prussian or a Pole; Prussians belonged in Prussia and Poles in Poland. The provinces of West Prussia and Poznania were part of Poland. The Orędownik felt that the Goniec was a pathetic relic of bygone years that was engaging in empty rhetoric rather than working seriously for the national cause. The categorical opposition to everything Prussian or German and the pompous boasting of a Poland "from sea to sea" were perhaps humourous but useless in coming to grips with modern social and economical realities.(108)

Although critical of many decisions made by the Central Committee the Coniec was actively involved in the Polish political process. Its editor-in-chief, Ludwik Rzepecki, was a member of Poznań's municipal committee from 1888-1893 and his son, Karol, was a key figure in the politicized "Sokół" organization (Turnverein) and later a leading National Democrat. The Goniec faithfully printed all the statements and election coverage issued by the Central Committee, and apart from its call to reject Kościelski, never spoke out directly against other Polish candidates.

Because it was the only consistent opponent of blind loyalism its authority in Poznania rose with the evident failure of the reconciliation attempt during the Caprivi years. With Caprivi's resignation and the onset of a harsher Polish policy on the part of his successors, the Goniec was ready to join in the new, fiercer phase of the Polish-German struggle under Hohenlohe and von Buelow. It went so far as to suggest that too much kindness had endangered the national spirit and that the return of the truncheon would rekindle resistance and patriotic fervour. "The 'Neue Kurs' has been a hundred times more dangerous to us than Bismarck was", it declared in June, 1894.(109) Here, it had something in common with determined German nationalists. Both emerged from the Neue Kurs stronger and convinced that mutual hostility rather than reconciliation was the only natural course in the German-Polish relationship.

2.4.5 The Orędownik

The most dynamic force in Poznań's Polish political life during the 1890s was the growth of a populist opposition party centred around the radical editor-in-chief of the Orędownik, Dr. Roman Szymański. Szymański is the only newspaperman in Prussian Poland to have generated any biographical interest and his reputation among future generations as the "father of Poznań's middle-class awakening" has been considerable.(110) It is tempting to portray him as a resolute burgher triumphing over the decadent aristocracy, a sort of latter-day David challenging and eventually overcoming Goliath. He took on the whole weight of the traditional gentry power groups: the political orgainization, the newspapers, the Catholic hierarchy, and the Peasants' Societies. In doing so he incurred a great number of enemies who saw him as nothing more than an egotistical demagogue with no scruples and no clear programme. To highlight the frequent confusion evident in his political views his critics contemptuously called him a "Schwarzweisser".(111)

After studies in Germany, Szymański decided to enter the priesthood. He registered at a seminary in 1862 but left soon afterwards and joined a secret society, the "Towarzystwo Narodowe" (National Association) in 1863. The association's purpose was to aid the uprising in Russian Poland, but it was broken up by the Prussian police and Szymański spent one month in prison.(112) During the 1880s he struck up a friendship with Józef Ignacy Kraszewski in Dresden, and likely met his future arch-enemy and journalistic rival, Dobrowolski.

In the late 1860s Szymański decided upon a career in journalism and secured his first major appointment as editor of the cultural weekly Sobótka (1869-1870) before moving on to the Gazeta Toruńska in mid-1870.(113) Hired by Maksymilian Jackowski to edit the newly-founded organ of the middle class, the Orędownik, Szymański soon quarrelled with his employer over the paper's policy and decided to run it himself. By the end of 1873 he had paid off his considerable debt to Jackowski and was the Orędownik's sole owner.(114) For the next two decades

Szymański engineered various minor miracles to keep his newspaper going, a great challenge in view of the hostility of the Polish landowners and the watchful eye of the Prussian press authorities. In the 1870s he spent a good deal of time in prison (115), which may have convinced him to concentrate less on the nationality struggle and more on the cause of the expanding middle class. After an unsuccessful attempt to organize Poznań's Polish urban voters into a viable pressure group in the mid-1870s, Szymański turned to long-term enlightenment and organic work as his key themes. His message that modernization required a greater middle-class participation in national affairs made slow but steady progress into the towns.

Szymański was more than simply a newspaperman. He was a politician, a lecturer on economics and business organization and chairman of the Society of Catholic Craftsmen. He also directed an informal school for editors and journalists, and his students included such future press leaders as Adam Napieralski Bernard Milski, Józef Siemianowski (his protegee and assistant editor of the Orędownik) and Franciszek Krysiak.(116) Szymański was particularly interested in Polish organizations in Upper Silesia and the Ruhr Vally, urging all middle-class Poles to form their own associations rather than join German ones.(117)

The final break with the Central Committee and the gentry leadership came in 1888, when Szymański resigned his seat on Poznań's municipal committee and, in the words of his biographer, Lech Trzeciakowski, "issued a declaration of war on the gentry".(118) He tried to organise a boycott of the 1888 Landtag election, and when this failed urged his followers to stop making financial contributions to the Party coffers.(119) After the Caprivi era his popularity continued to grow and he became a late convert to the National Democrats before his death in 1908. However one felt about Szymański's views, it had to be admitted that he constituted a dynamic causal factor in Polish social and political life. He certainly did more than any other journalist to politicize the middle class in Poznania. One of the first German scholars to appreciate his importance was Ludwig Bernhard, who wrote in 1907, "Alle heute erscheinenden demokratischen oder populaeren polnischen Blaetter in Preussen haben vom Oredownik einen Teil ihrer Farben und Tone und Ideen entnommen, und so ist der Oredownik, der niemals viel Leser hatte, sondern sich meist mit 3 bis 4000 Abonnenten begnuegen musste, dennoch als das pfadweisende Blatt der polnischen Demokratie zu beachten."(120)

Richard Blanke has recently written that Szymański's programme, "if any, was to 'buy Polish'".(121) True, an economic boycott of German and Jewish businesses was part of the Orędownik's program. "No German or Jew will hold it (the boycott T.K.) against us because we have been forced into this position. Otherwise, we should die."(122) But a boycott was only one element in a sophisticated, if not always consistent, socio-political platform. The final goal was the emancipation of the middle class; to set the Polish middle class on an equal standing with the German, and satisfy all the economic needs of the Polish community. The middle class had to be elevated in size, prestige and political significance. Initially, he felt that the gentry class had a natural predisposition to rule and should guide national policy while granting an increasingly greater share of political responsibility to the middle class. The task of the gentry was to educate, strengthen and speed along the rise of the new power base which so clearly represented the wave of the future. However, with the passage of time Szymański saw that the landowners were unwilling to broaden the base of the Polish political decision-making process. Landowners had thus forfeited their role as leaders of Polish society. They had engaged in bombastic rhetoric for decades, and were inhibiting the processes of economic development and urbanization. They had 'betrayed' the Polish nation by clinging to power longer than their economic strength warranted, and would go to any length to maintain their monopoly.

Szymański blamed the Polish gentry for the poor state of trade and commerce in the Polish community. Development required capital and investment; yet the Polish gentry, rather than cultivate the growth of Polish commerce, were buying from German shops and investing scarce capital in German enterprises. "Ultimately, we are part of Germany, and therefore our fate is not a happy one", wrote the Orędownik in February, 1890, "nevertheless the sad plight of our nation should not be complicated by the creation of even sadder economic conditions. If we must be part of Germany, let us at least take material advantage of this union and better ourselves. If our community falls deeper into poverty, it will become increasingly difficult to defend our national interests, and at some point it may become impossible."(123)

A wealthier Polish community required not only capital and investment, but also an effective political lobby in Berlin. Polish deputies should be pressing for greater government patronage in the poorer eastern provinces, greater protection for small enterprises, easier credit and improved modes of transportation and communication. Instead, the deputies were loudmouthing about a Poland from "sea to sea" and making useless protests against the violation of the treaties of Vienna, while at the same time squandering Polish capital in the bars and shops of Berlin and selling Polish soil to the Colonization Commission.(124) More representatives of the middle class had to be present in the Polish Reichstag and Landtag Parties to draw attention to the needs and interests of the growing urban sector.

While the Orędownik sharply criticized the way the gentry conducted the defence of the national cause, it offered only a few novel suggestions. One of these was a sharper distinction between Roman Catholicism and the national interest. It was critical of the disproportionately strong influence held by the Catholic hierarchy in political life and expressed disapproval when clergymen made unequivocal political statements, usually supportive of the landowner leadership.(125) During the Caprivi era the Orędownik-led populist movement was frequently accused by the Church of being anti-Catholic, and Szymański had to hold demonstrative "Catholic populist rallies" to prove his adherence to the Catholic Faith. The Orędownik also showed unqualified support for the early signs of a national awakening in Upper Silesia. Upper Silesia was a sensitive issue because it formed part of the political domain of the German Centrum Party, the Poles' most consistent and powerful parliamentary ally. Other newspapers were hesitant to deal directly with the Silesian problem because of the impact this might have on the German Catholics. A formula was devised to disguise the quarrel over Silesia; since it was not part of Poland in 1772 it was not subject to the guarantees of the treaties of Vienna and of no concern to the Poles in Poznania and West Prussia. The Orędownik, however, felt that the need to assert the Polish character of the Upper Silesians was more important than the parliamentary alliance with the Centrum. In 1889 it wrote, "(Polish) national feeling is perfectly natural in Upper Silesia. It results from German unification and from the forces of modernization."(126) A year later it heralded the beginnings of the Polish Electoral Committee for the German Reich when it wrote, "Poles all over Prussia must feel as one and have one common program." (127) Later on the concern over Polish rights in Upper Silesia was taken up by all Polish newspapers and became a matter of Polish policy among the National Democrats.

In other areas, however, the Orędownik shared the mainline policies of the gentry. It agreed that Poles should protest when their rights were violated by the Prussian bureaucracy but insisted that the leadership was managing the demonstrations all wrong.(128) It voiced the concerns of the gentry press over the growth of Social Democracy and similarly ordered its followers to destroy socialist voting cards on sight.(129) In unison with the other papers it was dismayed by the grim prospects for Poles in the event of a general European war and warned against any breakdown of the existing nation-state alignments. In 1889 it wrote, "It seems certain that no Pole desires a war because our blood would be shed on both sides. (In addition) we have nothing to gain."(130) An independent Poland could arise in the future, but this depended on the will of Providence. "If Almighty God wills it, a future free and independent Poland will arise as a result of a new European order."(131) The Poles, however, should do nothing actively to force the issue. "We feel that our best policy is to keep far away from a war against Russia, and we should also decline to join a Slavic federation. We must defend our existence in our own Polish lands."(132)

The Orędownik charged that the loyalist initiative was seeking a war against Russia as a final desparate manoeuvre to push aside the rising challenge of the middle class. "The 'partya dworska'('Hofpartei' or court party, the gentry loyalists led by Kościelski) is looking for a war to create an independent Poland without Great Poland... We shall remain in our ancient lands as we are. (This policy would signify) our national extinction in Great Poland. This is what Kościelski's loyalism is leading to."(133)

The Orędownik's resolute promotion of the middle class in Poznań earned it the hostility of all the gentry papers. Its abusive and aggressive style was matched word for word by the Kuryer and the mass-circulation Wielkopolanin. Szymański had a personal grudge against Dobrowolski of the Dziennik and spared no effort to ridicule him as a servile lackey of the landowners. The Orędownik also made fun of the Goniec, but later formed an uneasy alliance with it in a common war against Kościelski and the loyalists. Its only firm ally during the 1890s was Knapowski's anti-Semitic Postęp, which openly joined the battle against the political establishment in mid-1893.

In stressing the importance of the Orędownik, one should remember that during the Caprivi years it survived a fierce boycott and was able to triple its circulation by 1900.(134) Szymański may not have been a great theoretician or altogether consistent in his views (ein doktrinaerer Eigenbroter Ludwig Bernhard)(135) but he was the undisputed leader of the Polish middle class during an era when its influence dramatically increased in tandem with the rise of urbanization and industrialization.

2.4.6 The Postęp

The most dynamic growth during the Caprivi years was enjoyed by the virulently anti-Semitic Postęp. Its editor-in-chief and owner was Stanisław Knapowski, a working-class native of Poznań whose career depended on wholesale Jew-baiting and sensational publicism. Knapowski was a vain egotist who possessed a strong personality and a shrewd ability to manipulate base emotions. His abrasive character, however, made many enemies, especially the urban intellectuals in Poznań.(136)

Knapowski began his work in publishing as a printer in the workshop of the Dziennik Poznański. He then travelled to several German cities and wrote articles for the Orędownik during the 1870s. After returning to the Dziennik's printshop for a while Knapowski set up his own in 1886, concentrating mostly on pamphlets and religious catechisms.(137) The Postęp appeared twice weekly from January, 1890, and six times weekly from September of that year.

Knapowski described the Postęp as, "A newspaper dedicated to matters of industry, trade and craftsmanship, and directed against the Jews." On New Year's Day, 1892, his new motto was, "Polish and Catholic, the only anti- Semitic organ under Prussian rule in Polish".(138) Two themes dominated the headlines until the domestic crisis in Poznań in mid-1893: the Jewish 'menace' and the need to upgrade the standards of trade and industry among the Polish population.

The popularity of anti-Semitism as evidenced in the soaring circulation of the Postęp is surprising in the light of statistics. In 1890 there were only 44,346 Jews in the whole province of Poznania (total population ca. 1,700,000, of whom 542,013 were Protestants and 1,164,067 were Catholics) and their numbers steadily dropped to 26,412 in 1910.(139) Their percentage of the total population declined from 3.3% in 1880 to 2.2% in 1895 to only 1.2% in 1910.(140) However, though not great in number, Poznań's Jewish community was influential in the town's municipal council, its Progressive Party organisation and its local businesses.(141)

The anti-Semitism espoused by Knapowski did not differ substantially from similar currents in other European countries. In brief, all the world's problems were in some way caused by International Jewry. In Prussian Poland anti-Semitism was also used to explain the overall weakness of the Polish middle class and commerce. The Jews were using their influence to prevent the growth of Polish retail businesses and seduce affluent Polish landowners away from Polish shops. Initially, Knapowski seemed to feel that the gentry class would respond to his cries of alarm if properly informed. In addition to his newspaper, he went on speaking tours all across the province, and as soon as he was accepted into the Polish municipal committee in Poznań in 1891 he seized the podium to denounce the 'Jewish conspiracy'. When it became apparent that the gentry were not interested in his exaggerated anti-Semitism, Knapowski reached for a straightforward explanation "The Kuryer and the Wielkopolanin (i.e. the gentry papers T.K.) have clearly gone over to the side of the Jews."(142)

Even more than its 'elder brother' in the Polish press constellation, the Orędownik, the Postęp editorialized the need to boycott Jewish and German shops and support Polish commerce. At times its tone was rather sharp. In June, 1890, it wrote, "Among our craftsmen voices are heard saying that the Polish gentry need the townspeople only at election times or to attend patriotic rallies... They eagerly buy things from Berlin rather than support local industry."(143) Like the Orędownik, it argued for a more assertive role for the middle class but looked to the landowners for leadership, investment and capital in promoting a more nationalistic economic policy. When it became apparent that the gentry were dithering, despite all their assurances to the contrary, Knapowski broke completely with the leadership, stopped taking part in meetings of the Polish committee in Poznań, and, together with Szymański, set up the opposition "partya ludowa", the Populist Party, in August, 1893.

A forum for Knapowski's interest in the modernisation of the Polish economy was the "Towarzystwo Młodych Przemysłowców", the Society of Young Industrialists, of which he was chairman. (144) His lectures combined economic and political themes: the 'Jewish menace', business organization, insurance policies, the threat of Social Democracy, marketing strategy and the need to modernize production techniques with new technology to keep up with the German and Jewish competition. Roman Szymański was often the Society's guest lecturer. Members of this Society included Tomasz Drobnik and Stanisław Mniszewski, who were later to be faithful deputies to the two editors in the populist revolt of 1893.

On other matters of interest to Polish society the Postęp did not diverge greatly from other papers. Its attitude to the loyalist initaitive was moderately critical at first and it was not averse to the idea of loyalty vis-à-vis the Prussian government as such. At times the Postęp offered its readers sound and balanced political analysis. In late 1892 it wrote, "The policy of unequivocal loyalty is only stirring up confusion in our minds... Our best policy will always be the middle road. We should not harp on the treaties (of Vienna) to boredom, but we should also not bend our knees in abject obedience and vote against the material interests of our people. The 'New Era' has not brought us many benefits and can do a lot of damage... We have faith in our deputies but feel it is in the interests of our nation that they do not burden us with new taxes."(145) Had this line of thought been dominant among the parliamentarians in Berlin, a great deal of friction within the Polish community might have been avoided.

The Postęp was also not interested in any military intrigues to reunite Polish lands. Although it shared the antipathy towards Russia common to Prussian Poles ("Show me a Muscovite and I shall show you a thief and a liar!")(146) it frowned on any war speculation. In answer to an Austrian newspaper that was urging a combined German-Austrian strike against Russia and promising an independent Polish buffer state, the Postęp wrote, "None of these theories interest us. Let Germany and Russia fight to the finish - it is not our affair. We shall not be exploited. Just treat us like equal citizens, make our language legal in the schools and the courts and give us equal access to the civil service. Leave Poland's resurrection to whoever God decides."(147)

At the outset the Postęp downplayed the Social Democratic 'threat' and was not particularly excited over its growing electoral successes. In late 1890 it wrote, "The Church and the Catholic Faith are the best defences against socialism. But when Germanization is propagated by the Church, and when the Polish language is banned from the schools, then the door is open for the socialists to reach the poor."(148) In agreement with other Polish newspapers it rejected the idea of combating Social Democracy through the promulgation of emergency laws. "The Kaiser is contemplating passing laws to stop the encroachment of socialism into our schools. This is unnecessary. What is needed is for religious instruction to be taught forcefully and in a manner which is comprehensible to the children (i.e. in the Polish language T.K.)... Making socialism forbidden only makes it more attractive."(149) After the small socialist demonstration in Poznań on May Day, 1891, the Postęp expressed satisfaction that permission had been given by the police. "(Now they have) shown Poznania how weak they are and what sort of riff-raff they represent."(150) Later on, though, the Postęp was quick to re-interpret the potential danger after examining the list of Jews prominent in the leadership. In October, 1891, it wrote, "This dangerous newspaper (the socialist Gazeta Robotnicza T.K.) is being distributed among the Polish community. Should we not use all means available against these false prophets?...who are helped in their devilish work by the Jews?...At the head of the Erfurt Congress sat the Jew Singer."(151)

The meteoric rise of the Postęp was part of a phenomenal growth in anti-Semitism world-wide. In Poznań, Knapowski managed to exploit the issue to rise above the masses and create a career for himself as a public spokesman. He satisfied a need produced by growing resentment on the part of urban Poles of the perceived Jewish stranglehold on retail commerce. Anti-Semitism was a popular force and became an integral part of the National Democratic platform at the turn of the century. Although less sophisticated and imaginative than the other leader of the populists, Roman Szymański, the sheer power of Knapowski's aggressive, simple and unrelenting style made him a force to be reckoned with.

2.4.7 The Przegląd Poznański

By late 1893 the growing body of Poznań's Polish professionals and men of letters were begining to register their aversion to and alarm at the deep fissures evident within the Polish community and the poisonous atmosphere it had injected into the press. On 19 November, 1893, sixteen members of the intelligentsia led by the lawyer Bernard Chrzanowski, leader of Poznań's "Sokół" and Reichstag deputy from Poznań from 1901 (152), and the physicians Tomasz Drobnik and Bolesław Krysiewicz, met in Poznań to organize the founding of a new literary and cultural weekly.(153) The group calculated that it would need about 20,000 Mk. to start up the paper, but was able to launch it with far less in the end. As editor-in-chief the paper's shareholders chose Władysław Rabski, an aspiring writer and holder of a degree from the University of Berlin at present employed at the Dziennik Poznański.(154) Rabski was dissatisfied with the heavy-handed manner in which Franciszek Dobrowolski was managing the Dziennik and objected to the slander routinely hurled at the populist papers. His young age (29 at the time of his appointment) and the corresponding youth of other key writers and employees (Drobnik was only 36, Krysiewicz 32, Chrzanowski 33) signified that a new generation was emerging in Prussian Poland, not tied to the policies and conflicts of the past and willing to take up the national banner with more energy and resolution.

The first issue of the Przegląd Poznański appeared on 1 April, 1894. It comprised twelve pages and cost 3 Mk. per quarter, too expensive to be within the reach of the working classes. It was clearly written for a select group of urban intelligentsia, educated landowners and professionals. Because it was never able to increase its circulation beyond these circles and because of the open hostility of the two leading gentry papers, the Dziennik and the Kuryer, the Przegląd was forced to give up publication in 1896.(155) Nevertheless, many of its chief contributors such as Chrzanowski, Krysiewicz and Marian Seyda were later to become leading spokesmen of the National Democrats in Prussian Poland and this brief experience with journalism undoubtedly helped their careers. (156)

The Przegląd has been considered by many scholars as the 'prototype' of the National Democratic movement in Poznań.(157) Szymański wrote that the Przegląd represented a "national achievement" and urged that it be supported. (158) Similarly the Goniec Wielkopolski, whose young editor Karol Rzepecki was also destined to be one of the leaders of the National Democrats, wrote that the Przegląd would be a "progressive paper that will have a unifying effect upon our society."(159) The Prussian police described the Przegląd as the "Organ der liberalen, gebildeten polnischen Kreise".(160)

In its editorials, the Przegląd assured its readers that it was primarily a literary and cultural weekly and was interested in politics only in so far as it influenced the social and intellectual development of the Polish community. At the outset it declared itself neutral in the feud between nobles and populists, but neutrality in Poznań in 1894 was hard to maintain in light of the incredible emotions that had been generated during the Neue Kurs. Before long the Przegląd began to tilt markedly towards the populists, bringing upon itself the wrath of Rabski's former employer and editor of the Dziennik, Dobrowolski.(161)

The Przegląd accused the landowners of manipulating the local electoral committees and exploiting the slogan of 'national solidarity' to maintain their own anachronistic dominance over political affairs. "Solidarity has been forged into a weapon against all forms of opposition in our society. Solidarity has been used to prevent the social and political emancipation of the great majority of our lower classes... Every protest against the activities of the Central Committee or local committees has been labelled "secession" and an attack upon solidarity."(162)

The failure of the loyalist initiative signalled to all the need to infuse the old structures with new blood and ideas. Although not supportive of all populist tactics and offended by Knapowski's demagogy, the Przegląd stated that the accomodation of new forces into the existing political apparatus was necessary to secure the future. Within a decade of the inglorious Kościelski initiative and the end of the short life of the Przegląd, the National Democrats had managed to unite a majority of Poles behind the values that the Przegląd had stood for.

****

An analysis of the individual newspapers will allow the reader to better appreciate the significance of each in Polish politics. They all represented clearly defined political programs and their editors and shareholders were key figures in the provincial political apparatus and the Polish Parties in Berlin. Just as the newspapers needed to reflect the views of their patrons, so also the Polish Parties could not wholly disregard the views of the press lords.

Newspapers also acted as the principal propaganda organs for the Polish political oranisation. They directed pre-election campaigning in unison with local committees and the Central Committee. They ordered the Polish community when to vote and for whom; sternly worded articles appeared forbidding 'patriotic' Poles to vote for a German candidate on pain of betraying their national identity. This rule could only be broken if the Central Committee arranged a 'deal' with German Catholics or Progressives not to field rival candidates and combine their strength to oppose Kartell candidates.

The tight discipline and apparent national solidarity among the Poles made them seem a formidable obstacle to German observers. Many Germans, convinced that the Poles were born intriguers and deceivers, refused to believe that serious differences existed among them. As Wilhelm von Massow wrote in 1902, "Der Orędownik hat also auf das sachliche Programm des Dziennik nichts zu sagen. Er hat tatsaechlich dasselbe Arbeitsprogramm; was er bekaempft ist nur die soziale Schicht, in der der Schwerpunkt der nationalen Arbeit liegen soll. Deutlicher kann kaum gezeigt werden, dass der Parteiunterschied innerhalb des

Polentums fuer das Deutschtum eigentlich gar nicht in Betracht kommt."(163)

Indeed, as the survey above indicates, there was little disagreement among the Polish newspapers on the most important issues facing the Polish community in Prussia. The high pitch of rhetorical aggression and insuperable conceit evident in their chronic feuding should not be taken to mean that their visions of the future were wholly incompatible with one another. Nevertheless, as we shall now see, the Caprivi era resulted in perhaps the most formidable cleavage within the Polish community in the history of Prussian rule, and there is no better source through which to study this than the Polish press.

Notes to Chapter Two

1. The last decades before World War One were also favourable for the growth of German-language newspapers in the eastern provinces. During the period 1870-1910, 24 new German papers were founded in the province of Poznania. See Michel, Handbuch deutscher Zeitungen..., p. 85; Schultze, Die politische Tagespresse..., p. 27. Gerhard Muser writes that the average circulation increased from 1445 to 4188 from 1885-1906. Muser, Statistische Untersuchung... pp. 8-12, 58-62.

2. Grot, Hipolit Cegielski..., pp. 92-95 calls Cegielski the "creator of Poznań's national press". Circulation of the Gazeta Polska has been estimated at from 1300 to 1500 copies. See Zygmunt Dulczewski, "Prasa 'ludowa' w Wielkiem Księstwie Poznańskim w okresie Wiosny Ludów 1848-1850", in: Studia i Materiały do Dziejów Wielkopolski i Pomorza, 2 (1956), p. 114.

3. "Libelt, Karol", in: PSB, vol. 17.

4. Andrzej Wojtkowski, "Karol Libelt", in: Wybitni Wielkopolanie XIX Wieku Witold Jakóbczyk, ed. (Poznań, 1959), p. 177.

5. On the effects of the 5 June press legislation see Eichhorn, Geschichte des Zeitungswesen..., p. 80; Trzeciakowski, Pod zaborem pruskim..., pp. 36-37; Dulczewski, "Prasa 'ludowa'...", p. 151.

6. The ultramontane Przegląd Poznański (not to be confused with the literary and cultural weekly from 1894-1896 of the same name) appeared from 1845-1865 under the guidance of Jan Koźmian. The 1850 press law obliged it to reduce its frequency to once in six weeks. See "Koźmian, Jan", in: PSB, vol. 15. See also Maria Szymańska, Bibliografia miasta Poznania (Poznań, 1960), p. 29; Stanisław Karwowski, "Historya Dziennika Poznańskiego", in: Książka jubileuszowa Dziennika Poznańskiego 1859-1909 (Poznań, 1909), p. 13; Laubert, Die preussische Polenpolitik..., p. 118.

7. Grot, Hipolit Cegielski..., pp. 148-152. See also "Kwilecki, Mieczysław", in: PSB, vol. 16. Kwilecki put up the sum of 3000 talers to start up the Dziennik Poznański. See also Laubert, Die preussische Polenpolitik.., p. 111.

8. Boras, Trzeciakowski, W dawnym Poznaniu..., p. 284; Teresa Tyszkiewicz, Sobótka 1869-1871 (Poznań, 1961), pp. 20-21, 50-53.

9. "Merzbach, Ludwik", in: PSB, vol. 20.

10. Tyszkiewicz, Sobótka..., p. 15.

11. For a scholarly study of the Kulturkampf in Prussia, see Wilfrid Loth, Katholiken im Kaiserreich (Duesseldorf, 1984); Erich Schmidt-Volkmar, Der Kulturkampf in Deutschland 1871-1890 (Goettingen, 1962); Lech Trzeciakowski, Kulturkampf w zaborze pruskim (Poznań, 1970).

12. Wetzel, Presseinnenpolitik im Bismarckreich..., pp. 139, 304-305.

13. Karwowski, Historya Wielkiego Księstwa..., vol. 2, p. 454.

14. Witold Jakóbczyk, Patron Jackowski (Poznań, 1938), pp. 80-81; Trzeciakowski "Roman Szymański 1840-1908"..., p. 348.

15. Dzieje Wielkopolski, vol. 2, p. 599.

16. Jakóbczyk, Patron Jackowski..., pp. 84-85.

17. Karwowski, "Historya Dziennika Poznańskiego"..., pp. 61-62; Boras, Trzeciakowski, W dawnym Poznaniu..., p. 289; Grot, Hipolit Cegielski... p. 201; Jakóbczyk, "Wielkopolska 1869-1918"..., p. 183.

18. "Niegolewski, Władysław", in: PSB, vol. 23; Laubert, Die preussische Polenpolitik..., pp. 109, 123. See also Niegolewski's career as chairman of the Polish Party in the Reichstag in Zdzisław Grot, "Prezesi kół polskich w parlamentach niemieckich w latach 1867-1918", in: Rola Wielkopolski w dziejach narodu polskiego, Stanisław Kubiak, Lech Trzeciakowski ed. (Poznań, 1979), pp. 264-265.

19. See Mieczysław Łyskowski's obituary in Dziennik Poznański, 19.1.1894, no. 14. See also Karwowski, "Historya Dziennika Poznańskiego"..., p. 81. On Julian Bukowiecki, see Jakóbczyk, "Wielkopolska 1859-1918"..., p. 184.

20. Dzieje Wielkopolski, ...vol. 2, p. 601.

21. Mai, Die preussisch-deutsche Polenpolitik..., p. 174.

22. Wielkopolanin, 12.8.1893, no. 183, reprinted a story first published in the Goniec that Cegielski had given Knapowski one donation of 1500 Mk. to start up the Postęp, and then another in mid-1893, just before Knapowski broke with the Poznań municipal committee and joined forces with Szymański and the populists.

23. BK., Ms. no. 1456/1457, meeting of 24.2.1893.

24. Goniec Wielkopolski, 23.10.1894, no. 242.

25. Dziennik Poznański, 1896, no. 71.

26. The Polish newspapers themselves generally kept quiet about their own circulation and financial resources, perhaps to deceive the Prussian monitoring authorities. In 1889, the Orędownik claimed to have 1000 subscribers in the city of Poznań alone, about 25% more than the police had calculated. Orędownik, 20.11.1889, no. 267. The following sources have been consulted to construct the figures on page 35. For those of 1886 and 1890, see PP-Posen, file no. 4877, "Akta betr. die polnische Tagespresse, ihre Haltung und Verbreitung". For those of 1902, Guenzel, Die nationale Arbeit..., pp. 23,26. There is some dispute over figures for the Dziennik. Guenzel places its circulation at only 2500 in 1902.

Jakóbczyk in Dzieje Wielkopolski..., vol. 2, p. 590, places it at 3000 in 1900, while Molik, "Dziennikarze polscy..., p. 136, places it as high as 4500. The figure in the table is, therefore, an arbitrary one. Polish-language newspapers had circulations well below that of German ones. For example, Der Gesellige had a circulation of 14,000 in 1889, 17,000 in 1891, and 25,000 in 1895. See Schultz, Die politische Tagespresse..., p. 27. Equivalent figures for the large Warsaw papers were about seven times as great. See Witold Giełżyński, Prasa warszawska 1661-1914 (Warszawa, 1962), p. 360.

27. Danilczuk, Działalność SPD i PPS zaboru pruskiego..., pp. 18-21. This figure is confirmed by Thomas Gey, Die preussische Verwaltung des Regierungsbezirks Bromberg 1871-1920 (Koeln-Berlin, 1976), p. 138, who states that rural labourers earned only 1.50 Mk. per day as late as 1913. William Hagen, Germans, Poles and Jews. The Nationality Conflict in the Prussian East 1772-1914 (Chicago, 1980), p. 215, writes that 80% of then working class earned less than 900 Mk. in 1896. The Polish population had a much smaller income than the German. Leo Wegener, Der wirtschaftliche Kampf..., p. 158, writes that in 1897-1898 the Poles paid only 13.5% of all income taxes in Poznania, although they were in the majority.

28. Mai, Die preussisch-deutsche Polenpolitik...pp. 173-174.

29. For example, in the two-week period from 29 April to 12 May, 1893, the Prussian monitors translated only one article from the mass-circulation Wielkopolanin, in comparison with 12 for the Dziennik Poznański, and 8 each for the Orędownik and the Kuryer Poznański. See PP-Posen, file no. 4806a, pp. 196-224. See also Orędownik, 11.11.1890, no. 259.

30. PP-Posen, file no. 4877, report of 28.1.1890.

31. Orędownik, 11.11.1890, no. 259.

32. Postęp, 25.10.1892, no. 245, and 3.10.1893, no. 225.

33. Kuryer Poznański, 2.5.1890, no. 101, noted that the Poznanian Poles had raised 40,000 Mk. for the Galician Relief Fund, and stated that its owners had donated 12,000 Mk. of this amount. The Dziennik Poznański, 27.4.1890, no. 97, gave a more modest figure of 30,000 Mk. All newspapers regularly appealed for support to aid Polish public libraries, for example, Dziennik Poznański, 27.4.1890, no. 97, and the Kuryer Poznański of the same day. The newspapers made regular donations to the public libraries. PP-Posen, file no. 4806b, pp. 136-137, noted that the Dziennik had contributed 372 Mk. and the Kuryer 316 Mk. in 1893. See also Massow, Die Polen-Not..., p. 91.

34. For example, Mieczysław Łyskowski and Władysław Łebiński, two residents of Poznań, provided the funding and organizational talent for the newly-founded Gazeta Gdańska in 1891. Its first editor-in-chief was Bernard Milski, also a native of Poznań, who moved back to take over the Goniec Wielkopolski in 1901. See Cieślak, Z dziejów prasy polskiej..., p. 104; Michel, Handbuch deutscher Zeitungen...p. 160; "Milski, Bernard", PSB, vol. 21.

35. Molik, "Dziennikarze polscy...", p. 121.

36. Ibid., p. 122. Bernard Milski suffered 12 court cases as editor of the Gazeta Gdańska and this cost him a total of 6000 Mk.

37. Karwowski, "Historya Dziennika Poznańskiego"..., p. 81.

38. Jerzy Marczewski, Narodowa Demokracja w poznańskim (Warszawa, 1967), p. 58; Grot, Dezydery Chłapowski..., pp. 181, 187.

39. The estate of Józef Kościelski was estimated at about 30 million Mk. by contemporaries. See Hans Pfeiffer, Der polnische Adel und die preussische Polenpolitik von 1863-1894 (Wuerzburg, 1939), p. 78.

40. Trzeciakowski, "Roman Szymański 1840-1908...", p. 357.

41. Dziennik Poznański, 1.1.1893, no. 1.

42. Eichhorn, Geschichte des Zeitungswesen..., p. 80; Trzeciakowski, Pod zaborem pruskim..., p. 36.

43. Chojnacki, "Niemieckie tłumaczenie...", p. 382.

44. "Es sind nur drei Elemente welche in Russland zum Kriege hetzen: die Presse, die Polen und die Juden. Die Presse nur insoweit, als sie vom Auslande, von Polen und Juden beeinflusst ist, oder von Polen und Juden bedient wird. Die Seele aller Kriegshetzerei in Russland sind aber die Polen...Wie viele Polen in der russischen Presse, in hohen russischen Aemtern, selbst in der russischen Armee sich einzunisten verstanden haben, das waere genauerer Forschung wert." Bismarck, GW, vol. 9, p. 277. See also Heinz Schulze, Die Presse im Urteil Bismarcks (Leipzig, 1930), p. 251.

45. Reichsgesetzblatt (1874), no. 16, pp. 65-72. For analyses, see Wetzel, Presseinnenpolitik...,pp. 1-3; Jakóbczyk, "Wielkopolska 1859-1918"...p. 199.

46. Wetzel, Presseinnenpolitik..., pp. 97, 303-305.

47. Irene Fischer-Frauendienst, Bismarcks Pressepolitik (Muenster, 1963), p. 58.

48. Wetzel, Presseinnenpolitik...p. 304, has calculated that 65% of court cases concerned charges of "Beleidigungen", and 22% "Vergehen gegen den Staat".

49. Ibid., p. 138.

50. Ibid., p. 232.

51. Mai, Die preussisch-deutsche Polenpolitik..., pp. 27, 175-176.

52. Chojnacki, "Niemieckie tłumaczenie...", p. 384. See also Blanke, Prussian Poland...pp. 46, 113. In West Prussia, the activities of Heinrich Rex (+1887) paralleled those of Zacher in Poznania. Kuryer Poznański, 13.7. 1890, no. 159.

53. PP-Posen, file no. 4806a (1893) and 4806b (1894). See also Chojnacki, "Niemieckie tłumaczenie..., p. 384, and Galos, "Działalność antypolska... p. 239.

54. Wielkopolanin, 30.9.1890, no. 224, welcomed the fact that during Caprivi's first six months not a single case of slander had been brought against the Polish press.

55. Kuryer Poznański, 4.9.1894, no. 203.

56. Ibid., "It is no secret that at the Decher printshop here in Poznań a publication intended for government circles is being printed...Its main concern is the Goniec, which is deliberately supplying our enemies with ammunition. Plainly put, this is a crime that calls out to heaven for punishment...it should convince everyone of the need to cancel their subscriptions (to the Goniec)."

57. Karwowski, "Historya Dziennika Poznańskiego"..., p. 90. In 1909, the Dziennik's board of executives included three deputies or former deputies: Stefan Cegielski, Roman Komierowski and Mieczysław Kwilecki. See also Orędownik, 4.9.1890, no. 203, "Some of the Dziennik's owners are sitting in Berlin making declarations (a reference to Józef Mielżyński in the Prussian Herrenhaus T.K.) while the others in the editorial offices do not know how to react to them." Henryk Szuman, a deputy to the Landtag for almost 50 years and its chairman from 1871-1887, was a steady contributor to the Dziennik. See Henryk Szuman, Wspomnienie berlińskie i poznańskie z roku 1848 (Warszawa, 1894), pp. 4-5; Grot, "Prezesi kół polskich...p. 264.

58. Karwowski, "Historya Dziennika Poznańskiego..." p. 42. See also "Dobrowolski, Franciszek", PSB, vol. 5. For Dobrowolski's role in the later stages of the January Uprising, see Stefan Kieniewicz, Powstanie Styczniowe (Warszawa, 1983), pp. 512-521, 634-646.

59. Tyszkiewicz, Sobótka..., p. 81 lists his publications.

60. Karwowski, "Historya Dziennika Poznańskiego"...,p. 81; Molik, "Dziennikarze polscy...", p. 143. The Orędownik, 14.8.1890, no. 186, and Kuryer Poznański, 15.8.1890, no. 186, list the wages paid by Poznań's newspapers to printers. The Dziennik Poznański led both lists at 30 Mk. per week.

61. Franciszek Dobrowolski belonged to the following associations during the years 1890-1892, in addition to his position as editor of the Dziennik Poznański and his two important political functions: the Marcinkowski Education Fund, the Committee to Transfer the Remains of Adam Mickiewicz to Cracow (secretary), the Polish Orphans' Relief Committee (chairman), the Committee to Support Private Polish Language Lessons, the Polish Theatre (director), the Committee to Legalise the Jesuit Order in Prussia, and the Polish Industrialists' Society. See Karwowski, "Historya Dziennika Poznańskiego"...p. 83; Dziennik Poznański, 4.5.1890, no. 103. Nevertheless, his popularity shrank as he threw himself ever more deeply into the defence of the landowner class in light of their disappointing behaviour in Berlin. See Bernard Chrzanowski, Wspomnienie, B. Racz. Ms. no. 1375, p. 321; Molik, Wokół 'Przeglądu Poznańskiego'..., p. 221.

62. Trzeciakowski, Polityka polskich klas..., p. 39.

63. Lech Trzeciakowski, "Polskie ugrupowania polityczne zaboru pruskiego wobec Niemiec 1871-1918", in: Dzieje Najnowsze 4 (1972), p. 26.

64. "Imperative for our Political Conduct and Solidarity", Dziennik Poznański, 13.5.1891, no. 107.

65. Ibid., 22.10.1890, no. 243.

66. Ibid., 9.6.1893, no. 129.

67. Ibid., 2.2.1888, no. 27. See also Wrzesiński, "Oblicze polityczne..." p. 96.

68. Dziennik Poznański, 6.2.1890, no. 30.

69. Wiegand, Die anti-deutsche Propaganda..., p. 8, stated that the Dziennik categorically refused to print any extra-parliamentary speeches made by Kościelski. The present study confirms this.

70. Dziennik Poznański, 19.9.1893, no. 213.

71. Ibid., 23.1.1891, no. 18.

72. Orędownik, 20.9.1888, no. 216. See also Postęp, 6.7.1894, no. 151. See the report by the Poznań police in PP-Posen, file no. 4877, report of 28.1.1890.

73. Wielkopolanin, 27.3.1889, no. 71.

74. Ibid., 13.6.1893, no. 132; 3.8.1893, no. 175; and 14.10.1893, no. 235.

75. Ibid., 28.12.1890, no. 297.

76. Ibid., 26.1.1888, no. 21.

77. Ibid., 6.12.893, no. 273.

78. Orędownik, 18.8.1893, no. 187, called them the "wychowankowie Wielkopolana", the pupils of the Wielkopolanin.

79. Trzeciakowski, Walka o polskość miast..., p. 179; J. Kusztelan, Ks. Piotr Wawrzyniak, B. Racz., Ms. no. 1527, p. 801.

80. Wetzel, Presseinnenpolitik im Bismarckreich...,p. 139.

81. "Kantecki, Antoni", in: PSB, vol. 11.

82. Kuryer Poznański, 31.8.1890, no. 200.

83. Kultusminister von Gossler to Graf Zedlitz-Truetzschler, Oberpraesident of Poznania, on 29.5.1888: "Auch die Hoffnung, welche sich an die Entfernung des Geistlichen Kantecki aus der Redaktion der Kuryer Poznanski und seiner Uebersiedlung nach Gnesen knuepfte, hat sich nicht erfuellt... Als Redakteur hat Kantecki so viel gelesen und geschrieben, wie er in keinem geistlichen Amt Anlass hat, auch gibt es fuer einen Geistlichen zahlreiche andere Gelegenheiten, seine Faehigkeiten zu verwerten;..." Gatz, Akten zur preussischen Kirchenpolitik..., p. 67.

84. "Kantecki, Maksymilian", in: PSB, vol. 11; "Kantecki, Maksymilian", in: WSB, p. 314.

85. In keeping with the practise of covering all controversial events affecting Polish political life with a veil of secrecy, M. Kantecki's resignation as secretary of the municipal committee was not announced. It can only be noticed when tracing the composition of the committee throughout 1890 and 1891.

86. Kuryer Poznański, 15.4.1892, no. 87.

87. Ibid., 1.10.1890, no. 225.

88. Ibid., 12.4.1890, no. 84.

89. Ibid., 3.1.1891, no. 2.

90. Ibid., 17.5.1890, no. 112, in answer to an article in Die Gegenwart, "Die Polen und der Weltkrieg".

91. Ibid., 6.4.1890, no. 153.

92. Ibid., 6.12.1892, no. 280, in commenting on a speech by Kościelski in the Reichstag of 2.12.1892. Berichte Rtg. 1892, vol. 1, pp. 93-95.

93. Ibid., 26.2.1893.

94. Ibid., 11.11.1893, no. 258.

95. Ibid., 22.1.1890, no. 17.

96. Ibid., 3.3.1894.

97. Orędownik, 16.7.1892, no.

98. Blanke, Prussian Poland...p. 134; Jerzy Marczewski, "Zmiany polityczne wśród polskiej burżuazji poznańskiego 1900-1907" in: Studia i Materiały do Dziejów Wielkopolski i Pomorza 3 (1957), p. 186.

99. Schulthess'... 1895, p. 183.

100. "Rzepecki, Karol", in: WSB, p. 641.

101. PP-Posen, file no. 4806b, p. 268. See also Wiegand, Die anti-deutsche Propaganda..., p. 16.

102. PP-Posen, file no. 4806a, Goniec Wielkopolski, 1.1.1893, no. 1.

103. Ibid., Goniec Wielkopolski, 11.11.1893, no. 258.

104. Ibid., Goniec Wielkopolski, 26.11.1893, no. 270.

105. Ibid., Goniec Wielkopolski, 10.5.1893, no. 106.

106. Ibid., Goniec Wielkopolski, 12.4.1893, no. 83.

107. Ibid., Goniec Wielkopolski, 15.4.1893, no. 86.

108. Orędownik, 30.8.1891, no. 197; Kuryer Poznański, 28.10.1894.

109. PP-Posen, file no. 4806b, Goniec Wielkopolski, 3.6.1894, no. 124.

110. Lech Trzeciakowski, "Roman Szymański 1840-1908", in: Wybitni Wielkopolanie XIX wieku, Witold Jakóbczyk, ed. (Poznań, 1969), vol. 2, pp. 340-361; by the same author, "Roman Szymański, poglądy i praktyka polityczna", in: Acta Universitatis Wratislaviensis 543 (1981), pp. 421-432.

111. Karwowski, "Historya Dziennika Poznańskiego"...p. 74.

112. Trzeciakowski, "Roman Szymański 1840-1908..., pp. 342-343.

113. Tyszkiewicz, Sobótka..., pp. 5, 9-10.

114. Jakóbczyk, Patron Jackowski..., p. 85.

115. Trzeciakowski, "Roman Szymański 1840-1908..., p. 350; Wielkopolska, wybór źródeł 1851-1914, Witold Jakóbczyk, ed., (Wrocław, 1954), p. 139.

116. Molik, "Dziennikarze polscy...", p. 145.

117. Orędownik, 12.2.1890, no. 35; Krystyna Murzynowska, Polskie wychodźstwo zarobkowe w zagłębiu Ruhry w latach 1880-1914 (Wrocław, 1972), pp. 69-70.

118. Trzeciakowski, Polityka polskich klas..., p. 44.

119. Orędownik, 26.10.1889, no. 247: "We know what the Central Committee is - it is the editorial board of the Dziennik...We should refuse to give a penny to the treasury until the right people are chosen." See also the issue of 16.2.1890.

120. Bernhard, Das polnische Gemeinwesen..., p. 146.

121. Blanke, Prussian Poland..., p. 104.

122. Orędownik, 1.11.1890, no. 252.

123. Ibid., 2.2.1890, no. 27.

124. See for example the strong reaction to the sale of the Landtag deputy Ludwik Graeve's property to the Colonisation Commission in Orędownik, 19.6.1890, no. 138 and 22.6.1890, no. 141. In the issue of 30.7.1890, no. 173, Szymański wrote, "One after another leading executives of the Dziennik Poznański are selling their properties to the Colonisation Commission."

125. Szymański had a long-standing quarrel with Florian Stablewski, Landtag deputy, a dedicated loyalist and later Archbishop of Gniezno-Poznań from 1892-1906, charging that Stablewski was using the Catholic Church to further the programme of the loyalists. See Orędownik, 19.5.1893, no. 113.

126. Ibid., 27.1.1889, no. 23.

127. Ibid., 12.2.1890, no. 35.

128. Ibid., 23.2.1889, no. 45. This was a report on about a public rally held in Poznań on 20.2.1889 attended by some 3000 to protest the ban on teaching Polish in the public elementary schools. It was addressed by the editors of the Dziennik and Kuryer, Dobrowolski and A. Kantecki.

129. Ibid., 22.1.1889, no. 18.

130. Ibid., 17.4.1889, no. 89.

131. Ibid., 12.2.1890, no.35.

132. Ibid., 29.3.1891, no. 72.

133. Ibid., 10.6.1893, no. 130, and 8.6.1893, no. 128.

134. PP-Posen, file no. 4806a, p. 342. See also Richard Perdelwitz, Die Posener Polen 1815-1914 (Schneidemuehl, 1936), p. 81.

135. Bernhard, Das polnische Gemeinwesen..., p. 146.

136. "Political Suicide", Przegląd Poznański, 4.11.1894, no. 32. The intellectuals linked to the Przegląd Poznański were incensed at Knapowski's insolent behaviour at the Poznań meeting of 27.10.1894, that was supposed to reconcile the populist and gentry rival electoral committees. See also Postęp, 3.11.1894, no. 251, for Knapowski's attack on the Przegląd Poznański's editor-in-chief Władysław Rabski. See also Molik, "Wokół 'Przeglądu Poznańskiego'...", p. 233.

137. "Knapowski, Stanisław", in: PSB, vol. 13.

138. Postęp, 1,1,1892, no. 1.

139. Hagen, Germans, Poles and Jews..., p. 324; Wegener, Der wirtschaftliche Kampf..., p. 237.

140. Marczewski, Narodowa Demokracja...p. 20. Moritz Jaffe, Die Stadt Posen unter preussischer Herrschaft (Leipzig, 1909), pp. 310,410, states that in the town of Poznań itself Jews comprised 9.7% of the civilian population in 1885, but only 5.1% in 1900.

141. Postęp, 21.10.1891, no. 240. Wegener, Der wirtschaftliche Kampf..., p. 157, has calculated that of 760 "Handelsfirmen, Gesellschaften und Genossenschaften" in Poznań in 1894, as many as 490 were owned by Jews, 155 by "German Christians", and 115 by Poles.

142. Postęp, 23.10.1894, no. 242. Earlier, the Postęp had criticised the Dziennik Poznański for "Shunning anti-Jewish propaganda". On 6.11.1891, no. 254, Knapowski wrote, "Open your eyes and look around at the evils of Jewry."

143. Ibid., 12.6.1890, no. 47.

144. Orędownik, 6.3.1891, no. 53.

145. Postęp, 21.10.1892, no. 242.

146. Ibid., 6.5.1892, no. 104.

147. Ibid., 13.9.1891, no. 208.

148. Ibid., 18.10.1890, no. 94.

149. Ibid., 20.11.1890, no. 121.

150. Ibid., 5.5.1890, no. 102.

151. Ibid., 25.10.1891, no. 244.

152. Karol Rzepecki, Pobudka Wyborcza (Poznań, 1907), p. 66 offers a brief biography.

153. Kuryer Poznański, 21.1.1894, no. 16. Of the 16 founders, 12 were either lawyers or physicians and none were landowners. See also Molik, "Wokół 'Przeglądu Poznańskiego'...", p. 222.

154. "Rabski, Władysław", in: Nowy Korbut 15 (1978), pp. 358-359.

155. Molik, "Wokół 'Przeglądu Poznańskiego'...", p. 238; Boras, Trzeciakowski, W dawnym Poznaniu..., p. 303.

156. Marczewski, Narodowa Demokracja... outlines the later journalistic work of the Przegląd's editors.

157. Marczewski, "Zmiany polityczne...", p. 185; Dzieje Wielkopolski, vol. 2, p. 603.

158. Orędownik, 3.10.1894, no. 225. See in particular Szymański's speech at the populist rally of 13.11.1894, in Postęp, 20.11.1894, no. 265.

159. PP-Posen, file no. 4806a, Goniec Wielkopolski, 23.9.1893, no. 217.

160. Ibid., Goniec Wielkopolski, 23.9.1893, no. 217.

161. Dziennik Poznański, 25.4.1894, no. 94.

162. Przegląd Poznański, 23.9.1894, no. 26.

163. Massow, Die Polen-Not..., p. 83.

Chapter Three: The First Phase of Loyalism 1884-1890

3.1 The Press and the Formation of a Loyalist Faction 1884-1889

The relationship between Poznań's Polish newspapers and the Party deputies in Berlin had never been entirely satisfactory. The tremendous growth in circulation and the rising importance of public opinion represented a threat to the deputies' monopoly of power and a potential source of dissension at home. Consequently, in 1879, the Reichstag and Landtag Parties combined to adopt a resolution forbidding deputies to giveunauthorized interviews or disclose any details of deliberations when in closed session.(1) Henceforward, the activities of both Parties were to be shrouded in a veil of strict secrecy.

However, a combination of several factors made it impossible in practice to keep the press out of political life: friendships between politicians and newspapermen; animosities and jealousies among deputies; and the professionalism of journalists looking for a good story. It was inevitable that the newspapers would soon take sides in disputes evident within the Berlin Parties or the Central Committee in Poznań.

During the 1880s the composition of the Reichstag and Landtag Parties underwent a significant change. Younger and more pragmatic Positivists were replacing the veterans of the 1863 Uprising and those brought up in the tradition of gentry revolution. The new men showed a willingness to break with the policy of abstention and protest that had dominated political thought heretofore, and urged a greater Polish participation in the affairs of Prussia and Germany. Almost immediately, the newspapers began to take sides. The Kuryer Poznański favoured greater co-operation with the state, while the Goniec Wielkopolski demanded that Poles stand firmly behind their traditional opposition, which, if unsuccessful, was at least dignified.(2) The controversy came to a head in 1884 when the outspoken irreconcilable Władysław Niegolewski, a veteran of the 1863 Uprising and formerly chairman of the Reichstag Party, challenged the nomination of the young industrialist Stefan Cegielski to represent Poznań in the upcoming Reichstag election. This confrontation well illustrates the clash of generations; Niegolewski, born in 1819, had been deeply involved in revolutionary activity before Cegielski's birth in 1858. His challenge was supported by the Goniec Wielkopolski but bitterly opposed by the Central Committee and by Poznań's other Polish newspapers, in particular A. Kantecki's Kuryer. Because Cegielski had been nominated and sponsored by the Party machinery, Niegolewski, for all his prestige and unquestioned former service to his country, was badly beaten on election day.(3) His death in 1885, along with the passing away of another great irreconcilable, Kazimierz Kantak, in 1886, removed two fierce critics of the growing Positivist trend towards constructive co-operation with the Prussian state.

The accession to power of Friedrich III in March, 1888, gave the necessary impulse to the proponents of constructive co-operation to state their case. As press accounts show, Friedrich was immensely popular with the Poles. His first public statements were very well-received and awoke desperate hopes in those looking for a change of direction in Berlin's systematic Germanization efforts.(4) His short reign witnessed a number of events that gave Poles heart and hope for a better future.

In early April, 1888, the Empress Victoria visited Poznań to show sympathy with the residents affected by a serious flood. To the chagrin of many German nationalists the English-born Empress was enthusiastically greeted by the Polish community and was made aware of its seperate identity.(5) The reception committee formed to welcome the Empress included the editors of the Dziennik, Kuryer and the Orędownik, one of the last times Dobrowolski, Szymański and M. Kantecki were able to work together in Poznań's social and political life. It issued the following address to the community: "Countrymen! We call upon you to come out and welcome Her Majesty with all the respect she is entitled to. Let us forget our national suffering for this one day and hope that our sad fate will be improved in the future."(6)

Almost despite their better judgement the Polish newspapers fawned over a critically ill Emperor who had never made any specific reference to Prussia's Polish minority. After Victoria's departure the Polish press took issue with German newspapers that had spoken ill of her visit and her decision to speak French to the Poles rather than German. The Dziennik wrote on 15 April, "The German press is upset that Polish women used the occasion of the Empress's visit to display the national colours. Why should we be ashamed of calling ourselves what we are? The Vienna treaties of 1815 guarantee us the right to feel like a nation. And we respect the words of monarchs, not like some who feel they are worth no more than a 'Pfifferling'".(7) The Orędownik complained of the way Victoria was being mistreated by the German newspapers. "First the Empress cannot marry off her daughter to whoever she wants, then she cannot travel wherever she wants... Where will all this end?"(8) Throughout Friedrich III's short reign the Polish newspapers took pride in aligning themselves with the 'Court party' against the semi-official Bismarck-dominated press.

Emboldened by Victoria's visit to Poznań the leading Polish politicians decided to go ahead with a projected address to the ailing Emperor, assuring him of their loyalty to King and country. Obviously they hoped that attention would be drawn to their misery through this direct communication with their monarch. The decision to draft the address was taken on 22 March 1888, though it was over a month before the final version was put together. Every word was the subject of scrutiny and dispute; was the language too timid and hence meaningless, or was it too strong and perhaps offensive? Finally two versions were drafted, and the more moderate one prepared by Ferdynand Radziwiłł prevailed over a more assertive version written by Władysław Wierzbiński by a vote of 13-10.(9) The Radziwiłł version avoided any mention of specific Polish grievances and hence was felt by its critics to be too obsequious. The address was signed on 3 May by all deputies of both Parties and presented to Chancellor Bismarck for the Emperor's perusal the following day.(10)

At the same time it was debated whether or not to publish the address in the Polish papers. No clear decision could be reached. On 8 May, however, the Wielkopolanin reported that German papers had learnt that the Poles were "intending to communicate directly with the Emperor" from a German artist in Berlin hired to frame the address.(11) Concerned that a premature publication and raucous debate within the Polish community would ruin the prospects for success, the Parties ordered it be kept secret until after German newspapers had published the Emperor's reply.(12)

The position of the newspapers was ambiguous to say the least. Many editors knew of the text adopted by the deputies and were strongly tempted to disclose it in the interests of journalistic freedom. The Goniec was opposed to the tame language of the final draft and the Dziennik felt it should have been designed as a declaration of all Poles in Prussia. (13) When the deputies made their decision not to publish the address on 14 May, the Dziennik seemed to go along, but as early as 19 May wrote that, "We hope the Polish Party will disclose the text to our papers soon as it is a matter of importance for our whole community."(14) The Orędownik commented, "All Poles will be grateful to our deputies for this. It was correct to undertake this with the accession of Friedrich III, and it is the right way to convince the monarch that Poles are not disrespectful or dangerous suspects, as is reported in German newspapers and in the Landtag."(15) Soon, however, the Orędownik was also demanding publication. But the Party deputies remained firm.

At the beginning of June, 1888, as Friedrich III was on his deathbed, Bismarck presented Ignacy Bniński, a member of the Herrenhaus, with a reply to the Polish address. It was written by Bismarck himself and calculated to throw some cold water on Polish aspirations. To the deputies, the reply was interpreted as an insult and for a short time cooled the enthusiasm for reconciliation with the Prussian government. The question again emerged of publishing the address before the German newspapers got hold of it. Afraid to display their poor judgement before Polish society, the Parties put off publication indefinitely, hoping perhaps that their constituencies would forget all about it.

Friedrich III's last days saw the dismissal of the Minister of the Interior, Robert Victor von Puttkamer, one of Bismarck's key ministers and one of the trio upon which the anti-Polish legislation of 1885-1887 was constructed.(16) His dismissal was greeted by the Poles and was portrayed as a step in the right direction. Unfortunately, Friedrich's death on 15 June, 1888, ended the brief period of high expectations and frustrated the plans of Kościelski's faction and the Kuryer to declare a full break with the past.

Now pressure began to mount from the newspapers to clear up the affair of the address once and for all. Leading the fight for disclosure were the Dziennik and the Orędownik, a strange alliance of two declared enemies. The Orędownik wondered aloud on 17 June, 1888, "Whatever happened to that address sent to the deceased Emperor? We have a right to know what was in it."(17) A week later the tone was sharper, "There is no reason to withhold the (contents of the) address and the reply. Even if the reply was negative it should be published... This is taking the voters for granted."(18) The Dziennik, with good connections to the deputies, announced on 15 June that a reply had been received by the Landtag Party chairman Ignacy Zakrzewski and would be published "within a week".(19) But it was soon forced to retract and stated that, "In view of recent events (the Party) has decided not to disclose either the address or the answer."(20) This state of affairs continued through July, as speculation about the contents increased within the German and Polish newspapers. The Orędownik portrayed the Party's reluctance to publish the text as proof of its condescending view of the voters. "The middle class is evidently not mature enough to have the texts revealed... How can the deputies expect support from the voters when they thus conduct affairs?"(21) The Dziennik was similarly exasperated at the Party's attitude and rose to defend the inherent prerogative of journalism to access to information. "Journalists have the right to state their view of the tactics employed by our Party, and our observations can only benefit policy-making."(22) Clearly pressure was being put on the Party members to respect the public's desire for honesty and full accountability.

What had been intended as a pledge of loyalty to a fair-minded, newly-crowned monarch turned into a nasty domestic squabble which forced the resignation of Landtag chairman Ignacy Zakrzewski and damaged the Party's already questionable reputation for political maturity. Under great pressure from the newspapers, the Parties finally agreed to release the texts of the address and the reply, but only after both were first published in the Norddeutsche Allgemeine Zeitung.(23) Apart from the Goniec, which called the deputies "renegades" and "Germans"(24), no other newspaper was upset by the contents, but all objected to the stubbornness and arrogance of the deputies in needlessly delaying publication. Yet the very fact that the texts were published at all attests to the growing significance of public opinion and the role of the press.

The outcry over the address had little effect upon the 1888 Landtag election campaign, though it was often brought up by critics at rallies. (25). In March 1889 another issue divided the Polish press. In honour of Helmuth Graf von Moltke's 70th anniversary of Prussian military service, senior members of the Landtag sent him a congratulatory note, signed, among others, by the Polish deputy Szuman. As a senior member of the Landtag Szuman felt duty-bound to sign the note, thus laying himself to hostile criticism at home. Did a Pole have to honour a Prussian general whose 70 years of service had kept them dismembered? The uproar over Szuman's act well illustrates the dilemma that faced all Polish deputies: how far could they go in carrying out the normal functions of a Prussian deputy without transgressing upon the sacred area of Polish national honour?

Strangely enough, it was the Kuryer that led the criticism of Szuman, though he was a respected parliamentarian of many years service who had once been chairman of the Landtag Party.(26) Szuman was also criticized by the Goniec, but was defended by the Dziennik, for which he occasionally wrote articles.(27) The Orędownik pointed to the quarrel within the Party machinery to buttress its repeated argument that the gentry was no longer capable of managing the nation's affairs and must hand over power to the middle class.(28) Szuman was authorized to issue an explanation to the Dziennik why he had signed the congratulatory note. Nevertheless, public opinion took its toll; Szuman was reprimanded and removed from the three-man Convent of Seniors.(29) To the aid of Szuman came Kościelski, who had earlier got into trouble with the press for attending banquets given by Chancellor Bismarck. Kościelski urged Szuman not to resign under pressure and to endure the misplaced criticism of the Party and the press.(30)

3.2 The Reichstag Election of February, 1890

Bismarck's difficulties in both domestic and foreign policy during his last two years of rule did not go unnoticed in the Polish press. Strict monitoring of Polish newspapers by the Prussian authorities and Bismarck's quick temper muted overly passionate jubilation that the aging statesman could no longer hold on to the reigns of power. Instead, the press and the political machine in Poznania quietly but effectively prepared itself for the crucially important Reichstag election of February, 1890. Under the leadership of a newly-elected Central Committee headed by Stefan Żółtowski and Dobrowolski, the electoral agitation proceeded smoothly. From 11 January, 1890, when the election date was announced, until election day on 20 February, Polish newspapers concentrated almost exclusively on this theme. Agitation consisted of: stressing the importance of the election; the need to attend meetings and choose three candidates for deputy; make donations; and finally, to make absolutely sure that every Pole knew who to vote for on election day. To the outsider, there appeared little variance in Polish campaigns from election to election. Deprived of a real say in Berlin and not compelled to engage in serious debates with German rivals, issues played a small role in campaigning. Success or failure depended on how many Poles went out on election day and what strategy the German parties adopted to prevent a Polish victory.

The 1890 campaign, however, was plagued by the stubborn protest of the Orędownik, which called for a boycott on contributions to the Central Committee but stopped short of boycotting the election itself. On 4 February, the Orędownik began to take part in the distribution of campaign leaflets and notices approved by the Committee, but at the same time told its readers to withhold donations.(31) "They are in no need of money... they go to expensive balls and fund their own newspapers, like the Wielkopolanin", it wrote on 11 February.(32) The obstinate behaviour of the Orędownik infuriated the two principal organs of the gentry. On 24 January the Kuryer wrote, "What blind partisanship can lead to!... Who would have thought that this pseudo-tribune of the middle class would go so far in spreading the disease of discord?... These are anarchic declarations... criminal slogans. We do not intend to enter into a polemic with him or refute the obvious lies he wrote about the Committee because it is simply beneath our dignity."(33) Similar statements came from the Dziennik and the Wielkopolanin. On 23 January, the Dziennik wrote, "It is a waste of our time to argue with the obscene behaviour of the Orędownik. (Our readers) will also treat his demand to boycott our funding drive with the contempt it deserves. We see that the Orędownik, a Polish newspaper, is engaging in a very broad sense in electoral nihilism. It is becoming a thoroughly German electoral agent."(34)

In contrast to Poznań itself, the rest of the province experienced a typically low-key campaign, with few disputes over candidates' lists or Party policy.(35) The countryside was firmly in the hands of the gentry and clergy, and it would be some time yet before a grass-roots populism made any headway into the small towns and villages of Poznania.

The highlight of the 1890 campaign was the rally held in Poznań on 26 January in the Bazar building, the centre of Polish social and political life in the province. Before a crowd of 1000 Dobrowolski, as chairman of the Poznań municipal committee, opened with a speech lauding the incumbent deputy, Cegielski, and nominating him for another term. Cegielski, who was also treasurer of the Central Committee, then delivered an impassioned speech touching on everything from peace in a troubled world to the dangers of Social Democracy and the need to preserve national solidarity. He was nominated by acclamation and given three cheers.(36) Sensing that he stood no chance of overturning Cegielski's candidacy, Szymański and his followers stayed away from the rally but continued to hurl criticism at the handling of the campaign.(37) As it was the Orędownik's opposition to Cegielski lowered his total vote on election day by about 300-500, and caused Dobrowolski to complain at a post-election meeting of "intellectuals who had made things difficult."(38)

The 1890 Reichstag election was one of the milestones of late Imperial Germany, which the historian Erich Eyck described as the "Absage des Volkes an sein (Bismarck's T.K.) ganzes politisches System."(39) The Poles did better than many observers had predicted; they polled over 246,000 votes and increased their share of the national vote from 2.8% to 3.4%, picking up three additional seats. (40) Poznań's Polish newspapers were overjoyed. Despite the fury of Bismarck's latest anti-Polish legislation they had not only survived but had grown stronger, an example to the world that repression against a national minority simply did not work.

The post-election editorials emphasised the ruin of the Kartell and the bankruptcy of Bismarck's domestic policies. The Dziennik of 26 February wrote, "We have now seen unmistakably how false the policies pursued heretofore were. They were based on police measures and emergency laws that were at variance with the principles of equal rights for all."(41) Something in Germany had to change now, the Dziennik surmised, and Bismarck had to adopt a different posture towards the former opposition parties. At around the same time, the Dziennik and the Kuryer arrived at the same hypothesis - that a Conservative-Centrum coalition together with either the Poles or Alsatians could form a parliamentary majority.(42) The Kuryer delighted at the collapse of the Kartell. "There will come a time when the broken Kartell will admit that it has to move away from emergency laws and stop stripping people of their native culture", it wrote on 25 February.(43) On 14 March it was openly predicting great changes ahead in Prussia's Polish policy. "The results of the election are opening the eyes of even the most dedicated Kartell politicians. They are becoming convinced that the policies vis-à-vis the so-called opposition parties, and in particular the Poles, are not only immoral and unjust, but also, and this is more important, produce results diametrically opposite to those projected." (44) Both the Dziennik and Kuryer showed concern over the tremendous growth in support for the SPD and emphasised that it fully illustrated the folly of the extra-legal laws. The SPD polled 400 votes in Poznań and as many as 2000 in Bromberg, but the Polish press contented itself with the assertion that most of those votes had come from Germans.(45) Similarly the Orędownik celebrated the collapse of the Kartell parties and hinted at the possibility of another coalition - Centrum, Progressives, Poles, SPD and Alsatians.(46)

3.3 Bismarck's Dismissal and the Onset of the Loyalist Initiative

By early March, 1890, there were unmistakable signs that Bismarck's position had become increasingly untenable, and on the 18th he was compelled to resign. The Dziennik noted as early as 4 March that Bismarck could no longer hold on to power and that everyone in Berlin was not asking "if" but only "when".(47) An era of great significance for Prussia's and Germany's battered opposition parties was approaching. When the Iron Chancellor indeed stepped down the joy in all sectors of Polish society was immesuarable. Roman Komierowski, a Reichstag deputy at the time, later wrote in his semi-official Party history, "The dismissal of Prince Bismarck meant a change in our political program for the future. Were we not allowed to believe that new winds were blowing even at the highest levels toward us?... The political situation signalled that a total change of direction would have to take place. The former awesome power of the Kartell that had dominated the Reichstag crashed in early 1890. Bismarck's domestic programs were slowly beginning to disintegrate."(48) Many Poles saw Bismarck's fall as the consequence of his clash with the young, fair-minded Wilhelm II. Witold Skarżyński, a former Reichstag deputy and leading loyalist spokesman, compared the Kaiser to the Archangel Michael, "der mit seinem Schwert die ganze Welt und besonders die Polen auf preussischem Gebiet von dem Drachen Bismarck befreite."(49)

After being ridiculed and persecuted by Bismarck for over a quarter of a century the feeling within the Polish community over his dismissal was a mixture of relief, joy and great expectation. Bismarck had been in charge for so long that few could remember the happier days before his appointment. Whoever came after him was bound to be more attentive to the grievances of the Poles. The second and most important of the seemingly invincible trio that had devised the Kulturkampf and the anti-Polish campaigns of the 1880s had fallen. Von Puttkamer had been replaced by Ludwig Herrfurth as Minister of the Interior, clearly a more moderate man who had won the respect of all Germans by forbidding gerrymandering in the 1890 election.(50) Bismarck was now being replaced by an unknown military man, General Leo von Caprivi, about whom the Kuryer wrote at his appointment, "What we know about Caprivi is that he will not block the winds of change from above."(51) Only von Gossler, the Kultusminister remained, and educated opinion ventured that he could not last long without the protection of his lord and master Bismarck.

But the most important personal influence in the eyes of the Poles was that of Wilhelm II, the "Emperor of the Workers", whose early years awoke much admiration and hope in Germany among all those groups that Bismarck had despised: workers, Catholics, Progressives and the national minorities. In placing their trust in Wilhelm II, the Poles were only sharing the general feeling among the so-called "staatsfeindliche" groups - a conviction that the days of arbitrary rule were over and that Germany would now enjoy a popular constitutional monarchy. In this belief the Poles greatly overestimated Wilhelm II's awareness of their difficult position and his willingness to recognise their special status accorded at Vienna in 1815 and sworn to by his forefathers. Throughout the Caprivi era, until September, 1894, the Emperor made no clear reference to Prussia's Polish question, and the Polish loyalists misinterpreted his silence to indicate he was supportive.(52)

The stalemate between loyalists and irreconcilables among the Polish powerholders was broken with the collapse of the Kartell in the 1890 election. At the same time as changes at the highest ministerial levels were taking place in Berlin, a group of 16-18 Poles assembled in Poznań to reconsider the whole framework of Polish politics in Prussia and Germany. The meeting was so sensitive that a complete news blackout was imposed; not even the usually well-informed Orędownik printed a word about it. Present at the meeting were Poznania's wealthiest landowners - Stanisław Żółtowski, Kościelski, Ludwik Mycielski, Kwilecki and Skarżyński - and the editors of the Dziennik, Kuryer, and Wielkopolanin.(53) Kościelski and the Kuryer's editor, M. Kantecki, dominated the session and claimed to have emerged with a mandate for a break with the past, though not everyone there was in full agreement. Interestingly enough, the Prussian authorities had a full report of the "secret" meeting the next day, while the Polish public was kept in the dark.(54) This indicates how thoroughly the Prussian police monitored all aspects of Polish political life.

Two days later, on 19 March, Poznań's Polish community was stunned by a lead article in the Kuryer, "A Program for the Not-Too-Distant Future". The article noted that for over forty years the policy of protest and opposition had led the Poles in Prussia nowhere and that it was no longer enough to invoke the Vienna treaties as the legal framework for Polish political life. "This is a call for action, not words... Together with Germans we shall work for the general good of the state...We cannot make impossible demands, but will look reality in the eye and move forward step by step."(55)

The program (afterwards simply called the 'program Kuryera') was not an abject surrender of Polish rights nor an unconditional pledge to support Caprivi in every possible undertaking, but it deviated so markedly from Polish policy heretofore that it electrified the Polish community. Szymański was overjoyed. In a lead editorial entitled "A Ray of Bright Light from the Kuryer" the Orędownik wrote, "It is difficult to believe what we are reading. Has the Kuryer finally seen the error of its policies to date? We hope that the Kuryer continues to promote this new policy."(56) The Dziennik waited three days before mentioning the Kuryer's article and then came down strongly against it. Dobrowolski had been present at the 17 March meeting but had not been convinced of the need to embrace Caprivi. On 23 March the Dziennik wrote that there was essentially nothing new in the Kuryer's article, and that the Poles would never agree to their second-class citizen's status.(57)

The quarrel over the Kuryer's article was to last several months and temporarily re-arrange the constellation of press alliances in Poznań. The Dziennik, in normal times an ally of the Kuryer, remained critical of the programme, writing that it would result in the co-operation of Poles in promulgating new anti-Polish laws.(58) It was "working hand in hand with those planning our destruction," wrote the Dziennik in June.(59) The Dziennik felt that unconditional support for Caprivi would convince many Germans that it was the Poles and not they who had to take the initiative in seeking a reconciliation. Besides, the Poles had never been disloyal in the past, so why the great fuss? The Kuryer answered that the Dziennik was adopting the tactics of the obstreperous Goniec and noted, "We need a calm and substantive discussion, not polemics...(the article was written) because of Bismarck's fall and the convictions of the young monarch - justice and compassion for all. We repeated what all serious groups in our society hold true...We wanted to make an address to G e r m a n s (emphasis in the original). Our article has already been successful. (It has) reached Germania and the whole German press. Now comes the question, will Germans follow our lead?"(60)

The Orędownik originally praised the Kuryer's initiative but after only two weeks returned to its chronic criticism. By mid-April it was charging that the Kuryer had retreated from its original position and had given in to the pressure of the Dziennik and Goniec.(61) The split within the gentry newspapers over how to react to Chancellor Caprivi seemed to confirm the Orędownik's main theme that the landowners had lost the ability to steer the Polish ship of state in the modern era. The reaction of the Goniec to the Kuryer's program was short and predictable: it was an act of treason.(62)

Bismarck's dismissal and Caprivi's appointment actually converted very few irreconcilables into loyalists; rather it split the ruling classes into loyalists and sceptics. For the moment the elation at Bismarck's dismissal gave the loyalists the initiative. In the Prussian Abgeordnetenhaus Florian Stablewski made a speech in early April assuring the new leadership that the Poles would be patriotic Prussian citizens if the government moved forward in redressing some fundamental grievances.(63) A month later Józef Mielżyński made a similar speech in the Herrenhaus.(64) Once again, the Kuryer and the Orędownik applauded these declarations of loyalty, while the Dziennik and Goniec opposed them. The Dziennik saw no reason to make these public statements since it gave Germans a false idea that Poles had been playing a double game all during Bismarck's rule, and because it promised unconditional support for the Caprivi administration.(65) The Kuryer praised Mielżyński's speech and took pleasure in noting that the Dziennik had been forced to print the Landtag speech even if a week late.(66) The Orędownik voiced its support for Mielżyński's declaration and noted that, "The moral bankruptcy of the loudmouth politicians (krzykacze) is clearly evident. We agree with the salient points of both the Mielżyński speech and the Kuryer's program".(67) A week later it wrote, "The speech was virtually a slap in the face to the Dziennik and the Goniec. We have always said that loyalty vis-à-vis Prussia was necessary and a precondition for rescuing our national spirit."(68)

Caprivi's moderate maiden speeches in the Reichstag and Landtag helped the Kuryer to promote its initiative.(69) The Dziennik stressed the Chancellor's statement in a Landtag speech that the new government would listen to all sides of public opinion, and noted in mid-June that, "The tone (toward us) has changed. It is more peaceful and pleasant."(70) In addition the Poles were quietly informed by the Minister of the Interior that the expulsion of non-Prussian Poles would be halted during the harvest season because, "The existing reality (of the shortage of labour T.K.) is stronger than government decrees".(71) The suspension of the expulsions during harvest season was a response to petitions made by numerous East Elbian landowners who were suffering from a shortage of cheap labour and not necessarily a gesture towards the Poles, but to those looking for signs that Berlin was testing the waters of a new Polish policy it was a welcome move.(72)

An important source of strength that worked in favour of the loyalist initiative was the attitude of German newspapers to the Neue Kurs in general and the Polish question in particular. Bismarck's fall resulted in highly critical editorials in many German newspapers. (73) The Catholic, Progressive and Social Democratic press was understandably pleased by the turn of events in Berlin, but criticism also flowed from an unexpected source - the Conservative press, especially the Kreuzzeitung. The normally sceptical Dziennik noted as early as 3 April, 1890, that many formerly hostile Germans were now conceding that, "Our legal opposition in the battle to gain our just rights is completely valid."(74) The Dziennik took heart in the statements of the new chancellor and predictions in the German papers that old policies could not be continued. On 27 April it noted, "We still cannot be sure if the government is going to seriously come to grips with the Polish question. The former anti-Polish barriers have collapsed ...We can note a change in German public opinion, e.g. the admission in the Landtag that the expulsions (of 1885-1886) were wrong. A substantial number of deputies have changed their tune on anti-Polish legislation. Let us not give up hope that what certain individuals today are articulating will one day be earnestly taken up by the parties."(75)

Approval of the Kuryer Poznański's program came quickly from the Catholic press and to a lesser extent from the Progressives. The Progressive Party had voted against some of the more illiberal anti-Polish measures under Bismarck, and with his dismissal seemed to expect a fundamentally new answer to the Polish question.(76) While unhappy with the strong social and religious conservatism of the Poles, the Progressives in principle sympathised with the plight of Prussia's national minorities and felt Bismarck's harsh Germanization was both wrong and a failure.(77)

Yet the most encouraging turnaround came with the Conservative Party. It had been part of the Kartell and had approved all previous anti-Polish legislation. By mid-1890, however, many Conservatives appeared ready to consider a milder

Polish policy, though there was a good deal of debate within the Party on this. (78) In a series of articles from its Poznań correspondent entitled "Ein Woertchen ueber unsere Polen", the Kreuzzeitung hinted at a willingness to suspend some of the harsher anti-Polish laws, such as the expulsion policy and the total ban on the use of Polish in the schools.(79) This apparent policy modification was connected to the increasingly fierce anti-Russian tone adopted by the newspaper and growing speculation that a German-Russian war was imminent All Polish papers welcomed the more tolerant language of the Kreuzzeitung during 1890, though by the end of the year the Dziennik was questioning its sincerity and suggesting that German Conservatives merely wanted to exploit the Polish minority for Germany's imperial war aims.(80)

3.4 The Army Bill of 1890

Having been conditioned by Bismarck's consistent denunciations of Polish aspirations, German public opinion needed some sign that the "conversion" to law-abiding Prussian citizens was sincere. The loyalist leaders realized that the declarations friendly to the Prussian state in the Landtag would not be enough; a dramatic, unequivocal signal had to be given.

An opportunity to manifest their departure from protest and opposition came to the Polish parliamentarians in June, 1890 with the introduction of a bill in the Reichstag that would increase the peace-time strength of the armed forces. This legislation had been originally planned by Bismarck but enjoyed the full support of Caprivi, who was more concerned than his predecessor with the threat of a war on two fronts.(81) Taxes imposed for increasing the strength of the German armed forces had never been popular among the Poles and Reichstag Party with full social backing, had consistently voted against new increases before. As late as January, 1890 the Poznań deputy Cegielski had solemnly stated that Poles, lacking representation in the decision-making levels of government and treated as second-class citizens, would play no part in building up Germany's military might.(82) How could Poles contribute to the military might of their partitioners?

The new circumstances brought about by Bismarck's dismissal, however, confronted the Polish deputies with a difficult choice between honouring tradition and political manoeuvring. Chancellor Caprivi had been in office only three months and this was his first important domestic bill. As a military man he was bound to be especially sensitive to a Polish rejection of measures intended to ensure Germany's security. How could the new Chancellor take the Polish statements of loyalty seriously if they rejected a strong German army? The Polish vote either for or against would make no difference in the final outcome; Caprivi had managed to win over the decisive support of the Centrum Party. Yet while in Berlin the Polish vote was largely a symbolic act, in Poznań it constituted a moral question of supreme importance. Could the deputies sacrifice an important point of principle in order to send the right signal to the new chancellor?

The debate among Poznań's newspapers was heated. The Dziennik, Wielkopolanin and Goniec strongly argued that the bill should be rejected, though for different reasons. For the Dziennik, sceptical of the great importance attached by the loyalists to the Neue Kurs, a stronger German army had nothing to offer Prussia's Polish minority. As late as 12 June, Dobrowolski and his editors were hoping that the Reichstag Party would vote against the bill, noting, "We are certain that in this issue as in all others, the Party will act in accordance with the real needs of our land and our people and not be guided by legends or fantasies."(83) The 'fantasies' was a reference to the bold prophesy made by the Kuryer that breaking fully with the past would lead to a Prussian-Polish accomodation. The next day the Dziennik explicitly called upon the Party to reject the bill. "We do not know how the Party stands on this issue, and from our information it appears they have not yet made a decision. But we desperately pray that the voices of those few propagating unconditional support for government bills are not heeded. Our deputies must weigh all the factors with an open mind and will appreciate what a difficult material and political situation our society faces. They must ask themselves if they can burden us with new taxes without obtaining any compensation in our moral and national needs."(84) The 'moral and national needs' was doubtless a reference to the lifting of the emergency laws passed during Bismarck's last years in power. The Dziennik's message: await concessions from the government before supporting a bill that would bring no positive benefits to the Polish minority. One could be loyal in the sense that one did not engage in conspiratorial activity and regularly paid his taxes, without losing all sense of pragmatism. As the days passed leading up to the vote, the editorial line of the Dziennik became more urgent. On 20 June it wrote that militarism threatened Polish social and political life as much as Social Democratic revolution, a remarkable statement coming from well-to-do landowners who were the descendents of former insurgents and the self-appointed guardians of "sacred Polish traditions". "All astute politicians must confront militarism", it concluded.(85)

Fear that the Party in Berlin would disregard public opinion and vote for the Army Bill sent off a wave of alarm in the Polish community, and on 19 June an extraordinary meeting of the Poznań municipal committee was called by the 'Goniec supporters' to debate the issue. After heated debate a resolution, composed by the Goniec's editor Rzepecki, was adopted which formally requested the Party in Berlin to vote against the bill. The vote within the committee was 6-5 in favour of sending the resolution, with both M. Kantecki of the Kuryer and Dobrowolski of the Dziennik opposed. The resolution was signed by 44 citizens present and sent to Berlin, where, like other earlier attempts to influence the opinion of the deputies, it was ignored.(86)

The Orędownik was opposed to the bill for economic reasons. Szymański advocated a pragmatic loyalism vis-à-vis Prussia and in mid-1890 was still wholeheartedly behind the Kuryer's program. But the Orędownik objected to the increased taxation which the bill entailed. It noted that Chancellor Caprivi's version of the bill went even farther than anything Bismarck had proposed.(87) Two weeks before the vote, the Orędownik wrote, "The Party should be guided by our principles and our interests. It should absolutely vote against the Army Bill... The money is more difficult to come by here among us Poles."(88) On 18 June, it noted that all centres of public opinion were against the bill. "This bill will pass anyway but we should say no. If our society could be sure that the system built up by Bismarck over 20 years would change at least a little, then the Polish people would do everything to support His Majesty."(89) Like the Dziennik, the Orędownik seemed to be waiting for some credible statement from Chancellor Caprivi or the Prussian officialdon that an overhaul of the sad state of affairs in the eastern provinces was forthcoming.

Only the Kuryer urged the acceptance of the bill. This was a doubly difficult stand to take for a strongly clerical paper that had been mishandled during the Kulturkampf; the Kuryer had to overcome not ony Polish nationalist sentiment against a stronger German army but also religious opposition to endless armaments and unhappiness with the inferior status of Catholicism in Prussia. Yet in the spirit of reconciliation, the Kuryer plunged fully into a campaign to win over at least a modicum of public approval. It was important for the loyalists to silence some of the more strident opposition to the Army Bill in other newspapers, for they knew that summaries of the Polish press were being sent off to Berlin and that Chancellor Caprivi was likely reading them to determine if the Poles were really serious about their "conversion" to loyal Prussian subjects. Thus the Kuryer was writing as much for the government as for its Polish readers.

A number of arguments were used to support the bill. While recognising that it entailed increased taxation the Kuryer wrote that it would pass anyway and that there could be no possible advantage in supporting a losing cause. It laid great emphasis upon the acceptance of the bill by the Centrum Party, and linked the fortunes of the Poles under Chancellor Caprivi's administration to those of German Catholics. Without a common front with German Catholics the Poles could not expect the rapid changes for the better that everyone was demanding.(90) Another clever tactic was to defend the prerogatives of the deputies in Berlin. The Kuryer demanded that Polish society not attempt to influence their decision by emotional resolutions and editorials. On 17 June it wrote, "We are disappointed that other newspapers are telling our Party how to vote, discouraging, threatening and terrorizing them. The Party does not seek to be popular in the manner of those winning a popularity contest, but is supposed to promote our needs... The bill will be approved anyway - how can we remain in opposition allied only to the Progressives and the Social Democrats?"(91) The next day, in solemn tones, it informed its readers that the times had greatly changed and that the only ones capable of understanding what was best for Polish society were the deputies. "Whoever understands the new state of affairs, or even vaguely understands it, cannot argue that we should stand back now and play a passive role. By a resolute and unmistakable act we want to bring about a full shift in our situation. The sooner the better... We shall never convince our enemies, but we shall make new friends."(92)

The Poles, then, had to swallow a bitter pill and vote for an unpopular act in order to send the clear signal to Chancellor Caprivi and his ministers that the days of protest and irredenta were over and that they were a reliable, conservative element. Once notified, the Prussian government could not ignore an honest partnership, just as it could not ignore the Centrum Party and its just demands that the last vestiges of the Kulturkampf be eliminated from Prussia. Caprivi was obliged to build a wórking majority out of the ruins of the Kartell, and Polish loyalists wanted to be part of his coalition. They had to prove that they could be relied upon. After all, had not the Poles always been faithful to the throne and the alter?

Once resolved to support increased military spending the Kuryer tried to convince other Poles, and undoubtedly the Prussian authorities that the bill really enjoyed general popularity. It printed letters from readers that applauded its editorial stance but steadfastly refused to identify its "correspondents", making it virtually impossible to determine whether the letters were authentic or written by the Kuryer's employees. On 26 June it printed two suspicious letters from Poznań under the title, "An About Face in Public Opinion". The gist of the letters was that all Poznań now supported the bill and disgruntled residents should allow the deputies in Berlin to make their own decision. (93)

Having decided to vote for the Army Bill, it only made sense for the Reichstag Party to publicize its action to make the most favourable impression on decision-making circles. On 25 June, Komierowski, the Party's spokesman on military affairs, surprised his German colleagues with a stirring declaration of loyalty to Prussia and its monarch. He further challenged Caprivi to improve Polish-German relations on the basis of full equality for Poles as Prussian citizens who were willing to do their part to strengthen the Reich against its external enemies.(94) The Polish vote seemed to catch German public opinion off guard; it had been assumed that the Poles would automatically vote against all military bills. Reaction to the vote was positive all throughout the land but for the National Liberal and Free Conservative camps who felt the vote was some sort of a 'trick'. The Kuryer was quick to praise the vote and pointed out, "Now at least we have a bargaining point with the government... In our opinion, all mature elements in our society that are not under the influence of the 'loudmouth' politics of our irreconcilable chauvinists, are thankful to our deputies for this forceful sign that has decisively broken with ancient traditions that had brought us nothing but defeat."(95)

Throughout the summer and autumn of 1890 the Kuryer reprinted articles from friendly German newspapers that were intended to show how the vote had indeed made new friends and blunted the attacks of their sworn enemies. "We are certain", it wrote on 28 June, "that if we had voted against the bill, or abstained, our enemies surrounding the Emperor would not have passed up the chance to compare us with the socialists - as enemies of the state."(96) Virtually all important German newspapers had correctly interpreted the Army Bill vote as a sign of loyalty towards Prussia and an unequivocal rejection of Pan-Slavism.(97) The Kuryer was particularly delighted by the change of tone in the Kreuzzeitung, which, fearful of an imminent war against Russia, argued that the Poles should be incorporated into the Prussian state mentality by persuasion rather than by force. There was good reason to believe that the Kuryer's ideal coalition of Conservatives, Catholics and Poles seemed within the realm of the feasible.(98)

The nationalists centred around the Goniec were incensed and saw the vote as an act of betrayal. On 15 July it wrote that 99% of Polish society were cursing the Party and that its vote represented an insult to Polish traditions and principles.(99) In an insightful analysis it concluded that the Reichstag Party would win its great gamble only if four demands were met: 1) that education of Poles had to be once again provided in Polish, 2) the Polish language had to win recognition in the courts, 3) Polish officials had to return to the Polish provinces and assume duties there, and 4) a Polish 'namiestnik' (Statthalter) had to be named as an intermediary between the monarch and the Polish nation (as Fuerst Antoni Radziwiłł had served Friedrich Wilhelm III from 1815-1830 T.K.)(100) The analysis of the Goniec called for a full and immediate recognition of the Vienna treaties. Yet the Goniec had no faith at all in loyalism. "Since the Party voted for the bill", it wrote, "Germans are treating Poles only as a rag with which to slap the face of Russia."(101) Obsequiousness vis-a-vis Prussia would not lead to greater concessions but to greater exploitation; the only way to counter Germanization was to guard every piece of national property, religion and tradition, whatever the cost.

The needless provocation of Russia was also of great concern to the Orędownik. Szymański had opposed the Army bill for economic reasons but agreed with the Kuryer's stand on the rejection of fruitless negation and protest.

It did not, however, approve of the needless antagonism of Russia. "Why grate at Russia when we have several million of our countrymen there?", it asked on 29 June, 1890.(102) It suggested that the Polish gentry, desperate to hold on to their monopoly of political power, was making an exaggerated show of anti-Russian feeling to impress German public opinion, to the detriment of the oppressed Poles in Russia. On 12 July, the Orędownik wrote, "The Kuryer is presenting the vote on the Army Bill as an attempt to increase Germany's strength against Russia. It is writing as if it wanted to go to war with Russia in two weeks... Why is it blowing up the importance of this vote when it was not really so important?"(103) In response to further articles in the Kuryer, the Orędownik wrote on 17 July, "The Kuryer is saying that the Poles are the front line against Russia. But (the fact is) we are not interested in Russia at all! We are only interested in saving our own skins - to break down the anti-Polish legislation."(104) Szymański approved of the main theme of the Komierowski Reichstag speech, writing that, "Its principal fault is that it was not made 20 years ago".(105) Nevertheless, it was sheer delusion to believe that the government would respond to such a declaration, for the simple fact that the Poles possessed no political clout. The deputies had no business provoking Russia when the fundamental battle over the Polish identity in Prussia was being lost. "We have to look to ourselves (to preserve) our national existence."(106)

The Dziennik was ambiguous in its appraisal of the Party's vote. Its earlier opposition to the bill had been taken to heart by the deputies and Komierowski mentioned it in his 25 June Reichstag speech.(107) Yet the Dziennik had always seen itself as the spokesman for gentry leadership and was reluctant to damage the splendid image of national solidarity by post-vote recriminations. On the day after the vote the Dziennik reminded its readers of its earlier opposition but then added, "We are not making any accusations because we are firmly convinced that the Polish Party had, and still has, important reasons for its position."(108) Having lost its bid to convince the deputies of the folly of their act, the Dziennik now hoped that their outstretched hand would be grasped by Chancellor Caprivi and that some immediate concessions were forthcoming. It was ready to employ some of the loyalists' arguments so long as they brought about the repeal of the detested anti-Polish legislation. On 20 July, in the midst of the uproar over the Party's vote and Komierowski's declaration the Dziennik wrote, "Our deputies voted for the Army Bill only because they are good loyal Prussian subjects, not for any other reasons. We did not want Wilhelm II to be deprived of a strong army needed to balance (the threat of) Russia."(109) The Dziennik was willing to give the loyalist initiative a chance but would not go so far as to repudiate its oppositionist stand since 1871. On 23 July, in answer to charges in the Hamburger Nachrichten that the Poles' vote on the Army Bill was a 'trick', the Dziennik wrote, "Let us hope that now with this hostile force (Bismarck T.K.) out of office, mistrust of Poles among the authorities will be replaced by a mutual feeling of trust and a degree of justice."(110) The Dziennik's client paper, the Wielkopolanin, dealt with Bismarck's articles in simpler terms. It denounced him for accusing the Poles of duplicity in their vote, and concluded in an atmosphere of self-confidence, "Our cause is just and sooner or later we shall win, whether Prince Bismarck likes it or not."(111)

One can appreciate the difficult position of Dobrowolski of the Dziennik. A veteran of the 1863 Uprising, like so many of the irreconcilables, Dobrowolski could see no reason why the Poles should take part in strengthening the armed forces of a partitioning power that had shown no respect for Polish aspirations. What possible interest could Poles have in a stronger German army?

Was Germany really planning a pre-emptive strike against Russia, and if so, how should Prussian Poles react if ordered to fight against their brothers in Russian Poland? On the other hand, Dobrowolski was a leading powerbroker in the Polish community in Poznania and had always stressed the need to maintain national solidarity and the legitimate hegemony of the gentry. The prestige and standing of the Reichstag deputies had to be upheld; only as a solid unit could the Poles in Prussia constitute any sort of power factor in Berlin. The principle of Party unity was so sacred that Dobrowolski and the sceptical gentry refrained from outright criticism of the loyalists at this stage. Their reasoning at this stage was: if they are successful, all the better, if not, let us limit the damage, but whatever the case let us not sacrifice the unity which we have enjoyed since the beginnings of parliamentarism in Prussia. The key question which the Dziennik was trying to answer in 1890 was: would Chancellor Caprivi and Wilhelm II change direction in their Polish policy? Would Bismarck's strategy of "Ausrotten!" be continued or would Prussia's Polenpolitik undergo a "new era" as part of a broader political, social and economic reorientation in Prussia and the Reich? It took two years before the Dziennik arrived at the definitive answer, and even then the principle of national unity prevented an outright break with the loyalists.

The signs during the last half of 1890 were confusing. The Dziennik, in constant touch with German newspapers and very sensitive to anything written about the Poles, noticed a substantial improvement in attitudes after the Army Bill vote. Sympathy with the plight of the Poles coincided with a surge of articles criticizing Bismarck's legacy, a theme all Polish newspapers delighted in exploiting.(112) So long as Bismarck was fair game for criticism in leading Conservative, Catholic and Progressive newspapers, there was reason for hope. Yet as Chancellor Caprivi failed to come to grips with the Polish question, the patience of the Dziennik began to grow thin. If the new government could take a more moderate view of the aspirations of the Alsatians and allow the anti-socialist laws to lapse (as they did at the end of September, 1890), then why was nothing being done for the Poles?(113) Were the law-abiding, peaceful Poles less deserving than the revolutionary socialists?

3.5. The Rentengutsgesetz of 1890

Interestingly enough, one of the most important pieces of legislation enacted by the Prussian Landtag (in two stages, the Rentengutsgesetz of 27 June, 1890 and 7 July, 1891) passed almost unnoticed in the pages of the Polish press, in spite of the fact that Poles were able to profit handsomely from it.(114) Indeed, the legislation, designed to place Prussian state financial resources at the disposal of enterprising farmers willing to take part in the dismemberment of deficit estates, was open to Poles and Germans alike and was quickly exploited by the Polish "Bank Ziemski" (Land Bank) to defend against the encroachments of the Ansiedlungskommission. Future German historians lamented the liberalism of the Rentengutsgesetz and deplored the fact that two German institutions in the eastern provinces, the Ansiedlungskommission and the Generalkommission, operated simultaneously and to each other's detriment. As Richard Perdelwitz noted, "So arbeiten also waehrend dieser 5 Jahre (1891-1896 T.K.) in beiden Provinzen Posen und Westpreussen die beiden staatlichen Einrichtungen mit staatlichen Mitteln nebeneinander, die Ansiedlungskommission an der Staerkung des deutschen Bauernstandes, die Generalkommission an der Vermehrung des polnischen Bauernstandes."(115) It was not before 1894 that public opinion was alerted to this paradox, and an appropriate clause to the Rentengutsgesetz in 1896 made its activities conform with the interests of the Ansiedlungskommission.(116)

The silence of the Polish newspapers on the passage of this beneficial piece of economic legislation invites analysis. Writing directly after independence the historian Stanisław Karwowski felt that Chancellor Caprivi intended the bill as a "gesture of reconciliation between the Polish people and the Prussian government."(117) If so, it may have been the opening move that Poles were waiting for so earnestly as a reply to their declarations of loyalty in the Prussian Landtag and Reichstag. The Landtag Polish Party's secret deliberations reveal that the legislation had been under consideration even before Caprivi became Prussian Ministerpraesident.(118) In fact, when the Landtag Party deliberated on the bill there was some opposition among the wealthy landowners and general scepticism as to its effectiveness. On 10 June, it was finally decided to vote for the bill, "One member of the Herrenhaus advised not to bog ourselves down in details but to vote for the bill so that our constituents could not say that the government wanted to give them the chance to buy property and their own deputies opposed." (119) The Party, it appears, was less interested in whether or not the bill would work than it was in preserving its reputation at home.

The most plausible explanation for the silence over the Rentengutsgesetz in the Polish press, as well as silence over later economic bills favourable to the Poles, is that contemporaries, both Germans and Poles, did not consider economic measures that worked to the benefit of both the Polish minority and the German majority as a "concession". Attention from both sides was invariably turned to "national" concerns: language lessons in the schools, religious instruction for the young, place-name changes, Germanization or Polonization of youth, the 'great-Polish agitation' in Upper Silesia, and the hostility of the Prussian bureaucracy. This framework for the nationality conflict in Prussia's East had been promoted by Fuerst Bismarck during his years as Ministerpraesident in 1862-1890. Bismarck felt the greatest enemies among the Poles were the aristocrats and upper clergy; he praised the peasantry and ignored the urban class. (120) It took another decade before the importance of the economic organisations and self-sufficiency of the Poles became evident. From the Polish point of view, the Rentengutsgesetz was passed in the Prussian Landtag at the height of debate over the Army Bill vote, an issue whose intense emotional involvement excluded all other issues. Not even the middle-class papers dedicated to economic matters took any notice of the passage of this new law. The Postęp was absorbed in anti-Semitism during its first year and had little to offer on current events, while the Orędownik was rejoicing over the split within the gentry over the Army Bill.

A second interpretation for the Polish silence is that they were indeed aware of the positive benefits but refrained from jubilation for fear of alerting the Prussian government and suffering the bill's revision to exclude Poles.(121) Remembering that the newspapers were closely monitored by the Prussian police and the 'Bismarckpresse', the Polish papers may have struck a quiet bargain to keep silent on this important bill which they knew was a windfall to their hard-pressed low-income farmers. Whatever the case, the silence on economic benefits gained under Chancellor Caprivi was to be repeated during the crucial year 1892 when Polish co-operatives were given the right to conduct their own financial auditing without government supervision.

3.6 A Polish Archbishop for Gniezno-Poznań. Phase One (to Oct. 1890)

On 30 May, 1890, Julius Dinder, a kind-hearted but irresolute German churchman, died, thus vacating the all-important Archbishopric of Gniezno-Poznań. Dinder had been virtually forced into accepting the office in 1886 by Bismarck and never seemed comfortable as spiritual overlord of a predominantly Polish Catholic population.(122) The previous Archbishop, Mieczysław Ledóchowski-Halka had been imprisoned during the Kulturkampf and expelled from Prussia, and was now a Cardinal who constituted a Polish lobby within the Roman Curia. Dinder's performance as Archbishop seemed to satisfy no one; the Poles, against his appointment from the outset, fiercely resented his collaboration with the Germanization measures in the Church, while Bismarck felt Dinder did not pursue this policy with enough fervour.(123) Polish opposition to Dinder resulted in an embarrassing confrontation with the Schlesische Volkszeitung. As Leonhard Mueller noted, "Bereits im Jahre 1888 das fuehrende Zentrumsorgan Schlesiens energisch Front machen musste gegen die polnische Presse, weil diese schon damals einen systematischen Kampf begann gegen die ostdeutschen Bischoefe von Posen, Kulm und Ermland wegen deren angeblichen Germanisierungsbestrebungen."(124)

Dinder's death presented a prize occasion to initiate a new course in German-Polish relations. A speedy appointment of a qualified Pole would have strengthened the resolve of Poznań's loyalists and constituted an unmistakable sign that the Caprivi government wanted a full break with Bismarck's legacy. As the Dziennik wrote in Dinder's obituary on 1 June, 1890, "The government should take advantage of the moment and, learning the proper lessons from past experience, it should be aware that it is in the interests of the state that a shepherd and his flock be of the same origin and blood".(125) And yet Caprivi demurred. Instead of speedily appointing a Pole he hesitated for over a year before acting, and in so doing disappointed the Poles while giving his German critics the opportunity to make a major issue of it all. Von Hutten-Czapski wrote in his memoirs, "Die Frage der Besetzung des Erzbistums von Gnesen und Posen beruehrte alle Verhaeltnisse meiner Heimatprovinz und ihre politischen, nationalen und kirchlichen Probleme aufs engste."(126)

A brief review of events leading up to the appointment of Florian Stablewski will help to place the role of Polish public opinion in better focus.(127) Immediately upon hearing of Dinder's death, Graf von Zedlitz-Truetzschler, Oberpraesident of Poznania, wrote to Kultusminister von Gossler presenting and evaluating a list of candidates for the vacant see. He listed Edward Likowski as the strongest Polish candidate but considered Likowski an ultramontane and anti-state to a high degree.(128) Gossler, the last of Bismarck's convinced anti-Polish ministers, dominated a cabinet meeting of 5 June, 1890, and successfully excluded all potential Polish candidates. Likowski was described as "streng polnisch und klerikal" and too strongly linked to the Polish national movement.(129) Caprivi was impressed by these arguments and agreed to promote the nomination of Leo Redner, the German bishop of Kulm, a reputable churchman but disliked by the Poles. Throughout June, however, movements were afoot to convince Pope Leo XIII not to agree to a German candidate. In mid-June Mielżyński travelled to Rome and secured an interview with the Pope thanks to the intervention of Cardinal Ledóchowski-Halka, and was given assurances that the Pope would not agree to a German candidate.(130) Later on, both Kościelski and Stablewski, who was not considered a candidate at this time, also visited the Pope to put forward the Polish cause.(131)

In the meantime the Poznań Capitula presented its list of candidates to the government for consideration on 2 July, 1890. All six candidates were Poles. Caprivi dismissed them as "Polen schroffster Richtung" and showed no preference for any candidate.(132) Throughout the critical months of July and August key German statesmen were putting strong pressure on Caprivi and Wilhelm II not to agree to a Polish candidate. Gossler wrote to the Chancellor on 29 July, "Alle Kandidaten sind nicht allein der streng ultramontanen Richtung angehoerig sondern... sind polnisch-national gesinnt."(133) Similar advice was being given to Caprivi and Wilhelm II by Ludwig Raschdau, diplomat and courtier who was one of Bismarck's most faithful followers.(134)

A cabinet meeting of 5 August rejected the Capitula's list and Wilhelm II concurred on 13 August. A delegation of Poles that met secretly with the Chancellor were told that all the candidates were too anti-government, but that the state would not object to a Pole who was "apolitical".(135) From mid-August 1890 to September, 1891 virtually no progress was made in the matter of a new Archbishop; the government preferred a German saying it could not find a suitable Pole, while Rome demanded a Polish candidate.

It was only natural that the Polish press would be fully behind a Polish Archbishop, and all newspapers were shaken by the decision of both the Chancellor and Emperor to reject the Capitula's list. It seemed out of place in all the talk of a Neue Kurs and appeared as a deliberate rejection to the outstretched hand offered by the vote on the Army Bill only two months before. Why should not the Archbishop of Gniezno-Poznań, who carried the title "Primate of Poland", be a Pole? Until the decision was announced at the end of August the newspapers acted as though an appointment of a Pole was beyond discussion - even the Kreuzzeitung had editorialized that a loyal and patriotic Pole would be a better candidate than an incompetent German.(136) The Catholic Germania strongly supported a Pole, arguing that the alternative would be an increase in the alienation of the Poles and the rise of Social Democracy and Pan-Slavism. (137) With both the Conservative and Catholic newspapers behind them the Poles had good reason to believe that the government would surely accede.

The most hard-hit by the rejection of the Capitula's list was the Kuryer Poznański. On 17 August it wrote in an atmosphere of exasperation "It is a violation of the rights of the Capitula, out of place and unjust."(138) Almost immediately its chief rival, the Goniec Wielkopolski, ridiculed the evident failure of the Kuryer's program and assured Poles that the Germans only thought of themselves and would never consider a Pole.(139) Defending loyalty in the face of the rejection considerable journalistic skill. On 26 August the Kuryer wrote, "All of Polish society is deeply hurt. We had expected a positive reply because the (Capitula's) list was one of moderates."(140) To manifest the disappointment of Prussia's Polish minority the Kuryer proposed to hold an open rally, an idea that met with little public support and eventually floundered. (141) It vigorously defended the Capitula's list of candidates, "Would 100,000 German Catholics be upset by a Polish Archbishop in light of over 1,000,000 Polish Catholics? The claim that a German Archbishop is necessary to defend German Catholics (from Polonization) is ridiculous. The existing system favours Germans anyway."(142) The Kuryer could not accept the notion that Chancellor Caprivi and the Emperor had no intention of abandoning Bismarck's Polish policy, as this would strike at the very foundation of loyalism, and preferred to lay the blame on Gossler. "Gossler is not identical with the new era", it wrote on

11 September, 1890. "The new era has not really begun but it is in the process of creation. In both parliamentary constellations and in the composition of the ministers the new era has first to bloom over the ruins (of Bismarck's legacy T.K.)... The more Gossler continues Bismarck's policies the more out of line he is with the new order."(143) To bolster its argument the Kuryer reprinted articles from the German press critical of Bismarck and suggested that a large part of German public opinion wanted Gossler to resign. In November it was openly calling for Gossler's resignation. "Komierowski's declaration should do away with all suspicions of Polish disloyalty. Polish 'agitation' simply does not exist... We feel that the resignation of Herr Gossler, the last relic and faithful disciple of Bismarck's fallen system, would do a great deal to bring the Polish population closer to the throne and do away with the intolerable conditions that exist in the Polish districts."(144) As early as August the Kuryer ran a column entitled "We are Waiting" (Czekamy) in which readers contributed letters demanding Gossler's departure. One such letter read, "We are praying for Gossler's dismissal and for that of Kuegler (Gossler's chief deputy T.K.). We pray to God that He speed up the dismissal and allow us all to breathe easier and more freely."(145) It is interesting to note the more assertive tones adopted by the Polish press towards Prussian officials after Bismarck's dismissal. Similar remarks about a Prussian minister under Bismarck's iron rule would simply not have been tolerated. Clearly, Polish newspapers feared the ill effects of the German press law less under Caprivi, and their sharper tones reflect a confidence that the press authorities were now more tolerant.

Equally disappointed at the government's decision was the Dziennik Poznański. Its first comment on the Emperor's rejection was, "deep pain and regret in our whole society. This is an unprovoked blow against us, just as we were trying to win the good graces of the government."(146) The government's action seemed proof that, "The Kulturkampf has not ended... The Germans are treating the whole affair as a political matter... They want to form a state-run Church."(147) Like the Kuryer, the Dziennik did not have to look far to arrive at the conclusion that the principal rogue was von Gossler. "Our Army Bill vote should have made the right opinion about us (in government circles). Gossler does not think so... It is all his fault."(148) In early September it found a sympathetic article in Germania that similarly blamed the disliked Kultusminister for the rejection of the Capitula's list. "We agree with Germania that the main burden of blame falls on Gossler. He wants to prevent Poles from following the road of loyalty."(149) Like Bismarck in the Hamburger Nachrichten, Gossler was seen as sabotaging the Polish loyalist initiative by provoking Polish outrage, thus preventing the government from developing the bond of trust so badly needed to dismantle the anti-Polish laws. Gossler's opposition to a Polish Archbishop was not merely a desire to defend the interests of German Catholics but a desperate attempt to destroy the good faith built up by the positive vote on the Army Bill. This was the view expressed by the correspondent of the Kreuzzeitung based in Poznań in his regular contribution "Ein Woertchen ueber unsere Polen", who remarked that the movement towards loyalty signalled by the Army Bill vote was being offset by anger at the rejection of the Capitula's list.(150) Yet such a strategy was easy to defeat: one had only to keep calm, moderate the level of disappointment, and hope that Gossler would soon be forced out of office. By December, 1890, as Gossler was beginning to come into disagreement with the Chancellor over a Prussian school reform bill, the Dziennik was openly calling for his dismissal.

"The Freisinnige Zeitung writes that Gossler's days are numbered. It is not the only one waiting for his resignation."(151)

Throughout the stormy first half of 1890 the Dziennik had urged a reserved, cautious stance towards the Caprivi administration, waiting for the Chancellor to make the first move in improving relations. After all, it was not the Poles who had declared war on Prussia, but Prussia that under Bismarck had pursued a barely-concealed "Ausrotten" policy. By October, 1890, there was still no sign that Caprivi was interested in changing course. In an analysis of mid-October entitled "Which Way to Agreement" the Dziennik stressed that virtually no progress had been made to put an end to the warlike conditions. "The rejection of the Capitula's list was a blow to our efforts at reaching an understanding," it wrote, and asked why, given the Army Bill vote and the expiration of the anti-socialist laws, nothing positive in the eastern provinces had happened.(152)

The Dziennik acknowledged the support for a Polish candidate from the Catholic but took a critical view of the Conservative position. Throughout 1890 the Dziennik cast doubt on the sincerity of the conversion of German Conservatives to a fairer and more moderate Polish policy. It strongly hinted that the Conservatives, even on an issue so sensitive as an Archbishop for Gniezno-Poznań, were primarily interested in the Polish military factor in the event of war against Russia. "Why is (the Kreuzzeitung) linking this appointment to a future rebuilt Poland?" it asked on 12 October.(153) On 16 October, in a major analysis of the Conservative stand vis-à-vis the Poles, the Dziennik wrote, "We are indeed happy to see a new wind blowing in some of the Conservative papers, notably the Kreuzzeitung... A certain part of German public opinion has changed its tone since Bismarck's departure. But, in truth, it is comical that the Kreuzzeitung should poison and confuse the issues of politics and the just treatment of a national minority by bringing up concepts of creating a future Poland on the Dnieper and the Black Sea... This is pure fantasy and we have not said a word about this anywhere (in our press)".(154) Ultimately, the Dziennik concluded that the only sincere support the Poles in Prussia could count on was the Pope himself. "We place our hope in the Holy Father, who, we trust, will never choose an Archbishop who is not of our flesh and blood."(155)

The Orędownik lamented the relative powerlessness of the Polish minority and was less hopeful than other papers that a Pole would be named Archbishop. Because of their lack of economic strenght and the pathetic policies of the Parties in Berlin, no one took Polish desires seriously. Only the personal intervention and good grace of the Kaiser could overcome the hostility of Prussia's officials.(156) Although the Orędownik had urged a declaration be made to the new Chancellor earlier in the year, it now spoke out against demonstrations on the issue of a new Archbishop. It rejected the Kuryer's notion of holding a mass rally, feeling it would give the impression that Poles always remained in opposition and erase whatever good feeling had been generated by the Army Bill vote and Komierowski's Reichstag address.(157) In effect the Orędownik believed that all forms of pressure were useless as they would only serve to irritate Gossler and other members of the cabinet. At the root of the problem lay the absence of an authentic Polish power base. Like the the Dziennik, it urged the believed faithful to place their trust in the Pope and the Capitula.(158)

The question of a new Archbishop awoke a responsive chord in both low-price popular newspapers. The Wielkopolanin, usually abrasive in editorial comment, had been portraying the "new liberal tendency is higher levels of government" in a positive light and had led its readers to believe that under Caprivi things would be different.(159) When news of the rejection of the Capitula's list came out, the Wielkopolanin could not hide its displeasure. "Although we had never been overly optimistic that the postion taken by the Prussian government towards us would change in a short time, we felt that at least in the question of a new Archbishop-Primate we would not be disappointed".(160) Nominating a German would be a great injustice and, "It would be a continuation of Bismarck's anti-Polish policy. A German would be regarded as an intruder".(161) Before long the Wielkopolanin was also calling for the resignation of Kultusminister Gossler and his deputy Kuegler. After Kuegler had told the Schlesische Zeitung that the ministry would never retreat from Germanization in the school system, the Wielkopolanin noted wryly, "So much for our 'educators'...These kinds of 'never' are many in history; all of them see their day and then fade away."(162) In the pages of the Wielkopolanin and its mentor, the Dziennik, one can see the confusion reigning among the editorial staff during 1890 over the much-heralded Neue Kurs. After a period of friendly gestures towards the Poles and friendly articles in German newspapers both papers wrote about a reversal of the Bismarckian legacy; yet after a sharp blow, such as the rejection of the Capitula's list, both papers were quick to stress that they had "never really believed" in a better future.

Finally, the urban anti-Semitic Postęp took its first clear stand on national affairs. Stanisław Knapowski had spent most of his first year in building up his readership and propagating his chief themes: anti-Semitism and economic modernisation. The lapse of the anti-socialist laws and the rejection of the Capitula's list, however, moved the Postęp to comment on the specific unfairness shown the Poles. If socialists could be trusted to behave as law-abiding citizens (and so many of them were Jews, as the Postęp never failed to remind its readers), then why not the Poles?(163) Like the Orędownik, the Postęp did not place much faith in the politics of the landowner-dominated Party and saw the only salvation in the Papacy and the chief Polish spokesman in Rome, Cardinal Ledóchowski-Halka.(164) The Postęp was irritated by the condition set by the Prussian government that any Polish candidate needed to be a "moderate in national affairs".(165) How could anyone be a 'moderate' when, "The Polish people are sentenced to a slow extermination. Everything that the world has given to us has been taken away. We are left only with our Faith in God."(166) After listing the benefits other groups in Germany had come to expect from the Caprivi government, the Postęp complained, "Things for us will never get any better. The evil that has predominated so long continues to rule. We can expect even a sadder fate and can only dream of better times."(167)

As the first year of the Neue Kurs came to an end, emotions in Prussian Poland can best be described as mixed. The Poles had begun with an impressive electoral victory in February and were overjoyed when Bismarck had stepped down in March. Overnight the aristocratic loyalists took command of the Reichstag Party and through the Kuryer Poznański tried to convince their voters that the time had come to become a pro-government party. In its year-end review, the Kuryer lauded the first year of Caprivi's chancellorship. "A complete turnaround has taken place in the domestic political scene in Germany."(168) It was only a matter of time, the Kuryer concluded, before a reversal of policy was set into motion in Prussia's Polish policy as well.

The irreconcilables centred around the Goniec were not convinced. Their great fear was that loyalism would diminish the national resistance to Germanization and delay the day of national independence. The majority of the landowners linked to the Dziennik and the Wielkopolanin failed to see the "complete turnaround" which the Kuryer was publicizing with such enthusiasm but were temporarily out-manoeuvred by the loyalists and were willing to give Chancellor Caprivi support if he addressed the Polish question quickly and substantially. They were content at the end of 1890 with a wait-and-see attitude. In its year-end review the Dziennik wrote, "The changes that have taken place... have had a greater effect upon our illusions and hopes than in an objective modification of conditions. After Bismarck's fall we tried to cool the expectations (of Polish society) despite the loyalist leanings of our Party. Yet our list of candidates for an Archbishop was rejected. There has been no withdrawal of the extra-legal laws."(169) The Wielkopolanin was more pessimistic, "Another year has gone by, and our lot has not got better only worse, though Bismarck has gone... there has been no let-up in anti-Polish legislation."(170) The national-liberals were waiting for clearer evidence of a change of heart in Berlin.

Notes to Chapter Three

1. Goniec Wielkopolski, 28.5.1895, no. 121. The secretary of the Landtag Party Father Piotr Wawrzyniak, referred to the 1879 decision in answer to an appeal by the populist deputy Józef Głębocki, supported by nine newspapers, to form a regular flow of information directly from the Party to the press. See also Akta PKW, Ms. no. 784, "Papiery po przewodniczącym PCKW Ks. Piotra Wawrzyniaka". Vol. 1.

2. Mai, Die preussische Polenpolitik..., p. 30, "Das Gutsbesitzermehrheit in der Polenfraktion fand mit den preussischen Junkern auf parlamentarischer Ebene eine gemeinsame Sprache... Damals (1884) verurteilte Dr. Kantecki die bisherige Taktik des staendigen Protests als unfruchtbare Politik und forderte volle Mitwirkung im parlamentarischen Leben... So wurde die Loesung von der organischen Arbeit auf politischem Gebiet zur Loyalitaet gegenueber der preussischen Regierung." See also Schinkel, Polen, Preussen und Deutschland..., p. 163.

3. Dzieje Wielkopolski... vol. 2, pp. 511-512 gives the election results as: Cegielski-9801, Niegolewski-1093. See also Blanke, Prussian Poland...,p. 111.

4. Dziennik Poznański, 14.3.1888, no. 61; 15.3.1888, no. 62; 22.3.1888, no. 68. See also Orędownik, 14.3.1888, no. 61; 21.3.1888, no. 67.

5. Schulthess' Europaeischer Geschichtskalender, 1888, p. 81: "Ihre Majestaet empfing in Posen ein Deputation von Damen unter der Fuehrung der Graefin Honorina Kwilecka. Die Graefin, obwohl der deutschen Sprache voellig maechtig, richtete an die Kaiserin eine franzoesische Ansprache, in welcher - und auch dies ist charakteristisch - nicht von Preussinnen, sondern von den Polonaises die Rede ist. Eine solche Demonstration verdient zumal unter den Umstaenden, unter denen sie in Szene gesetzt worden ist, in der That die schaerfste Verurteilung." For a more favourable account of Victoria's visit, see Hutten-Czapski, Sechzig Jahre...vol. 1, p. 167; Komierowski, Koło Polskie w Berlinie..., pp. 180-181; Karwowski, Historya Wielkiego Księstwa...vol. 2, p. 476.

6. Dziennik Poznański, 10.4.1888, no. 83.

7. Ibid., 15.4.1888, no. 88. The term 'Pfifferling' is a reference to Chancellor Bismarck's famous response to a Polish-Centrum interpellation in the Prussian Landtag on 26 January, 1886, concerning the violations of the 1815 guarantees, "Ich gebe meinesteils keinen Pfifferling auf irgendeine Berufung auf die damaligen Proklamationen." Bismarck, GW. vol. 13, pp. 145-146.

8. Orędownik, 13.4.1888, no. 86.

9. Benyskiewicz, Posłowie polscy..., pp. 201-202.

10. Karwowski, Historya Wielkiego Księstwa...vol. 2, p. 476.

11. Wielkopolanin, 8.5.1888, no. 107.

12. Benyskiewicz, Posłowie polscy..., p. 203.

13. Karwowski, "Historya Dziennika Poznańskiego"..., pp. 73-74.

14. Dziennik Poznański, 19.5.1888, no. 115.

15. Orędownik, 19.5.1888, no. 115.

16. Dziennik Poznański, 10.6.1888, no. 132; 12.6.1888, no. 133; Wielkopolanin, 9.6.1888, no. 131. The other two were Chancellor Bismarck himself and the Kultusminister Gustav von Gossler.

17. Orędownik, 17.6.1888, no. 138.

18. Ibid., 23.6.1888, no. 143.

19. Dziennik Poznański, 15.6.1888, no. 136.

20. Ibid., 21.6.1888, no. 141.

21. Orędownik, 18.7.1888, no. 163.

22. Dziennik Poznański, 24.7.1888, no. 168.

23. Schulthess'...1888, pp. 114 and 116 offers a full text of both the address and the reply drafted by the Chancellor.

24. Orędownik, 31.10.1888, no. 251.

25. For example, Chłapowski at Kościan on 30.9.1888, reported in Orędownik, 2.10.1888, no. 226; Józef Kościelski at Inowrocław, reported in Wielkopolanin, 22.8.1888, no. 192; Ignacy Zakrzewski at Ostrów on 28.8.1888, reported in Orędownik, 31.8.1888, no. 200; Władysław Różański at Jarocin reported in Wielkopolanin on 30.8.1888, no. 199.

26. Kuryer Poznański, 19.3.1889, no. 65.

27. Trzeciakowski, Polityka polskich klas..., p. 38.

28. Orędownik, 20.3.1889, no. 65; 27.3.1889, no. 71.

29. Benyskiewicz, Posłowie polscy..., p. 208.

30. Kościelski to Szuman, 15.4.1889, in: B.Racz., Ms. no. 1636, "Korrespondencja Henryka Szumana". For Kościelski's difficulties with other members of the Landtag Party, see BK., Ms. no. 1456/1457, minutes of the meeting of 6.2. 1890 and 27.2.1890; Orędownik, 2.4.1889, no. 76; Kucner, "Polityka Koła Polskiego"..., pp. 48-49.

31. Orędownik, 4.2.1890, no. 28.

32. Ibid., 11.2.1890, no. 34.

33. Kuryer Poznański, 24.1.1890, no. 19.

34. Dziennik Poznański, 23.1.1890, no. 18. See also Wielkopolanin, 23.1.1890, no. 18. It is instructive to note how both these newspapers commented on the same topics at the same time, suggesting a co-ordinated effort.

35. Akta PKW, Ms. no. 877 (Pleszów), 28.1.1890; Ms. no. 869 (Srem), 19.1.1890. See also the report on the rally at Kepno on 5.1.1890 in Wielkopolanin, 17.1.1890, no. 13; rally in Inowrocław on 26.1.1890, reported in Wielkopolanin, 31.1.1890, no. 25.

36. Dziennik Poznański, 28.1.1890, no. 22; Kuryer Poznański, 28.1.1890, no. 22; Wielkopolanin, 28.1.1890, no. 22.

37. Orędownik, 5.2.1890, no. 29.

38. Wielkopolanin, 11.3.1890, no. 58; Orędownik, 23.2.1890, no. 45.

39. Erich Eyck, Bismarck. Leben und Werk (Zuerich, 1944), vol. 3, p. 580.

40. Statistisches Jahrbuch fuer das Deutsche Reich. Hrsg. vom Kaiserlichen Statistischen Amt. 1891 (vol. 12), p. 133.

41. Dziennik Poznański, 14.3.1890, no. 47.

42. Ibid., 27.2.1890, no. 48; 28.2.1890, no. 49.

43. Kuryer Poznański, 25.2.1890, no. 46.

44. Ibid., 14.3.1890, no. 61.

45. Ibid., 22.2.1890, no. 44 gives the figures for the socialist vote. For commentaries, see Dziennik Poznański, 25.5.1890, no. 46; Kuryer Poznański, 6.3.1890, no. 54.

46. Orędownik, 6.3.1890, no. 54.

47. Dziennik Poznański, 4.3.1890, no. 52.

48. Komierowski, Koło Polskie...p. 185.

49. Witold Skarżynski, Nasze Sprawy (Poznań, 1897), quoted in: Wiegand, Die anti-deutsche Propaganda..., p. 21.

50. Dziennik Poznański, 26.2.1890, no. 47.

51. Kuryer Poznański, 23.3.1890, no. 69.

52. And yet Wilhelm II did keep the Polish factor in mind when discussing the possibility of war against Russia. See J.G.C. Roehl, "A Document of 1892 on Germany, Prussia and Poland", in: Historical Journal 7 (1964), pp. 143-149.

53. Deutschland und Polen, ed. Brackmann..., p. 233; Trzeciakowski, Polityka polskich klas..., p. 60

54. Muenstermann, Die preussisch-deutsche Polenpolitik..., p. 9.

55. "Z programu niedalekiej przyszłości", Kuryer Poznański, 19.3.1890, no. 65.

56. Orędownik, 20.3.1890, no. 66.

57. Dziennik Poznański, 22.3.1890, no. 68.

58. Ibid., 25.3.1890, no. 70.

59. Ibid., 13.6.1890, no. 71.

60. Kuryer Poznański, 27.3.1890, no. 71.

61. Orędownik, 5.4.1890, no. 79.

62. Ibid., 27.3.1890, no. 71.

63. Florian Stablewski in the Abgeordnetenhaus on 18.4.1890: "Wenn der Herr Ministerpraesident auch abwesend ist, ... will ich, wenn auch in seiner Abwesenheit, Namens meiner Landsleute die Hoffnung und gleichzeitig unser Vertrauen zu ihm aussprechen,... Wir haben das Vertrauen, dass der Herr Reichskanzler auch diese Frage in Erwaegung ziehen werde, wobei er sich auch ueberzeugen koennte, dass wie alle unsere Pflichten dem Staate gegenueber treu erfuellen, dass wir, wo uns die Gelegenheit dazu geboten wird, auch an den Aufgaben des Staates mitarbeiten wollen..." Berichte Abg.H., 1890, vol. 2, p. 1163.

64. Józef Mielżyński in the Herrenhaus on 7.5.1890: "Meine Herren, ich moechte mich ebenso wie meine Landsleute im Abgeordnetenhause dem Ausdruck des Vertrauens an den Herrn Ministerpraesident anschliessen,... Wir strebten nach Frieden auf dem Boden der natuerlichen und der goettlichen Rechte eines Volkesstammes und auch unserer Pflichten, die wir nie missachten werden." Berichte Herrenhaus, 1890, vol. 1, pp. 175-176.

65. Dziennik Poznański, 10.4.1890, no. 82.

66. Kuryer Poznański, 15.5.1890, no. 111.

67. Orędownik, 11.5.1890, no. 108.

68. Ibid., 18.5.1890, no. 113.

69. Ministerpraesident Caprivi in the Abgeordnetenhaus on 15.4.1890: "Wir werden das Gute nehmen, von wo und durch wen es auch kommt, ... Wir werden gern mit allen denjenigen zusammenarbeiten, und wir hoffen auf einen engeren Zusammenschluss aller derjenigen angesichts der immerhin schwierigen Lage im Innern, vor der wir voraussichtlich stehen werden, mit allen denen, die ein Herz fuer Preussen haben, und die gesonnen sind, den Staat im monarchischen, das Reich im nationalen Sinne weiter zu fuehren und ausbauen zu helfen." Berichte Abg. H., 1890, vol. 2, p. 1049. See the comment in the Dziennik Poznański, 17.4.1890, no. 88.

70. Dziennik Poznański, 14.6.1890, no. 134.

71. BK. Ms. no. 1456/1457, meeting of 9.6.1890.

72. Helmut Neubach, Die Ausweisungen von Polen und Juden aus Preussen 1885-1886 (Wiesbaden, 1967), p. 135.

73. For a more detailed description, see Karl Lange, Bismarcks Sturz und die oeffentliche Meinung in Deutschland und im Auslande (Stuttgart, 1927).

74. Dziennik Poznański, 3.4.1890, no. 77.

75. Ibid., 27.4.1890, no. 97.

76. Eugen Richter in the Abgeordnetenhaus in reference to the Ansiedlungsgesetz on 11.3.1890: "Meine Herren, eine solche Politik ist nicht die Politik der Versoehnung, welche man Staatsbuergern gegenueber, die einstweilen noch dieselben Rechte haben wie wir, beobachten muss ...Mit diesen Polen- gesetzen, meine Herren, hat er (Bismarck T.K.) die Polen zurueckdraengen wollen, und das Polenthum gewinnt von Tag zu Tag und Schritt fuer Schritt mehr Boden." Berichte Abg. H. 1890, vol. 1, p. 612.

77. Kuryer Poznański, 28.8.1890, no. 197; Wielkopolanin, 29.8.1890, no. 198.

78. Orędownik, 25.4.1890, no. 95. For an analysis of the complex relationship between the German Conservatives and the Poles, see Hanne-Lore Land, Die Konservativen und die preussische Polenpolitik 1886-1912 (Berlin, 1963).

79. Orędownik, 23.9.1890, no. 218; Dziennik Poznański, 19.7.1890, no. 164.

80. Dziennik Poznański, 26.10.1890, no. 247.

81. For a more detailed study of the war factor in Caprivi's chancellorship, see Johann Werdermann, Die Heeresreform unter Caprivi (Greifswald, 1928); Robert Geis, Der Sturz des Reichskanzlers Caprivi (Berlin, 1930); Heinz Goebel, Die Militaervorlage 1892-1893 (Leipzig, 1935). A more recent work which stresses this theme is Heinrich Otto Meisner, Der Reichskanzler Caprivi (Darmstadt, 1969).

82. Wielkopolanin, 28.1.1890, no. 22.

83. Dziennik Poznański, 12.6.1890, no. 132.

84. Ibid., 13.6.1890, no. 133.

85. Ibid., 20.6.1890, no. 139.

86. Kuryer Poznański, 20.6.1890, no. 139.

87. Orędownik, 24.5.1890, no. 118.

88. Ibid., 14.6.1890, no. 134.

89. Ibid., 18.6.1890, no. 137.

90. Kuryer Poznański, 13.6.1890, no. 133.

91. Ibid., 17.6.1890, no. 136.

92. Ibid., 18.6.1890, no. 137.

93. Ibid., 26.6.1890, no. 144.

94. Roman Komierowski in the Reichstag on 25 June, 1890, "Wenn wir hier der Militaervorlage folgen, so thun wir es, weil die Thronrede mit bestimmtem Nachdruck, mit ihrem vollen Vertrauen sich an das ganze Reich wandte mit dem Appel, die Militaervorlage, wie es gestern der Herr Reichskanzler sagte womoeglich einstimmig durchzubringen... Und nun, meine Herren, nehmen Sie diese schlichte Erklaerung in ihrem vollen Inhalt und mit dem vollen Wunsche an, der uns berechtigen moege zu der Zuversicht, welche nunmehr auch die Bundesregierungen gegenueber unserer polnischen Bevoelkerung bethaetigen moegen. Sollten wir uns in dieser Zuversicht geirrt haben, so trifft nicht uns Polen die Schuld, dass wir schwierigen Aufgaben nicht gerecht zu werden verstanden, und dass es nicht unsere Schuld ist, dass ein Einverstaendnis zwischen der Regierung und der polnischen Bevoelkerung nicht zu erzielen war." Berichte Rtg., 1890, vol. 1, p. 582.

95. Kuryer Poznański, 27.6.1890, no. 145.

96. Ibid., 28.6.1890, no. 146.

97. Ibid., 16.7.1890, no. 161.

98. Ibid., 12.7.1890, no. 158; 23.9.1890. no. 218.

99. Cited in the Kuryer Poznański, 17.7.1890, no. 162. See also Orędownik, 4.9.1890, no. 203.

100. Cited in Orędownik, 16.7.1890, no. 161.

101. Ibid.

102. Ibid., 29.6.1890, no. 147.

103. Ibid., 12.7.1890, no. 153.

104. Ibid., 17.7.1890, no. 162.

105. Ibid., 2.9.1890, no. 202.

106. Ibid., 28.9.1890, no. 223.

107. Roman Komierowski in the Reichstag on 25.6.1890: "Ein Theil unserer Presse und der oeffentlichen Meinung hat in Folge dessen direkt gegen die Vorlage Stellung genommen;..." Berichte Rtg. 1890, vol. 1., p. 582.

108. Dziennik Poznański, 27.6.1890, no. 145.

109. Ibid., 20.7.1890, no. 165.

110. Ibid., 23.7.1890, no. 167.

111. Wielkopolanin, 24.7.1890, no. 168. See also Orędownik, 24.7.1890, no. 168.

112. Dziennik Poznański, 26.7.1890, no. 170; 29.7.1890, no. 172; 12.8.1890, no. 184.

113. Ibid., 24.5.1890, no. 118; 25.5.1890, no. 119; 15.8.1890, no. 187. See also Wielkopolanin, 23.5.1890, no. 117.

114. Trzeciakowski, Polityka polskich klas..., p. 111; Blanke, Prussian Poland..., p. 128.

115. Perdelwitz, Die Posener Polen..., p. 84. See also Baier, Der deutsche Osten ..., p. 20; Muenstermann, Die preussisch-deutsche Polenpolitik..., pp. 39-41; Schinkel, Polen, Preussen und Deutschland..., pp. 199-200; Hans-Ulrich Wehler, Krisenherde des Kaiserreichs 1871-1918 (Goettingen, 2nd edition, 1979), p. 192; Henryk Sitarek, Rola kredytu w rozwoju gospodarki Wielkopolski na przełomie XIX i XX wieku (Poznań, 1977), p. 25.

116. Laubert, Die preussische Polenpolitik..., p. 139; Wegener, Der wirtschaftliche Kampf..., p. 187.

117. Karwowski, Historya Wielkiego Księstwa..., vol. 3, p. 7. See also Buzek, Historya polityki narodowościowej..., p. 228.

118. BK. Ms. 1456/1457, meeting of 20.3.1890.

119. Ibid., meeting of 6.6.1890.

120. Bismarck addressing a group of West Prussian Germans at Varzin on 23.9. 1894: "Wir koennten ohne den Adel und die Geistlichkeit mit der Masse der polnischen Bevoelkerung vollkommen in Frieden leben. Sie wuerde fuer die Wohlthaten eines geordneten, gesetzmaessig lebenden Staates, fuer die Moeglichkeit, auch gegenueber den staerksten Magnaten Recht zu finden, dankbar sein. Das sehen sie und verlangen nicht mehr. Sie sind auch nicht offensiv gegen das Deutschtum. Offensiv ist nur der Adel, und das Deutschtum hat sich bisher gegen diese Angriffe immer defensiv verhalten." Bismarck, GW., vol. 13, p. 546.

121. Personal interview with Professor Lech Trzeciakowski, 5.8.1984.

122. Helmut Neubach, "Julius Dinder, der einzige deutsche Erzbischof von Gnesen-Posen", Jahrbuch Weichsel-Warthe 11 (1965), p. 75.

123. Ibid., p. 77: "Bismarck, der Dinders Amtseinfuehrung und ueberhaupt sein ganzes Auftreten gegenueber den Polen mit grossem Interesse verfolgte, liess sich dessen Ansprache in deutscher Uebersetzung vorlegen und versah sie mit der Randbemerkung, 'Wenn dies genau ist, so hat er unnoetig polonisiert und zu Polen, nicht zu Preussen, gesprochen'." See also Wielkopolanin, 1.6.1890, no. 124; Orędownik, 1.6.1890, no. 124.

124. Mueller, Nationalpolnische Presse..., p. V.

125. Dziennik Poznański, 1.6.1890, no. 124.

126. Hutten-Czapski, Sechzig Jahre..., vol. 1, p. 188.

127. For a more general discussion of the appointment, see Lech Trzeciakowski, Geneza powołania Floriana Stablewskiego na stolicę Arcybiskupią Gnieźnieńsko-Poznańską", in: Polska Niemcy Europa..., ed. Czubiński, pp. 185-196; Harry Rosenthal, "The Election of Archbishop Stablewski", in: Slavic Review 28 (1969), pp. 265-275; Adam Galos, "Tragizm Ugody. Władze pruskie a arcybiskup Stablewski", in: Przegląd Zachodni 31 (1975), pp. 235-256; Gatz, Akten zur preussischen Kirchenpolitik..., Introduction.

128. Gatz, Akten zur preussischen Kirchenpolitik..., p. L.

129. Ibid., p. 112; Rosenthal, "The Election...", p. 267.

130. Trzeciakowski, "Geneza powołania...", p. 189.

131. Ibid., p. 192.

132. Gatz, Akten zur preussischen Kirchenpolitik..., p. LIV.

133. Ibid., p. 135.

134. Raschdau, Unter Bismarck und Caprivi..., pp. 214, 210.

135. Trzeciakowski, "Geneza powołania...", p. 191.

136. Kuryer Poznański, 11.7.1890, no. 157.

137. Muenstermann, Die preussisch-deutsche Polenpolitik..., p. 32.

138. Kuryer Poznański, 17.8.1890, no. 188.

139. Cited in ibid., 22.8.1890, no. 192.

140. Ibid., 26.8.1890, no. 195.

141. Ibid., 4.9.1890, no. 203.

142. Ibid., 31.8.1890, no. 200.

143. Ibid., 11.9.1890, no. 208.

144. Ibid., 16.11.1890, no. 264.

145. Ibid., 6.8.1890, no. 179.

146. Dziennik Poznański, 27.8.1890, no. 196.

147. Ibid., 2.9.1890, no. 201.

148. Ibid., 28.8.1890, no. 197.

149. Ibid., 5.9.1890, no. 204.

150. Ibid., 21.9.1890, no. 217.

151. Ibid., 4.12.1890, no. 279.

152. Ibid., 21.10.1890, no. 242.

153. Ibid., 12.10.1890, no. 235.

154. Ibid., 16.10.1890, no. 238.

155. Ibid., 8.10.1890, no. 231.

156. Orędownik, 11.7.1890, no. 157.

157. Ibid., 27.8.1890, no. 196.

158. Ibid., 11.9.1890, no. 208.

159. Wielkopolanin, 5.8.1890, no. 178.

160. Ibid., 27.8.1890, no. 196.

161. Ibid., 12.9.1890, no. 209.

162. Ibid., 13.11.1890, no. 261.

163. Postęp, 3.10.1890, no. 81.

164. Ibid., 7.10.1890, no. 84.

165. Ibid., 29.10.1890, no. 103.

166. Ibid., 14.12.1890, no. 141.

167. Ibid.

168. Kuryer Poznański, 3.1.1891, no. 2.

169. Dziennik Poznański, 3.1.1891, no. 3.

170. Wielkopolanin, 1.1.1891, no. 1.

4. Initial Successes of the Loyalists: January 1891-Spring, 1892

4.1 The Relaxation of the Expulsion Laws

The first change in the nationality policies in the eastern provinces initiated by the Caprivi administration was the decision in late November, 1890, to relax the expulsion laws against non-Prussian Poles and Jews who had illegally taken up residence within Prussia. (1) Having driven out some 32,000 "foreigners" from 1885-1886 and having barred the entry of new immigrants from Russia and Austria-Hungary, the East Elbian landlords found themselves critically short of seasonal labour at harvest time. Bismarck had been prepared to accept yield losses in order to prevent the "flooding" of Prussia's East by Poles from Russia and Galicia. He expected the Junker estates to sacrifice part of their earnings in view of the greater danger to the German element from unlimited immigration of Polish labourers. But his successor was of a different opinion.

In late December 1890, the Oberpraesident of Poznania, Graf von Zedlitz-Truetzschler, told a delegation of Polish and German landowners concerned over their drastic losses in unreaped yields in the harvest just concluded that Poles from Russia would soon be allowed into the Reich to replace those emigrating to Brazil and America.(2) With Caprivi's approval, Minister of the Interior Herrfurth announced that as of 1 January, 1891, seasonal labourers could be admitted into the Prussia for the harvest season provided that they came without their families and left by the 15th of November.(3) In mid-March the Minister defended the ruling in the Landtag from both the criticisms of the National Liberals, who felt he had gone too far, and from the Polish deputy Leon Czarliński, who felt he had not gone far enough.(4) The ruling proved beneficial for the economic well-being of the Prussian east and was one of the few administrative measures under Caprivi to survive the sharp turn to national antagonism following his resignation.

The decision to relax the expulsion laws was above all a measure to alleviat the difficult economic position of the East Elbian landowners, and it was not portrayed by the government as a concession to the Poles. But the decision clearly had a special national dimension for the Polish community. The expulsions of 1885-1886 were considered "barbaric" by Poles everywhere because of their brutality and their "illegal" nature, i.e they restricted the freedom of movement within the zones of partition guarenteed through the Congress of Vienna and violated the solemn promises given by successive Prussian monarchs throughout the century. The modification of the expulsion practice in 1891 was the first move that went against the flow of the Germanization policies followed by Bismarck. Yet the Polish press was not as favourably impressed as might be expected. The edict was recognized as a break with Bismarck's legacy, which had placed the Prussian state interest above the economic interests of Prussian Junkers, but it was roundly criticized as a half-measure which failed to address the problem in its wider constitutional context.

Only the landowner-oriented press gave the ruling of Minister Herrfurth much notice. The Dziennik Poznański was initially critical of the limited relaxation, claiming it was "not in essence a reversal of Bismarck's line but only a milder enforcement of it."(5) What the Poles wanted was a "total turnaround", i.e. the repeal of the 1885 law. In February the Dziennik ran a major editorial comparing Prussian policies in Alsace-Lorraine with the Polish provinces, and concluded that the French element in the former was being given preferential treatment. The relaxed expulsion policy announced by Herrfurth was not the same as the decision to lift passport requirements for the French.(6) Throughout 1891 the Dziennik stressed the alarming depopulation of the rural areas in the eastern provinces and warned that unless "free movement were allowed between Poles of all sectors as foreseen at the Congress of Vienna " Poznania and other provinces would turn into an economic wasteland.(7) Introducing a more humane enforcement of the expulsion law was an improvement but did not go far enough. Similarly, the Dziennik's client paper, the Wielkopolanin, complained that Polish seasonal labourers who could not bring in their families and had to leave Prussia's borders every year after harvest time would not solve the problem of rural impoverishment and depopulation. What was needed was a steady flow of legal Polish immigrants from the other partitioned zones to take up the load left by departing emigrants.(8) This would not only make economic sense but would conform to the spirit of Vienna Treaties of 1815.

The Kuryer Poznański wrote that Herrfurth's ruling was a "clear admission" that previous policies had failed. The German Junkers and conservatives were now suffering from the consequences of the forceful measures they had earlier supported, and the Poles were being avenged.(9) Later in the year, after Herrfurth had stated that no further relaxation would be enacted until the 'experiment' was tested over years, the Kuryer wrote, "The November decree (of 1890, T.K.) is simply insufficient", and that "further shortages of labour will convince the government to go farther."(10) In fact, Caprivi and his ministers held firmly to Bismarck's notion of stemming the inflow of Poles from other countries and confirmed their intention to strengthen the German element in the East. In a major policy speech in the Reichstag on 28 November, 1891, Caprivi addressed the seasonal labour question head on, "Nun hat die preussische Staatsregierung nicht verkannt, dass, wenn sie russische Arbeiter herueber laesst, damit eine gewisse Gefahr fuer die Germanisierung verbunden ist; sie macht den Versuch sie im Herbst immer wieder zurueckzufuehren".(11)

After this Reichstag speech, which dispersed any illusions of full freedom of movement for Poles, the Polish press quietly dropped the matter. The Polish parliamentarians brought it up at every review of the Interior Ministry's budget, but made no concerted effort to embarrass the Chancellor and force his hand. Questions of language teaching and land acquisition were much more important for the moment.

4.2 The Resignation of Gustav von Gossler and his Replacement by Graf von Zedlitz-Truetzschler

Poles from all sectors of Poznań's political spectrum agreed that little could be done to reverse the accumulated sufferings under Bismarck until a series of personnel changes, inspired by the highly-regarded Wilhelm II, swept away not only the Iron Chancellor but his obedient ministers as well. The last of Bismarck's faithful disciples was von Gossler, Kultusminister since 1881, and regarded as more hostile to the Poles than his mentor. Proponents of loyalism were blaming him for the slow pace of change in the Neue Kurs; once Gossler was swept aside, argued the loyalists, the "new era" would gain momentum. As the Kuryer wrote in February, 1891, "We are convinced that the noble-minded Germans in Poznania would give us their hands in agreement if it were not for that phalanx of officials who do not want to see the end of these intolerable conditions... These officials have formed a wall between the Polish people and the throne, and this wall must be pulled down."(12)

Gossler's position was indeed in trouble by the early months of 1891, though not because of his opposition to a Polish-German reconciliation. He was rapidly losing the confidence of both Caprivi and Wilhelm II for failing to draw up a Prussian public school bill that satisfied the powerful Centrum Party, a mainstay of support for Caprivi in the early part of his rule.(13) Furthermore, the minister had enraged the Catholics by rejecting outright a full return of the 16 million marks Sperrgeld that had been withheld from the Catholic Church since the days of the Kulturkampf.(14) As early as December, 1890, the Polish and German press began to comment on Gossler's growing unpopularity and speculated on how long he could remain in office.(15) In late February, 1891, Gossler admitted to his close friend and political ally Raschdau that his position was untenable on the school reform bill, but that he would have preferred to resign over the Polish question.(16)

Gossler's resignation on 9 March, announced on 11 March, was naturally well-received by the Polish community. Just before his fall the Kuryer fretted that Wilhelm II had given encouragement to all disadvantaged groups in Germany - except the Poles. "Our deputies should be congratulated for their patience and endurance but they cannot hold the line forever unless something happens."(17) The timing of Gossler's removal freed the loyalist spokesmen from the thankless task of explaining the lack of progress to their electorate. No one regretted the resignation and all papers welcomed his replacement, Graf von Zedlitz-Truetzschler, Oberpraesident of Poznania and head of the Ansiedlungskommission. He was regarded by Poles and Germans alike as open-minded.(18)

Similarly, the majority of Polish public opinion was content with Zedlitz's replacement as Oberpraesident of Poznania, Hugo von Wilamowitz-Moellendorf, who was to survive the Caprivi era and stay in office until 1899 despite the hostility of the Ostmarkenverein after 1894. His appointment was interpreted by many Germans and Poles as an act of friendship towards the Polish community, though not everyone agreed on its wisdom.(19) The historian Thomas Gey has written, "Ausschlaggebend fuer seine Ernennung war der mit Caprivi einsetzende Richtungswechsel in der Polenpolitik. Die Bereitschaft des neuen Oberpraesidenten, die sogenannte Versoehnungspolitik vorbehaltlos zu vertreten fand nicht ueberall Zustimmung."(20)

The personnel changes seemed to point to a change for the better in German-Polish relations, but many Poles held back from demonstrating any exuberance too strongly. The cautious Dziennik welcomed Gossler's departure but reminded its readers that, "What is needed is an end to the system, not the replacement of individuals."(21) On 15 March, in a long editorial, the Dziennik refuted the allegation that the appointment of Zedlitz constituted a "concession". It praised his fairness as Oberpraesident of Poznania and hoped that, "he would look favourably on our spiritual needs", an unmistakable reference to the inclusion of Polish language rights in the new Prussian public school reform bill.(22) Later on Gossler's appointment as Oberpraesident of West Prussia rekindled the Dziennik's innate suspicion about the Neue Kurs. In mid-July it wrote, "It is difficult to resist the notion that the 'old course' is to be retained when today one of its chief exponents takes over the administration of a province and all its school matters."(23) The Wielkopolanin contented itself with the remark that "There is justice in the world", but refused to speculate on what Graf Zedlitz would do as Kultusminister. (24)

The middle-class newspapers seemed unsure of how to respond to the new currents and ministerial changes at this point. On 13 March the Postęp wrote, "We have reason to be happy, but should wait and see because in Prussia individuals change but the course of politics does not." (25) Speculation as to why Gossler had been eased out, and interpretation of the personnel changes within the greater context of the Polish condition in Prussia was avoided. "Never mind who (brought down Gossler T.K.) as long as he is finally gone."(26) The Postęp's reaction to the new Oberpraesident of Poznania was positive.(27)

Szymański was very ambivalent about the change of ministers. On 13 March he wrote in the Orędownik, "Zedlitz will certainly be no better than Gossler. If he does us no greater harm it will not be because of his integrity but because of the changes taking place at the highest levels in Berlin."(28) Yet on the very next day, 14 March, he wrote, "Zedlitz knows our conditions and knows we represent no danger to the German state, hence he will likely give us back our rights."(29) Like the Dziennik, the Orędownik regretted Gossler's appointment in West Prussia and predicted he would ruthlessly further Germanization.(30)

4.3 The 11 April 1891 Private Language-Teaching Edict

It is with the private language-teaching edict of 11 April, 1891 that one may begin to speak of Prussian government concessions towards its Polish residents. 31) The relaxation of the expulsion laws was evidently a move in response to distressed East Elbian landowners burdened by labour shortages at harvest time; but the decree of April 1891 was the first direct reference to the Polish question since Bismarck's dismissal. Like Herrfurth's relaxation of the expulsion laws, the ruling by Zedlitz was a half-measure; it permitted the instruction of the Polish language in German schools (thus enraging German nationalists and the Bismarck press) while setting so many limitations that it failed to satisfy the Poles. Furthermore, it was restricted to the province of Poznania, making no provision for the Poles in West Prussia. Polish sceptics saw the ruling as a move to detach the Poznanian Poles from their fellow-countrymen in West Prussia, East Prussia and Upper Silesia, creating "first-class" and "second-class" Poles. The loyalist publicists who had said that with Gossler's dismissal the "new era" would enter its age of achievement, were confident that Zedlitz would re-introduce the Polish language into the school curriculum; they were caught off guard by the concession which had to be financed by an impoverished Polish community that was already support numerous national causes. Many German publicists were upset by the decree. Bismarck called it a "weitgehende

Nachgiebigkeit"(32); the Conservatives, Progressives and Centrum parties had no great objections to the decree (33) but it encountered tremendous opposition among the National Liberals and Free Conservatives.(34) Komierowski wrote later that the Zedlitz edict, coming only a month after Gossler's dismissal, "seemed to signal the beginning of a more fortunate turnaround for us and the first step of the government along the road we so passionately desired." (35)

The Kuryer, anxious to show that the Caprivi administration was reacting to Polish loyalty , rejoiced at the announcement. In an optimistic mood it wrote on 16 April, "We send the government our warm thanks for this first step along its new road."(36) Two days later, in reaction to criticism by the Posener Zeitung, it wrote ,"How good that government circles have come to recognise the worthless Jewish pseudo-liberalism of this paper. We trust that the new Kultusminister will treat these voices with the indifference that they deserve."(37) Before the month was over the Kuryer and other Polish newspapers were defending Zedlitz from the harsh criticism of German publicists and denounced the resistance of the local Prussian bureaucracy which blocked implementation of the decree. In particular the Bromberg Regency under the leadership of von Tiedemann did all in its power to prevent the setting up of private Polish-language teaching.(38) On 29 April the Kuryer lashed out at the intransigent bureaucrats. "Zedlitz's decree does not permit regents to block private lessons. It is not up to them (to decide)."(39) The article further went on to state, "There can now be no doubt that the government will adopt a new strategy towards us. It cannot act against the wishes of the Kaiser, as Gossler did, and in any case Zedlitz is a completely different person".(40) Before long, however, the Kuryer joined others in questioning the practicality of the decree. After surveying the financial hardships involved it lamented on 22 May that the "Lessons will be costly, and where will we get the teachers and the money?"(41) Indeed, the Poles soon discovered that the private language ruling was, as the Orędownik remarked on 17 April, "the equivalent of a new tax on us."(42)

No one wanted to confront the difficult task of financing the private teaching. After two and a half months of dithering a meeting of Poznań's notables, chaired by Dobrowolski, was finally called at the Bazar to discuss implementation of the Zedlitz decree in the city. The assembled clerics and notables gave many fine speeches on the need to take advantage of the decree, but could not escape the hard fact that at least 8000 Mk. per annum would be required to teach the 4000 children in the city.(43) It was decided to pay teachers from 150-160 Mk. per year and that the lessons would begin in September, 1891.(44) The assembly appointed a committee headed by two priests, Woliński and Antoni Stychel, to organize the lessons. Despite regular appeals for donations and a flurry of patriotic editorials on the need to make the private lessons work, the committee was able to raise only 2885.85 Mk. in the first year, enough for only 2365 children to take part, and was chronically short of money.(45)

The difficulty in financing the lessons attests to how overburdened Poznań's Polish community was with various social, cultural and national causes. Poles were called upon to donate to the support of the Polish theatre, Polish public libraries, Polish orphanages and the Central Electoral Committee, not to mention various causes in other Polish lands, like the Galician Famine Relief Fund or the Fund to Transfer the Remains of Adam Mickiewicz to Cracow. Private language lessons were likely to succeed in the countryside where wealthy landowners like Kościelski, Radziwiłł, the Czartoryskis and the Kwileckis could easily pay for them. For the working-class poor in Poznań, however, with an average wage of from 50-65% of the Reich medium, the question looked altogether different.

The Dziennik was initially happy about the decree but quickly became dissatisfied when its full implications were appreciated. On 16 April it warmly praised the decree, writing that the initiative definitely came from the Emperor himself. "It is the first step that will lead to more. The government is convinced that the present schooling system is inadequate. It will find its way to the right road now. This reform is necessary for the good of our children as well as for the state."(46) A week later it vigorously defended the new legislation against hostile German opinion. In an article entitled, "The Polish Question in the German Press" it noted, "We have faith that the government will go further along the course it has begun and will receive the support of (German) public opinion."(47) Later on, the Dziennik minimized the significance of the decree but continued to defend its enactment. In mid-July it praised the stand taken by the Conservative Kreuzzeitung against the hostile Free Conservative Post and concluded, "Let us hope that the Kreuzzeitung and the government come to the conclusion that the language lessons must be included in the school program."(48) After Graf Zedlitz's second decree of 2 October, 1891, that allowed German children to take part in the lessons, the Dziennik noted that it was necessary to make the first effective and accepted the ruling with "respect and thankfullness".(49) Centuries of co-existence in the Prussian East had produced many mixed marriages and numerous cases of Polonization and Germanization. This was evident in many family names; thus there were two "von Dziembowskis" in the Berlin parliaments , one a Pole and the other a German Free Conservative, while the German Army featured such generals as von Bogusławski and von Leszczynski. Hostile Prussian officials tried to exclude as many children from the private lessons as possible to protect their German character, hence the need for the 2 October ruling. The Dziennik approved of the second edict yet, "We do not consider this a concession, rather an admission that Gossler's policies were in error".(50) The Kuryer, while insistent that the Zedlitz decrees were "concessions" wrote at the end of October, "Now he (Zedlitz T.K.) should not stop half-way but go on and let parents decide who will learn religion in Polish and German."(51)

The Wielkopolanin welcomed the ruling and the fact that the government was now acting for "the good of the nation and a concept of justice acceptable to all citizens".(52) It was quick, however, to make recommendations on how the decree could be improved. It should a) include all three provinces in Prussia where significant numbers of Poles lived (i.e. Poznania, West Prussia and Silesia) and b) should bring back all Polish teachers from other parts of Prussia. (53) Similarly, it refuted hostile German newspapers and denounced the "unconstitutional" acts of officials impeding the implementation of the decree.(54)

The urban newspapers were troubled primarily by the cost of the private lessons but felt that every effort should be made to implement them. The Orędownik, disturbed at the unequal burdens set on the larger towns and the sparcely populated countryside, urged landowners to make donations to urban areas.(55) When the campaign to raise money failed to satisfy Poznań's needs the Orędownik blamed the wealthy landlowners, whose patriotism evidently did not extend to their pocketbooks. At the end of May, 1891, the Orędownik sadly concluded that the Zedlitz decree was of little practical value but that the Polish community had to try and "make the best of it".(56)

The Postęp questioned what use "voluntary private lessons" could have and immediately concluded that the decree was not much of a concession at all. "We shall only be satisfied when the teaching of Polish finds its way into the school curriculum".(57) Throughout the year it singled out Prussian officials who either blocked the lessons altogether or who excluded children with German-sounding names, and demanded that special enquires be set up to determine the nationality of children. When Zedlitz's second decree was announced the Postep breathed a sigh of relief. "This is only reasonable as it is impossible to forbid the learning of other languages."(58)

Many German contemporaries and later historians made a great affair over the Zedlitz decrees, intimating that the Poles had "tricked" the good-hearted but naive Prussian minister. Hermann Oncken wrote, "Es dauerte eine gewisse Zeit, bis der neue Polenkurs in Berlin sichtbar wurde. Der Erlass vom 11 April, 1891...war das erste Vorspiel; die polnischen Erklaerungen von Treue und Dankbarkeit kannten keine Grenzen."(59) In fact, as has been shown, Polish public opinion, while appreciative of Zedlitz's noble intentions, was hardly jubilant. Their hope that the Prussian government would quickly see the need to institutionalize the lessons suffered a setback when Caprivi addressed the question in the Reichstag in late November, 1891.(60) In the end, the two decrees of 1891 satisfied neither German nor Pole and were replaced in early 1894 by an even more restricted reintroduction of Polish language lessons into the school curriculum.

4.4 Confrontations in Berlin: Ludwik Jażdżewski against Józef Kościelski

The accession of Graf Zedlitz to Kultusminister in March 1891 and his quick action in allowing private language lessons stimulated several members of the Polish Landtag Party to try and force the government to deliniate just how far the "new course" was to affect the Polish minority in Prussia. The leader of this group was Father Ludwik Jażdżewski, a parliamentarian of almost 20 years service in both the Prussian Landtag and German Reichstag.(61) At the end of April he decided the time had come to confront Chancellor Caprivi during a Landtag session on the state of the Ansiedlungskommission. On 30 April at a meeting of the Landtag Polish deputies in Berlin, he was advised to "speak in general and polite language in view of the new Kultusminister".(62) Jażdżewski replied that he intended to "speak briefly but energetically, listing all our demands to the new minister."(63) On 2 May he took the podium and challenged Caprivi to do away with the Ansiedlungskommission altogether.(64) His long speech was hardly "general and polite" as his colleagues had specified a few days earlier. Caprivi was provoked into making a stern reply in which he categorically refused to disband the Commission and, in a manner reminiscent of Bismarck and von Puttkamer that drew many cheers from the right, defended its activities and fundamental assumptions. (65)

The loyalists among the Poles were distraught at Jażdżewski's speech. Florian Stablewski, their spokesman in the Abgeordnetenhaus, tried to convince the Party in caucus on 3 May to publicly dissociate itself from it, but he was told instead to deliver a more soft-spoken speech that restated the Polish position in gentler terms.(66) He used the occasion of a speech on 4 May to proclaim once again the fundamental loyalty of the Poles.(67)

Far from feeling censured, Jażdżewski pushed ahead and on 8 May confronted Zedlitz in the same harsh manner that had irritated the Chancellor a week earlier. Rather than praising the edict, Jażdżewski demanded that the Prussian state pay for the private lessons.(68) The minister was surprised and annoyed. After having risked a political crisis by permitting the private teaching of Polish, he was now being challenged by the Poles for not going far enough. Visibly irritated, he rose to defend his decree and in the process delivered a sharp rebuke to Polish aspirations.(69)

Jażdżewski's speeches set off a furor within Polish public opinion. The Kuryer, though normally very circumspect about the dignity of priests, called for Jażdżewski's removal from the Party. It had been carrying on a campaign for over a year to convince the new Prussian leadership that the Poles in Prussia were ready and willing to serve the state and withdraw from their traditional politics of protest and negation; now in two Landtag speeches, poorly planned and harshly worded, Jażdżewski had set the Polish-German dialogue back to the polemics of Bismarck's era. On 10 May the Kuryer wrote, "The results (of these speeches T.K.) have been absolutely negative. It is impossible to comprehend how a politician could have so conducted himself as to endanger the clear friendship shown to us heretofore... Jażdżewski did not have authorization ...(he) was acting all on his own. ... Thanks to the irresponsible utterances of individuals our cause may now be more difficult. We cannot keep silent in view of chauvinistic designs."(70) Two days later it continued its attack upon Jażdżewski, "Father Jażdżewski's behaviour cannot be justified in any way...(he) has been criticized for keeping faith with the unfortunate notions of the era of protest. How could other deputies allow him to go so far? Is not pessimism a sin, now that so many positive signs are evident?"(71) The pressure against Jażdżewski was applied until mid-July 1891, when the Kuryer declared the affair over and admitted that it had gone too far in its ignoble smear tactic. "Those who disagreed with Father Jażdżewski's behaviour did not act in the best way."(72)

The Dziennik was very upset by Caprivi's intention to maintain the Ansiedlungskommission and noted that, "If he really wants to act against external danger and prevent unrest at home then he should really make peace with the Poles."(73) The Dziennik was reluctant to criticize Jażdżewski on the grounds of maiming national solidarity. Nevertheless, on 13 May, 1891, it stated that the outspoken priest had committed a tactical error and that he had acted against a resolution reached earlier not to antagonize Minister Zedlitz.(74) Jażdżewski and Party chairman Leon Czarliński answered the newspapers in an open letter to the Dziennik. They denied violating a predetermined resolution and stated that no such resolution existed.(75) The Dziennik printed the open letter but added that there had indeed been a resolution agreed upon. It knew all about the intense quarrels going on within the Party "from our own Party sources", suggesting that a deputy was reporting all goings-on directly to editor-in-chief

Dobrowolski.(76)

The Dziennik took no comfort in criticizing the outspoken but popular priest, however, and on 20 May urged the public to forget the quarrel, noting that, "The only way out of such squabbling is to make records (of Party caucus meetings T.K.) public".(77) Jaździewski continued to send letters defending his speech well into July, 1891. The Dziennik finally admitted that ,"His remarks were badly timed and tactical errors, but it was what we all felt."(78) On 17 July the Dziennik announced the affair at an end. "We do not disagree with Jaździewski", it wrote, and called for the Party to inform the press fully and promptly about its deliberations to avoid unnecessary polemics.(79) It should be added that the Wielkopolanin contained not a word about the quarrel; likely its owners wanted to prevent discussion among the urban and rural poor on such a sensitive subject as a split in the Party. Such quarrels were reserved for the gentry powerbrokers.

While the landowner-dominated papers criticized Jaździewski's speeches, the middle-class Orędownik and Postęp rose to his defence. The Postęp wrote on 10 May in its first comment, "We can be sure that although this minister is different and more moderate the policies are the same. Nothing essential has changed."(80) The Postęp derided the Kuryer's campaign against Jaździewski and charged that anonymous letters to the Kuryer ridiculing Jaździewski were the work of Florian Stablewski, jealous of his rival's popularity.(81) "He has not done anything wrong or out of touch with the public mood", editorialized the Postęp on 13 May. "We Poles cannot seem to find the 'golden mean'. When we opposed the government we did so almost to excess; but now that we have repudiated the policy of protest, we fall into a servility that is a disgrace to our personal and national honour."(82)

But it was the Orędownik that protested the most fiercely against the concerted pressure against Jaździewski. It was particularly incensed at a remark made by Stablewski, in his 4 May Landtag speech, which described the Kuryer and Dziennik as the only reputable Polish papers in Poznań and ignored completely the middle-class press.(83) The Orędownik attacked Stablewski's anti-Russian references and noted, "Reminding everyone of our obligations to the state but neglecting our just national demands, we are degrading ourselves to the level of second-class citizens, simple helots in the Prussian state."(84) In reference to Jaździewski's controversial 8 May speech the Orędownik wrote, "Father Jaździewski is perhaps the only statesman in the Party who has been working in the spirit of the declarations (of loyalty made by Komierowski and Mielżyński the year before T.K.) for the past 20 years."(85) The whole affair was "totally incomprehensible and a scandal"(86), and seriously discredited the two main landowner newspapers and the whole political apparatus.(87) On 15 May, Szymański wrote, "The Dziennik does not know what to do... It is concerned only with Party solidarity. It wants to hush up the affair and uphold the dignity of the Party because it manufactures the candidates and deputies."(88)

Jaździewski's most serious opponents among the Polish deputies were Stablewski and Kościelski, leaders of the loyalist factions in the Landtag and Reichstag respectively. Stablewski's priesthood did not enjoin him from writing letters to other deputies complaining of Jaździewski's behaviour.(89) Kościelski, a member of the Prussian Landtag Party by virtue of being a deputy in the Herrenhaus, realized early on that Jaździewski would present the Landtag loyalists with great difficulties. In early 1890, he had tried to have Jażdżewski secretly removed from political affairs by a direct appeal to Minister Gossler, and via the then Oberpraesident, Graf Zedlitz, to Archbishop Dinder.(90) This plan came to nought when Dinder died, but Kościelski was successful in preventing Jażdżewski from speaking in the Reichstag, where the loyalists enjoyed a firmer standing. In early 1891, Kościelski's personal standing in the Reich rose significantly when Wilhelm II asked him to be the government spokesman on the naval expansion program, and his fine work earned him a personal citation from the Kaiser.(91) After Jażdżewski's 8 May speech Kościelski, aided by Stablewski, tried once again to have the outspoken priest silenced at a Party caucus in Berlin of 9 June. He introduced a resolution urging his public censure, but the Party would only agree, by a 9-5 vote, to say that "His speech, in regard to form and tactics, did not meet the needs of the moment."(92) This milder statement was adopted only because 7 of the 9 members of the Herrenhaus, all declared loyalists, did not bother to show up and vote.

Feeling that a public repudiation of Jażdżewski was necessary, Kościelski decided to do it himself. In a speech in the Herrenhaus only three days after the Party caucus vote, (12 June, 1891) Kościelski described Jażdżewski's speech as personal aggrandizement and unrepresentative of the Polish nation as a whole. (93) His speech was ultra-loyal in tone and went so far as to refer to the Poles as "diejenigen Preussen, die sich zu polnischen Nationalitaet bekennen".(94)

Kościelski's speech aroused another storm in Poznania both among his colleagues and within the Polish press. In a long, tension-filled caucus of 18 June Kościelski was censured for his remarks, but it was decided not to make his humiliation public.(95) The strongest criticism came from Jażdżewski and Czarliński, still sensitive over the furor begun by him a fortnight ago. Kościelski got into further controversy due to an exchange of letters with the new leader of the Centrum party, Graf Ballestrem (who had succeeded to the party leadership following the death of Ludwig Windthorst in March, 1891), in which he failed to draw a clear dividing line between "Poles" and "Prussians".(96) His conduct went much farther in the direction of loyalty than Polish opinion would allow; indeed many accused him of being only a step away from voluntary Germanization. Dobrowolski at the Dziennik had had serious objections to Kościelski's loyalist platform ever since the 17 March, 1890 Bazar meeting, and now he took him to task for his public statements. The Dziennik pointedly repudiated Koscielski's speech, "not for its friendliness to the government but because he criticized a colleague in the Herrenhaus, which is never done in public, and because he used the word Prussian rather than Pole."(97) On 16 July, 1891, it refuted the suggestion that Poles and Prussians were identical. "One is either a Prussian or a Pole but not both... We are subjects of the Prussian crown, that is correct, but we were born Poles and shall always feel Polish."(98) Having once rebuked Kościelski the Dziennik then began to print "letters from the provinces" (mostly unsigned) critical of his remarks.(99)

The urban papers were highly outraged by Kościelski's statements. The Postęp remarked wryly that the Herrenhaus was the highest platform for the Poles to make their just demands, but that Kościelski "had passed up an excellent opportunity", and "had made no demands whatsoever."(100) Szymański at the Orędownik wanted to combine Kościelski's attack on Jażdżewski with the more general crisis of the ruling landowner class, so obviously divided on how to respond to Caprivi. "It is unbelievable that he could have said such a thing (criticizing Jażdżewski T.K.), picking a quarrel with a deputy in the Herrenhaus... He has totally lost his political orientations."(101) The next day Szymański wrote, "The whole policy of loyalty as practised by the Kuryer, Dziennik, and Kościelski, with Stablewski along to help, will bring us nought. The integrity of the Party has been shattered... We have deputies in Berlin but no Party."(102) Already at this stage Szymański was beginning to argue that "loyalty" in the version of the Kuryer was "only the last chance for the ruling classes to save their position of power".(103)

Kościelski's only support came from the the Kuryer, which may have been the result of his secret funding. The Kuryer defended his references to Poles as Prussians by stating that, "In fact, a 'Prussian' as a nationality does not exist. It exists only as a legal term to describe the state."(104) There are only Prussian subjects, but not Prussian nationals. Hence it followed that every "Prussian subject" was also a "Prussian". On 22 July, 1891 it wrote concerning the controversial exchange with Graf Ballestrem, "We really are 'Prussians' by virtue of being subjects of the Prussian monarchy. We can be Prussia's most loyal subjects and still retain the name 'Poles' ."(105) Needless to say this bit of sophistry convinced no one, and the Kuryer quietly dropped the matter. It made no attempt to defend Kościelski's statements against Jażdżewski.(106)

The events of May to July 1891 well illustrate some of the major dilemmas of the Polish-German Versoehnungsaera. The lively polemics pointed to the disharmony between the Landtag and Reichstag Parties. Jażdżewski and Czarliński were both members of the Abgeordnetenhaus, where the real decisions on how the Poles were to be ruled in Prussia were made. With so little progress being made in the reversal of Bismarck's emergency laws, the assertive deputies in the Landtag saw little basis for a true reconciliation. They did not share the optimism of their countrymen in the Reichstag, where the numerical superiority of the non-Kartell parties fed their illusions of constitutional monarchy and equal status for all citizens. It is important to note that the major loyalist parliamentarians: Kościelski, Radziwiłł, Komierowski, Dziembowski and the Kwilecki brothers were all members of the Reichstag but not the Prussian Abgeordnetenhaus, where all the decisions affecting the Polish community were made. Here, leadership was in the hands of hardened veterans of the Kulturkampf and the last stage of Bismarck's anti-Polish legislation: Czarliński, Jażdżewski, Szuman and Motty. While "loyal" in the sense that none believed in conspiratorial activity or insurrection, the realists in the Landtag Party never fell prey to the visions of a "second Galicia" that seemed to dominate the Reichstag deputies.

Secondly, the disputes of May-July 1891 revealed to the careful eye that the seemingly invincible front of Polish "national solidarity" was not impervious to the human failings and political infighting that all parties were subject to. Nor was Polish solidarity immune to the deeper undercurrents of social change that were rapidly coming to the forefront at the end of the 19th century. Caprivi's Neue Kurs gave these divisions occasion to rise after being suppressed for so long due to Bismarck's anti-Polish laws. Now that a friendly government was in power, the Poles were divided on how to proceed, unsure of ultimate objectives and short-term tactics. Finally, the public statements of Caprivi and Zedlitz showed how cautious the new leadership was in the Polish question and how reluctant it was to retreat from Bismarck's legacy.

4.5 Loyalism and Socialism

The expiration of the anti-Socialist laws in October 1890 and the formation of a Society of Polish Socialists in Berlin in December, the forerunner of the "PPS-zaboru pruskiego", offered Poles and Germans an ideal opportunity to work together on a matter of deep concern to both. There was no greater critic of Social Democracy in Germany than Chancellor Caprivi; again and again he denounced their aims and brought up the spectre of civil war. For example, on 27 February, 1891 he said in the Reichstag, "Als die verbuundeten Regierungen darauf verzichteten, ein Sozialistengesetz wieder einzubringen, waren sie sich ueber zwei Dinge klar, einmal, dass der Kampf gegen die Sozialdemokratie die ernsteste Frage unserer Zeit ist, eine Frage, die Jahrzehnte lang die Welt beschaeftigen kann, und deren Erledigung des Schweisses der Edelsten werth ist;... Und wenn ich nun auch den aeussersten Fall beruehren darf, dass es mal zum Kampf mit den Sozialdemokraten kaeme, so beduerfen wir fuer einen solchen Kampf einer viel besseren Disziplin als fuer den Kampf vor dem Feinde."(107) Caprivi's strong aversion to socialist doctrine and behaviour was further evident in his struggle to return school inspection and curriculum under clerical supervision.(108)

In taking aim at Social Democracy Caprivi could find no better ally than the Poles. Alarmed at socialist thought spreading into the Polish community, all sectors of public opinion stressed the need to combat it. Indeed, the Berlin-financed Gazeta Robotnicza, which appeared in 1200 copies on 3 January, 1891, made painstakingly slow progress in Prussian Poland, and in 1895 had only 174 subscriptions in all of Poznania.(109) To the impoverished Polish farmer and urban labourer, strongly influenced by the Catholic Church and national traditions, Social Democracy was portrayed as repulsive, subversive, atheistical and anti-Polish.

The Polish press reacted with varying degrees of alarm to the declaration of Berlin's Social Democrats that a Polish wing was being prepared for agitation among the community. The supercilious Dziennik, feeling that carrying on a polemic against such riff-raff was beneath its dignity, dismissed the threat as inconsequential. On 16 December, 1890, it wrote, "Of 60,000 Poles in Berlin 70 socialists is nothing to get upset about. Most of its adherents here will be Germans."(110) Bashing the socialists was left for the mass-circulation Wielkopolanin. The Kuryer, however, was alarmed at the very idea of a Polish socialist. On 17 December, 1890, it wrote "O peril! O humiliation! O shame! For many years Polish workers, with the help of God, have been honestly and successfully resisting the Satanic temptations of the socialist emissaries. Finally in 1890 the power of evil is winning out over honest principles... Despite its divisions socialism is today a powerful subversive force, a negative evil, but powerful just the same."(111) All newspapers stressed the need to promote traditional values of patriotism and religion to ward off the evil, and warned that the continuation of discriminatory laws against the Poles were alienating them and making them susceptible to Social Democracy.

The common antagonism against socialism by Germans and Poles in Poznania following the 1890 election was voiced in the formation of a Society to Combat the Activities of Social Democracy. Some of its more well-known Polish founding members were Kościelski, Cegielski, Komierowski and Mycielski (Reichstag and Landtag deputies), and Władysław Łebiński, secretary of the Society, an editor and journalist who seems to have worked for both the Kuryer and the Wielkopolanin. Some well-known German members were: von Unruhe, chairman, an influential Conservative deputy in the Reichstag and Prussian Landtag, Nathusius, vice-chairman, director of the Poznań municipal police force and von Tiedemann, Regent of Bromberg.(112)

Polish alarm at the spectre of Social Democracy was well articulated in a brochure by a teacher in Brodnica, Antoni Chudziński, entitled "Kwestja Polska w Prusiech" (Die Polenfrage in Preussen). Chudziński warned that the socialist revolution was not far away and that only a broadly-based German- Polish reconciliation could prevent its growth in the eastern provinces.(113) Similarly, in October 1891 Mielżyński published an "Offener Brief eines Polen an die deutschen Einwohner der ehemals polnischen Landestheile", a restatement of the loyalist position that placed great emphasis upon the mutual need to combat the socialist danger.(114) Another inspiration to act was undoubtedly the Papal encyclical "Rerum Novarum" of May 1891 which called for modernization and Christianization of human and economic interactions to forestall socialism.

Yet despite the fanfare and the long list of German and Polish notables who agreed to co-operate, the Society got nowhere. Almost from the outset the divisive issue proved to be language; the Poles demanded that the Society be bilingual while the Germans insisted that only German sufficed. Without the press and the weight of public opinion , Polish members might likely have given in and recognized the German demand, but the newspaper editorials made it a point of honour to incorporate the Polish language. Apparently both Cegielski and Józef Grabski, two key members, wanted equal rights for the Polish language in the Society but Kościelski was not interested in pursuing the point and the Polish position was abandoned.(115) The Dziennik, already angry at Kościelski for publicly criticizing Jaździewski in the Herrenhaus on 12 June, 1891 and disturbed by his attempts to equate Pole and Prussian printed "letters from correspondents" critical of him for not standing firm on the equal language rights issue.(116). The Wielkopolanin was permitted to address its editorials against the loyalist leader as well.(117) Szymański felt that the language issue was insignificant as the society would not amount to anything because it excluded the middle class.(118) Without middle-class involvement and plagued by the language problem the anti-socialist society indeed floundered, and in the words of Lech Trzeciakowski, "soon died a natural death".(119)

The inability of Poles and Germans to cooperate on a local level to combat a universally perceived common enemy raises serious questions about the resources of strength that the era of reconciliation could draw upon. The Kuryer, feeding its readers a daily diet of editorials proclaiming the ultimate victory of reconciliation, failed to notice, or chose not to concede, the weak foundations upon which mutual trust and co-existence were supposed to function in Prussia's eastern provinces.

4.6 A Polish Archbishop for Gniezno-Poznań, Phase Two

After almost a year of immobility, the question of an appointment to the vacant archbishopric of Gniezno-Poznań was raised once again in the late summer of 1891. Throughout the year, with Gossler's resignation and the gathering war clouds sparked by the visit of a French naval squadron to Kronstadt, more and more reasons were adding up to appoint a Polish archbishop. In January, 1891, Pope Leo XIII agreed to the Prussian government's candidate for the archbishopric of Strassburg; hence it was only natural for Berlin to make the return gesture and accept the Vatican's suggestion in the Gniezno-Poznań affair. By August, 1891, there was still no movement in Berlin and the Vatican sent a note protesting the extended vacancy.(120) Everyone, it seemed, was now agreed to the idea of a Polish candidate - the only question was, who would be acceptable to both Rome and Berlin?

At this juncture, Caprivi, in close contact with Kościelski throughout the year, hinted to him that if a Polish prelate made an unmistakable statement of loyalty towards the Reich the appointment would be his.(121) Kościelski seized the initiative and promoted the candidacy of his colleague Stablewski, who had previously not been seriously considered by either Rome or Berlin. The two composed an ultra-loyal speech that was delivered on the last day of the three-day mass Catholic rally in Thorn on 29 September, 1891. The speech was a familiar restatement of loyalist themes: admiration for king and country, anti-socialism and firm adherence to traditional Catholic values. But a new twist was added by directing several openly hostile remarks towards Russia, likely with the prospects of a dual Franco-Russian threat against Germany in mind. "Russland mit seiner fremdartigen Kultur, mit seinem offiziellen religioesen Fanatismus, mit seinem Rassenhass und seinem Bestreben, eine universal-slawische Monarchie zu gruenden oder wenigstens eine drueckende Hegemonie aufzurichten. Auf welche Seite wir uns nun stellen sollen, darauf antwortet unsre Geschichte, unsre Erziehung, unsre Kultur. Wir sind die Soehne eines Volkes, dass seine Zugehoerigkeit zum Westen nie verleugnet hat, wir sind Soehne der katholischen Kirche, deren erbittertster Feind Russland ist."(122)

The effect of Stablewski's speech was strong enough to break the long deadlock over a successor to Julius Dinder. Kultusminister Zedlitz had the speech translated and sent it to Caprivi, who relayed it to Wilhelm II for his perusal.(123) By mid-October it was decided to appoint Stablewski provided the Papacy agree to a Cardinal's hat for Fuerst Georg Kopp, bishop of Breslau.(124) Stablewski wrote a finely-worded memorandum to Caprivi on 26 October, repeating the main themes of the Thorn speech and to finance minister Miquel.(125) On 2 November, 1891, the news was made public, and Stablewski was officially Archbishop on 14 December.(126)

The appointment of one of Bismarck's most quarrelsome parliamentary enemies to the highest religious office in the Prussian East infuriated the German nationalist press to no end.(127) Anger was so great that Caprivi was obliged to defend himself in the Norddeutsche Allgemeine Zeitung and in the Reichstag in late November.(128) Critics were angry for two reasons: the conspicuous concession to the Polish community and the open affront to Russia. Former Army Chief of Staff Graf von Waldersee wrote in his journal, "Ich weiss nun wohl, dass Caprivi angefangen hat, mit den Polen zu rechnen, um sie gegen Russland zu verwenden, bin ja selbst ueberzeugt, dass wir ohne polnische Hilfe nur schwer den Krieg gegen Russland zu Ende fuehren koennten, aber die jetzt beliebte Methode muss die Russen argwoehnisch machen und eine noch staerkere Bedrueckun der russischen Polen zur Folge haben"(129) The Free Conservative Post wrote on 2

December, 1891, "Alle verstummten Hoffnungen leben mit einem Schlage wieder auf, und alle Moeglichkeiten scheinen wieder voellig erreichbar. Das Sprichtwort von dem kleinen Finger und der ganzen Hand passt auf niemand besser als auf den Polen".(130) Many German publicists seemed convinced that Caprivi was favouring the Polish element to the German. The Dresdener Nachrichten wrote on 6 November, 1891, "Dass mit diesem Schritt (der Ernennung Stablewski's) das muehsame Gebaeude welches vom Fuersten Bismarck zur Germanisierung der Polen errichtet wurde, zusammengepulvert wird, liegt um so mehr auf der Hand, als auch die Zugestaendnisse auf dem Gebiete des polnischen Sprachunterrichts die Perspektive auf ein vollstaendiges Nachgeben des Staates zu Gunsten des Polenthums und zu Ungunsten des Deutschthums eroeffnen"(131)

The Polish press was, as could be expected, jubilant at Stablewski's appointment. He was the first Polish prelate appointed to the Archbishopric since the arrest of Ledóchowski in 1875. The fact that it had taken Caprivi almost 18 months to reach a decision that many Poles felt should have been made right away was seemingly forgotten in the general atmosphere of gratefullness and appreciation. Stablewski's appointment constituted indeed the high point of Polish-German reconciliation under Caprivi.

The Kuryer rejoiced at the moment of its greatest victory, for it had consistently argued the merits of the loyalist position from the outset. Knowing full well Kościelski's strategy to get Stablewski appointed, the Kuryer prepared the Polish of community for the inevitable appointment and idealized the candidate. Thus, immediately after the Thorn rally, it began to print articles praising Stablewski's speech and emphasizing that German public opinion wholly approved of it. On 7 October it wrote, "We are happy that Catholic papers and the Kreuzzeitung were satisfied with the rally... The Muenchner Allgemeine Zeitung saw the rally as a total Polish victory. Now is clearly the time to change course".(132) With undisguised joy it reprinted an article from Germania that foretold the total turnaround in Prussia's Polish policy and applauded the Poles for their thoughful and reasonable loyalist course.(133) "Father Stablewski", wrote the Kuryer on 17 October, "was the leading spirit of the first Catholic rally in Thorn. His speech was the quintessence of the three day rally, and it succinctly defined our activity for the future... He was not challenged by anyone at the rally; instead he was greeted with unsurpassed enthusiasm"(134) In answer to charges from the Orędownik that Stablewski's speech was political and not religious in tone, the Kuryer noted that all of the references to Russia concerned matters of Faith, and that his speech was fully in line with the Galician thinkers Józef Szujski (a historian at the Jagiellonian University and one of the most famous "Stańczycy") and Stanisław Tarnowski (rector of the Jagiellonian University).(135) The height of the hero-worship came on 20 October when the Kuryer wrote, "The golden thoughts of Father Stablewski's program will be embedded into our memories for a century."(136)

The Dziennik reported Stablewski's Thorn speech but added no comment. Dobrowolski was obviously annoyed at the needless provocation of Russia but he likely saw the reasoning of Kościelski's strategy to have Stablewski appointed Archbishop and did not want to impede the effort. If the loyalists succeeded, so much the better. As the announcement of the appointment neared the Dziennik contented itself with appreciation that the government had arrived at the justice.(137) On 30 October it wrote, "In our opinion the choice of a Pole is not a concession, but an act of justice as natural as all our national and political demands."(138) When the choice of Stablewski was announced, the Dziennik wrote that it was a "satisfactory solution" and that Stablewski had been instrumental in the improvement of the Polish-German relationship.(139)

Both the Goniec and the Orędownik were dissatisfied with Stablewski's speech; the former because of its ultra-loyal obsequious tone and the latter because it needlessly provoked Russia. The Goniec hinted that the Thorn speech had been written for him in Rome, for which it was strongly berated by the Kuryer for insulting the dignity of the Church.(140) Szymański, who had a long-standing grievance against the prelate from Września, was appalled at the speech. On 10 October the Orędownik wrote, "We can boldly say that Father Stablewski's excursion from a strictly interpreted Catholic rally to international politics and his extraordinary war fever against the Muscovites not only found no support at the rally itself but also were regarded as completely out of place by serious social spheres."(141) In a major article entitled "Russia in Stablewski's Speech at the Thorn Rally" Szymański repeated his charge that no one at the rally was behind Stablewski's attacks on Russia. "Irritating Russia will not help our countrymen there... He should not have touched on the Russian problem. He wants to bind our society to the Triple Alliance and claims that we shall happily march off to war against Russia. He is demanding those things of us that not even the government is."(142)

When the appointment was announced the Orędownik noted that it had nothing against the candidate but was disturbed that he had got it because of the Thorn speech.(143) It opposed any loud celebrations because it would only anger Germans and urged the Polish community to send a thank-you note to the Emperor and the Pope instead. In regard to the general relationship the Orędownik was cautious, "Germans will remain Germans", it wrote on 15 November, 1891, "They will always look at us from a conviction of superiority."(144) In a major article "The Faces of Loyalism", it concluded that the present government had not done anything spectacular for the Poles and argued that unconditional acquiescence in every government initiative did not constitute real loyalty. On 3 December it warned its readers, "When manifesting our loyalty we should keep to certain limits for the sake of the Germans. With total, unconditional loyalty we shall win ourselves no friends"(145)

Szymański's cautious tone was echoed in the Postęp. It also shied away from the term "concession", feeling that the appointment was recognition of a Polish national right.(146) German nationalists were wrong to feel that Poles would repay the government by now happily marching off to war against Russia. On 17 November it wrote, "It is taken for granted that we Poles, with a Polish Archbishop, will now happily battle the Muscovites in the event of war. Let the Germans burn their own fingers in such a war, we do not have to have ours burnt for them. In any case the question remains - where are conditions better for Poles, in Russia or Prussia?" (147) In regard to Kościelski's 30 November, 1891 speech in the Reichstag the Postęp wrote, "It was perhaps too loyal in tone. We do not feel like Prussians or Germans. Let us not go too far in our loyalty."(148)

The Kuryer continued to monitor German public opinion and felt that apart from Bismarck and the Koelnische Zeitung voices of approval were unanimous.(149)

On 14 November it wrote in an air of triumph, "Bismarck had claimed that Poles could never be good subjects of the Kaiser. Wilhelm II has proven this a lie by his immediate (!) appointment of a Pole as Archbishop. The Conservatives are openly and bravely discarding the standards of Bismarck and going over to the Kaiser's banner... In our opinion the change has come from the top. The ruin which Bismarck brought to the country has been halted. With time voices from below will also fall silent when they recognize their impotence and irrelevance."(150) On 28 November it challenged its critics that it was conducting an anti-Russian campaign. "Perhaps Wilhelm II's policies are isolating us within the Slavic world. This does not trouble us. We can see no benefit from Slavophilism either in the past or in the future."(151)

The Dziennik, which had oscillated between hot and cold on Caprivi and the chances of a German-Polish reconciliation throughout 1891, wavered in its analysis between bright optimism and grim forebodings. On 5 November, 1891 the Dziennik wrote, "In our opinion the appointment was not a surprise and does not constitute a 'new era'. One cannot speak of a new era until Poles achieve complete equality with their German fellow-citizens."(152) Yet the very next day it wrote in optimistic tones, "From the government's decision we draw faith that we shall finally be granted full justice."(153) Following Chancellor Caprivi's Reichstag speech of 27 November the Dziennik moved to a more optimistic mood. "We cannot but give him our respect. We take faith (from the speech T.K.) that the methods and basic policies will change. We can only hope that the government will remain on this course and all will benefit."(154) Yet the day after, 3 December, it advised the deputies to vote on each measure in the Landtag and Reichstag according to the needs of the Polish community, a signal that it dissaproved of unconditional loyalty.(155) By the end of December it had changed its mind once again and congratulated the Reichstag deputies for approving Caprivi's trade treaty with Austria-Hungary. "It will mean certain sacrifices for Poles, but it is for the general good."(156) This confusing position was the closest the Dziennik ever came to outright support for loyalism.

The sequel to the Stablewski appointment was the conflict over his replacement in the Prussian Abgeordnetenhaus. The local Srem committee, dominated by landowners, proposed Jan Żółtowski to run for Stablewski's seat, but in a surprising move the citizenry rejected Żółtowski in favour of the popular priest, Piotr Wawrzyniak, already a key figure in the Polish co-op movement which he was to dominate in later years. On 10 January, 1892, Wawrzyniak accepted the nomination; yet within two weeks he withdrew from contention and tried to prove that he had never accepted the nomination in the first place.(157) Szymański was overjoyed that the "people" had rejected the candidate of the gentry and deeply disappointed when Wawrzyniak announced his non-candidacy.(158) Without mentioning any specifics the Orędownik hinted that the withdrawal was the result of intervention from higher clerical circles, likely the new Archbishop himself who did not want another popular priest like Jażdżewski in the Prussian Landtag. (159) The Central Committee speedily recognized Wawrzyniak's resignation and authorized the candidacy of Żółtowski.(160)

4.7 The High Point of Polish-German Reconciliation

During the winter of 1891-1892 it seemed to a great many Poles, and almost all non-Poles, that the Prussian government had indeed decided to do away with Bismarck's anti-Polish policy and improve their social, economic and national condition. That this change in Prussia's Polenpolitik was linked to the Franco-Russian reconciliation and the grim prospects of an impending European war escaped no one's attention. The fact that Polish loyalists were making brilliant careers in Berlin by verbally thrashing Russia gave everyone the impression that the Poles were being rewarded in advance for future services on the battlefield. Russian newspapers were forbidden to print the Polish Primate's name because, in the words von Hutten-Czapski, "Dennoch hatte seine Programmrede, (the speech in Thorn T.K.) in der er sich gegen Russland und fuer Deutschland aussprach, in Tausended von heimlich eingefuehrten Exemplaren ihren Weg durchs Land und überall Beifall gefunden."(161) General Lothar von Schweinitz, German ambassador in St. Petersburg was gravely disturbed at the "complete turnaround" from Bismarck's Polish policy and fretted about the angry Russian response. In a memo on 20 February, 1892, he restated some of the fundamental priciples of the German-Russian relationship. "Die preussisch-russischen Beziehungen sind seit hundert Jahren vornehmlich durch die Konsequenzen der Teilung Polens bestimmt worden, welche die Interessengemeinschaft der beiden nichtkatholischen Teilungsmaechte begruendete,... jede Aenderung in den polnischen Dingen sich bald, nicht bloss an der 1000 km langen unnatuerlichen Grenze fuehlbar, auf den Gebiet der Gesamtpolitik."(162) A week later Schweinitz reported that, "Fuerst Lobanov, Botschafter in Wien, kam zu mir; in vertraulichem Gespraeche sagte er ganz offen, Polen erwarte seine Wiederherstellung von Kaiser Wilhelm II.".(163) His successor in St. Petersburg, General Bernhard von Werder, told a group of statesmen in 1893, "dass die Auszeichnung, mit der Kaiser Wilhelm die polnischen Abgeordneten seit einiger Zeit behandle - unter anderen hatte Kościelski einen Orden erhalten - die politischen Kreise in Russland lebhaft beschaeftigte."(164) Bismarck's oft-repeated maxim that solid Prussian-Russian relations depended on a common suppression of Polish aspirations seemed to be substantiated.

Yet how close were the Poles to the Germans under Caprivi in 1891-1892? In contrast to international opinion, the voices within the Polish community were divided, though there was no question that the general mood had improved greatly since early 1890. Polish newspapers began to take notice of the Neue Kurs in many ways: in the Emperor's and the Chancellor's dispositions, in the friendlier tones of the German newspapers and German political parties, in the more moderate behaviour of the local bureaucrats and in the personalities of the new ministers who had replaced Bismarck's old crew: Graf Zedlitz, von Berlepsch, Herrfurth and von Miquel.(165) All papers took note of the second phase of the Rentengutsgesetz of July, 1891, praising the fair-minded intentions of the law's formulators and urging Poles to take advantage of its generous terms.(166) Teachers were no longer being sent to non-Polish provinces, and court cases against Polish newspapers virtually ceased.(167)

The high point of mutual good will was well-illustrated in a mixed German-

Polish meeting held at the Bazar in Poznań on 13 January, 1892. A government official addressed the directors of the Bank Ziemski and, in the ironic report of Ludwig Bernhard, declared that, "die Spannung welche zwischen den beiden beisammen wohnenden Nationalitaeten bisher geherrscht habe, im Schwinden begriffen sei, und erklaerte sich bereit, an der Versoehnung mitzuwirken und den polnischen Besitzern mit Rat und Tat bei Bildung der von Rentengutern behilflich zu sein.". (168) One only has to refer briefly to any speech by Bismarck on the Polish question to realize how remarkable such a statement was. A Prussian civil servant giving advice to Polish landowners on how to combat the negative effects of the Ansiedlungskommission was unthinkable only a few years ago.

Yet, apart from the Kuryer, no other Polish newspaper in Poznań declared itself satisfied with the state of affairs. There were still too many grievances: the continued existence of the Ansiedlungskommission, the lack of any Polish officials in the local administration, the hostility of school inspectors and Landrats, the exclusion of Polish from the school curriculum, the maintenance, in principle, of the expulsion policy, and the refusal of the government to extend what few privileges the Poles in Poznania had received to those in West Prussia, who were hardly aware of a Neue Kurs at all.

The turn of 1891-1892 found most newspapers optimistic about further concessions.(169) Both domestic and foreign policy seemed to presage better days for the Poles in Prussia. By aligning themselves unmistakably behind the Triple Alliance, the Polish question in international affairs could no longer be ignored; indeed the French fleet had visited Kronstadt in July 1891, paving the way for a Franco-Russian military pact and a more rigid division of European powers into hostile blocks. At home Caprivi had launched a sharp campaign on Social Democracy that stressed education and religion rather than repression. The backbone of anti-Polish sentiment, the Kartell of Conservatives and National Liberals, were feuding, and Bismarck remained a recluse in disfavour.

A closer look at the Polish position, however, reveals some fragile it really was. Few Poles seemed to be aware of how closely their position was linked to the political fortunes of Chancellor Caprivi because most preferred to identify the Emperor as the source of all power in Prussia. Caprivi was well-meaning but ambivalent towards the Poles; in any case he was beset by a multitude of more important issues and never felt fully secure in office. He was dependent on the whims of an erratic Wilhelm II, who had given no evidence whatsoever of an open disposition to Polish aspirations. Perhaps most important was the continued hostility in the Prussian Abgeordnetenhaus to redressing Polish grievances. Almost no headway had been made in changing the positions of the Kartell majority. Doubtless, the Reichstag, dominated by Catholics, Progressives, Social Democrats and the minorities would have undertaken a major review of the Polish question if it had belonged to their prerogatives; but it could not because the issue was an internal Prussian affair. Progress in dismantling Bismarck's anti-Polish legislation depended on friendly ministers in Berlin and winning over at least one of the Kartell parties in the Landtag, preferably the Conservatives. In the long term, these objectives could not be attained. Thus, as shall be seen, the Polish press was surprised by the lack of further moves in their favour after Caprivi's humiliation over the Prussian school reform bill and his clumsy handling of the "Uriasbrief" affair. The optimistic mood from the appointment of Stablewski in November, 1891 to the resignation of Zedlitz in March, 1892, was never to occur again.

NOTES TO CHAPTER 4

1. For a detailed study of the expulsion laws of 1885-1886 see Helmut Neubach Die Ausweisungen von Polen und Juden aus Preussen 1886-1886 (Wiesbaden 1967); Joachim Mai, Die preussisch-deutsche Polenpolitik 1885-1887 (Ost-Berlin, 1962); Klaus J. Bade, "Kulturkampf auf dem Arbeitsmarkt. Bismarcks Polenpolitik 1885-1890", in: Innenpolitische Probleme des Bismarck-Reiches, ed. Otto Pflanze (Muenchen, Wien, 1983), pp. 121-142.

2. Postęp, 28.12.1890, no. 151.

3. Karwowski, Historya Wielkiego Księstwa ..., vol. 3, p. 5. The ruling was adhered to conscientiously; Gey, Der preussische Verwaltung..., p. 86 states that there were only 89 expulsions in the whole of 1894. See also Bade, "Kulturkampf auf dem Arbeitsmarkt..., p. 141.

4. Wielkopolanin, 19.3.1891, no. 64.

5. Dziennik Poznański, 9.1.1891, no. 6

6. Ibid., 18.2.1891, no. 39.

7. Ibid., 26.7.1891, no. 168.

8. Wielkopolanin, 8.2.1891, no. 31; 16.6.1891, no. 134.

9. Kuryer Poznański, 10.1.1891, no. 7.

10. Ibid., 18.6.1891, no 136.

11. Reden des Grafen von Caprivi im Deutschen Reichstage, Preussischen Landtage und bei besonderen Anlaessen, ed. Rudolf Arndt (Berlin, 1894), p. 152.

12. Kuryer Poznański, 5.2.1891, no. 28. See also Blanke, Prussian Poland..., p. 74.

13. J. Alden Nichols, Germany After Bismarck..., p. 110; Meisner, Der Reichskanzler Caprivi..., p. 33.

14. Massow, Die deutsche innere Politik unter Kaiser Wilhelm II. (Stuttgart, Berlin, 1913), p. 120.

15. Dziennik Poznański, 13.12.1890, no. 286; 31.1.1891, no. 25.

16. Raschdau, Unter Bismarck und Caprivi..., p. 209.

17. Kuryer Poznański, 11.3.1891, no. 57.

18. Ibid., 13.3.1891, no. 59; Gey, Die preussische Verwaltung..., p. 164.

19. Trzeciakowski, Polityka polskich klas..., p. 103; Rosenthal, "The Election of Archbishop Stablewski...p. 271; Lotte Kaminski, Die Auseinandersetzung um die polnische Frage zur Zeit der Reichskanzlerschaft des Fuersten Hohenlohe (Hamburg, 1938), p. 15.

20. Gey, Die preussische Verwaltung..., p. 18.

21. Dziennik Poznański, 14.3.1891, no. 60.

22. Ibid., 15.3.1891, no. 61.

23. Ibid., 30.7.1891, no. 171.

24. Wielkopolanin, 13.3.1891, no. 59.

25. Postęp, 13.3.1891, no. 59.

26. Ibid., 15.3.1891, no. 61.

27. Ibid., 20.3.1891, no. 65.

28. Orędownik, 13.3.1891, no. 59.

29. Ibid., 14.3.1891, no. 60.

30. Ibid., 22.7.1891, no. 164.

31. A transcript of the 11 April Zedlitz decree is found in Schulthess'..., 1891, p. 69.

32. Fuerst Bismarck nach seiner Entlassung, ed. Johannes Penzler (Leipzig, 1897) vol. 2, p. 340.

33. Muenstermann, Die preussische-deutsche Polenpolitik..., p. 36.

34. Ibid., pp. 35-37.

35. Komierowski, Koło polskie w Berlinie..., p. 201. The total number of Polish schoolchildren eligible for private lessons was 186,346 in 1891, of whom 34,994 lived in towns and 151,352 lived in the countryside. At their disposal were 2399 schools. The 3756 teachers in Poznania were chronically underpaid, earning an average of 800 Mk. per year, in comparison with 2082 in Berlin. Preussische Statistik 1891, vol. 20, Das gesammte Volksschulen im preussischen Staate im Jahre 1891, pp. A4, A9, A15, A44, A70, A77.

36. Kuryer Poznański, 16.4.1891, no. 86.

37. Ibid., 18.4.1891, no. 88.

38. Gey, Die preussische Verwaltung...p. 164.

39. Kuryer Poznański, 29.4.1891, no. 97.

40. Ibid.

41. Ibid., 22.5.1891, no. 114.

42. Orędownik, 17.4.1891, no. 87.

43. Karwowski, Historya Wielkiego Ksiestwa..., vol. 3, p. 6; Lech, Maria Trzeciakowski, W dziewiętnastowiecznym Poznaniu..., p. 301.

44. Postep, 28.6.1891, no. 119; Dziennik Poznanski, 2.7.1891, no. 147.

45. Lech, Maria Trzeciakowski, W dziewiętnastowiecznym Poznaniu..., p. 301. The Polish community paid only 13.5% of the province's income tax (1897); average wages for a rural labourer came to only 1.5 Mk. per day; urban factory workers earned only 600 Mk. per year; 80% of landowners were indebted to over 50% value of their estates; and Poles had a long list of other national causes to support, like the Polish libraries, educational foundations, and socio-economic organizations. See Wegener, Der wirtschaftliche Kampf..., pp. 119, 133; Łuczak, Życie gospodarczo-społeczne..., pp. 240-241.

46. Dziennik Poznański, 16.4.1891, no. 86.

47. Ibid., 22.4.1891, no. 91.

48. Ibid., 11.7.1891, no. 155.

49. Ibid., 3.11.1891, no. 251.

50. Ibid.

51. Kuryer Poznański, 29.10. 1891, no. 247.

52. Wielkopolanin, 19.4.1891, no. 89.

53. Ibid., 2.5.1891, no. 100.

54. Ibid., 28.8.1891, no. 195; 3.11.1891, no. 251.

55. Orędownik, 18.4.1891, no. 88.

56. Ibid., 20.5.1891, no. 112.

57. Postęp, 17.4.1891, no. 87.

58. Ibid., 1.11.1891, no. 250.

59. Deutschland und Polen, ed. Brackmann..., p. 235.

60. Reden des Grafen von Caprivi..., ed. Arndt, p. 153.

61. "Jażdżewski, Ludwik", PSB, vol. 13; Grot, "Prezesi kół polskich...", p. 263.

62. BK, Ms. no. 1456/57, meeting 30.4.1891.

63. Ibid.

64. Jażdżewski in the Abgeordnetenhaus, 2 May, 1891, "...glaube ich, sind wir bei dem Zeitpunkt angekommen, wo die Koenigliche Staatsregierung sich reiflich ueberlegen sollte, ob man mit dem Ansiedlungsgesetz in seiner jetzigen Form und mit seiner Tendenz nicht Schicht machen sollte...Meine Herren, ich richte nun an den Herrn Ministerpraesidenten der ergebene Frage, mir mittheilen zu wollen, ob die Koenigliche Staatsregierung noch auf dem Standpunkt steht, auf welchem der Ministerpraesident Fuerst Bismarck stand, als er 1886 diese Sache befuerwortete." Berichte Abg.H., 1891, vol. 4, p. 2105.

65. Caprivi in the Abgeordnetenhaus, 2 May, 1891 "Die Staatsregierung ist nicht gewillt, das jetzige Gesetz zu veraendern...Die Verhaeltnisse in der Provinz Posen haben sich im Laufe der 5 Jahre nicht so geaendert, dass die Regierung diejenigen Mittel, die sie damals fuer noetig gehalten hat, um die Zugehoerigkeit der Provinz Posen zum preussischen Staate zum vollen Ausdruck zu bringen, aus der Hand geben koennte." Ibid., p. 2105-2106.

66. BK., Ms. no. 1456/57, meeting of 3 May, 1891.

67. Berichte Abg. H., 1891, vol. 4, p. 2147-2148.

68. Jażdżewski in the Abgeordnetenhaus, 8 May, 1891 "Nach meinem Dafuerhalten ist das einzige Mittel, um auf dem Gebiete unseres Schulwesens gedeihlich zu wirken, das, dass der polnische Sprachunterricht wieder obligatorisch in die Volksschule eingefuehrt wird." Berichte Abg. H., 1891, vol. 4, p. 2231.

69. von Zedlitz-Truetzschler in the Abgeordnetenhaus, 8 May, 1891 "...wir machen Sie darauf aufmerksam, dass, wenn Sie den kleinen Finger geben, sehr bald von Ihnen die Hand gefordert werden wird. (Sehr wahr! Hoert! rechts) Meine Herren, an diese Stelle kann ein Mann treten, wie er will,- die ganze Hand kann er Ihnen niemals geben;...Ibid., p.2232.

70. Kuryer Poznański, 10.5.1891, no. 105.

71. Ibid., 12.5.1891, no. 106.

72. Ibid., 5.7.1891, no.

73. Dziennik Poznański, 6.5.1891, no. 103.

74. Ibid., 13.5.1891, no. 107.

75. Ibid., 17.5.1891, no. 111.

76. Ibid.

77. Ibid., 20.5.1891, no.

78. Ibid., 12.7.1891, no. 156.

79. Ibid., 17.7.1891, no. 160.

80. Postęp, 10.5.1891, no. 105.

81. Ibid., 13.5.1891, no. 107. The charge was denied by Stablewski in an open letter to the Dziennik Poznański, 16.5.1891, no. 110.

82. Postęp, 13.5.1891, no. 107.

83. Florian Stablewski in the Abgeordetenhaus, 4 May, 1891 "Der Herr Kultusminister wird mir zugeben, dass in Polen die zwei Hauptblaetter, der Dziennik und der Kuryer Poznański, thatsaechlich der Ausdruck der oeffentlichen Meinung sind und dieselbe beherrschen." Berichte Abg. H., 1891, vol. 4, p. 2148.

84. Orędownik, 12.5.1891, no. 106.

85. Ibid., 14.5.1891, no. 108.

86. Ibid., 7.7.1891, no. 157.

87. Ibid., 21.5.1891, no. 113.

88. Ibid., 15.7.1891, no. 109.

89. Stablewski to Henryk Szuman, 21.5.1891, B. Racz., Ms. no. 1636.

90. Trzeciakowski, Polityka polskich klas..., p. 62.

91. Schulthess'...1891, p. 56; Postęp, 8.3.1891, no. 55.

92. BK., Ms. no. 1456/57, meeting of 9.6.1891.

93. Józef Kościelski in the Herrnhaus 12 June, 1891, "Ich wuerde dieses Vorgehen fuer einen grossen politischen Fehler halten, den nur derjenige begehen kann, dem seine eigene Popularitaet bei einer gewissen Art von Presse hoeher steht, als die normale Entwicklung des versoehnlichen Verhaeltnisses zwischen der Regierung und den polnischen Unterthanen Seiner Majestaet." Berichte Herrenhaus, 1891, vol. 1, p. 307. For a more comprehensive view of Kościelski's political philosophy, see his essay "Prussia and the Poles", in: The National Review 43 (July, 1904), pp. 740-764.

94. Ibid.

95. BK., Ms. no. 1456/57, meeting of 18.6.1891.

96. Kościelski's open letter was in response to a remark critical of Polish aspirations in Upper Silesia by Graf Ballestrem (Wasserpolaken). Copies of the letter were printed in the Dziennik Poznański, Kuryer Poznański (16.7.1891) and in Germania (21.7.1891).

97. Dziennik Poznański, 12.7.1891, no. 156.

98. Ibid., 16.7.1891, no. 159.

99. Ibid., 17.7.1891, no. 160.

100. Postęp, 16.6.1891, no. 134.

101. Orędownik, 25.6.1891, no. 142.

102. Ibid., 26.6.1891, no. 143.

103. Ibid.

104. Kuryer Poznański, 27.6.1891, no. 144.

105. Ibid., 22.7.1891, no.

106. Ibid., 5.7.1891, no.

107. Caprivi in the Reichstag, 27 February, 1891. Berichte Rtg., 1891, vol. 3, p. 1767.

108. Caprivi in the Abgeordnetenhaus, 29 January, 1892: "Ich glaube, es handelt sich hier in letzter Instanz nicht um evangelisch und katholisch, sondern es handelt sich um Christentum und Atheismus." Reden des Grafen Caprivi ed. Arndt, p. 405.

109. Trzeciakowski, Walka o polskość miast..., p. 183; Wehler, Sozialdemokratie p. 115; Danilczuk, Dzialalność SPD i PPS-zaboru pruskiego..., p. 95-98.

110. Dziennik Poznański, 16.12.1890, no. 288.

111. Kuryer Poznański, 17.12.1890, no. 289.

112. Wielkopolanin, 18.7.1891, no. 161; Wielkopolska, wybór źródeł 1851-1914, ed. Witold Jakóbczyk, (Wrocław, 1954), p. 223.

113. Excepts of the brochure are reprinted in ibid., pp. 23-26. For reactions in the Polish press, see Dziennik Poznański, 21.5.1891, no. 113; Orędownik 3.5.1891, no. 101 and 22.5.1891, no. 114.

114. Kuryer Poznański, 28.11.1891, no. 273; Dziennik Poznański, 28.11.1891,no. 273.

115. Orędownik, 21.8.1891, no. 189.

116. Dziennik Poznański, 19.8.1891, no. 187.

117. Wielkopolanin, 22.8.1891, no. 190.

118. Orędownik, 21.8.1891, no. 189.

119. Trzeciakowski, Polityka polskich klas..., p. 95.

120. Trzeciakowski, Geneza powołania..., p. 194.

121. Trzeciakowski, Polityka polskich klas ..., p. 104.

122. Schulthess'...1891, p. 130 gives excerpts in German; Komierowski, Koło polskie w Berlinie pp. 216-229 offers the speech in full in Polish.

123. Trzeciakowski, Polityka polskich klas..., p. 105.

124. Caprivi to Schloezer, German envoy at the Vatican, 18.10.1891: "Gleichzeitig wollen Ew. pp. Seiner Heiligkeit ganz vertraulich bemerken, dass Seine Majestaet die Verleihung des Kardinalshutes an Fuerstbischof Kopp gern saehe und gegenwaertig auf Erfuellung dieses Wunsches umso mehr Wert lege, als die Ernennung eines Polen zum Erzbischof von Posen die deutsche Bevoelkerung sehr unangenehm beruehren und letztere in der Ernennung eines deutschen Kardinals ein gewisses Aequivalent dafuer finden werde." Gatz, Akten zur preussischen Kirchenpolitik..., p. 146.

125. Ibid., p. LVIII; Hans Herzfeld, Johannes von Miquel (Bielefeld, 1938) vol. 1, p. 496 "In den Kreisen der polnischen Herrenhausfraktion hat man jedenfalls geglaubt, dass die im Oktober 1891 erfolgte Ernennung hauptsaechlich der wohlwollenden Unterstuetzung Miquels beim Kaiser zu dankbar gewesen sei."

126. Schulthess'...1891, p. 130.

127. Komierowski, Koło polskie w Berlinie..., p. 212.

128. Caprivi in the Reichstag 28 November, 1891, "Es fand sich anfangs keiner, es fand sich aber auch kein Deutscher, und nach den Ereignissen in Thorn war es nun fuer uns nicht zweifelhaft, dass der Mann, der da eine Rede gehalten hatte, die so weit preussisch und preussisch-patriotisch war, als wir es ueberhaupt von den Einwohnern polnischer Zunge in der Provinz Posen erwarten koennen, den Anforderungen soweit genuegte, als es moeglich war." Reden des Grafen Caprivi..., ed. Arndt, p. 153.

129. Waldersee, Denkwuerdigkeiten..., vol. 2, p. 221.

130. Bismarck nach seiner Entlassung..., ed. Penzler, vol. 2, pp. 352-353.

131. Ibid., vol. 2, p. 305.

132. Kuryer Poznański, 7.10.1891, no. 228.

133. Ibid., 14.10.1891, no. 234.

134. Ibid., 17.10.1891, no. 237.

135. Ibid. The "Stańczyk" group in Cracow represented Galician magnates and intelligentsia who repudiated the notion of insurrection and propagated loyalty to and co-operation with the Habsburg administration.

136. Ibid., 20.10.1891, no. 239.

137. Dziennik Poznański, 29.10.1891, no. 247.

138. Ibid., 30.10.1891, no. 248.

139. Ibid., 3.11.1891, no. 251.

140. cited in Kuryer Poznański, 13.12.1891, no. 285; the originals of the Goniec for this period have been lost.

141. Orędownik, 10.10.1891, no. 231.

142. Ibid., 15.10.1891, no. 235.

143. Ibid., 12.11.1891, no. 259.

144. Ibid., 15.11.1891, no. 262; 25.11.1891, no. 270.

145. Ibid., 2.12.1891, no. 276.

146. Postęp, 30.10.1891, no. 248.

147. Ibid., 17.11.1891, no. 263.

148. Ibid., 4.12.1891, no. 257.

149. Kuryer Poznański, 10.11.1891, no. 257.

150. Ibid., 14.11.1891, no. 261.

151. Ibid., 28.11.1891, no. 273.

152. Dziennik Poznański, 5.11.1891.

153. Ibid., 6.11.1891, no. 254.

154. Ibid., 2.12.1891, no. 276.

155. Ibid., 3.12.1891, no. 277.

156. Ibid., 18.12.1891, no. 289. See also Komierowski, Koło polskie w Berlinie..., p. 232.

157. Akta PKW Ms. no. 869, Srem nos. 4, 6, 11; Kuryer Poznański 23.1.1892, no. 18.

158. Orędownik, 12.1.1892, no. 8.

159. Ibid., 24.1.1892, no. 19.

160. Kuryer Poznański, 24.1.1892, no. 19.

161. Hutten-Czapski, Sechzig Jahre..., vol. 1, p. 168.

162. Die Grosse Politik der Europaeischen Kabinette 1871-1914 (Berlin, 1922), vol. 7, pp. 382-384.

163. Schweinitz, Denkwuerdigkeiten..., vol. 2, p. 441.

164. Raschdau, Unter Bismarck und Caprivi..., pp. 293-294.

165. Dziennik Poznański, 25.6.1891, no. 142; Wielkopolanin, 29.1.1892, no. 23; Orędownik, 25.3.1891, no. 69 and 27.1.1892, no. 21.

166. Kuryer Poznański, 25.12.1891, no. 295; Wielkopolanin, 22.10.1891, no. 241; Dziennik Poznański, 27.10.1891, no. 245; Orędownik, 29.12.1891, no. 296.

167. Wielkopolanin, 26.2.1891, no. 46.

168. Bernhard, Das polnische Gemeinwesen..., p. 491.

169. Postęp, 1.1.1892, no. 1; Wielkopolanin, 14.2.1892, no. 36; Dziennik Poznański, 6.1.1891, no. 4; Kuryer Poznański, 2.10.1891, no. 224.

5. The Turning of the Tide, Spring, 1892-Spring, 1893.

5.1. The Collapse of the Zedlitz-Truetzschler School Bill

For much of late 1891 and early 1892 attention in Prussia was focused on the heated debate over the School Reform Bill, which polarized German society and eventually forcced Caprivi to resign. Gossler had been dismissed in early 1891 for his failure to draft a bill satisfactory to both the Conservative and the Centrum parties. His successor, Graf von Zedlitz-Truetzschler, worked on a new bill with great zeal and staked his entire political career on its outcome. His emphasis on clerical influence in education together with Caprivi's frequent references to the bill as being a "choice between atheism and Christianity" alarmed the Progressives and National Liberals and stimulated an unprecedented lobbying effort to have the bill withdrawn.(1) From all over Prussia petitions from urban councils, teachers, and universities were drawn up urging its rejection. The Emperor, initially intimating that he was fully behind Zedlitz and Caprivi, succumbed to the ceaseless appeals and at a ministerial meeting of 17 March, 1892, withdrew his support, adding that the bill had to be redrawn to win over the support of the moderate parties.(2) Caprivi, who had worked so hard to assure the powerful Centrum party of the government's sympathy in order to win their support for his trade treaties and military bills, saw his hopes of building a steady pro-government coalition in the Reichstag dissolve. For him every law that failed to gain the support of the Centrum was worthless.(3) Zedlitz was completely disillusioned and on 18 March submitted his resignation; on the same day Caprivi offered to resign but was prevailed upon to remain as Reichskanzler.(4)

The collapse of the School Bill in Prussia was a serious blow to Caprivi's standing in the Reichstag. The Centrum party, which had heartily welcomed Caprivi's appointment, now returned to the opposition.(5) The quarrel had alienated everyone; the left felt Caprivi was too clerical and obsequious towards the Catholics, while the right felt let down by the bill's withdrawal. In the words of Friedrich von Holstein's biographer, Norman Rich, "The failure of the School Bill meant the destruction of every kind of pro-government party alignment in either the Prussian Landtag or the Reichstag."(6) Eugen Richter was not far from the truth when he said in the Reichstag that, "Der Reichskanzler ist heute vor uns erschienen wie ehedem; aber er ist doch heute nicht mehr derselbe wie frueher. Er ist in seinen politischen Funktionen sozusagen halbiert worden."(7) Indeed, from March 1892 one can trace a unmistakable decline in Caprivi's earlier popularity. Although his greatest successes still lay before him - the Russian trade treaty and the Great Army Bill of 1893 - his removal from the Prussian ministry signalled a break with the centre of power in Germany, for, as he and his supporters were to learn to their chagrin, a German Chancellor without support from the Prussian power-base could never really be effective.

The Polish community followed the arguments concerning the Zedlitz School Bill intensely. Promising greater clerical control over education and returning to the Catholic Church a good deal of influence that it had lost during the Kulturkampf coincided fully with the Polish world-view. Thus, when Zedlitz twice rejected Polish requests to get a language clause into the bill to assure that teaching of religion be conducted in the mother tongue, the reaction in the Polish press was subdued.(8) Perhaps recognizing the tremendous pressure the Kultusminister was facing from the National Liberals and the Progressives, the Poles hid their disappointment knowing that their outcries would be used by their enemies to discredit the minister. Once again, self-censorship was imposed to make the proper impression in German public opinion. The Orędownik, however, lost its enthusiasm over the bill when the Polish demands failed to pass. "(The bill) makes no contribution to our national identity. Why, then should we demonstrate for it?" it wrote on 27 February.(9) After the bill's withdrawal the Orędownik noted that, "In all the debates on the school bill no one mentioned or even thought of us. The Germans only fought for themselves. We Poles should learn from this."(10)

Polish support of the bill began when it was introduced by Zedlitz in the Landtag on 15 January, 1892. The Dziennik wrote on 28 January, "No one can really call returning clerical control over schools 'clericalism'. In his project the minister is adhering only to the notions of international law and the principles of great thinkers... The Poles, Centrum and Conservatives form a large enough majority to pass the bill."(11) The Dziennik was infuriated that "Opponents are linking the school bill to a concession for the Poles", (5 February) and on the next day charged that the "German press in Poznania is using the school bill as another vehicle in anti-Polish agitation...It is seen as a gift to the Poles."(12) The Dziennik basically agreed with Caprivi's and Zedlitz's notion of portraying the question as one of atheism and Christianity. "Mixed schools lead to secular schools - atheism."(13) In a similar tone the Postep wrote on 4 February, "We are strongly in favour of the school bill and denominational schools... liberal schools are secular schools... liberalism has many of the same qualities as socialism; both reject God and both hunt only for material goods."(14) Szymański originally greeted the bill, "Zedlitz's new proposals will benefit Catholics and Poles and do away with the structures of Falk and Gossler."(15) The Kuryer welcomed the bill as an example of the new Polish-Centrum-Conservative majority in operation. It was a great improvement on Gossler's earlier proposals, but the Kuryer was not satisfied with the compromises made to secular authority, and urged that the Church retain the right to appoint teachers for religious instruction.(16)

The German and Jewish communities of Poznania, like many other Prussian provinces, were alarmed at the tone of the bill, and on 18 March the Poznań municipal council sent a petition to the Kaiser complaining of the bill. Even the mayor, Richard Witting, a Progressive who had earlier been welcomed by the Poles, signed the petition and complained of Polish criticism of him.(17) The petition enraged Poznań's Polish community. "Municipal treason!", thundered the Postęp on 20 February, "From yesterday's deliberations we Poles and Christians should learn that we must defend our Christian values with full consciousness in the face of the growing Jewish usurpation."(18) Three days later Knapowski charged that the Jews were instrumental again in manipulating Bromberg's town council to sign a similar petition.(19) Significantly, Knapowski's anti-Semitic sentiments were shared by almost all sectors of Polish society, who perceived Jewish influence in the service of Germanization. The growing resentment was to manifest itself in fierce anti-Semitism among the young, hot-headed National Democrats at the end of the century. The Kuryer complained that the "Jews who are masterminding the petition... are pushing all good Christians to anti-Semitism. 6000 Jews are dominating 65,000 Christians...We warn the Jews not to fan the flames of anti-Semitism."(20) The Orędownik wrote, "Who in Poznań could be against confessional schools? Jews. Jews should not get involved.(21) The blame for the petition was placed squarely upon the Jews, who were also accused of furthering Germanization.(22) The Wielkopolanin wrote in early June, "If on the one hand it is incontrovertible that Poles really are holding to their friendly disposition towards the Jews, then on the other we see, unfortunately, that the conceit, domination and eternal dislike of the Jews to everything Polish is spreading and growing at every occasion."(23) It was a dark time for Polish-Jewish relations and undoubtedly contributed to the growing anti-Semitism in Prussian Poland that later found its expression in National Democracy.

Threatened with a fundamental assault on their rights, the Poles decided to draft a counter-petition and held a huge rally at the Bazar on 7 March. Chaired by Franciszek Dobrowolski and addressed by a number of Polish notables, the rally drafted a protest against the Jewish-German petition which unfortunately arrived at Berlin just as the School Bill was withdrawn.(24)

The withdrawal of the bill and the ministerial resignations in Berlin disappointed all the papers. The Dziennik recognized the move as a clear victory for the National Liberals and deplored the "heavy cloud that has settled on the whole constitutional system".(25) It wrote highly of the departing Zedlitz and regretted that Wilhelm II had bowed to external pressure. (26) The Postęp noted that the bill's withdrawal was a sign that "atheism and impiety had grown ever stronger roots" in Germany and that, "This will be a unique event in parliamentary proceedings. The government withdrew a bill that had the overwhelming support of Catholics and Christians behind it."(27) The Orędownik wrote in grave tones that "the changes (in Berlin) will not be without effect on Polish conditions", and that Zedlitz's departure should not be regretted too much because he was, "a sly person who, acting like a gentleman was able to safegaurd Prussian state interests and was therefore dangerous to us Poles."(28) The Kuryer was shocked at the bill's withdrawal as it had felt that its passage was assured. It urged the Conservatives to make a clear break with the National Liberals and align themselves even more strongly to the "Christian" parties. "A strict Christian-monarchical power block, based on the constitution, on positivism and on conservatism has a future and is necessary in Germany", it wrote in early April.(29)

In later years the Poles came to recognize Zedlitz's successor, Robert Bosse, as one of their greatest enemies, but in the first months after his appointment many hoped that he would continue the promising policies of his successor. Thus, the Dziennik wrote on April 2, 1892, "We have no reason to doubt the new minister. He will be directed by thoughts of equal rights and good will. He will carry on the work begun by his predecessor."(30) The Kuryer wrote at the end of July, "We have iron faith and unwavering trust in the Prussian government, whose educational affairs are in the hands of a man of dedicated Christian convictions."(31) The new minister, unfamiliar with Polish affairs, reserved comment on the fiercely disputed issues of Polish language and religious rights for many months and gave the Poles reason to believe he was basically on their side. In June, 1892, Bosse made a four-day tour of Poznania to see the situation of the schools for himself, and the Poles took advantage of his presence to submit a memorial complaining of their second-class status.(32) "The truth cannot be hidden", wrote the Kuryer on 28 June, and instructed the Poles, "We must be armed with patience. Bosse will know how to handle the chauvinists."(33) The Dziennik expressed joy at Bosse's visit and faith that he would see the inequalities and uselessness of conducting religious classes for Polish children in German.(34) "The enactment of that which simple justice dictates depends on the good will of the minister. We must wait to see what the government does but not cease in our national efforts."(35) The Orędownik protested that the memorial to Bosse was drawn up exclusively by notables and demanded that its contents be made public. "What reasons do we have to hope from Bosse?" it asked on 29 June, "Our hopes are built on Bosse's 'Christian convictions'. How many other such ministers have we known?... If he did not decide about language classes in Berlin, he will not when he is here."(36) As no visible response from Bosse's visit materialized throughout the year the Orędownik became more disillusioned. In mid-September it wrote that "We cannot count on our loyalist deputies. ...We can depend only on ourselves. We have no idea what was in the memorial... There should be no secrets! Everyone knows what we want!"(37)

Throughout 1892 the Poles kept up their campaign both at home and in Berlin to further their aims in the crucial area language teaching. The Postęp in early December 1892 wrote that re-introducing the obligatory teaching of Polish was "our alpha and omega"(38). The Kuryer lamented that poor attendance and the difficult financing of private lessons would lead many children to crime, prostitution and, the worst of all possibilities, Social Democracy. "We need obligatory lessons to save these souls by a religious education, "it wrote in December, 1892.(39) The Kuryer was thankful for the freedom to hold private lessons but pointed out that these were simply not working out. In part, hostile Prussian school inspectors were to blame; but the main reason was the shortage of funding.(40) Some hope was awoken through the publication of an interview with Archbishop Stablewski conducted by Maximilian Harden and printed in September 1892 in the first issue of Die Zukunft.(41) Stablewski stressed the need for obligatory lessons at all levels of public schooling but indicated the Poles would be satisfied with at least 2 hours per week. Public concern over the language issue was so great that even the Goniec, which had shown a haughty disdain for all government "concessions" to date, urged its readers to take advantage of the ability to hold private lessons.(42)

During 1892, The Dziennik printed many articles pointing out the inadequacy of the existing system and its discriminatory policies towards the Poles. On June 10 it wrote in an ironic tone, "The chronicle (of injustice) which is being compiled here in the areas of education is becoming thicker - all this despite the 'new era'. In fact we do not see this new era at all. On one side, beautiful promises, but on the other old methods! What a comedy! And bitter irony!" (43) It deeply regretted the inability of the community to meet the financial burdens of private teaching, and was adamant that the minimum the Poles could expect from the government for their loyal behaviour was adequate language teaching for their children. "It is in the interest of the state as well as ours", it wrote on 21 September, "What sort of justice is it when we Poles, fulfilling our civil obligations and paying our taxes, must also raise money for something so important for us? Every subject of a law-abiding state has the right to demand justice... It is time to repair this damage."(44)

The Orędownik favoured a more militant position by the deputies in Berlin and bitterly complained of the private teaching decree as simply a "new tax that the government has levied on us. It can be seen as a tariff duty which we must pay for our own language, much like sugar or coffee." (45) It praised the stance taken by Jaździewski in sharply addressing the question in the Prussian Landtag and denounced the loyalists for making many promises in the areas of language and religion that were not being met. "The Zedlitz 'concesion' of 11.4.1891 was supposed to help all citizens against Socialism... The belief that the government would soon return Polish into the schools was unfounded. Now, a year and a half later, we still have no lessons. The fact is that we are politically great paupers".(46) It stressed that the government would only promote policies in its own interest and would never give up Germanization. "The Prussian government will make no concesion for Polish children in the schools unless it is in its own interest. We should never doubt this for a moment."(47) Much of the blame for public disenchantment was levelled at the loyalist deputies in Berlin. "Our loyalists are trying to tell us that the Archbishop will act as an intermediary for us in Berlin. It will not work... The Germans recognise his position as an element in strengthening Prussia... The government has done nothing for the Archbishop in the way of language teaching."(48)

It is important to note that of the two areas in which the Poles felt themselves discriminated against the most in Prussia, language and land purchases, the urban sector tended to be more concerned about the former, while the landed gentry took the latter more to heart. Urban residents were not as concerned about the inroads being made by the Ansiedlungskommission as they themselves had no land to lose; but they were thoroughly angered by the refusal of the government to do anything about Polish language lessons in the school curriculum. Survival of the language meant survival of the nation; possession of land reflected the gentry power structure. Here the pace of social change in Prussian Poland is evident again. The growing urban class was willing to accept gentry claims that land possession represented the most important national treasure no longer; the very notion of wealth was becoming more flexible and diversified.

Whatever hopes the Poles may have placed in Robert Bosse to continue in the spirit of Zedlitz evaporated in January, 1893, after a sharp exchange with Jaździewski in the Prussian Abgeordnetenhaus that reminded many of the frequent Polish feuds with the departed Gossler. The spark that ignited the sharp exchange was a ruling by Poznań's school inspector Schwalbe on 5 January 1893, to seriously restrict the implementation of private language lessons. Citing misuse of the lessons, Schwalbe ordered that a) only those who already knew some German could attend b) only 2 hours per week per child c) pupils could not be forced to attend lessons d) homework was to be limited and e) pupils who performed poorly in other subjects could be refused lessons.(49) The enforcement of Schwalbe's ruling would be, as the Polish press realized, the virtual end to private language lessons.(50) Reaction ranged from deep anger to helpless prayers to heaven. The Kuryer had complained of Schwalbe's intervention with the Zedlitz decree as early as September, 1892, charging that he was illegally preventing children from attending lessons because he felt them to be Germans.(51) After the 5 January 1893 ruling the Kuryer demanded that he be removed and confidently predicted that a dismissal order from Berlin would arrive any day.(52) "(Schwalbe's edict) was written by pupils of the Falk-Bismarck school... The order to keep German children out of lessons is a direct contradiction of Zedlitz's decree of 2.10.1891... It has awoken a great amount of disappointment and anger here among citizens... Are Poles worse than the Jews? Why not investigate them?"(53) it asked on 11 January. The Orędownik pointed to the decree as proof that nothing more was forthcoming in educational and ecclesiastical affairs from the ministry in Berlin. "These restrictions will not hamper us too much - we have survived many similar restrictions before. What is more damaging is the constant delusion which our court party (Hofpartei) with the aid of its newspapers is trying to maintain. Only these delusions can save the political careers of our court party... The Archbishop's influence has been no help... Bosse's visit to Poznań and the memorial have had no results. The Kuryer and Dziennik are telling us that people in high places in Berlin love us, and that only the local officials are slow to catch on. This is a legend."(54) The Goniec wrote of the Schwalbe ruling, "Diese kalte Wasserstrahl wird die Nerven derjenigen beruhigen, welche 'neue' Stroemungen empfanden und denen die Augen oeffnen, welche 'neue' Horizonte sahen."(55)

On 11 January, 1893, Jażdżewski delivered a long speech in the Landtag on the unfairness of the educational system in Poznania and West Prussia and ended with a direct enquiry of Minister Bosse about the Schwalbe ruling.(56) Bosse replied that he knew nothing at all about the ruling, but added a long list of accusations against Polonization of German youth and the offensive nature of Polish agitation.(57) The ruling was eventually overturned by Bosse as being an illegal curtailment of the Zedlitz decrees, but so much ill will had been generated by his remarks critical of the Poles that the fortunes of the loyalists in the Prussian Landtag seemed buried forever. In February Bosse's quarrel with Jażdżewski dominated the five-day debate over the ratification of the budget (20-25 February). All Polish interpellations were rejected; all Polish arguments were countered in a way that reminded everyone of Gossler.(58) Tempers between Jażdżewski and the Kultusminister rose so high that only a superb self-control and linguistic nuances prevented open insults. An extra argument developed when Handelsminister Hans von Berlepsch ruled out Polish language classes in evening craftsmanship classes telling the Poles they should be happy with what they had.(59)

The clashes in Berlin over Schwalbe's ruling and the Ministry's budget cast a deep, dark shadow over German-Polish relations and signalled to a great many Polish and German observers that the "era of reconciliation" was over. A year before, the Dziennik had criticized Jażdżewski for speaking in an offensive manner to Minister Zedlitz; now it applauded his more offensive tone towards Bosse. "Jażdżewski's remarks in the Landtag were correct and necessary. Is this a sign of equality? Is this evidence that the government is seeking an understanding? ... We would not be worthy of our past or our dignity if we remained silent through all this and humbly tolerated our loss of nationality. Never! Never ever! (nigdy! przenigdy!) Whether the minister likes it or not we shall not take a step back from our adherence to the Prussian crown but at the same time will not cease demanding that which human and divine law assures us, codified and sworn to by (Prussian) monarchs".(60) After wavering between hot and cold on the Neue Kurs throughout 1890-1891, the Dziennik seemed to be finally taking a firmer stand against the loyalists.

The Postęp had never expected much from Bosse and wrote on 13 January, "Let the Minister's remarks be a lesson to us never to count on the good graces of Germans and count only upon ourselves. This attempt to win over the good will of Germans will harm us more than help us."(61) It is interesting to note the increasingly similar tones taken on a wide number of social and political issues by the Postęp and the Orędownik, both urban newspapers and both nearing the point of a complete break with the gentry political organization by early 1893. The events in educational and ecclesiastical matters from early 1892 through to the heated Landtag clashes between Bosse and Jaździewski had proved to both the "fundamental unchangeable character of today's system".(62)

5.2 New Currents in Prussia and Germany

The changes that took place in Prussia's cabinet in March 1892 after Wilhelm II withdrew the School Bill shows how closely the fate of the Poles was tied to the fortunes of ministers in Berlin. That the Poles were slow to recognize this attests to their firm belief that the Emperor was personally committed to reconciliation. In the words of the Kuryer in an article of 19 June, 1892, "The Kaiser himself stands at the head of the government and directs its machinery; it is from him that the real course emanates."(63) In this, however, the Poles were mistaken. Decision-making remained in the hands of three ministers: the Prussian Ministerpraesident, the Kultusminister, and the minister of the Interior. During 1892 all three positions received new leadership; Botho Graf zu Eulenburg was named Ministerpraesident and, when Herrfurth resigned in August, minister of the Interior, while Zedlitz was replaced by Robert Bosse. Both Bosse and Eulenburg believed in the growing danger of Polish agitation and frowned on Caprivi's policy of granting them concessions for votes in the Reichstag.

Leo von Caprivi was a most unlikely choice to succeed Bismarck in 1890 and from the outset evidenced little joy in his new role. He admitted to his adjutant, Carl von Wedel, in June, 1890, "Dass er seine jetzige Stellung weiss Gott nicht erstrebt habe und gluecklich sein wuerde, wenn er schon morgen als Pensionaer in Wiesbaden leben koenne."(64) As the months passed Caprivi's disillusionment grew with the difficulties of running a divided Reich and catering to the Emperor's ideosyncracies. In March 1891 Marie Radziwill noted, "Caprivi... sagte mir, dass er nicht mehr koenne, dass die Unruhe ihm den Schlaf raube und dass er sehr schlechte Tage hinter sich habe."(65) Schweinitz, returning from St. Petersburg wrote after meeting Caprivi in October 1892 that he seemed listless and tired, and lacked the will to go on.(66) During his four and a half years as Chancellor he tried to resign 10 times(67), and was never able to reconcile his high ideals with the political infighting characteristic of post-Bismarckian Germany. Most contemporaries felt that he was honest and conscientious, a man of great integrity, yet, as Radziwill wrote, "Tatsache ist, dass er von parlamentarischer Taktik nichts versteht."(68) After the collapse of the School Bill the Kaiser's mother, Victoria, wrote, "Caprivi is certainly not a statesman, but he is so honest and well meaning and conscientious and a safe man."(69) With the Centrum alienated by the withdrawal of the School Bill and the Conservatives beginning to voice ever greater concern over his promotion of free trade policies, Caprivi found himself increasingly isolated, encountering crisis after crisis. Von Holstein noted on 13 July, 1892, "The Chancellor is absolutely alone."(70) From 1892 onwards Caprivi's quarrel with Bismarck entered a new and more vociferous stage, and he was troubled further by the almost open rebellion of von Miquel and Graf Eulenburg in the Prussian government.(71) The last thing he needed was added controversy over an alleged liberal Polish policy which was not nearly so sympathetic to the Poles as his critics charged.

In August, 1892, Herrfurth resigned as minister of the Interior and the ministry was placed under the control of Graf Eulenburg.(72) Eulenburg came to be regarded in Prussia as a reactionary and his frequent quarrels with the Chancellor led to their mutual resignation in 1894.(73) He had no sympathy for Polish demands and took advantage of a Landtag appearance in March 1893 to dispel any Polish hopes that he would abandon the work of the Ansiedlungskommission.(74) Holstein wrote to his cousin,"There is one good thing about the selection (of Eulenburg to replace Caprivi).The coquetting with the Poles will probably cease, for there can surely be no such thing as an East Prussian who pursues a pro-Polish policy."(75) As with Kultusminister Bosse, Eulenburg was convinced that Polish "agitation" in Poznania and Upper Silesia had to be brought under control regardless of how the Polish Reichstag party voted.

The Polish press was not blind to the new leadership in Berlin and worried that the new ministers were not in the same mould as Caprivi and Zedlitz. The Orędownik, emphasized that the tone emerging from Berlin was very similar to that of Bismarck. It warned that Herrfurth's resignation signalled the victory of the liberal-Jewish parties and that the Conservative Eulenburg was anti-Catholic.(76) In October it wrote that Caprivi was not secure in his office and hinted that he was about to resign. "It is possible that Graf Caprivi, under such great pressure, will resign, and then a cooler wind will blow upon us Poles. Graf Eulenburg could become chancellor and he does not like Poles at all. Thank God that we survived the deep freeze under Bismarck,... and we will survive Eulenburg if we have to."(77) On 11 October it asked, "What is happening with Caprivi?... Caprivi cannot carry on without the support of the Catholics. For us Poles it makes no difference whether or not the Army Bill passes because we will have to pay higher taxes in any case. But Caprivi is not an indifferent matter for us."(78) When Bosse made his celebrated charges of 'great Polish agitation' in the Landtag the Orędownik noted sourly, "After Bosse's remarks it would be a great mistake to entertain any more hopes."(79) The Orędownik charged that the court party and its newpapers were hanging onto a slender thread in placing their hopes in Berlin. "They know (the dismal prospects T.K.) but they will not admit it because it would signal the end of their policies and their power... They know their rule is finished."(80)

The Kuryer ignored the personnel changes, perhaps not knowing what to say, and promoted instead its pet theory of a 'grand alliance' of all Christian parties in Germany against the liberals and Bismarck. It used the term 'we' when speaking of the Centrum party and continued to stress the friendship of the Conservatives and the Kreuzzeitung. "What we need is a coalition of all real Christian forces respecting law and order", it wrote on 29 July, 1892.(81) In August it was writing of a 'clerical-conservative Kartell', of which the Poles were an integral part, that was defending the Emperor and the government from the attacks of the Bismarck-led liberals.(82) By the end of the year, however, it was beginning to voice disapproval of the Centrum's critical stance towards Caprivi, foreshadowing a painful quarrel over passage of the Army Bill in mid-1893.(83)

The Dziennik was the first to notice the clear defeat for parliamentary democracy in Prussia suffered by the withdrawal of the School Bill and regretted the ministerial changes. On 5 August it wrote, "We Poles accepted with thankfullness the relaxation of Bismarck's extermination policies, although we were disturbed by the indecisiveness in the former minister of Interior. Unfortunately, he moved so slowly away from Bismarck that we still have not caught our breath and are still suffering from the brutal 'ukaz' of the former chancellor."(84) In early 1893 it noted that the former Kartell forces were aligning with the agrarians to remove Caprivi. "We must be very careful in these troubled waters", it warned on 26 February.(85) The Postęp worried that Eulenburg was unfavourably disposed towards the Poles. "It appears that our lucky star is always hidden behind many clouds", it wrote in mid-October.(86)

Of great concern to the Poles during 1892 and 1893 was the growth of new organizations hostile to Polish aspirations. The first movement to vociferously protest against alleged government indifference to the fate of Germans living in the Prussian East was the Alldeutsche Verband, formed in 1891, which acted as a lobby in Berlin to safeguard the interests of Germans worldwide.(87) Although their first statements were very general on the Polish question, by 1893, under the leadership of Alfred Hugenberg, the anti-Polish aspect became more prominent.(88) Attracting a number of Prussian Junkers to their ranks the Verband early on pointed to the danger of the government concessions in economic matters in the East and called for a more energetic Polish policy. Later on many of their demands became part of the platform of the Deutsche Ostmarkenverein, a similar lobby dedicated to the defence of German interests in Prussia's East.

The growing influence of anti-Polish voices in German public opinion led to familiar charges of 'Polish agitation'. These played a prominent role in Bosse's feud with Jaździewski in January-February 1893 debates in the Prussian Landtag. All Polish newspapers took these charges very seriously and did their best to refute them. The Dziennik was particularly upset at the new flood of attacks upon the Poles in the German press. In August, 1892, it bitterly wrote, "If one were to compile all the voices about Poland and the Poles that German newspapers often spread 'urbi et orbi', one could write a terrible romance novel in which every Pole is a destructive demon."(89) The Dziennik vehemently denied Bosse's allegations of great Polish agitation in Poznania. "Where are these great Polish agitators?", it asked rhetorically on 14 January, 1893, "This shows how far agitation against us has developed. The real agitators are local Pole-haters (polakożercy), journalists and officials. There are no facts to support the charge of Polish agitation. Our calm and reasonable stand is being described as Polish agitation."(90) After Bosse denounced the "national" Polish-language press in Poznania and its appeal in other provinces with Polish minorities, the Dziennik wrote, "It is a sad fact that Bosse used many of the same arguments as Gossler. Bosse called the Polish press a hatchery of disturbance-creating bacteria. We remind the minister that since Bismarck's dismissal we have taken a very loyal stance."(91) Instead of sympathizing with just Polish demands for equal rights in Prussia, "Bosse could only find fault with agitators. Now we cannot count on introducing Polish into the school system."(92)

The Kuryer viewed the whole affair over "great Polish agitation" as a plot hatched by the liberal newspapers to discredit the Poles in the eyes of the Emperor and the government. In early September, 1892, it wrote that "We could not admit to such agitation without telling a lie... The strong national movement is the fault of the other side's offences. The real "great Polish agitators" are German officials, bureaucrats and the chauvinist press out to strike fear into everyone's hearts."(93) It claimed that serious Germans had had enough of this foolish talk and that the anti-Polish campaign of German chauvinists was intended to keep four million people who had adequately proved their loyalty away from the throne and the state. (94) The Kuryer took issue with Graf von Ballestrem and other Centrum politicans who were pointing to disturbing evidence of a growing Polish consciousness in Upper Silesia. "No one has ever heard of great Polish agitation in Upper Silesia", it wrote on 9 October, 1892, "but Silesians are Poles and are aware of their status... Bismarck should be condemned for disturbing the calm in Upper Silesia... The legal position of the Silesians is different from ours... Our party cannot accept Silesian Poles into its ranks."(95) On 11 October the Kuryer charged that an informal press bureau had been formed in Poznań whose purpose was to feed German chauvinists ar liberal papers with incriminating material against the Poles.(96) After Bosse's charges in the Landtag the Kuryer admitted that the road to full equal rights in Prussia was a long and hard one. "Those who felt that Germans would appear before us in white robes begging forgiveness (for previous injustices T.K.) were misled... We do not take part in anti-state agitation. Whatever we do is a drop in the bucket when compared with anti-Polish agitation... We will continue to fight against all chauvinism, whether German or Polish."(97)

In early 1893 an opportunity arose for Polish and German landowners to co-operate once again on an issue of fundamental importance to them. In line with Caprivi's more liberal economic policies Germany was preparing a trade treaty with Russia that would open up the Czarist Empire to imports of German manufactured goods while reducing the tariff barriers on Russian wheat. (98) As with the anti-Socialist league in 1891, a number of Polish notables shared a common interest with German Junkers to oppose the treaty and the subsequent dro in income from their agricultural yields. The Polish party in the Reichstag had approved of the first set of Caprivi's trade treaties with Austria-Hungary and Italy without much dissent. These arguably strengthened the Dreibund and in any case had a small volume of trade in foodstuffs with Germany. With Russia, however, the situation was completely different. Angered beyond measure, East Elbian landowners called a huge rally at the Tivoli in Berlin on 18 February, 1893, and formed the Bund der Landwirte, another powerful lobby alienated by Caprivi and insistent upon his removal. The Bund went so far as to charge that the Chancellor was a traitor to his class; how else could a Prussian conservative conspire to bring about the ruin of Prussian agriculture?

Poznania and West Prussia were predominantly rural communities and the Polish element was wholly dependent upon agriculture for a living. The question of a healthy agricultural sector was uppermost in the minds of the gentry. The first statement issued by the Poles on the agrarian movement came on 15 February, 1893, when the Reichstag Party wrote a formal letter to the Dziennik. Polish landowners recognized the Bund's commitment to agriculture but they could not join the agrarian movement officially because of its political nature.(99) On 16 February Jan Żółtowski in the Abgeordnetenhaus used the opportunity of an address on an agrarian petition sponsored by the Free Conservative von Dziembowski to complain of anti-Polish legislation detrimental to both German and Polish landlowners and confirmed the very central nature of agriculture to

Polish economic well-being.(100) Dziembowski and Zółtowski attended the Tivoli congress and read out a statement which stressed the common interests of both nationalities for a sound agricultural economy. "We shall consider the plan of the agrarians when it is presented... In the name of agriculture we wish the Bund der Landwirte success."(101) It should be pointed out that the two Poles were under strict orders to speak only for themselves and not for the community. A special session of both Polish Parties in Berlin was called on 24 February, where the deputies debated whether or not to show sympathy with the agrarians and what stance to take on the upcoming debates over the Russian trade treaty. It was decided, "Poles everywhere are dependent upon agriculture for a living. If the league of German agrarians were only a lobbying group dedicated to the interests of agriculture, and did not have the political aim of overthrowing the Chancellor, then we could join it... Today we cannot speak out either for or against the treaties (with Russia T.K.) The parties should declare forcefully that they will not join with the league of agrarians although we sympathize with the aim of improving agriculture."(102) Throughout the province of Poznania local rural clubs (spolki rolnicze), led by Maksymilian Jackowski and the landowner-dominated economic clubs, (Centralne Towarzystwo Gospodarcze) led by Stanisław Zółtowski, debated the treaties and the German Bund; at a common meeting of 22 June, 1893, it was decided to take a wait-and-see attitude.(103)

The Polish press echoed the doubts expressed by its deputies when speaking of the Bund der Landwirte. As with the question of the expulsion of non-Prussian Poles, only the landowner-dominated press focused its attention on the Bund; for the urban newspapers the theme was of little interest. At first the Polish press applauded the effort to form a lobbying group in Berlin to protect the interests of agriculture; Pole and German alike were aware of the rapid pace of economic and social change linked to industrialization, and were dismayed at the transfer of power away from the countryside to the factories and large urban centres. Landowners of both nationalities resented the undue influence held in Berlin by "liberal-Jewish capitalists and speculators". What was lacking was a voice to offset the lobbying of industry-based groups, to remind the government of the needs of agriculture, the traditional backbone of a healthy Prussian state. The Wielkopolanin wrote on 8 February, 1893 that the enemies of the agrarians were, "liberals, free-thinkers, socialists and speculators," and concluded that the agrarians shared many common values with Poles.(104) "Polish papers assure the agrarians of our support and sympathy as we share the same fate of economic depression as German agrarians," it added the next day but also warned, "so long as you remain an agrarian-political lobby we shall support you. But we shall not be drawn into your organization."(105) Many areas of co-operation were envisioned by the Polish papers. The Kuryer proposed on 11 March that German and Polish agrarians open up an academy in Poznan for agricultural research, pressure the government to improve roads and rail communications in the Prussian East, promote irrigation, grant easy-credit loans, discourage emigration to Brazil or America and abolish the expulsion laws completely to assure a steady supply of cheap farm labour.(106)

Yet from the very outset the press was sceptical of the formation and aims of the Bund. German agrarians were, after all, Prussian Junkers, who had been hostile to the Poles for decades and who had participated fully in Bismarck's detested anti-Polish policies. When the congress in Berlin was announced the

Kuryer and the Dziennik urged whoever wanted to attend to go, but not to speak as representatives of Polish society.(107) "We should not get involved in German interest groups", concluded the Kuryer on 15 February. The Dziennik noted that Poles would support "all programs leading to an improvement in rural conditions. But we warn that these programs not be used for more clearly political aims, for undermining the position of the Chancellor or other actions intended to bring back the former Chancellor or his supporters."(108) On 2 March, the Dziennik wrote that the Poles had an obvious alliance with the agrarians to uplift conditions in the economically depressed East and voiced its faith in the deputies in Berlin that they would vote against the Russian trade treaty. (109) But as the weeks passed by the ever greater nationalistic rhetoric of the Bund alarmed the Poles. Increasingly the program of the Bund amounted to little else but a reinforcement of Bismarck's call for Caprivi's removal. What had begun an anti-liberal movement was now repeating the slogans of the liberals' champion - Bismarck. "The Bund is running to Bismarck", complained the Kuryer on 9 March, "(It) wants to exert pressure to elect candidates to parliament, to sponsor political organizations. (It) should support the Poles as well, but whoever is aware of our conditions knows that the majority of Germans will never do this."(110) The Kuryer's article called upon the Central Committee to issue a definitive statement: support the Bund or dissociate the Polish community from it?

Polish disillusionment with the Bund was fortified during the Landtag deliberations of early March 1893 on the Ansiedlungskommission. The Poles had hoped that at least some of the Conservatives could be won over to their side, and the Landtag deputies contemplated trading off Polish support for the Bund if the Conservatives changed their minds on the Commission. During deliberations on the upcoming Landtag sessions on the activities of the Commission the Polish deputies concluded, "We must give the Germans to understand that if they want Polish support to change agricultural laws, then they should give us their hands as well."(111) Nevertheless, the same combination of National Liberals, Free Conservatives and Conservatives defeated the Polish attempts to abolish the Commission. As the Kuryer wrote on 10 March, "They want our support but will give us none... We pay our taxes like first-class citizens but are treated like second." (112) The Dziennik was also bitter at the failure of the agrarians to redress the grievances of the Poles. "Let us be honest. Both the government and all the German parties, with the exception of socialists and some Catholics, are consistantly striving to Germanize us. Some are more violent, some less."(113) The sad fact was, as the Dziennik noted, that the Poles had no real friends among Germans, whether they shared the same economic interests or not. As the campaign against Caprivi escalated the Dziennik's views became more pronounced. "The Bund definitely has nationalistic tendencies and declared political aims. For us Poles this is a sign - we cannot join the Bund for any reason and cannot identify ourselves with it."(114) On 28 April it wrote, "Remember yourselves! Do not become unthinking advocates of the Bund der Landwirte... We must be true to ourselves. From the beginning we declared ourselves against joining the Bund. This will break up our unity."(115)

The failure of Poles and Germans to unite in a common effort to lobby in Berlin for greater concern over agricultural conditions is easier to understand when the principal aims and tactics of the Bund der Landwirte are examined. It wanted the rejection of the trade treaties and a greater attention in Berlin given to questions of the land; so also did most Poles. But it also demanded the removal of Caprivi in unison with Bismarck and became increasingly nationalistic - here the common interests with the Poles ended. After the Conservatives failed to support the Polish motions to abolish the Ansiedlungskommission in March 1893 further speculation of co-operation ended. Once again, the weak basis of a real Polish-German reconciliation was pointed out for all to see.

5.3 Bismarck Re-enters the Stage: The Propaganda War against Caprivi's Polish Policy

A key element in the transition period of the Polish-German relationship under Caprivi was Bismarck's re-emergence on the national political scene. After a short period of inactivity following his dismissal in March 1890 the 'aging titan' began to voice his invariably cricital views of Caprivi's leadership. One of his greatest admirers was Dr. Emil Hartmeyer, owner of the Hamburger Nachrichten, who placed his newspaper at Bismarck's disposal. (116) Other newspapers followed suit: the Westdeutsche Allgemeine Zeitung, the Muenchner Allgemeine Zeitung and the Leipziger Neueste Nachrichten. On May 23, 1890, Caprivi tried to cut off this formation of a "Bismarckpresse" by sending a circular to all newspapers warning of the detrimental effects on foreign opinion of disseminating Bismarck's anti-government statements.(117) When this did not work he decided to counterattack and engaged Otto Hammann as government press spokesman. But by 1892 Bismarck's fierce press campaign and Caprivi's clumsy response had begun to undermine much of the good will originally given to the Neue Kurs.

The quarrel between Bismarck and Caprivi has been the subject of several academic studies.(118) Bismarck warred against the Caprivi administration because of both personal animosity and serious differences of opinion of the future of Prussia and Germany. Until 1892, Caprivi was able to keep his foe at bay; he prevented the Emperor from sending Bismarck a good wishes telegram on 1 April 1891, and kept him away from Graf von Moltke's funeral that same month.(119) Wilhelm II needed little persuasion to isolate the former chancellor; in June 1891 he accused Bismarck of high treason and dangerous indiscretions and left his listeners with the feeling that he would soon order his arrest.(120) Yet Wilhelm II soon changed his tone, leading to speculation of an 'Aussoehnung' in 1892. There is a visible connection between the Emperor's trust in Caprivi and his quarrel with Bismarck; in 1890-92, when the Emperor's suspicions of Bismarck were at their height, so also was Caprivi's influence. As Caprivi progressively lost his control over Prussian affairs and annoyed the Kaiser with his numerous concessions in the Reichstag (such as the two-year service in the 1893 Army Bill) Bismarck inched his way back into favour. The logic of this situation led to the formal reconciliation of Kaiser and ex-chancellor in January, 1894, and to Caprivi's resignation later in the year.

There is also a relationship between Bismarck's posture and the attitude of Prussia's Polish community. The high point of Polish-German reconciliation came in 1891, when Bismarck was still in the Emperor's disfavour. In 1892, however, as Bismarck began to take a more assertive role in the formation of German public opinion, Polish hopes sank and a good deal of pessimism set in. For the Poles the relationship was clear. Prussia had only two ways to proceed with its Polish community: either the government abandoned Bismarck's policies and granted Poles full citizenship in a reformed Prussian state, or it adhered to Bismarck's reasoning and refused Poles equal rights.

It is difficult to over-estimate the importance of Bismarck to the Polish community and the Polish national cause in Prussia. As Richard Perdelwitz astutely observed, "Die gesamte polnische Gedankenwelt der ersten 20 Jahre nach 1870/71 ist beherrscht von der Persoenlichkeit Bismarcks; ihn hat man gehasst, wie selten einen Deutschen, ihn hat man aber auch gefuerchtet, wie kaum einen andern, weil man fuehlte, dass die polnische Frage fuer ihn eine andere Bedeutung hatte, als es bisher der Fall gewesen war."(121) The feeling of tremendous importance was mutual. As a recent biographer of Bismarck has written, "It is imposssible to understand Bismarck's Prussia and therefore Germany without keeping Poland in view... its reconstruction as an independent state was an everpresent menace, indeed a problem more immediate for him than the Austrian one. This hostility towards Poland exaggerated almost to the point of insanity was a product of Prussian history."(122) Every statement of the former chancellor even remotely connected to Poland was immediately reported in the Polish press and condemned. Berthold Wiegand noted, "Jedesmal wenn Bismarck in den Reden oder in Artikeln, die seine Feder errichtete, zu politischen Fragen Stellung nahm, fanden seine Worte in der polnischen Presse ein Echo, das den ganzen Hass dieser Nation gegen den grossen Staatsmann offenbarte."(123)

During the first part of Caprivi's administration, Polish press coverage of the former chancellor was characterized by ridicule and an irresistable urge to view his downfall as a just reward for many decades of unconstitutional rule. The consensus seemed to be that Bismarck should be happy he had not been called to account for his misdeeds and should stop meddling in Prussian affairs. As the ex-chancellor stepped up his criticism of the Neue Kurs the Poles began to perceive the threat in more serious tones and decried the impact his outrageous statements were having on the already bleak prospects for Polish-German reconciliation. An indication of the strong feelings held by the Poles about Bismarck can be seen in an article in the Postęp of 19 February, 1891, "Bismarck is a despot who cannot get used to being a normal mortal. His life' goal was to punish and destroy our poor nation... His hate-filled statements about us drove us to the point where we could no longer cry and protest against the hurt and injustice. So long as Poland remains Poland and Poles live in it, mothers will tell their children that Bismarck was the darkest spirit associated with the Polish cause."(124)

Poland's role in Bismarck's politics and worldview have been exhaustively examined elsewhere (125); only his contribution to the general decline of the Polish-German reconciliation under Caprivi need be recounted here. The relaxation of the expulsion laws and the permission for private language teaching was perceived as as a reversal of Bismarck's twenty-year Germanization policy and a threat to the German community in the Prussian East; while the nomination of Stablewski, one of Bismarck's greatest enemies in the Landtag, to the key position of Archbishop of Gniezno-Poznań touched a raw nerve and stimulated an unprecedented volley of attacks upon both Caprivi and the Poles.

The campaign carried on into the hot summer of 1892, when Bismarck journeyed to Bad Kissingen for his annual health treatment and onwards to Vienna to attend the wedding of his son, Herbert. Caprivi added fuel to the fire when he commanded the ambassadoror in Vienna, Prince Reuss, to treat Bismarck as a private citizen, and prevent an audience with Franz Joseph.(126) This letter, the infamous "Uriasbrief", smacked of personal intrigue that most observers had not credited Caprivi with, and it seriously undermined his prestige with conservative groups who had taken his earlier statements praising Bismarck's achievements at face value. Bismarck's return journey to Friedrichsruh turned into a triumphant procession of huge rallies, patriotic speeches and honours. Wherever he spoke, Bismarck attacked the Caprivi administration at its weakest points - the emergence of the Franco-Russian reconciliation and, linked to this, the Polish policy.

Thus, in an article in the Westdeutsche Allgemeine Zeitung of 26 June, 1892, Bismarck reportedly told guests at Friedrichsruh, "Das Schlimmste nun, was unter Caprivi geschehen ist, das ist die kopfueber erfolgte Abreissung aller Faden mit Russland... Unserer auswaertigen Politik konnte nichts verhaengnisvolleres angethan werden, als ein Einlenken in eine preussische Polenpolitik, welche Aehnlichkeit mit der oesterreichischen hat und den Russen fuer den Kriegsfall eine polnische Legion, fuer den Fall einer russischen Niederlage das Koenigreich Polen am Horizont zeigt. Das musste ein Kronstadt herbeifuehren. ... Caprivi hat aber unser Verhaeltnis zu Russland gerade an der Stelle vergiftet, wo Russland am allerempfindlichsten ist: in der Polenfrage." (127)

While in Vienna Bismarck granted an interview to Moritz Benedikt, editor-in-chief of the Neue Freie Presse, in which he stated, "Der deutsche Botschafter in Petersburg hat jetzt viel weniger Einfluss als frueher. Dazu treten noch andere Umstaende, insbesondere die Wandlung in der polnischen Politik Preussens. Man hat einen Polen zum Erzbischof gemacht und ihm eine Stelle gegeben, welche im Interesse der deutschen Politik einem deutschen Katholiken gebuhrt hatte... Die Politik gegenuber den Polen in Posen hat das Vertrauen, welches unsere Regierung frueher in Russland genoss, geschwaecht und unseren Einfluss ebenfalls herabgemindert."(128)

Bismarck continued to pounce on Prussia's Polish community during his return trip from Vienna. On 31 July, 1892 he addressed a crowd in the market square of Jena and denounced the policy of building a pro-government alliance consisting of the Centrum and the Poles. He also admitted the central role of the Polish factor in the Kulturkampf, "Ich halte sie (the Centrum Party T.K.) fuer gefaehrlich, nicht bloss in konfessionellen Fragen, sondern hauptsaechlich in nationalen Fragen. Sie broeckelt uns alles ab, was wir im Osten unsrer Grenzen in Polen germanisch angebaut haben und anbauen haben wollen. Den ganzen Kulturkampf koennten wir entbehren, wenn die polnische Frage nicht daran hing. Sie hing daran."(129)

In September Maximilian Harden confronted Bismarck with the remarks of Archbishop Stablewski on the role of the Polish community in Prussia. Stablewski had described Bismarck's influence as "Abschliessung der Nationalitaeten gegeneinander, Misstrauen hier und Verkennung dort, und voellige Laehmung des geistigen und wirtschaftlichen Lebens der Provinz."(130) More than any other person, Bismarck had contributed to the creation of a 'Prussian Ireland'. Bismarck responded fiercely. In a reference to present Polish loyalty he objected, "Diese Tonart kenne ich!... Sie zeigen uns freundliche Gesichter, weil sie wuenschen, wir moechten Russland schlagen und dann den 7 1/2 Millionen Polen -mehr gibt es ueberhaupt nicht auf der Welt- das ganze Gebiet der Ruthenen und Weissrussen restituiren, so etwa das, was sie im 14 Jahrhundert bei der Teilung Russlands in die Tasche steckten, bis ueber Kiev, Tschernigov und Smolensk."(131) In reference to Prussia's Polish provinces, Bismarck told Harden: "Die Polen betrachten Posen und Westpreussen nur als ein Uebungsterrain, wo sie ihre nationalen Besonderheiten bewahren konnen. Darum macht unsere neueste polnische Wirtschaft auch in Russland so viel boeses Blut, weil man da gleich den Glauben verbreitet, wir speculieren auf die Revolution der russischen Polen."(132)

Many of Bismarck's statements dealt with the 'Polish character'; the depiction of a stereotype Polish 'szlachta' or priest. The Pole was invariably charming - hence the success of the "Radziwilsche Einfluss" at the court of Wilhelm I(133) - clever, conspiratorial, and proud. He was also lazy, hopelessly romantic, tyrannical towards lower social classes, and incapable of directing his own political affairs in the days of modern nation states. Seeing his country partitioned among three powers the only logical course the Pole could follow was to turn the three against each other. Hence, Polish moves were part of a master plan to re-establish an independent Polish state. The idea that a Pole could be 'loyal' in either Prussia, Russia or Austria was plainly absurd; this suspect loyalty was only a tactical ploy to ruin the good relations among the partitioning powers. Thus, he said in the Muenchner Allgemeine Zeitung on 18 May, 1892, "Der politische Pole kann seine Ideale nur durch Krieg zwischen Deutschland und Russland verwirklichen, der Krieg ist seine Hoffnung, freilich auch nur dann, wenn Russland den Kuerzeren dabei zieht. Der Pole ist geschickter und klueger als der Russe... koennten die Namen veroeffentlicht werden, so wuerde man ueber die vielen Polen in der russischen Presse erstaunen."(134)

In late October 1892 Bismarck told his authorized biographer Hans Blum during a walk in Friedrichsruh: "Die Feinde des Friedens mit Deutschland sind aber in Russland in Wahrheit nur die Juden und namentlich die Polen... Mit unglaublicher Geschicklichkeit haben sich die Polen in alle Stellungen des russischen Reiches hineingelegt. Ihre alleinige Hoffnung ist der Krieg gegen Deutschland, bei dem Russland den kuerzeren zieht und das polnische Reich wiederstehen soll. Freilich wuerden wir auch bei einem sehr glanzenden Siege dazu am wenigstens die Hand bieten, dieses Reich wieder aufzurichten."(135)

Little of what Bismarck had to say in 1892 was new to the Poles; they had heard the same or similar charges since the January Uprising and the Alvensleben Convention of 1863. What was particularly disturbing was the enthusiasm shown Bismarck during his summer journey to Bad Kissingen and Vienna - and the numerous delegations from cities and districts who travelled to Friedrichsruh and Varzin to pay homage to the 'old master'. The situation was so serious that Kościelski felt obliged to refute the charges of false loyalty hurled at the Poles by Bismarck in a major Reichstag speech of 2 December, 1892.(136) The Polish press in Poznań followed Bismarck's statements with a mixture of fear and spite. The press had to refute Bismarck's charges and save what elements of good will that Germans still had to the Polish cause. In surveying their defence, one fails to find a well-thought out strategy or common line; rather each speech or article by the ex-chancellor was duly reported, analyzed and condemned statement by statement. The Dziennik felt called upon to lead the defence efforts as it was the voice of the gentry, and it was no secret that Bismarck's chief whipping post among the Poles was the 'Adelstyrannei'.(137)

The Dziennik rejected outright all of Bismarck's accusations. It attacked him as the greatest enemy of constitutionalism that Germany had ever known, reminding its readers that he had often opposed the monarchs as well as the majority of elected opinion in Berlin. "It is a strange thing when one who swept aside all constitutional considerations as chancellor now emerges as the defender of the constitution," it wrote in November, 1891.(138) It described the passage of the trade treaty with Austria in December, 1891, as a defeat for Bismarck and a visible triumph for Caprivi.(139) The Dziennik could not understand why the German press centred around Bismarck was making such a large affair over the Stablewski nomination. In March, 1892, it noted that Bismarck's anger at losing the struggle with Rome had turned into a persecution mania against the Poles. "But we cannot close our eyes to the fact that, apart from a few meagre relaxations which we received last year, the whole extermination campaign carried out by the government apparatus set into motion by the chauvinistic fury of the last administration, continues to exist... Many voices are calling for a return to the old policies. Everyday we receive new evidence that there is no question of a fundamental change in the direction of granting us justice and freeing us from the state of emergency that we find ourselves in."(140) In mid-June the Dziennik described the idea that Bismarck's removal was a misfortune for Prussia and Germany as "a fairy tale". "The changes that have taken place since his downfall in domestic politics have striven for general harmony and can only be for the general good."(141) By the end of June, when Bismarck was in Vienna for his son's wedding, the Dziennik was running two articles a day on the story. In response to Bismarck's interview in the Neue Freie Presse of 23 June the Dziennik called the ex-chancellor the "apostle of hatred and brutality", and went into some detail to prove that it was Bismarck who had begun the decline in German-Russian relations.(142) The Dziennik rose to support Caprivi in his weak defence against Bismarck's accusations. "There will be no reconciliation with Wilhelm II", it confidently predicted on 29 June, 1892. (143) Yet the Dziennik could not deny that Bismarck's triumphant return home from Vienna proved that his message of might over right had a large following within the Reich. On 8 July it wrote, "Bismarck is politically dead, but the harvest of anti-Polish hatred which he sowed is offering increasingly rich yields. The principle of ruthless repression has become absorbed into the German nation, and today, when the old man calls out with brutal cynicism that might goes before right, today, the fruits of his hatred are beginning to effect our position."(144) The Dziennik showed it could match the fierceness of German press attacks upon the Poles in full measure. In an angry article of 31 July its lead editorial was entitled, "Silence!", ordering the anti-Polish newspapers to cease their relentless campaign.(145) "Bismarck is criticizing just to criticize", it wrote on 1 November. "He is trying to frighten Germany and Russia over the Polish question. The idea of Bismarck as a great friend of Russia is ludicrous."(146) In a further article of 6 November, in response to the publication of Bismarck's interview with Hans Blum in the Leipziger Neueste Nachrichten of 4 November, the Dziennik called the ex-chancellor "the bushwhacker! (Napastnik!) ... It is he who initiated the Franco-Russian reconciliation".(147)

The Kuryer felt that it had the most influence of any Polish newspaper on the Prussian government, and here,in the direct confrontation between Caprivi and Bismarck, lay yet another excellent opportunity to express in no uncertain terms on whose side the Poles stood. Bismarck's criticisms were troubling because their ever-larger audience seemed to shatter the notion that all rational Germans were in favour of a Polish-German reconciliation. Already on the defensive because of the collapse of the School Bill and the lack of any further concessions in 1892, the Kuryer tried simultaneously to combat its Polish rivals and prove that Bismarck's statements were the rantings of a bitter old man who had absolutely no influence any longer in Berlin. In mid-April it charged that Bismarck's anti-Polish legislation was the real reason behind the existence of a Polish proletariat in non-Polish German states.(148) He had driven the Poles off the land and forced them to emigrate either to other parts of Germany or across the ocean. During the height of the Bismarck-Caprivi quarrel in July-August, 1892, the Kuryer saw itself in the front lines as part of the "government press", and accepted Bismarck's "declaration of war". Like the Dziennik, the Kuryer charged that it was Bismarck who had driven Russia into the arms of France and not Caprivi. "Bismarck is the one who ruined relations with Russia", the Kuryer wrote on 3 July, "The whole nation is behind the trade treaties. The question of war with Russia is as far away today as it ever was under his rule. Indeed, there are less military moves on our borders today."(149) The Kuryer laid great stress on the position of the Centrum party, and its chief organ Germania, for a central theme in Bismarck's fierce attacks upon Caprivi was his alleged pro-Catholic policy. It portrayed the whole quarrel as one between the ex-chancellor and the Emperor. "Bismarck's attacks are upon the government and Wilhelm II... His rallies have a clearly anti-Kaiser trend... Germans must decide either for Bismarck or for Wilhelm II."(150) In a major article of 17 August, 1892, "The Ex-chancellor and the Poles", the Kuryer described the Polish question as the most dangerous of Bismarck's attacks upon the government and called him as the "old father of lies". "We know how to appreciate the good will shown by the present government towards its Polish subjects. But Bismarck's policies must be removed! We are earnestly waiting for a full measure of justice."(151) The interview with Blum published in the Leipziger Neueste Nachrichten moved the Kuryer to compare Bismarck to Attila and Robespierre. "This is the unmasking of the wild, brutal aims of Bismarck's policies vis-a-vis the weak... We are at present going through a period of great trial, but we have faith in God that we shall emerge victorious. Through our patience and perseverence we are proving to the government that all the premises held by Bismarck were based on the same falsehoods as those he is now levelling at his monarch and his government."(152)

The middle-class newspapers were also upset at Bismarck's anti-Polish campaign of 1892, though it was less emphasized than in the gentry press. The Postep wonderered why Bismarck was not penalized for his blatant opposition towards his own government and monarch. "The effrontry of the man! When he was chancellor he tolerated no opposition. Now he is the leading opponent."(153)

Orędownik wrote early on that Bismarck should keep quiet and stay out of German politics, and felt his criticisms of Caprivi's Polish policies were "an insult to the Poles, to Caprivi and to the government".(154) The Orędownik followed his triumphant march home from Vienna through Jena, Weimar and Erfurt, but treated his anti-Polish statements less seriously than the gentry press. "He is philosophizing about something he knows nothing about. The old man is bored and needs to speak."(155) On 5 August, 1892, it called the Bismarckian press "liberal-Jewish", surprisingly, since Bismarck had also made some anti-Semitic statements during his travels. (156) What concerned Szymański the most was the charge that the Poles were anxious to bring about a war against Russia. In this aspect the Polish press was united; no speculation on a future war, a future Polish state, its future boundaries or alliances, and no pro-war sentiments. "Bismarck is charging that we want war... How many villages and cities would be burnt? (There would be) plunder, destruction and violence, all on our territory. Heaven help us!."(157)

Along with the genuine rage, what seemed to surprise the Polish press was the reception Bismarck was receiving throughout Germany and the inability of the Caprivi administration to effectively counter it. Like it or not, the Poles had to admit that the national mood in Germany had changed since the happy spring of 1890, and that the Polish minority could no longer count on the good will of their fellow German citizens.

5.4 The Notion of the Polish Factor in a European War

On 23 November, 1892, a weary but determined Chancellor Caprivi introduced his most important military bill in the Reichstag. In a long and convincing speech the Chancellor stressed the need for a major rearmament program in the face of the combined military might of France and Russia, who had just concluded a military convention in August.(158) Himself a professional soldier who needed no instruction on military matters, Caprivi made passage of the "Grosse Armeevorlage" his principal domestic concern from the end of 1892 to July of 1893, when the bill was finally passed. Many contemporaries observed that he seemed obsessed with the threat of a two-front war and a number of scholars of his chancellorship have stressed its very strong role in his policies.(159) General talk of war between Germany and Russia was nothing out of the ordinary in the last quarter of the 19th century and had been of great concern to Bismarck during the Bulgarian crisis of 1885-1888, but the soldierly way in which Caprivi went about improving Germany's armed forces combined with the non-renewal of the Reinsurance Treaty of 1887 and Wilhelm II's bombastic rhetoric of an imperial navy truly alarmed many Russian statesmen. Bismarck added to the Czar's suspicions when he told the Russian ambassador in Berlin, Shuvalov, that he was being dismissed for being too friendily disposed towards Russia.(160)

In the last decades of the 19th century many Austrian and German military men toyed with the 'Polish card' in the event of war against Russia. The strongest exponent Graf von Waldersee, a favourite of the Kaiser and Army Chief of Staff from 1888-1891. In November 1888 Waldersee wrote in his diary, "Der Kaiser gab zu, dass diese allgemeine politische Lage zu einen Krieg im Laufe des naechsten Jahres hinweise... Ich wies darauf hin, dass bei dem Ernst der Lage uns nichts uebrigbliebe, als die Polen auf unsere Seite zu bringen, indem wir eine Wiederherstellung Polens anstrebten."(161) Waldersee's successor as Chief of Staff, Alfred von Schlieffen, was also interested in the Polish card, and in early 1892, sent Hutten-Czapski on a fact-finding tour of Galicia and Russian Poland to determine the mood of the Poles. Hutten-Czapski reported that the Russian Poles were extremely restless and placed their hopes in German military might to rebuild a Polish state. "Diese koennte aber nur ein Weltkrieg herbeifuehren, und in einem solchen erscheint den russischen Polen Deutschland als die allein entscheidende Macht."(162) Wilhelm II received the same information from his American friend Poultney Bigelow, who travelled extensively throughout Russia in 1892 and noted the war-readiness of the Poles.(163)

The Polish response to combining with the Triple Alliance in an all-out war against Russia is one of the most intriguing in the long and troubled Polish-German relationship. Virtually everyone in Germany, whether well disposed towards the Poles or not, was convinced that Caprivi's milder Polenpolitik was tied to the Polish card in the event of a war against Russia.(164) Broadly speaking, it was felt that at the outset of hostilities Prussian Poles would instigate an insurrection in the Congress Kingdom, thus paralyzing Russian communications, while Prussian and Austrian Poles would lead the offensive to 'liberate' their cousins from Russian tyranny. Afterwards, a semi-independent Poland formed out of Galicia and conquered Russian territory under a Habsburg monarch would act as a German buffer state against future Russian adventurism.

The ever-present danger of a two-front war and the need to make use of the Poles affected even such confirmed opponents of Polish aspirations as Kultusminister Bosse. Bosse told Raschdau that he would have protested more energetically against Caprivi's Polish policy, but, "Freilich, gegenueber so hochpolitischen Erwaegungen wie dem Fall eines Krieges gegen Russland koenne er seine Auffassung schwer verteidigen."(165)

There is some evidence that Prussian statesmen held many high-level secret talks with Polish politicians on the war question. On 21 June, 1890, von Miquel told Graf von Wedel, "Der Vorsitzende der polnischen Fraktion, Herr von Kościelski, den er vor einigen Tagen in dieser Hinsicht befragt, habe ihm offen erklaert, dass die Polen unbedingt auf Posen und Westpreussen verzichten, dass sie sich mit einer eventuellen Wiederherstellung des Koenigreiches ausschliesslich auf Kostens Russland zufrieden erklaerten."(166) Not long after, Wedel and Miquel had a meeting with Kościelski in a Berlin Hofbrauhaus, of which Wedel left the following account: "In der langen Unterhaltung die ich mit ihm und Miquel fuehrte, bestaetigte mir Koscielski im wesentlichen das mir von Miquel mitgeteilte... Er betonte auch mir gegenueber, wie sie ein fuer allemal auf Posen und Westpreussen verzichteten und wie ihr ganzes Ziel auf einen engen Anschluss an Deutschland, als der Vormacht westlicher Kultur, gerichtet sei."(167)

Von Tiedemann told Chancellor Caprivi about a conversation he had had with a Polish deputy in 1890 in which the latter had said that a war with Russia was inevitable and that an independent Poland was needed, one that would reach out not for Prussian territory but for Kiev and Odessa.(170) Before his quarrel with Caprivi over the Pussian school bill, Miquel seemed open to the idea of using the Poles against Russia. Waldersee noted in his diary on 23 February, 1891, "Fuer den Kriegsfall mit Frankreich und Russland taucht meine alte Idee auf, Polen wiederherzustellen. Miquel interessiert sich dafuer."(169) On 6 November, 1891, Kościelski sent a memorandum to the Chancellor in which he promised that the Poles would act as "Treu Wacht an der Weichsel", provided they were treated as equal citizens.(170). As relations with Russia improved after passage of the Russian trade treaty in early 1894, Prussian statesmen lost interest in the question, and tried to cover up their earlier contacts with Polish deputies. Waldersee wrote on 30 September, 1894, "Ich fuerchte jetzt nur zahlreiche Indiskretionen, da man seinerzeit mit einflussreichen Polen in sehr leichtfertiger Weise ueber die Insurrektion des Koenigreiches gesprochen und ihnen allerhand verhiessen hat."(171)

It is important to keep the high-level, secret discussions between leading Poles and Germans in mind when reviewing the Polish attitude towards an imminent war between Russia and Germany and the prospects for resurrecting an independent Polish state. Once again, as in the case of anti-Socialism and common agrarian interests, influential Poles and Germans evidenced at least an awareness of the need to act together towards mutual interests. All of this, however, was unknown to the average Pole in Prussia, and from the press accounts one can gauge no trace of it. The Polish newspapers were unanimous in declaring their disinterest in a future Poland and their abhorence at the very idea of war. The strongest criticism were found in the Dziennik. Faced with a torrent of reports about Polish eagerness for war and a new Poland, the Dziennik replied, "It is a great falsehood that Poles are entertaining any hopes in a rebuilt Poland, as the National Zeitung tells us... Polish publicists have always treated such programs as empty fantasies and can only express their surprise that the National Zeitung links the new Archbishop to the rebirth of Poland." (172) The Dziennik consistently refuted the notion that Poles were ready to give up their claims to Poznania in a future Polish state. "It is a lie that our deputies in Berlin spoke about an independent Poland without Poznania", it declared in November 1891.(173) In December 1891 the Dziennik took issue with Hans Delbrueck, who had argued for a milder Polish policy in view of the need to utilize the Poles in a war situation. "He would eagerly rebuild Poland in the boundaries of the Congress Kingdom while Germanizing Poznania and West Prussia, at least to two-thirds. We can never agree to these sorts of ideas and there will never be agreement between us and academics like Delbrueck until the other side (the German T.K.) gives us equal rights as citizens alongside Germans."(174)

In 1892 speculation about an imminent war grew as France swung more closely towards Russia and as the German-Russian tariff war escalated. The Dziennik did all in its power to counter such talk. In January 1892 it wrote, "No one can claim that any Polish organ has brought up the idea of a resurrected Poland. All this is speculation in the German press... We have no need to enter into this sort of speculation."(175) In response to Bismarck's claims that the Poles were insiduous intriguers conspiring to disturb the peace of Europe, the Dziennik retorted fiercely, "We feel that a war between Germany and Russia can come about due to severe economic rivalry, but we attach no hopes at all to such thoughts of war. We are far removed from using any means to fan the flames of hatred between nations because we know that we shall have to pay the costs. We cannot stop militarism and war fever, and only the blind can accuse us of being European troublemakers."(176) The idea of exacting "promises" from Germany in an upcoming war, as Bismarck had insinuated, was similarly denied by the Dziennik. "Poles (are accused) of pushing towards war against Russia. A successful war... would create a dangerous threat to Germany in the form of a pro-French independent Poland. We will not enter into the speculation on Polish designs on Germany in the event of war - what sort of logic do (German) authors use? They are moved by hatred."(177) As the government prepared to introduce its new Army Bill, the Dziennik voiced its disapproval of increased military spending and warned that unlimited armaments resulted in the impoverishment of the country.(178) When the Bill was being hotly debated in the Reichstag the Dziennik made its position clear - it opposed the Bill because of the great economic hardships it would impose upon Prussian Polish society. On December 1, 1892, it wrote in hopeful tones that the Polish deputies would vote to defeat the bill. "We have been impoverished to the absolute minimum, impoverished due to the policies of the Prussian government towards us and the eastern provinces."(179) The Dziennik rejected the idea of voting for the bill to "reward" the Caprivi administration for its relaxation of Bismarck's anti-Polish legislation. On 11 December it wrote bitterly, "Despite the loud proclamations of a new era everything has remained the same. As before, we are second-class citizens. We can only vote for a bill if a real dismantling of Bismarck's system follows."(180) After Komierowski's statement in the Reichstag of 7 December tentatively rejecting the bill, the Dziennik wrote approvingly, "The Party rightly stated it would vote against the bill in view of the conditions in which we are forced to live, conditions that have not changed for the better despite the procalmation of the new era. We thank the Party for its clear and firm decision which is in full agreement with the convictions, feelings and opinions of all Poles."(181)

In repudiating the notion of the "Pole-intriguer" the Dziennik was following its long-upheld policy of organic work and positivist philosophy. From its inception in 1859 the Dziennik had rejected the tradition of conspiracy and insurrection linked to the Uprisings of the first half of the 19th century. This determination was reinforced by the utter failure of the desperate January Uprising of 1863 in Russian Poland. Poles had been deluded too long by dreams of their own invincibility and outside intervention on their behalf. Independence, it it ever came about, would be linked to a new European order that recognized the self-determination of all nations and undid the injustice of the partitions. Quite likely this could only take place through a major conflagration in which the Poles would be called upon to fight for opposing sides; but in any case it was out of Polish hands and not worthy of speculation. Certainly war should not be welcomed with any enthusiasm. The duty of Poles in Prussia was to struggle peacefully and legally for full civil and national rights, not get involved in anyone's war games, and not dwell tpp long on eventual independence. It is on the last point that the conservative gentry worldview was to clash violently with the more forceful National Democrats, who viewed independence as a self-evident national goal.

The Orędownik was fatalistic about the position of Poles in a future European conflict and discounted the views of many sympathetic German newspapers like the progressive Frankfurter Zeitung, which held that the Poles' only hope lay with Germany. "There are a few among us who think in this way, but surely no one who thinks politically can be taken in by such talk. In a future war, Prussian Polish subjects will stand by Germany, and the Czar's subjects will stand by Russia. And when it comes to a bloody encounter Poles will fight against Poles; some will be fulfilling their duties to the German Emperor and others to the Russian Czar. This is how Poles who think politically feel today, and from the hard fate we have to face, we draw the correct lesson that for Poles here and there the only answer is to do one's duty vis-à-vis the state and at the same time work hard at the strengthening of our national, social and religious basis."(182) Taking the side of one partitioning power against the other was futile. Rather than the salvation that Poles should be waiting for, war promised only suffering and the cruel fate of brother combating brother.

The Orędownik ridiculed German press speculation on a future Poland and denied that the Poles would fight with any enthusiasm. All such theories, whether voiced by Polish deputies in private or found in the pages of German newspapers, were promptly repudiated. Particular scorn was reserved for the warlike statements made by the loyalist deputies Kościelski, Mielżyński and Stablewski. They had no business touching on the question of Germany's external security until it was threatened, and senseless criticism of Russia could only worsen the fate of Poles in the Congress Kingdom.(183) Why should Poles in Prussia loudly proclaim their readiness to fight when they were not being called upon to do so by the government? The Poles should keep away from the war question and concentrate on the existing problems of second-class status within Prussia. In 1892 Szymański began to use the derogatory term 'partya dworska' to describe the loyalist initiative centred around Kościelski and the Kuryer. He argued that the gentry were trying to create of a Polish state without the Prussian territories, where they could emigrate with their capital and prolong their archaic domination over Polish society. The challenges posed by Germanization and the emerging Polish middle class in Prussia had proved too strong to combat; why not then give up the national cause in Prussia and move eastwards? The Oredownik defiantly proclaimed that the middle class would remain and carry on the fight.(184)

As attention in Germany focused on Caprivi's upcoming Army Bill in late 1892, the Orędownik dwelt on the dilemma of the Reichstag party on which way to vote. On 28 September it wrote, "Caprivi can count on the Centrum and the conservatives. What about the Poles?... The policy of do et des is impractical and unrealistic. We should not link the Army Bill to language teaching in our schools. The deputies should vote for the Army Bill to show that Poles meet their civic obligations. If no concession is given, then we shall have proof that the government does not care about us. Then we shall be able to play with an open hand... Today our whole society does not know what its political relationship to the government should be."(185) The Army Bill was important because of Caprivi's future. "The most important feature for us in the Army Bill is the chancellor. What will change towards us if he goes? He is the only one in the government who is not in favour of stronger measures. If he cannot get the support of the Catholics, then it is all over."(186)

In December the Orędownik again criticized Kościelski and the Reichstag deputies for engaging in needless anti-Russian rhetoric. "He (Koscielski) does not have the support of our society, because a large segment knows how meaningless it is when he states that we do not want war with Russia while the court party threatens her. We in Prussia have no need to think about how the Polish question will look after war against Russia breaks out. But we have a hundred important reasons to examine our state here and what our condition will be under Prussian rule."(187) In response to Komierowski's 16 January, 1893 Reichstag statement on the Polish position on the bill, the Orędownik wrote, "We cannot understand why our deputies continue provoking Russia... They have been told a hundred times that their threats are senseless and can only bring suspicion upon our fellow Poles in Russia; yet they continue to believe that these threats will win them approval in Berlin."(188) The middle-class opposition felt that the gentry powerbrokers were manipulating the war question to hold on to their positions in society. It was that the Polish people (lud) took matters into their own hands.

As the spokesman of the loyalists, the Kuryer was hard pressed to balance the two notions of Polish peaceful intentions and loyalty to Germany in a period of intense German-Russian rivalry. On the one hand, the Kuryer wanted its German neighbours to know that the Poles were fully prepared to defend the Reich against all external enemies, while on the other it vigorously denied that they constituted a war party. Thus it defended Stablewski's anti-Russian thrust at the Thorn rally in September 1891 while denying Bismarck's accusations of "Pole-intriguer" in 1892. In May 1892 the Kuryer wrote favourably about Julius von Eckhardt's book "Berlin-Rom-Wien", in which the Baltic German defended Caprivi's foreign policy against severe domestic critics. "If only the example of Austria triumphed in Prussia over the example of Russia (with regard to the Poles T.K.) Then the relationship between the Polish people and the Crown would surely meet his (Eckhardt's T.K.) expectations."(189) Yet, only a month later, the Kuryer dismissed a pamphlet by the Austrian von Ledersteger, "Die oesterreichische Mission im Osten", which urged that Poland be resurrected after a victorious war against Russia and that Germany give up Poznania in exchange for Russia's Baltic provinces. "These sorts of projects on paper to rebuild Poland are a dime a dozen and all of them up to now may be realized in heaven but not on earth."(190)

When Harden interviewed Archbishop Stablewski in August, 1892 the Kuryer noted the reference to a possible German-Russian conflict. "Of some importance is the remark about a future German-Russian war, in which Russia would be seriously weakened to the advantage of a new state between Russia and the present borders of Prussia. German chauvinists are appalled at the idea of a new Poland."(191) Yet when a German newspaper hostile to Polish aspirations, like the Leipziger Neueste Nachrichten, similarly hinted that Kościelski and Stablewski were counting on a rebellion in Russian Poland in the event of war and the set-up of a new Polish state, the Kuryer's ridiculed the story.(192) The full dilemma of the Kuryer's indecisive position on the war question emerges in an article commenting on Komierowski's 16 January, 1893, Reichstag speech. "We agree fully with the aims of the Triple Alliance. But we should be cautious when discussing Russia. Our speeches and their unfortunate interpretation in the press place tremendous pressure on our countrymen under Russian rule. We have our doubts about the Army Bill because of financial burdens, but the need for a stronger army is clear as we are faced with the Asiatic danger."(193)

One sees, then, a two-faced Polish attitude towards "tilting" in the direction of Germany in the event of a German-Russian war. In all fairness, it is difficult to conceptualize any other response. To say nothing at a time of German-Russian tension would leave the Poles open to the charge of Pan-Slavism and weak civic behaviour; yet to carry the banner of Prussian militarism too highly would alarm German public opinion and produce consternation within Polish society. That they were keenly aware of the possibilities in light of the Franco-Russian rapprochement and the growing German-Russian rivalry cannot be doubted. Wilhelm Muenstermann noted, "Nimmt es Wunder, wenn die Polen diese aussenpolitische Konstellation der europaeische Kraefte mit ihrem unverhohlenen Programm der Wiederherstellung des Polenreiches aufnahmen?"(194)

The Polish press routinely reported on atrocities and injustices which occurred in Russia were compiled by the Prussian police in a special file, "Secrete Akten betreffend die Haltung polnischer Presse gegenueber der Kaiserlichen Russischen Regierung".(195) However, from the pages of the Polish press one fails to discern a war party. The failure of the Caprivi administration to go farther and dismantle Bismarck's anti-Polish laws prevented the platform of Polish loyalism from becoming a war platform. In contrast to the Poles in Galicia, who were confident that the Habsburg monarchy would release hold of Galicia to a rebuilt Poland, Poles in Prussia knew full well that the Prussian monarchy would never give up Poznania and West Prussia, regardless of the outcome. The Polish press, then refused to be drawn into any enthusiastic pro-German warmongering, not only because much of the suffering would be felt by Poles in all three partitioned zones, but also because whatever the outcome they could not count on the inclusion of Prussian Poland into a new Polish state. With Caprivi's resignation and the onset of a new phase in German-Polish antagonism under Fuerst zu Hohenlohe-Schillingfuerst and in particular von Buelow, any thought of a 'Prussian orientation' similar to the Russian orientation of the National Democrats or the Austrian orientation of Pilsudski's revolutionaries vanished.

5.5 Loyalism in Crisis - the Significance of 1892 in the Versoehnungsaera

After the encouragement of 1891 Polish public opinion was truly disappointed and frustrated at the paucity of concessions in 1892. The only concession of that year was the decision in July by von Berlepsch to exempt Polish economic organizations from state controlled auditing. This allowed the Poles to appoint their own "Revisoren" and keep their own books without the fear of government manipulation. This concession was brought about by the efforts of the popular priest Piotr Wawrzyniak, head of the Polish "Związek Spółek Zarobkowych i Gospodarczych w W. Ks. Poznańskim i w Prusach Zachodnich.", the Polish co-op credit movement. Wawrzyniak was able to win the confidence of the minister because of his reliability, but the concession would never have been made had it not been for an improvement in Polish-German relations overall. (196)

The privilege was granted on 14 July, 1892 and was never repealed despite intense pressure from the Ostmarkenverein. Future German commentators viewed this concession as one of the most important, if not the most important, of the Caprivi era. Ludwig Bernhard wrote in 1907, "Durch diese Verleihung, die die preussische Regierung spaeter bereut hat, wurde das polnische Finanzwesen in Posen und Westpreussen juristisch einig, abgeschlossen und unabhaengig von der Kontrolle der Behoerden."(197) Wilhelm Muenstermann wrote in 1936, "Durch die Aufhebung des Genossenschaftsgesetzes vom Jahre 1889 wurden die polnischen Genossenschaften von jeder behoerdlichen Kontrolle befreit. Die Polen konnten jetzt unbehindert ihr national-politisches Ziel durch das Mittel eines wirtschaftlichen Staates im Staate verfolgen."(198)

Yet one would look in vain for any mention of this important economic concession in the pages of the Polish language press in Poznań. It went by unnoticed by all the newspapers, including the middle-class Orędownik and Postęp which were supposed to be dedicated to economic matters. Even the Kuryer, always looking for government concessions to bolster its loyalist platform, failed to take notice of the Berlepsch ruling. Hans-Christian Sievers has written that the failure of the Poles to respond to the Revisorenrecht of July, 1892 signalled the first breakdown in the Versoehnungsaera and discouraged the Caprivi administration from going any farther in its Polish policy.(199) One is sorely tempted to ask why the Poles failed to take notice of this very important privilege granted them. As with the case of the Rentengutsgesetz of 1890, the reason appears to lie with the fact that economic benefits did not seem to count as concessions. The Poles believed that they were being systematically impoverished in Prussia due to their second-class citizenship status, despite evidence of greater material prosperity. Caprivi, however, was prevented from granting any significant concessions in the areas of language and the Ansiedlungskommission by his own nagging doubts of Polish aspirations and by the fear of antagonising the Kartell parties and the Bismarckfronde, which, by late 1892, was beginning to play an increasingly active role in German affairs.

Throughout 1892 the attitude of most of the Polish press to the Neue Kurs shifted from enthusiasm to pessimism. This conversion was nowhere more evident than in the Dziennik, which had always been sceptical of the Neue Kurs, though it had moved towards greater government support after the appointment of Stablewski to the Archbishopric of Gniezno-Poznań. By mid-1892, however, with the collapse of the School Bill and the resignations of Caprivi as Ministerpraesident and Graf Zedlitz as Kultusminister, the prevailing tone of the Dziennik was once again reserved and gloomy. In response to an article in the Progressive Frankfurter Zeitung praising Caprivi's far-sighted Polenpolitik, the Dziennik observed, "We are struck by this somewhat optimistic view of the Prussian government's policy towards the Poles. The 'New Course' has been inaugurated, but up to now we are still waiting for it to be felt here. The concessions offered since the bankruptcy of Bismarck's policies are still insignificant, though very civilized. The interest of the state itself demands that it break fully with the persecution of the ex-chancellor. We demand full equality - only then will we believe in a new course."(200)

At the end of the year the Dziennik wrote, "We bid farewell (to 1892 T.K.) with less optimism than when we greeted it. We welcomed the year with great and genuine joy. We were convinced that loyalty would move the government to a more meaningful progress towards justice and equal rights... It must get rid of all emergency laws that were designed to exterminate our nationality."(201) Similar year-end statements are found in the Dziennik's surrogate paper the Wielkopolanin.(202)

Of the remaining gentry papers, the Goniec Wielkopolski had long ago stated its intractable opposition to the loyalist initiative and hence it showed little disappointment at the end of concessions in 1892. For the Goniec there was little to choose between Caprivi and Bismarck, just as there had been little to choose between Bismarck and his predecessors; the only solution to the Polish question in Prussia was Polish independence and the inclusion of Poznania and West Prussia into a new Polish state. Its disagreement with the loyalists changed to fury as the Reichstag deputies continued to promote trust in the government despite the evident failure of their policy. It compared the Reichstag and Landtag parties in April, 1893, "...denn die Landtagsfraktion ist das (cleverness, dignity and political acumen T.K.) voll und ganz, die Reichstagsfraktion dagegen ist nach wie vor eine Null. Die vorwiegend aus Magnaten zusammengefasste Reichstagsfraktion hat nicht den geringsten Sinn fuer unsere Nationalbeduerfnisse und sitzt in Wolken gehuellt da."(203) Such outbursts infuriated the more moderate Polish papers, especially the Kuryer, which accused the Goniec of undermining government confidence in the Polish community. Clearly, Kultusminister Bosse had the Goniec in mind when he spoke of the 'greater Poland agitation' in the Polish press.(204)

The Kuryer, so optimistic at the end of 1891 with the appointment of Stablewski, could only advise its readers to wait for better days ahead. The Poles had undertaken a great challenge, and they had to persevere in order to be victorious at the end. Other newspapers charged it with discounting Polish dignity and abandoning Polish national goals. All such criticism was met with the standard response, "Let us persevere! (Wytrwajmy!). Those who were expecting the government to surrender fully to Polish demands were being unrealistic, but with time and with unconditional loyalty towards the Crown and the state, Polish demands would eventually be met. The Kuryer's platform in late 1892 was spelled out in an article of 30 November, "Nasza Droga" (Our Way). "Our critics keep talking about losing our national dignity... The political position of the Poles as we see it is as follows: we shall support the government everywhere where the interests of the state, the general good and our own interests are concerned."(205) While all other Polish papers lost hope in further government concessions after the Landtag sessions in which Jażdżewski was sharply answered by Bosse on 11 January, 1893, the Kuryer refused to accept this as the end of an era. On 19 January it wrote, "The general charge is that Polish society has been duped and deluded by the politics of reconciliation (polityka ugodowa) We call it the politics of reason that is pursued by people who think correctly. The politics of reconciliation is not the politics of illusions, but that of hard work. This trial of patience is very difficult and exhaustive and often drives the statesman to despair. ... perseverant work and once again work (is necessary T.K.)".(206)

The middle-class newspapers counselled the Polish community to work hard in the direction of economic self-sufficiency and growth. Whereas the Polish loyalists in Berlin were counting on the Prussian government to improve their lot, the Postęp and the Orędownik felt that there was nothing to expect from the Prussian government. The Postęp wrote on 21 October, 1892, "Some of our political wizards expected that with a change of face the government would smile on them in a friendly manner. They were correct; the government smiled but it did nothing else... We cannot satisfy our dearest friends (nasi najserdeczniejsi, an ironic term for German neighbours T.K.) no matter what we do. Even if we stood on our heads; even if we enthusiastically contributed to a stronger army and navy; this would not help us because the Germans would not be grateful and the government would not re-introduce the obligatory teaching of Polish in our schools... If the government does not give us this then we will not believe in the new course at all and never will believe in it."(207) Szymański urged a practical loyalty, but was deeply concerned at the way in which the Party's loyalty was being expressed. "One has to be moderate and balanced in these statements of loyalty. Loyalty has to serve our existence and our interests. The sort of loyalty where one falls on one's knee at every opportunity and beats one's forehead not only stimulates disgust among Germans but also tremendous emotions among us... If we do not maintain a level of moderation in our declarations then after a while the Polish voters will cease to recognize their deputies and the deputies will cease to recognize their own society."(208) In June 1892 the Orędownik noted that, "No kind words will be of any practical benefit until language teaching is returned to the schools. The chances of this are becoming gloomier and gloomier...They (the loyalists T.K.) make promise after promise and then express regret when they cannot keep them." (209) The Orędownik was alarmed at the storm of anti-Polish publicism in Germany during 1892, in contrast to the friendlier tones that everyone had noted in 1890 and 1891. On 26 July, 1892, it wrote, "The slightest kind word by the government to the Poles evokes a flood of critical comment from the German press warning the government not to make concessions to us. This is how the Germans honestly express themselves about us, despite the 'new course', and despite the loyalism to Prussia which we trumpet from morning to night... The Germans are taking deadly aim straight at the hearts of the Polish middle and lower classes."(210) In its year-end review the Orędownik declared 1892 to be "disheartening". "We expected more after the promises of the court party. To a point a change is evident. The authorities are gentler, more pleasant and more understanding. But in essence all has remained the same. Bismarck's old course has remained the same. Colonization and the school system have not changed.(211)

The period begun with the collapse of the School Bill (March, 1892) and the refusal of the Landtag to repudiate the Ansiedlungskommission (March, 1893) signalled an important shift in Polish public opinion. In the words of Komierowski, "Poles in Poznania were discontented with the lack of success in 1892. Criticism at home made our job in Berlin that much more difficult."(212) This growing discontent led to the most severe domestic crisis in Prussian Polish history - the Populist secession of 1893.

NOTES TO CHAPTER FIVE

1. For a detailed study of the Prussian School Reform Bill of 1891-1892, see Kurt Richter, Der Kampf um den Schulgesetzentwurf des Grafen Zedlitz-Truetzschler vom Jahre 1892 (Halle, 1934). In regard to the effects in Prussian Poland, see Karwowski, Historya Wielkiego Księstwa..., vol. 3, pp. 17-24.

2. Schulthess'..., 1892, pp. 20, 75; Herzfeld, Johannes von Miquel..., vol. 1, p. 304.

3. Herzfeld, Johannes von Miquel..., vol. 1, p. 304. See also Richter, Der Kampf ..., p. 25.

4. Schulthess'..., 1892, p. 75.

5. Massow, Die deutsche innere Politik..., pp. 127-128; Nichols, Germany after Bismarck..., p. 187.

6. Rich, Friedrich von Holstein..., vol. 1, p. 391.

7. Eugen Richter in the Reichstag, 26 March, 1892. Berichte Rtg., 1892, vol. 7, p. 5014.

8. Dziennik Poznański, 13.2.1892, no. 35; 25.2.1892, no. 45; Kuryer Poznański, 14.2.1892, no. 36.

9. Orędownik, 27.2.1892, no. 47.

10. Ibid., 1.5.1892, no. 100.

11. Dziennik Poznański, 28.1.1892, no. 22.

12. Ibid., 6.2.1892, no. 24.

13. Ibid., 3.3.1892, no. 52

14. Postęp, 4.2.1892, no. 27.

15. Orędownik, 15.1.1892, no. 11.

16. Kuryer Poznański, 7.2.1892, no. 30.

17. Dziennik Poznański, 20.2.1892, no. 41; Orędownik, 19.2.1892, no. 40.

18. Postęp, 20.2.1892, no. 41.

19. Ibid., 23.2.1892, no. 43.

20. Kuryer Poznański, 18.2.1892, no. 39.

21. Orędownik, 14.2.1892, no. 36.

22. Ibid., 26.2.1892, no. 46.

23. Wielkopolanin, 10.6.1892, no. 132.

24. Postęp, 12.3.1892, no. 59; Dziennik Poznański, 6.3.1892, no. 54; 9.3.1892, no. 56; Kuryer Poznański, 9.3.1892, no. 56; 18.3.1892, no. 64.

25. Dziennik Poznański, 25.3.1892, no. 70.

26. Ibid., 29.3.1892, no. 72; 8.1.1893, no. 6.

27. Postęp, 24.3.1892, no. 69; 27.3.1892, no. 71.

28. Orędownik, 27.3.1892, no. 71; 6.4.1892, no. 79.

29. Kuryer Poznański, 7.4.1892, no. 80.

30. Dziennik Poznański, 2.4.1892, no. 76.

31. Kuryer Poznański, 26.7.1892, no. 169.

32. Bosse described his Poznań visit in the Abgeordnetenhaus on 11 January, 1893. See Berichte Abg.H., 1893, vol. 1, p. 299. For the memorial presented Bosse, see Karwowski, Historya Wielkiego Księstwa..., vol. 3, pp. 20-21.

33. Kuryer Poznański, 28.6.1892, no. 146; 1.7.1892, no. 148.

34. Dziennik Poznański, 23.6.1892, no. 142.

35. Ibid., 3.7.1892, no. 150.

36. Orędownik, 29.6.1892, no. 147.

37. Ibid., 10.9.1892, no. 207.

38. Postęp, 3.12.1892, no. 278.

39. Kuryer Poznański, 28.12.1892, no. 297.

40. Ibid., 16.10.1892, no. 238.

41. Ibid., 2.10.1892, no. 226.

42. Ibid., 17.1.1893, no. 13.

43. Dziennik Poznański, 10.6.1892, no. 132.

44. Ibid., 21.9.1892, no. 221.

45. Orędownik, 15.9.1892, no. 211.

46. Ibid., 14.9.1892, no. 210.

47. Ibid., 26.6.1892, no. 145.

48. Ibid., 26.10.1892, no. 246.

49. Dziennik Poznański, 11.1.1893, no. 8.

50. PP-Posen, file no. 4806a, p. 12.

51. Kuryer Poznański, 13.9.1892, no. 209.

52. Ibid., 12.1.1893, no. 9.

53. Ibid., 11.1.1893, no. 8.

54. Orędownik, 12.1.1893, no. 9.

55. PP-Posen, file no. 4806a, Goniec Wielkopolski, 11.1.1893, no. 8.

56. Ludwik Jaździewski in the Abgeordnetenhaus, 11 January, 1893. "Unter dem 5 Januar 1893 erlasst der Kreisschulinspektor Schulrath Schwalbe in Posen eine umfangreiche Verfuegung, worin er den Erlass des Herrn Ministers Zedlitz vollkommen einschraenkt, derartig einschraenkt, dass eigentlich die Wirkung desselben ganz lahm gelegt wird." Berichte Abg. H, 1893, vol. 1, p. 297.

57. Kultusminister Robert Bosse in the Abgeordnetenhaus, 11 January, 1893. "Ja, meine Herren, wenn alle Polen so loyale Preussen waeren, wie der Herr Abgeordnete Dr. v. Jaździewski und eine grosse Anzahl der, wie ich gern anerkenne, namentlich hier in Berlin lebenden Polen, auch manche Polen in der Provinz, dann wuerde man ueber diese Frage anders denken, dann wuerde die Regierung anders handeln, dann wuerde sie die straffen Zuegel vielleicht etwas nachlassen koennen. So liegt aber die Sache nicht. Die Agitation hat sich nicht gemindert, sondern sich verschaerft... Meine Herren, das kann uns, einer deutschen Regierung, doch auch niemand uebelnehmen, wenn wir heute die Kinder nicht zu national-polnischen Aspirationen erziehen. Wenn wir die national-polnische Agitation in der excessiven Form, in der sie jetzt in Posen auftritt, und sich sogar auf Oberschlesien erstreckt, auf eine Provinz, die niemals zum Koenigreich Polen gehoert hat, staerken sollen, dann saegen wir einfach den Ast ab, auf dem wir sitzen. Das kann keine deutsche Regierung, das kann kein deutscher Kultusminister jemals machen." Ibid., pp. 288-289.

58. For example, Bosse's rejection of the Polish appeal to eliminate state funds to further the education of exclusively German youth in the Abgeordnetenhaus on 21 February, 1893, "Meine Herren, wir haben gewisse Bezirke, in denen die Deutschen in der Minoritaet und die Polen in der Majoritaet sind, und in diesen Bezirken muessen wir die Deutschen stuetzen. Nur zum Schutze und der Stuetze der Deutschen sind diese Fonds bestimmt, und dazu koennen wir sie nicht entbehren." Berichte Abg. H., 1893, vol.2, p. 1011.

59. Handelsminister Berlepsch in the Abgeordnetenhaus, 25 February, 1893. "Ich bin nicht in der Lage, wie die Sachen einmal liegen, in den beiden Provinzen an den Fortbildungsschulen den polnischen Unterricht einzufuehren." Ibid., vol. 2, p. 1171.

60. Dziennik Poznański, 19.2.1893, no. 41.

61. Postęp, 13.1.1893, no. 10.

62. Orędownik, 3.3.1893, no. 51.

63. Kuryer Poznański, 19.6.1892, no. 139.

64. Zwischen Kaiser und Kanzler, ed. Wedel,..., p. 104.

65. Radziwiłł, Briefe..., p. 52.

66. Schweinitz, Denkwuerdigkeiten..., vol. 2, pp. 442-443.

67. Michael Balfour, The Kaiser and his Times (London, 1964), p. 178; Tyler Whittle, Kaiser Wilhelm II. Eine Biographie (Muenchen, 1979), p. 191.

68. Radziwill, Briefe...p. 71.

69. Letters of the Empress Frederick, ed. Sir Frederick Ponsonby (London,1928) ed. p. 234. See also Massow, Die deutsche innere Politik..., p. 104.

70. Rich, Friedrich von Holstein..., vol. 1, p. 392.

71. Nichols, Germany after Bismarck..., p. 183-184.

72. Schulthess'..., 1892, p. 130.

73. Röhl, Germany without Bismarck..., p.59; Balfour, The Kaiser..., p. 175.

74. Ministerpraesident Graf Eulenburg in the Abgeordnetenhaus on 7 March, 1893. "Ich muss sagen, in welchen Rechten sind sie denn durch dieses Gesetz beschraenkt? In gar keinem. (Zuruf bei den Polen: in allen!)...Irrthuemlich nach meiner festen Ueberzeugung ist aber die Meinung, dass, wenn wir das Gesetz aufheben wollten, damit die Wuensche unserer polnischen Mitbuerger befriedigt (sehr richtig! rechts) und die Agitationen desjenigen Theils unter ihnen, der sich denselben hingiebt, verringert oder auf ein anderes Gebiet uebergefuehrt werden wurden." Berichte Abg. H., 1893, vol. 3, pp. 1405-1406.

75. Rich, Friedrich von Holstein..., vol. 1, p. 385.

76. Orędownik, 13.8.1892, no. 185.

77. Ibid., 6.10.1892, no. 229.

78. Ibid., 11.10.1892, no. 233.

79. Ibid., 18.1.1893, no. 14.

80. Ibid., 14.1.1893, no. 11.

81. Kuryer Poznański, 29.7.1892, no. 172.

82. Ibid, 28.8.1892, no. 197.

83. Ibid., 15.11.1892, no. 262.

84. Dziennik Poznański, 5.8.1892, no. 178.

85. Ibid., 26.2.1893, no. 47.

86. Postęp, 15.10.1892, no. 237.

87. The standard study of the Alldeutsche Verband is Alfred Kruck, Geschichte des Alldeutschen Verbandes 1890-1939 (Wiesbaden, 1954). A more modern study is Roger Chickering, We Who Feel Most German. A Cultural Study of the Pan-German League (London, 1984). For the relationship of the Verband to Prussia's Polish minority, see Edgar Hartwig, Der Alldeutsche Verband und Polen in: Wissenschaftliche Zeitschrift der Friedrich Schiller Universitaet Jena, 19 (1970/1972), pp. 251-273. See also Witold Jakóbczyk, "Antypolski projekt Związku Wszechniemieckiego", in: Przegląd Zachodni 19 (1958), pp. 318-329.

88. Hartwig, "Der Alldeutsche Verband und Polen...", p. 252; Muenstermann, Die preussisch-deutsche Polenpolitik..., p. 47ff; Land, Die Konservativen und die preussische Polenpolitik..., p. 37ff.

89. Dziennik Poznański, 11.8.1892, no. 183.

90. Ibid., 14.1.1893, no. 11.

91. Ibid., 24.2.1893, no. 45.

92. Ibid., 17.1.1893, no. 13.

93. Kuryer Poznański, 3.9.1892, no. 202.

94. Ibid., 10.9.1892, no. 207.

95. Ibid., 9.10.1892, no. 232.

96. Ibid., 11.10.1892, no. 233.

97. Ibid., 25.2.1893.

98. Ludwig Bergstrasser, Geschichte der politischen Parteien in Deutschland (7 edition, Muenchen, 1952), p. 154.

99. Dziennik Poznański, 17.2.1893, no. 39.

100. Jan Żółtowski in the Abgeordnetenhaus, 16 February, 1893, "Meine Herren, als solche fuehlen wir uns hier sozusagen als geborene Vertreter der Interessen der Landwirthschaft ohne Ruecksicht auf den Beruf, den wir in unserem Privatleben haben. Wir werden deshalb immer mit denjenigen zusammengehen und ihre Bestrebungen unterstuetzen, die die Interessen der Landwirthschaft gewaehrt wissen wollen...Meine Herren, wir sind also mit Ihnen darin einverstanden, dass die Nothlage der Landwirthschaft eine grosse ist. Wir kennen die Verhaeltnisse genau, wir wissen, dass sie gerade zu trostlose sind. Wir wissen auch, dass die Rufe und Klagen, die jetzt aller Orten erhoben werden, nicht von nimmersatten Agrariern ausgehen, sondern von Leuten, die um ihr taegliches Brot ringen und die sich jetzt in ihrer ganzen Existenz gefaehrdet sehen." Berichte Abg. H. 1893, vol. 2, p. 918.

101. Dziennik Poznański, 19.2.1893, no. 41.

102. BK., Ms. no. 1456/57 meeting on 24.2.1893.

103. Jakóbczyk, Patron Jackowski..., p. 261; Trzeciakowski, Polityka polskich klas..., p. 132.

104. Wielkopolanin, 8.2.1893, no. 31.

105. Ibid., 9.2.1893, no. 32.

106. Kuryer Poznański, 11.3.1893, no. 58.

107. Ibid., 15.2.1893, no. 37.

108. Dziennik Poznański, 21.2.1893, no. 42.

109. Ibid., 2.3.1893, no. 50.

110. Kuryer Poznański 9.3.1893, no. 56.

111. BK., Ms. no. 1456/57 meeting on 2.3.1893.

112. Kuryer Poznański, 10.3.1893, no. 57.

113. Dziennik Poznański, 10.3.1893, no. 57.

114. Ibid., 23.3.1893, no. 68.

115. Ibid., 28.4.1893, no. 97.

116. Massow, Die deutsche innere Politik..., p. 106.

117. Full text in Schulthess'..., 1892, pp. 115-116.

118. For a more detailed study of the Bismarck-Caprivi rivalry, see Robert Geis, Der Sturz des Reichskanzlers Caprivi (Berlin, 1930); Wolfgang Stribrny, Bismarck und die deutsche Politik nach seiner Entlassung: (1890-1898) (Paderborn, 1977); Walter Held, Caprivi und Bismarck (Leipzig, 1931); Julius von Eckhardt, Aus den Tagen von Bismarcks Kampf gegen Caprivi (Leipzig, 1920); Adolf Rosinski, Fuerst Bismarcks Kampf gegen den Grafen Caprivi (Berlin, 1897); Lothar Gall, Bismarck. Der weisse Revolutionaer (Frankfurt, 1980), pp. 709-729.

119. Radziwiłł, Briefe..., p. 42; Meisner, Der Reichskanzler Caprivi..., p. 713.

120. Radziwiłł, Briefe..., p. 46. Lothar Gall writes, "Kaiser Wilhelm II erwog gelegentlich allen Ernstes Bismarck wegen 'Hochverrat' den Prozess machen zu lassen, und erklaerte wiederholt, wenn der ehemalige Kanzler so weiter mache, werde er 'doch noch eines Tages in Spandau endigen'". Gall, Bismarck Der weisse Revolutionaer..., p. 711.

121. Perdelwitz, Die Posener Polen..., p. 66.

122. Edward Crankshaw, Bismarck (London, 1981), p. 149. See also Ernst Engelberg Bismarck: Urpreusse und Reichsgruender (Berlin-Ost, 1985), p. 542.

123. Wiegand, Die anti-deutsche Propaganda..., p. 10.

124. Postęp, 19.2.1891, no. 40.

125. For a more detailed study of Bismarck and the Poles, see Hans Wendt, Bismarck und die polnische Frage (Halle, 1922) and Józef Feldman, Bismarck a Polska (Kraków, 1937). Most of Bismarck's statements about the Poles were compiled by Friedrich Koch for the Deutsche Ostmarkenverein in Bismarck ueber die Polen (Berlin, 1913). For Bismarck's Polish policies and Germany's neighbours, see Martha Pfeifer, Bismarcks Polenpolitik im Hinblick auf Russland (Marburg Diss. Phil. 1925), and Johannes Behrendt, Dis polnische Frage und das oesterreichisch-deutsche Buendnis 1885-1887 (Berlin, 1927).

126. The text of the letter to Reuss is found in Schulthess'..., 1892, p. 115. For the impact on public opinion in Germany, see Massow, Die deutsche innere Politik..., p. 106. For the reception of the "Uriasbrief" in the Polish community, see Komierowski, Koło polskie w Berlinie..., p. 239.

127. Bismarck, GW., vol. 9, pp. 205-206.

128. Interview with Moritz Benedikt in: Bismarck, GW., vol. 9, p. 217.

129. Speech at the Jena Main Square 31 July, 1892 in: Bismarck, GW., vol. 13, p. 474. See also vol. 15, "Erinnerung und Gedanke", p. 333: "Der Beginn des Culturkampfes war fur mich ueberwiegend bestimmt durch seine polnische Seite."

130. Maximilian Harden, "Erzbishof v. Stablewski ueber die Polenfrage", in: Die Zukunft 1 (1892), p. 7.

131. Bismarck to Harden in: Bismarck, GW., vol. 4, pp. 184-185.

132. Ibid.

133. "Dagegen war natuerlich der Radziwilsche Einfluss am Hof, nicht natuerlich mein Cultus-College, dessen Frau und Ihre Majestaet die Koenigin...Der Trager des Radziwilschen Einflusses war der juengere Bruder, Fuerst Bogislav, auch Stadtverordneter von Einfluss in Berlin." GW., vol. 9, p. 206.

134. Muenchner Allgemeine Zeitung 18.5.1892, in: Penzler, Bismarck nach seiner Entlassung...vol. 3, p. 233.

135. Bismarck to Hans Blum 31.10.1892, in: GW., vol. 9, p. 285.

136. Józef Kościelski in the Reichstag on 2 December, 1892, "Meine Herren, es ist in unser Aller lebhaftester Erinnerung, dass der Reichskanzler Fuerst Bismarck uns in diesem Hause vor einigen Jahren die ungeheuerliche Beschuldigung ins Gesicht geschleudert hat, wir arbeiteten darauf hinaus und wir sahen unser Heil darin, einen Krieg zu entfachen, wobei Preussen zertruemmert werden soll. Meine Herren, nun erfahren wir durch einen Leipziger Reporter, dass der Fuerst Bismarck seine Ansichten ueber uns geaendert und unseren Idealen oder unserem Trachten und Wirken diametral entgegengesetzte Ziele setzt: nun sollen wir angeblich als maachtige Intriguanten dahin arbeiten, einen Krieg heraufzubeschwoeren, der Russland vernichten soll." Berichte Rtg., 1892, vol. 1, pp. 94-95

137. Bismarck to Maximilian Harden in: GW., vol. 9, p. 285.

138. Dziennik Poznański, 17.11.1891, no. 263.

139. Ibid., 20.12.1891, no. 291.

140. Ibid., 16.3.1892, no. 57.

141. Ibid., 11.6.1892, no. 133.

142. Ibid., 26.6.1892, no. 145.

143. "The Government's Answer to the Assaults of the National Zeitung" Ibid., 29.6.1892, no. 147.

144. Ibid., 8.7.1892, no. 154.

145. Ibid., 31.7.1892, no. 174.

146. Ibid., 1.11.1892, no. 251.

147. Ibid., 6.11.1892, no. 255.

148. Kuryer Poznański, 17.4.1892, no. 89.

149. Ibid., 1.7.1892, no. 148; 3.7.1892, no. 150.

150. Ibid., 2.8.1892, no. 175.

151. Ibid., 17.8.1892, no. 187.

152. Ibid., 25.10.1892, no. 245.

153. Postęp, 4.8.1892, no. 177.

154. Orędownik, 22.12.1891, no. 292; 29.6.1892, no. 147.

155. Ibid., 3.8.1892, no. 176.

156. Ibid., 5.8.1892, no. 178.

157. Ibid., 3.11.1892, no. 252.

158. Chancellor Caprivi in the Reichstag, 23 November, 1892. Berichte Rtg., 1892, vol. 1, pp. 7-20.

159. Nichols, Germany after Bismarck..., p. 40; Ernst Deuerlein, Deutsche Kanzler. Von Bismarck bis Hitler (Muenchen, 1968), p. 66; Sigrid Kumpf-Korfes, Bismarcks 'Draht nach Russland' (Ost-Berlin, 1968), p. 134)

160. Schweinitz, Denkwuerdigkeiten..., vol. 2, p. 396.

161. Waldersee, Denkwuerdigkeiten..., vol. 2, p. 14. See also Waldersee to Graf Yorck von Wartenburg, 31.5.1888: "Um das Ziel, unsere Feinde gruendlich lahmzulegen, zu erreichen, bin ich nicht fuer einen Marsch ueber die Grenzen von Polen hinaus, sondern fuer eine Wiederherstellung Polens, so unbequem dies fuer uns auch ist. Dass die Polen spaeter Forderungen wegen Ostseehafen stellen werden, ist wahrscheinlich, wir koennen da aber etwas vorbeugen durch einen Zollverein. Gibt es keine Zollgrenze, so sind Danzig-Koenigsberg so gut polnische Hafen wie preussische. Vorlaeufig wuerde das wiederhergestellte Polen, dem man natuerlich eine ansehnliche

Groesse geben muesste, doch seine ganze Kraft zusammennehmen muessen, sich auf weitere Kriege gegen Russland vorzubereiten." in: "Briefwechsel zwischen dem Chef des Generalstabes Grafen Waldersee und dem Militaerattache in Petersburg Grafen Yorck von Wartenburg 1885-1894" ed. Hans O. Meisner, in: Historisch-Politisches Archiv 1 (1930), p. 164.

162. Hutten-Czapski, Sechzig Jahre..., vol. 1, p. 168.

163. J.G.C. Roehl "A Document of 1892 on Germany, Prussia and Poland" Historical Journal 7 (1964) pp. 143-149.

164. For example, see Hans Delbrueck, "Die Polenfrage",in: Preussische Jahrbuecher 78 (1894), and Herzfeld, Johannes von Miquel..., p. vol. 1, p. 495.

165. Raschdau, Unter Bismarck und Caprivi..., p. 290.

166. Wedel, Zwischen Kaiser und Kanzler..., p. 108.

167. Ibid., p. 109.

168. Georg von Weddern, Das schlafenden Heer der Polen (Berlin, 1912), p. 35.

169. Waldersee, Denkwuerdigkeiten..., vol. 2, p. 196

170. Trzeciakowski, Polityka polskich klas..., p. 62.

171. Ibid., vol. 2, p. 323

172. Dziennik Poznański, 26.9.1890, no. 221.

173. Ibid., 26.11.1891, no. 271.

174. Ibid., 18.12.1891, no. 289. For an in-depth analysis of the views of Hans Delbrueck on the Polish question, see Annalise Thimme, "Hans Delbrueck als Kritiker der wilhelminischen Epoche (Duesseldorf, 1955), especially pp. 77-100, and Jerzy Krasuski, "Zagadnienie polskie w publicystyce Hansa Delbruecka 1887-1917", in: Przegląd Zachodni 14 (1958), pp. 64-81

175. Ibid., 20.1.1892, no. 15.

176. Ibid., 10.6.1892, no. 132.

177. Ibid., 11.9.1892, no. 208.

178. Ibid., 6.10.1892, no. 229.

179. Ibid., 1.12.1892, no. 276.

180. Ibid., 11.12.1892, no. 284.

181. Ibid., 14.12.1892, no. 286.

182. Orędownik, 22.4.1892, no. 92.

183. Ibid., 19.1.1893, no. 15.

184. Ibid., 10.6.1893, no. 130.

185. Ibid., 28.9.1892, no. 222.

186. Ibid., 16.10.1892, no. 233.

187. Ibid., 8.12.1892, no. 282.

188. Ibid., 19.1.1893, no. 15.

189. Kuryer Poznański, 12.5.1892, no. 109.

190. Ibid., 9.6.1892, no. 131.

191. Ibid., 14.10.1892, no. 236.

192. Ibid., 12.11.1892, no. 260.

193. Ibid., 18.1.1893, no. 14.

194. Muenstermann, Die preussisch-deutsche Polenpolitik..., p. 10.

195. PP-Posen, file no. 4876.

196. BK., Ms.1527, J. Kusztelen "Ks. Piotr Wawrzyniak" vol. 2, p. 551; Sitarek, Rola kredytu w rozwoju..., p. 97.

197. Bernhard, Das polnische Gemeinwesen..., p. 139.

198. Muenstermann, Die preussisch-deutsche Polenpolitik..., p. 45. For further comments on the Berlepsch ruling, see Baier, Der deutsche Osten..., p. 20.

199. Sievers, Die Innenpolitik des Reichskanzlers Caprivi..., vol. 2, p.223.

200. Dziennik Poznański, 14.5.1892, no. 111.

201. Ibid., 3.1.1892, no. 2.

202. Wielkopolanin, 3.1.1893, no. 2.

203. PP-Posen, file no. 4806a, p. 771: Goniec Wielkopolski 18.4.1893, no. 88.

204. Kultusminister Bosse in the Abgeordnetenhaus on 13 February, 1893 "Sehen Sie sich die polnische Presse an! Mit ganz wenigen Ausnahmen ist es nicht eine ruhige, sondern eine wilde Agitation, die man dort gegen alles, was deutsch ist, einschliesslich aller Autoritaet fuehrt. Und dem sollte man nicht entgegentreten?" Berichte Abg.H., 1893, vol. 2, pp. 803-804.

205. Kuryer Poznański, 30.11.1892, no. 275.

206. Ibid., 19.1.1893.

207. Postęp, 21.10.1892, no. 242.

208. Orędownik, 1.4.1892, no. 75.

209. Ibid., 19.6.1892, no. 139.

210. Ibid., 26.7.1892, no. 169.

211. Ibid., 31.12.1892, no. 300.

212. Komierowski, Koło polskie w Berlinie..., p. 240.

Chapter 6. The Polish Community Divided Spring-Winter, 1893

6.1 The First Reichstag Vote of May, 1893 on the Great Army Bill

It would be instructive at this point to focus attention on the explosive controversies within Poznania's Polish community in the spring and summer of 1893 considering them in two aspects: a political struggle within the established ruling groups between sceptics and loyalists during the Neue Kurs, and a class struggle between the gentry and the rising middle class. The first of these was manifested in the quarrel between the Kuryer Poznański and its gentry critics, the Dziennik Poznański and the Goniec Wielkopolski, over the question of how the Poles should vote in the all-important issues of the Army Bill and the Russian Trade treaty; but the second, and without a doubt the more important, was manifested in an open challenge made to the Polish political apparatus in Poznania by Szymański of the Orędownik and his middle-class followers in Poznań, Bromberg, Inowrocław, and a number of smaller towns. Although the challenge in 1893 was not strong enough to knock the old order out of power, it stimulated a number of emerging currents in Prussian Poland that within a decade were to form a far more serious and unrelenting challenge - the National Democrats.

The Army bill votes of 1893 were without a doubt the most controversial issues faced by Polish parliamentarians since the founding of the Reich. Unlike the small Army Bill of 1890, whose passage was assured whichever way the Poles voted, the 1893 bill had as many opponents as advocates and its passage was in doubt from its introduction.(1) The main difference from 1890 was the Centrum's swing from Caprivi. It was angered by the withdrawal of the Zedlitz School Bill and found no reason at all to support a stronger German armed force in time of peace. At the outset all parties in the Reichstag found faults with Caprivi's bill, and it was not until January 1893 that the Kreuzzeitung announced its support.(2) The constellation of forces in the 1893 bill resembled closely the rivalry of the Kartell parties and the opposition under Bismarck; Caprivi could only win if he dislodged enough opposition deputies to the government's side.

The Polish deputies were well aware of the significance of their votes in 1893. When Bismarck introduced the Septennat in 1887, the Poles demonstratively walked out of the Reichstag in protest (3); in 1890 they decided to break with the tradition of protest on German armaments and voted for Caprivi's modification of the Septennat, but were well aware that their votes were purely symbolic in Berlin. In 1893, however, the Poles could, and eventually did, prove to be the decisive factor in the bill's passage. Debate within the Polish press began even before its introduction in the Reichstag in November 1892, and the newspapers divided in much the same manner as in 1890.

The Dziennik, which had opposed the 1890 bill because it felt that it was up to the Prussian government to make the first move of reconciliation, equally opposed the 1893 bill because it felt that Caprivi had not made a serious effort to dismantle Bismarck's anti-Polish legislation, particularly in the area of Polish language rights. Its position crystallized in February, 1893, after

Kultusminister Bosse rejected all Polish interpellations in the debates over the education budget in the Abgeordnetenhaus. It criticized Kościelski for his indiscreet remarks reprinted by Deutsche Warthe and Germania that the Party would vote for the bill. "Let us remind Pan Kościelski that no deputy is allowed to state his views separately (to German newspapers T.K.) This is against the statutes of the Party."(4) In the same issue the Dziennik appealed to the deputies to distingiuish between the difference between the concepts of "state" and "fatherland". "We recognize the interests of the state, but when speaking about the "fatherland" we recognize our national interest. We have only one beloved fatherland deeply embedded in our hearts, and codified in Prussian law (in the address of Friedrich Wilhelm III on 15.5.1815). Let us not confuse one with the other and openly declare our love for our fatherland."(5) This article was a critique of loyalist views that attempted to stimulate a "Prussian patriotism" in the Polish community while maintaining a separate Polish identity. On 21 March the Dziennik contented itself with the remark that "There is still no word on how our deputies will vote... Doubtless, our personal, and to a point political, sympathies lie with Graf Caprivi, because of all the statesmen who have been called upon to deal with us in recent times, he has proved himself a just and noble man. (But) our deputies should grant only those concessions (to Caprivi T.K.) which our economic and social conditions warrant."(6) On 29 March, the Dziennik declared that, "the military and technical aspects of the bill are not convincing. (The bill) must lead to militarism and would economically devastate our country. Windthorst had seen this earlier... We feel it is the responsibility of our deputies to reject the bill... In the Landtag we hear the same old story: despite assurances of peaceful, friendly intentions all our proposals have been rejected. Today, we know that the so-called 'new era' has not changed anything in respect to us, and that the old system continues in general despite our loyal posture."(7) Continued uncertainty within the Polish Party throughout the spring months exasperated the Dziennik, and by April it was demanding that the deputies take a public stand. On 2 April it announced in a lead editorial, "Time to Resolve the Matter", "Those who thought that support for the 1890 army bill would help us have been disabused both in the Reichstag and the Landtag. We demand justice, but we do not want to make justice an item for bargaining."(8) The Dziennik was referring to rampant speculation in the German press that the Poles had made a "deal" with Caprivi and Bosse - language lessons in the schools for votes on the army bill. In late April, it examined all the arguments both pro and con and came out strongly against the bill. Declaring confidently that "We represent more of our society than the Kuryer Poznański", the Dziennik refuted the idea of "passive" and "active" politics which the Kuryer was using to promote voting in favour. (9) Yet in this final flurry before the actual vote in the Reichstag, the Dziennik was forced to admit defeat. "As we have been told in Berlin, our Party has decided, by a small margin to vote in favour of the Huene compromise. Because we have voiced different views both due to political and economic factors, we shall reserve comment until a formal declaration is made."(10)

The Goniec was enraged at the way the loyalists had given their support to the government on a number of key issues and hurled all sorts of vile accusations at Kościelski, ranging from treason to political immaturity and egotism. On 25 March in a lead article entitled "Neue Laesterungen", the Goniec ridiculed Kościelski's faith in a German-Polish reconciliation and repeated its standard charge that the loyalists had sold out Polish interests. "Die Herren Polen sind in Berlin dazu da, um uns vor Unrecht zu schuetzen, und nicht dazu, um deutsche Huehneraugen zu kurieren."(11)

The Postęp's objections to the Bill vote were wholly pragmatic in nature. Voting yes would be both disruptive and expensive. "It is true", the Postęp wrote on 29 October, 1892, "that voting for the project will bring our deputies to the notice of the imperial court, but the nation will not receive anything... Poverty among our people is continually on the rise... The people (lud) are against increasing the armed forces of Germany. There is not enough to eat in Germany...." (12) The next day the Postęp wrote, "We are certain that our deputies will vote against the Army Bill and thus show that they cannot, in all good conscience, place greater burdens upon our society. Their constituency clearly demands this. Let them not get involved in 'great politics'."(13) The 'great politics' was an allusion to war threats critics had noted in the statements of loyalist deputies. The Postęp had early on voiced its concerns that loyalty under Kościelski had gone too far. "The bulk of our society is against the Army Bill. Our deputies cannot vote for it because of any greater political considerations, not after what Minister Bosse has been telling us in the Landtag", it wrote in mid-February, 1893, amidst reports that Kościelski was steering the Reichstag Party to vote for the bill.(14) As it became obvious that the bill would not pass the Postęp voiced its confidence that the Poles would emerge from the new elections with, "if not more, than at least the same number of deputies who with even greater determination will vote against the army bill burdens. Many of our citizens are disturbed at the conflicting positions taken by our deputies and rightly so. Economic burdens in Germany are so great that new taxes will result in the ruin of the country."(15) On 3 May, in response to many rumours in the German press, the Postęp wrote, "The word is going around that our deputies are ready to vote for the bill and new taxes in order to win the good graces of the government. The deputies want to be holier than the Pope, and more patriotic than Prussians and Germans. If this is the case... then our deputies have fallen to the level of servility. We feel, however, that our deputies have not fallen so low in their loyalty."(16)

Both the Orędownik and the Kuryer wanted the Reichstag Party to approve of the Bill, for largely similar tactical reasons but wholly different political principles. Both wanted to save whatever good faith the Party had been able to generate among Germans and keep Caprivi in office. But the Orędownik wanted to exploit the obvious split within the gentry ranks to advance Szymański's thesis that the days of gentry rule in Polish society were numbered. In early February he noted that the court party had lost all support in society, but that, "No one is available to take up their role. The middle classes are not yet ready."(17) Szymański's support of the Army Bill, however, was something of a mystery to many of his true supporters, as he himself sadly admitted (18). It contradicted the logic of his earlier stance in 1890 and apparently did not fit in with his otherwise pragmatic approach to political and economic affairs. On 4 February, 1893, the Orędownik noted, "We are still in favour of the Army Bill, but not for any of the reasons given by the court party'"(19). Why should the Poles vote for the Bill? The answer came on 8 February, "We recognize the arguments of the Bill's opponents, but nonetheless advise to vote for it. We have only a formal role to play in the vote, because we shall have to carry the burdens regardless of what we do. We should also vote for the Bill to save the honour and good name of our Party."(20) One might well ask why the radical tribune of the people, Szymański, would be interested in saving the honour of the landowner-dominated Party, and the reason is indeed difficult to fathom. He seemed to want to establish a priciple of basic allegiance to the Crown on a number of matters unrelated to the Polish question, such as military affairs, taxes, etc. As he wrote on 11 February, "A number of our readers do not agree with our stance... We should seek to establish principles in our politics and save the reputation of the Party. For these reasons we should vote for the Bill."(21)

On 4 May the Orędownik explained its reasoning once again. "We urge a vote for the Army Bill. We want the contents of the declarations of loyalty made by our deputies in 1890 to mean something. These declarations represent, in our view, the conditio sine qua non of the further survival and national development of our middle class and the whole Polish people."(22) To his confused supporters Szymański could only write, "We know most of our friends are against the Army Bill, and we can only hope that they will come around."(23) In fact it was Szymański who came around to the will of the people and after the general election in June, 1893, soon abandoned his reasoning. For now it rejoiced that "The Germania is justly criticizing Komierowski and the Party for not knowing what it really wants. It is a shame that this is being done by a German newspaper. It would be best if Komierowski said nothing at all."(24) "The Kuryer and Dziennik do not know what to do about the Army Bill", it concluded on 29 April.(25)

Unlike the other Polish papers, the Kuryer continued to believe in the progress of reconciliation despite the harsh remarks of minister Bosse in the Prussian Landtag in January-February, 1893, and showed no signs of pessimism in the ultimate outcome of its program. The press campaign to convince Poznań's Poles of the wisdon of the 1893 Army Bill was the last in which Antoni Kantecki took an active part, for he died in November, 1893. Kantecki knew all the political and psychological arguments necessary to convince people of seemingly undesireable policies, and in this campaign all his expertise was called upon. The Kuryer decided upon two principal lines of argument: a) the bill was, on balance positive for Germany and Poles living in Prussia and b) that only the deputies in Berlin, free from all fetters of Polish and German public opinion, could make such an important decision.

Such a strategy required that sceptics be convinced that the Bill was popular among Poles in Prussia. On 24 January, in an article entitled "The Voice of the People" it wrote that ordinary citizens wanted the introduction of the two-year military service. "The worst part of military service is its length. The people are happy that the two-year service is in the new Army Bill. ... Mature public opinion here looks with complete confidence in the work and efforts of our deputies."(26) On 25 February many of the Kuryer's arguments in favour of the Bill were summarized in a major policy article entitled, "Our Position". "The notion of 'terrorizing' public opinion by several members of the Party is truly ridiculous. The politics of reconciliation is not a new policy. but rather something very old. What did Wielopolski and the Whites (in the 1863 Uprising T.K.) want? What did Goluchowski and the Stanczyk party want? They wanted the same thing as the majority of Poles and the Party in Berlin. A very great segment of our society is in solidarity with the majority of our deputies... The political thought which we have always defended, that opposition for the sake of opposition should be avoided and that we should take a greater part in Prussian affairs to which fate has assigned us, today finds ever greater recognition in our society."(27) On 25 March the Kuryer vehemently denied charges in German newspapers that the Poles were making some sort of a "deal" with the government. "We shall not enter into deals, for this is not in our national spirit. We have a number of critics at home and in Berlin. What we need is patience and endurance."(28) A month later it repeated its denial in more assertive terms. "The decision on the Army Bill should be left up to the deputies... The sole thought of avoiding new taxes is childish. The Army Bill cannot be tied to do et des. Trade-offs are excluded; dispirited bargaining does not apply to the security of the state."(29) The Kuryer charged that extremists in both the Polish and German camps were out to wreck the hopes for reconciliation. "Polish chauvinists are trying to terrorize the Party into voting against the Army Bill. They want to sow discord between the Landtag and Reichstag Parties. This is having a dissasterous effect upon our German friends and foes...(Chauvinists) are not listening to those German ministers who have promised real changes if Polish chauvinism were stopped."(30) As the Reichstag vote neared, the Kuryer engaged in some disinformation. On 4 May it wrongly claimed that the Dziennik had come over to the adherents of the Bill, and confidently wrote, "This will make the decision of the Party much easier. ... There are no real expenses to be incurred for Poles in Poznan by passage of the Bill. The two-year service is a clear gain for our society."(31) Just before the vote the Kuryer made a last minute reference to fears of Russia. "Germans on the borderlands are especially susceptible to attack and need a strong army. We have to believe the generals."(32)

One of the unfortunate consequences of the Polish stand behind Caprivi's Army Bill in 1893 was the rift in relations with the Centrum Party. Under Ludwig Windthorst they had been excellent; but the new leadership of Graf Ballestrem, von Huene and Porsch was more suspicious of Polish aspirations. German Catholic politicians were particularly worried about the threat to their political domination over the Polish-speaking regions of Upper Silesia and East Prussia. Until 1893 many political observers had judged the Polish Parties in the German Reichstag and the Prussian Landtag as mere extensions of the Centrum; indeed they voted together on virtually every important issue under consideration. With Caprivi's 1893 Army Bill, however, the Poles, after a long and painful internal debate, decided to support the Chancellor, while the majority of the Centrum opposed the Bill. Doubtless it was the Kuryer which was most affected by the stinging criticism of Germania and other German Catholic newspapers. Since 1890 the Kuryer had based its strategy on an alliance of the "Christian" parties -

the Conservatives, Centrum, Poles and Alsatians against liberals, the SPD and progressives. Yet with the estrangement of the Centrum the prospects of the grand Christian alliance appeared to crumble.

Beginning in March, 1893, the Kuryer reassured the leading Catholic daily, Germania, that, "(You) can count upon us for support in all matters related to religion... (but) matters of state security are of greater importance to us than partisan considerations."(33) In late April after two distinctly disapproving articles in the Germania, the Kuryer wrote, "We are surprised at the rudeness in such a distinguished organ as the Germania. It is threatening to remember (our vote) in the future."(34) In early May the Germania wrote that it had "firm evidence" that the Polish Party was severely divided over the upcoming vote and urged the Party to release its deputies from their bond of solidarity. The Kuryer responded that all Party members held similar views and that the Germania had based its erroneous statements on the Orędownik's bold lies.(35) This seemed a poor line of reasoning for the Kuryer to take; it was well known that many influential Poles had ties to the Germania and that dissatisfied Polish deputies likely informed it of internal Party disputes. The Germania, for its part, was angry that the Kuryer had printed telegrams from Cardinal Ledóchowski and Archbishop Stablewski to the Polish deputies congratulating them for supporting the Bill. The Kuryer responded that its former ally was applying "unheard of pressure on Polish voters".(36)

Further bad blood emerged after the election of a Pole, the priest Wolszlegier, over the Centrum candidate Karkowski in Alleinstein in the 15 June general election. This was the first time that a Pole loyal to the Polish electoral organization had defeated a German Catholic in East Prussia, and it led to bitter charges in German Catholic newspapers of 'Polish agitation'. After the Polish vote in July which finally passed the Army Bill the quarrel between the Germania and the Kuryer escalated another notch. On 6 July the Kuryer wrote, "There is a good deal of egotism and barely disguised anger in its arguments against the independent position we are taking toward the Centrum... Our Party never swore allegiance to the German Catholic party... The Centrum press is accusing us of Polish agitation because of Father Wolszleiger's victory in Alleinstein, e.g. the Westpreussische Volksblatt. It would be best if the German press said nothing."(37) By the end of July, 1893, the Kuryer admitted that its "war with Germania is getting serious. ...The Germania is taking the side of the Orędownik... The Centrum has its own problems. Do not speculate on our Party's downfall; it might come to you instead. Poles in the east should stop reading Germania."(38)

The Dziennik joined the scrap with the Centrum press later in 1893 over the issue of Polish nationalism in Upper Silesia. It charged the leading Catholic organ in Silesia, the Schlesische Volkszeitung, with promoting Germanization(39), and in late October took aim at the Westpreussische Volksblatt over conflicts in West Prussia. "There is no such thing as Great Polish agitation in West Prussia! This paper and other German papers will have to get used to the idea that the Polish majority will not allow itself to be terrorized by a German minority."(40)

Significantly, the populist newspapers sympathized with the anger evidenced by the Centrum press over the ultra-loyal position taken by the Reichstag Polish

Party over the Army Bill. Stanisław Knapowski wrote in the Postęp on 29 June, "We agree with Germania. The principle of solidarity should be done away with ...(it) is usually necessary to defend our interests but not in this case."(41) The Postęp was angry that the loyalists had provoked an argument with the Poles' best ally. In late July 1893 it wrote, "(They) have repudiated our old, faithful allies and friends, the Catholics and in part deputies from other parties, who had formed a firm front and defended our national interests more eloquently than the Polish deputies themselves."(42) During the height of the civil strife among Poznań's Poles in the summer of 1893 the Postęp was happy to note, "German Catholic newspapers are standing solidly behind the Polish people and not behind the insignificant number of Polish lords."(43) The Orędownik, which had previously argued the case of Polish independence from the dominance of German Catholics, wrote in late April, "The Kuryer compares with Germania like a schoolboy who cannot count to three."(44) It voiced approval of the leading Catholic newspapers' accounts of the Poznań secession.(45)

The quarrel between Polish and German Catholic politicians and newspapers came to an end soon after the Army Bill vote. The community of interests between the two overrode the emotions aroused by the Polish vote. It was important, however, in that it seriously undermined the loyalist platform of a grand alliance of Christian parties against the atheistical and rebellious left. In addition it marked a significant decline in the credibility of the Kuryer. Having told the Polish community for three years that its hopes rested on a firm alliance with the Centrum in support of Caprivi, the Kuryer now found itself combating its former allies.

After months of internal debate the Poles decided to vote for the Army Bill. The spokesman on military affairs, Komierowski, announced the decision in the Reichstag on 5 May.(46) Loyalist arguments finally won out over national sentiment; Caprivi could not be abandoned; the Kaiser would be impressed by the Polish vote; German public opinion would be reassured after Bismarck's press campaign of 1892; one more sacrifice was necessary to renew the flow of concessions granted in 1891. There was never really any dispute about the need to maintain block voting within the Polish Party; the principle had worked very well since the beginnings of parliamentarism in Prussia and Germany and no one was ready to set the precedent by abandoning it. A dissenting minority could not vote against the majority according to the Party regulations. Nevertheless, the outcry over the bill had only begun, for it was rejected by a vote of 210-162 and Caprivi was forced to dissolve the Reichstag on 7 May and call for a new election. Most Polish newspapers in Poznań evidenced regret and anger over the Polish vote. The Dziennik wrote on 10 May, "We cannot agree with Komierowski's assertion that the two-year service is an economic concession... Friendly words are being juxtaposed with continual persecution. The old system has not changed It is denying us elementary rights, the postulates of our national life. Our deputies could only vote for this bill hoping for great concessions. We understand this reasoning but think it is wrong."(47) A week later the Dziennik printed a highly controversial article intended as a warning to the deputies. "Our economic situation is so critical and can hardly bear the extra burdens imposed by the Army Bill. If, then, our deputies, in the name of Polish society once again vote for the bill, they can only do so if they have a firm assurance of concessions which would make their vote worth it."(48) A vote for the bill had to bring forward concrete concessions from the Prussian government; otherwise Polish society would not tolerate it.

The Postęp was predictably angry at the Reichstag Party vote. On 11 May it wrote, "Loyalty can only go as far as society will condone. In this case our deputies have overstepped the bounds. At every meeting (for the upcoming Reichstag election T.K.) they must be told not to vote for the Army Bill. They cannot be the ones who turn the whips against their own countrymen."(49) The Orędownik tried to cover up its own ill-thought out support for the Bill by turning the upcoming election into a assault upon the court party. In an editorial of 17 May, 1893, entitled "The Struggle between the Polish People and the Court Party" the Orędownik wrote, "Now is the time to get rid of the court party. The Army Bill should not be the only reason to depose them. The key to the fight is to block the renomination of the deputies."(50)

Significantly, the Wielkopolanin downplayed the social tension generated by the vote. This is likely because its patrons did not want the urban and rural poor to be aware of the discord among the gentry class. It held true to its slogans of obedience to the gentry politicians and did not debate the merits of their Reichstag vote.(51) The Kuryer alone applauded the vote with enthusiasm. "From the beginning we had argued to give the deputies full freedom. Tying our deputies down by the restraints of public opinion would constitute returning to the worst days of Polish parliamentarism... Komierowski's speech has cleared up the political atmosphere. Let us take advantage of this... It is very easy to negate everything but more difficult to make the right decision."(52) On 14 May the Kuryer criticized the Dziennik for its demand to get some tangible concessions for their votes. "The Dziennik should know that the idea of 'I was a good boy and now I deserve a reward' is false. We reject the politics of bargaining. We and our readers know that the Army Bill is not a matter for bargaining."(53)

6.2 The Election Campaign in Poznań and Bromberg; the Populist Challenge

In many ways the 1893 Reichstag election taxed the Central Committee beyond its means. It had only one month before election day to organize the campaign and agitate to turn out the vote. Furthermore, it was plagued by financial difficulties, evidenced by the numerous calls for donations found in the Polish newspapers. Yet its greatest handicap was the unpopular vote of the Party on the Army Bill. For the first time in the history of Prussian Poland, an issue emerged which was important enough to crack the seemingly invincible bloc of national solidarity that justified the gentry's monopoly of social and political power. Seen from the perspective of the last quarter of the 20th century, the introduction of pluralism and political parties in a modern sense appears to be a great step forward along the road of democratization and modernization; yet for almost all contemporaries it was an unmitigated disaster which threatened the very survival of the Polish element in Prussia.

The returning deputies who were expecting an easy renomination received a mixed response from their constituencies. Most of Poznania's pre-election rallies went smoothly; candidates were renominated but reminded in various ways of the unpopularity of the Army Bill. Kościelski was renominated in Strzelno on 14 May, but "he received some very sharp questions"(54), and heard the customary three cheers only after making a vague promise that Polish recruits would soon be serving in their home provinces.(55) Kościelski also read out a letter by Archbishop Stablewski praising the Party's vote on the bill. In Kościan on 21 May the electors were evenly divided between supporters and opponents of the incumbent deputy Zdzisław Czartoryski. Czartoryski was finally renominated only after a supporter called on the Party to, "Remember the tremendous burdens we are already suffering from and the lack of significant concessions on the part of the government."(56) On 24 May, in Września, Dziembowski's candidacy passed only after the assembly adopted a formal resolution asking the deputies to reject the bill.(57) Speaking in Wągrowiec on 28 May, Komierowski and Cegielski persuaded the assembly to reject two successive resolutions against the bill, but that same day Kościelski faced a tough audience of 600 in Inowrocław, where his arguments on the need to strengthen Germany's eastern borders against the "dangerous neighbour to the East who is oppressing our countrymen." met with ridicule and a sharp riposte from Józef Czapla, the most influential populist in Inowrocław.(58) In other small towns rallies came off without a serious challenge; Komierowski was renominated unanimously in Gniezno; Czartoryski encountered no opposition in Opalenic; Dziembowski had an easy evening at Pleszew; and Kościelski had a quiet rally in Leszno.(59)

It was in Poznań and Bromberg that the populist challenge was the strongest. The rally in Bromberg on 14 May attracted 2000 participants, or about every third qualified Polish voter in the city. Komierowski attempted to defend the Party's voting record and received a poor reception; the assembly rejected his name on the list of candidates and demanded that a populist lawyer, Moczyński be placed first on the list of three candidates. Disorder forced the police to intervene and break up the rally before the issue could be resolved, and both sides blamed the other for the result. The Dziennik wrote that it was impossible to proceed because of "anarchists and socialists" (60), while the Kuryer charged that Moczyński and other populists had "broken up the meeting through their unruliness. They came with Germans and socialists... They are leaning towards the left and towards democracy'"(61). The Wielkopolanin reported that "Many voters did not know what they were supposed to do... As a result a noisy confusion ensued and the police broke up the meeting."(62) Szymański, on the other hand, was elated. "Long Live Bromberg!" announced the Orędownik on 17 May and praised the political maturity of Bromberg's Polish community as an example for all to follow.(63)

A major test for both sides came on 18 May when Dobrowolski called about 2000 Poznań voters to order. The description of the rally varied widely in the press. The Dziennik wrote, "The rally was broken up! Commanded by Dr. Szymański and his helpers, a small group shouted and terrorized the assembly to the point where the police inspector present, Herr Portaszewicz, found his tolerance exhausted and was forced to end the rally."(64) The Kuryer wrote, "The minority was the loudest, the majority of mature citizenry were in favour of peace. The solid phalanx of socialists found support in the person of Dr. Szymański. In his latest action Szymański has found no support among the middle class, but he has among the socialists. He is jumping on the deputies for doing that what he had urged them to do."(65) The Wielkopolanin, wrote, "The Orędownik's editor, Dr. R. Szymański, caused a cruel scandal at Thursday's rally in Poznań. The scandal was so terrible that the police were forced to break up the meeting. The speech by (the incumbent deputy) Stefan Cegielski was a masterpiece of political oratory... Dr. Szymański will never, but never, be the Polish candidate!"(66) The gentry newspapers wanted to place the blame for the unrest on Szymański and not on any serious rift within the Polish community. Predictably, Szymański's lead editorial on 20 May was, "Poznań has Retained its Honour!" "We have saved ourselves from the court party. Any one is better than Komierowski, and we shall not allow Cegielski to pass in Poznań... The assembly voiced its impatience with Cegielski's long speech which defended the Army Bill vote... The blame for the dissolution rests with the Committee."(67) In a follow-up article the next day, the Orędownik wrote, "It is a hundred times better to break up a meeting than accept a candidate who will follow the present policies of the Party. It is better to break up national solidarity than to tie the Polish people to the Committee that is leading us all to destruction. It is better to have no deputy at all than one like Dr. Komierowski. Cegielski must become a sacrifice to the politics of the Party. If the Central Committee nominates him again we shall forego solidarity because agreement would kill us."(68) Other newspapers critical of the Party did not go so far but expressed sympathy with the movement to reject Cegielski. The Postęp was critical of Cegielski's speech and angered by his reference to the socialists as "your friends", i.e. the friends of the political opposition.(69) It is important to remember that the Postęp had once received money from Cegielski to start up; but by 1893 it had built up a large circulation and felt free to break off the dependence. The Goniec wrote that the townspeople were trying to open the eyes of the rural community, that, "Ein Preusse polnischer Nationalitaet kann nicht Vertreter der mit Gewalt unter die preussische Herrschaft gebrachten Polen sein."(70)

Dobrowolski, chairman of the Poznań municipal committee, introduced a resolution addressed to the Party on the Army Bill question, partly to placate the supporters of the Goniec, and partly to express his own reservations about the Bill. Dobrowolski had consistently spoken out against the bill in the Dziennik; now he hoped to impress the deputies with the seriousness of public opinion. Against the wishes of the Kuryer and outpolling a counter-resolution proposed by Szymański, the committee's resolution passed. It read, "The voters of Poznań would like to express their deep conviction that our deputies are conscientiously defending our interests and we recognize their work and noble intentions. Nevertheless, in the hope of establishing greater contacts and understanding between the deputies and their constituencies, we should like to express our wish that our deputies defend us from any new burdens. The hard-pressed Polish community must already bear a tremendous load and is taxed with the need to defend our mother tongue."(71)

In the meantime, on the evening of May 18 forty of Szymański's hard-core supporters gathered in his home to plot strategy.(72) On the eve of Poznań's second rally, 22 May, Szymański called for another meeting, chaired by his long-time friend, the real-estate agent Stanisław Offierski, and attended by 150 people.(73) This meeting resolved that, "We shall use every means possible to prevent the re-election of Cegielski. We must save the Polish people from the court party."(74) Szymański's rallying call was "rozbić zebranie wyborcze" (break up election rallies), a desperate tactic to prevent the renomination of Reichstag deputies. At this point his candidacy was not yet formal, and his incomprehensible support for the Army Bill vote had alienated all but his most devoted followers. The establishment newspapers were enraged by his call to disrupt meetings. The Kuryer thundered on 24 May, "Szymański's cry to break up rallies means breaking up national solidarity. Through this one act he has committed political suicide. Let us not be afraid of him. Let us meet him head on and destroy him!"(75) The Dziennik called his strategy the "ultimate in demagogy" and blamed him for Polish electoral troubles all over the province.(76) In preparing its readers for Poznań's second rally, the Wielkopolanin wrote, "It would be very sad indeed if the guttersnipes were victorious over the sober and honest citizentry. We are convinced that our patriotic burghers and workers will attend today's rally and with one voice acclaim Pan Stefan Cegielski as Poznań's candidate!"(77)

All of Poznania awaited Poznań's second rally, held on 23 May, with great anticipation. Once again a tumult arose after the opening speeches, and the police were forced to end proceedings. The newspaper accounts varied according to their political posture, and with characteristic conceit all claimed to be in possession of the absolute truth. The Dziennik was alarmed at the chaos and joined the campaign against Szymański with a fury. "Szymański was accompanied by socialists who had journeyed all the way from Berlin!... He is a modern Cleon. It was a disgusting performance."(78) The Kuryer wrote in a similar vein but used the opportunity to criticize the decision to send the resolution drafted by Dobrowolski to the Reichstag Party.(79) Dobrowolski's chief ally on the resolution question was the fiery Rzepecki of the Goniec, also a member of the municipal committee. On 24 May the Goniec wrote that in view of the passage of the resolution the citizenry should approve Cegielski's candidacy.(80) Knapowski, also a member of the committee was drawing closer to Szymański and the populists. "The majority of those present were clearly against the Army Bill burdens. Yet the committee did not want to take this into consideration."(81) During the rally Józef Siemianowski, a junior editor at the Orędownik, tried to introduce a resolution condemning the Dziennik, Kuryer, and Wielkopolanin for "insulting the voters, but the rally was broken up before any decision was made." Szymański viewed the broken rally as a clear-cut victory for the Polish people. "The Glory of Poznań" ran the lead article on 25 March in the Orędownik. "The break-up of the second rally was all Dobrowolski's fault. With a few exceptions the committee is composed of open or silent supporters of the court party... This committee has been literally stopped in its tracks twice by the will of the people. An open opposition and disrupted rallies these are facts which in Berlin will shut Kościelski's mouth that the Polish people stand behind him."(82) About the only area in which all newspapers agreed was the size of the crowd: from 2500 to 3000 participants, a remarkable figure which attests to the aroused emotions within the Polish community. Szymański received more good news on 25 May when the populists in Bromberg, in an orderly meeting that avoided police intervention, rejected Komierowski once again and placed Moczyński on top of the list. "Upwards, Bromberg!" rejoiced Szymański on 28 May (83), while the Kuryer and Dziennik placed the blame on the Bromberg local committee headed by

Mieczkowski.(84) On 30 May Szymański gloated that voters in Inowrocław had given Kościelski such a rough time. "Pan Kościelski is the father of our modern Prussian loyalty. He is even more loyal than many Germans... He is the director and producer of the Polish Party, because he chooses many of the deputies and crushes the minority. Today, we can say that Pan Kościelski... is the most dangerous person to the cause of the Polish people."(85)

Before every Reichstag and Landtag election it was customary for Poles to hold a "general assembly" consisting of the Central Committee and representatives of the 38 local electoral districts to finalize the selection of candidates and outline campaign strategy. The assembly in theory was superior to the Central Committee, but in practice the inexperienced delegates from the countryside usualy deferred to the Poznanian powerbrokers. The assembly that preceded the June 15 election was scheduled for 30 May, and Poznań still had no candidate for Poznań, Dobrowolski, chairman of the Poznań committee as well as secretary of the Central Committee, decided to take matters into his own hands. He arbitrarily announced that, since there was no point in calling a third rally, Cegielski would represent Poznań. To avoid charges of despotism, Dobrowolski had a statement issued and signed by 200 of Poznań's most reputable citizens in support of his action.(86) The populists claimed that the nomination violated the regulations of the Central Committee, and hence was illegal. At this point Szymański's candidacy began to gather momentum, though he was not an announced candidate and refused to promote his cause in the Orędownik. His confusing reasoning on the Army Bill prevented his candidacy from expressing the full dissatision of Poznań's voters with the Bill.

On 30 May, 1893, Poznania's powerbrokers, accompanied by a representative of the ubiquitous police, determined the final list of candidates for the upcoming elections. Despite the lack of a formal endorsement from Poznań's electorate, the group approved of Cegielski's candidacy by a vote of 38-2 and thereby vindicated Dobrowolski. Kościelski's candidacy was opposed by 8 votes, indicating a degree of disapproval of his ultra-loyal stand, while the candidacy of the Party's nominal chairman, Radziwiłł, was approved by 37-1. When the delegates came to Bromberg on the order of business, however, the opponents of the populists with Dobrowolski at their head were able to overturn the candidacy of Moczyński by a vote of 27-11, and nominated Eugeniusz Rogaliński, a "safe landowner", instead.(87) Officially, the Assembly's reasoning was that Moczyński could never win in heavily Germanized Bromberg.(88) Populist supporters were outraged. In Bromberg a petition was quickly drawn up and signed by 350 voters protesting Moczyński's removal from the list of candidates. (89) The Goniec went on record as saying Moczyński was a "real patriot" and took pride in the fact that he was Czarliński's son-in-law.(90) Rogaliński then prudently announced that he would not accept the nomination, forcing the Central Committee to hold a third rally in Bromberg on 6 June. Significantly, the populist hero Czarliński was unanimously nominated.(91) The middle class had scored their first victory in breaking the gentry's monopoly. Szymański called the rally a "complete victory in Bromberg" in which the "candidate of the people had won."(92) Czarlinski, an old rival of Kościelski in the Prussian Landtag, went on record that he would vote against the Army Bill regardless of how the rest of the deputies voted.

The rest of the campaign was marked by feverish agitation at local levels to drum out as much of the vote as possible on election day, June 15. Kościelski received a very cool reception in Inowrocław on 30 May, and Szczaniecki got the customary three cheers in Środa only after admitting he was against the Army Bill.(93) Janta-Połczyński of West Prussia, thought to be in the ranks of the loyalists, told the Gazeta Gdańska in an interview on 9 June that he would "try and act according to the will of his constituency, that is to reduce the burdens placed on us."(94) In Poznań, the Goniec, though in favour of the Cegielski candidacy to prevent a break of national solidarity, called him a "government man", because of his position on the Bill. (95) The Postep undoubtedly expressed a popular view when it wrote on 31 May, "There is no one in Poznań who hates Pan Cegielski. On the contrary, we all like and respect him. People regret, however, that he has been converted to the policies of the Party which are driving our society to ruin. People are sad that he is in league with the likes of Kościelski and Komierowski, sharpening their knives against the rest of their colleagues in the Party".(96)

Meanwhile, Szymański's supporters decided to launch a campaign on his behalf. Officially, they received no help from him; unofficially he was heart and soul in the campaign. The reaction of the establishment press was close to hysterical. The Kuryer urged its readers to burn Szymański's voting cards and called on the clergy to "teach their parishioners of the benefits of the Army Bill and their voting responsibilities."(97) The Dziennik of 11 June wrote, "He has removed his mask. Szymański will run against Cegielski, although he said on the 22 May that he would not in the interests of unity. From 30 May, the behaviour of Pan Szymański can no longer be considered as opposition or agitation - it can only be described as a rebellion against our electoral authorities and secession!"(98) The Kuryer, Dziennik and Wielkopolanin issued emotional appeals for unity that resemble appeals to patriotism in times of war. "All true Poles! Arm in arm together!", wrote the Dziennik on 7 June, and produced another appeal signed by a large group of Poznań notables demanding unity and denouncing Szymański's campaign.(99) In a clever move, the Kuryer reminded its readers how Szymański had spoken out against the secession of Niegolewski in 1884. (100) The Postęp found Szymański's position on the Army Bill unacceptable and urged its followers to vote for Cegielski.(101) Szymański was isolated, but not intimidated.He spoke out against priests who used the pulpit to further the policies of the court party and continued to blame the gentry and, in particular, Dobrowolski, for the break in national solidarity. (102) As the Poles went to the polls on 15 June, Szymański's only declared support came from the readers of his own Orędownik.

The election of 15 June, 1893, disappointed many in Germany. Caprivi emerged with a shaky vote of confidence but was still unable to put together a reliable pro-government coalition. The big winners were the Social Democrats and the Anti-Semites, while the big loser was Richter and the divided Progressives. The strength of the large parties remained relatively unchanged.(103) The Poles could claim a qualified success because they had picked up three additional seats, including an important breakthrough in East Prussia, but their performance left something to be desired. Their total number of votes dropped from 246,000 in 1890 to 229,000, despite a continuously increasing population, and their percentage of the Reich total dropped from 3.4% to 3.0% (104). An analysis of the voting results indicates that all candidates who were known for their loyalist sentiments lost ground, while critics actually increased their support. Thus, in Inowrocław, Kościelski's votes dropped from 14,983 to 13,902; in Gniezno, Komierowski lost over 1000 votes, from 14,491 to 13,351; Radziwiłł lost almost 1500 votes in Ostrowo, from 14,307 to 12,855; in Września, Dziembowski lost some 900 votes, from 12,336 to 11,405; in Oborniki, Hektor Kwilecki lost 1300, from 12,986 to 11,675 and in Rawicz, Adam Czartoryski lost 700 votes from 8210 to 7578. On the other hand, the outspoken Jażdżewski picked up 300 votes in Krościen, from 7639 to 7959; Janta-Połczyński remained steady in Neustadt in West Prussia, from 13,962 to 14,105, and in Bromberg, to everyone's surprise, Czarliński forced a run-off with the German candidate in which the Pole won with 8388 votes, including some 2000 SPD votes.(105) In Poznań, the final results of the first ballot were: Cegielski- 9413, Hoffmeyer (Conservative)- 4539, Hesse (Progressive)- 3233, Szymański- 1869, and Morawski (a Polish Social Democrat)- 1102. (106) Cegielski had lost over 3500 votes since 1890 (12,841), a decline of 25%. Szymański's challenge was strong enough to force a run-off between Cegielski and Hoffmeyer, which Cegielski won handily but which cost the community an extra 30,000 Mk. The furious spokesmen of the Poznań municipal committee darkly hinted that Szymański should be charged with the bill.(107) The Dziennik lamented that, "This is the first time that a Polish candidate has not been elected on the first ballot in Poznań".(108) An important psychological barrier had been crossed- the aristocratic monopoly on candidates had been broken. "The notion that we (the populists T.K.) have made ourselves the self-appointed guardians of political power is nonsense. According to the constitution every Pole has the right to defend his political convictions." wrote the Orędownik on 22 June.(109) On 25 June Szymański wrote, "Our votes against Cegielski are a sign to the Party that 1) it should speak to its constituency as equals and 2) people in Berlin cannot take their positions for granted and should not conduct policy on their own without social support. And the Wielkopolanin calls this a war against the Church!"(110) In contrast to the partisan coverage of Poznań's campaign, all newspapers joined in celebrating the important victory in Bromberg, where populists and adherents of the political apparatus combined to win the seat from the Germans.(111)

One would have thought that after a close examination of the election rallies and results the newly-elected Polish deputies could not fail but to speak out against the Army Bill. As if they needed any analysis, all Polish newspapers except the Kuryer editorialized almost daily against the Bill in the three weeks between the election and the second vote in the Reichstag. The Goniec wrote, "Unsere Pflicht ist es, derselben das zu erklaeren, was bereits einige Generalversammlungen erklaert bezw. beschlossen haben, dass wir groessere Opfer an Geld und Menschen nicht haben wollen."(112) The Goniec pressed for another resolution to be sent to the Party, but could not convince Dobrowolski to call a special meeting of the municipal committee for this purpose. While Dobrowolski clearly sympathized with the concerns of the Goniec supporters, he had already challenged the Party once with the resolution adopted on 18 May, and this had been rejected.(113)

Through the Dziennik, however, Dobrowolski made his position very clear. On 2 July it wrote, "If the recent election has returned the same group of deputies to Berlin it is not because the Party voted unconditionally for the Army Bill, but in spite of their vote."(114) Five days later the Dziennik wrote, "Those who say we are honour bound to repeat our first vote in favour of the bill are wrong. The vote should be based on the social and economic conditions of our provinces."(115) Szymański now withdrew his support from the Bill, writing on 27 June, "There is no question now that the deputies should heed the national will and vote against the Army Bill. They must have got the message. If the deputies disregard the public will, then let them prepare themselves for another rough confrontation."(116) The Postęp was deeply disturbed at the upcoming vote. On 8 July it wrote, "German papers are saying that the Poles will vote as one bloc for the Bill. It is strange that the Polish deputies have given such information to German newspapers and omitted Polish ones. We can see from this that they are now so loyal that they feel it unimportant to inform their own voters through the Polish press. They seem to prefer German newspapers to Polish."(117) Only the Kuryer, urged that the Army Bill be supported. "We now have 19 votes and must keep on with the same policies", it wrote on 1 July.(118)

At this point one must turn to archival materials to understand the motives for the Polish vote. Both Kościelski and Archbishop Stablewski were furiously working behind the scenes to interest Chancellor Caprivi in a "deal" - Polish votes for language concessions. On 2 June Stablewski wrote to Caprivi asking for two hours a week in schools and Caprivi responded that he would take up the matter.(119) Prospects seemed bright until a three-man delegation consisting of Radziwiłł, Janta-Połczyński and Jażdżewski obtained an audience with Caprivi on the eve of the vote. Caprivi needed the Polish votes to pass the Bill, and the Polish aristocrats needed some concessions to keep loyalty within the Polish community alive. Caprivi was sympathetic but cautious. He ruled out concessions in West Prussia as the Emperor considered it an original Prussian province and pointed out that the question of language teaching was in the hands of the Prussian Landtag, of which he was no longer Ministerpraesident.(120) Despite this rebuff, Stablewski used his clerical authority to virtually order Jażdżewski to vote for the Bill, and sent other appeals to lay deputies.(121) Under such pressure the Party buckled and voted yes in a bloc. Only Czarliński, true to the word given his Bromberg voters, abstained. Jażdżewski delivered the address in the Reichstag announcing the vote, and the Polish votes pushed the Bill over the top at 201-185.(122) Of all the secret negotiations, including Stablewski's critical role, Polish public opinion knew nothing.

6.3 The Removal of the Dobrowolski Committee in Poznań and the Struggle Over its Replacement

It is difficult to over-estimate the emotions aroused over the Army Bill votes of 1893. In 1904 Komierowski wrote in his semi-official Party history, "Eleven years have now passed, and public opinion here has still not calmed down enough to make an objective evaluation." (123) Poznania's Polish community was virtually torn asunder by the vote. While Kościelski received yet another personal commendation from the Emperor for his Party's key role in the vote, Polish society seethed. The exasperated Dziennik weakly stated, "We are convinced that only very important and serious reasons could have influenced the declaration made by Jażdżewski in the Reichstag. We look to the future with full confidence."(124) The Orędownik wrote in an insightful analysis, "It looks like the Party had been caught in a devilish trap with no way out. It cannot get out of any situation without giving the government what it wants, regardless of the clear signals coming from the constituency."(125)

The Orędownik predicted that the Polish community would get nothing in return for the vote. "Our deputies pay no attention whatsoever to the Polish people, our poverty and our troubles. Hence the people view the deputies as no more than the servants of the Prussian government. We are sending people to Berlin who are playing at politics to the detriment of the Polish people."(126) The Goniec was infuriated beyond sensible criticism called Kościelski the "evil spirit of the Party", who had "expressly sold out the Polish people."(127) When a rumour began to circulate that Kościelski would be appointed a Prussian official, the Goniec wrote in biting satire, "How good this would be! Then he could represent a German district and give up his seat in the Polish Party. It would be a great move for the whole nation, Poles and Germans alike, and he would lose nothing!"(128) The extent of nationalist outrage can be appreciated in the Goniec's year-end review. "Ihr (the loyalists T.K.) habt das Recht, Euch auf koenigliche Worte zu berufen, und zieht es vor, um Gunst zu betteln. Schmach und Schande ueber Euch! Bisher wurden die Polen fuer eine patriotische Nation gehalten. Ihr Herren, ein zweites Targowica befleckt unseren Namen und fuehrt uns in den Schmutz und ins Verderben... schaendliche Kapitulation!"(129)

The Postęp called the vote "begging for mercy",(130) and warned on 15 July, "The Polish public is astonished at their stand and they will not be spared their well-deserved criticism."(131) Only the Kuryer congratulated the deputies. "It is true that various shrill voices tried to disrupt the unity and consistency of the Party, but who could believe that our representatives would be driven off the course or reason and responsibility by empty phrases and loudmouths propagating fear? The position taken by our Party... is the only rational course... We have won a great mutual (with the government T.K.) victory."(132)

The "victory" was immediately apparent to no one. Instead, an unprecedented groundswell of anger was generated throughout the province. For decades the electorate had accepted the decisions of the Central Committee and deputies meekly; now for the first time they were in open revolt. The powerbrokers had gone too far in ignoring the steadily growing mass national consciousness. Politics could no longer be limited to the backroom manipulations of the landed gentry. It was inevitably evolving in the direction of pluralism and greater democracy.

The chief defender of the battered prestige of the political machine was Dobrowolski. He called a rally for 19 July, to defend not the vote, with which he had never agreed, but the good name of the Party and the principle of national solidarity. However, the evening of 19 July was to be one of the low points of his career. He told the disappointed voters, "We know and feel that this vote will bring upon us new taxes, yet we also know that if our deputies voted for it a second time they must have had a very good reason."(133) Dobrowolski's speech was subjected to ridicule and Cegielski was booed by about 800 angry citizens. At this point, bowing to public pressure, Dobrowolski announced that the whole committee was resigning, as its five-year term was over. Critics said the committee had been given a vote of no-confidence, and that is the way the Prussian police recorded it.(134) The Dziennik blamed the unruliness of the populists and the flagrant abuse hurled at the Party by Rzepecki and the Goniec followers.(135) The Orędownik, which had ordered its readers on the eve of the meeting to "Overthrow the Committee!" was ecstatic.(136) On 21 July it wrote, "A vote of no-confidence in the Poznan committee represents a great victory for the citizenry and a humiliating defeat for the powerbrokers. Dobrowolski's speech was intended to drive the voters to boredom and fatigue... They had taken the voters for granted and violated the electoral regulations." (137) The next day the Orędownik denounced the attempt to describe the no-confidence measure as a voluntary resignation. "The vote of no-confidence was overwhelming. Only ten to fifteen people were against. This is something the Kuryer and Dziennik must reckon with."(138) Knapowski described the 19 July meeting in much the same manner. "The vote of no-confidence was unanimous. At yesterday's meeting the electorate settled accounts with the committee; at the next they will settle accounts with the deputies. Let the countryside follow the example of the capital."(139)

The Kuryer chose this inopportune time to launch an unsuccessful campaign to remove Czarliński from the Party for abstaining on the vote, which, in view of Czarliński's popularity, showed to all how removed the Kuryer had become from public opinion.(140) This ignoble campaign continued until 2 August, when Bromberg Poles issued their electoral committee a vote of no-confidence, but explicitly defended Czarliński.(141) The Dziennik did not join in criticizing Czarliński, but upheld the sanctity of national solidarity. On the eve of the 27 July Poznań assembly, the Dziennik wrote, "Patriotism means order and harmony, it means solidarity and not departing from the ranks. This has always been true but is especially so in our case. We are against any form of secession."(142)

The order and harmony that Dobrowolski sought eluded him. On 27 July about 1500 angry citizens jammed into the Kempf Hall to select a new committee. After half an hour of "unheard of tumults, insults and shouting"(143), during which nothing was settled, the police inspectors broke up the meeting. According to the police report, "Die Ursache der herrschenden Erregung bildete der Umstand, dass der Vorsitzende des bisherigen Komitees, Dobrowolski, gemaess der Vorschrift des Wahlreglements den Vorsitz beibehalten und ihn der von Mehrheit der Versammlung gewuenschten Persoenlichkeit nicht abtreten wollte."(144) The Orędownik wrote, "Dobrowolski broke up yesterday's meeting and showed us all that he will resort to any means to hold on to his power. Pan Dobrowolski disgraced, vulgarized and spat upon the national cause, the Polish cause, the citizen's cause."(145) The Postęp, moving ever closer to an open alliance with Szymański, claimed that Dobrowolski called upon the police to break up the meeting after he had seen that he could not remain as chairman.(146) As the meeting was breaking up one of the jurors, the priest Lucjan Skrzydlewski, a outspoken supporter of the Dobrowolski faction, made a deprecatory remark about the populists and was beaten by an enraged participant. A wholesale riot was averted by quick police action.

Poznań was shocked; there had never been a case of a Catholic Pole raising his hand against a Catholic priest. "An unheard of crime in Poznań!" raged the Kuryer on 2 August. "Sinful anarchy, trying to terrorize the clergy and remove it from public affairs."(147) Under the same title the Wielkopolanin wrote, "A priest has been assaulted by people impassioned with hate and destruction by the Orędownik and Postęp."(148) The Dziennik lamented, "This has never happened before. We have never had a priest beaten or clerics openly insulted. We also heard for the first time (from the populists T.K.) that here the law does not matter, that here there is no law, that what counts is the will of the people'".(149) The next day the Dziennik declared a "press war" against the Postęp and Orędownik. "He will end badly", predicted the Dziennik in a somber tone of Szymański.(150) Although the alliance between Knapowski and Szymański was not yet formalized, their opponents began to speak of them in the same breath, referring to the Postęp as the "servile lackey" of the Orędownik.(151)

The situation in Poznań seemed to be at an impasse. Dobrowolski's position was critical. His post on the Central Committee was coming up for renewal in October and he wanted the Poznań secession cleared up as soon as possible. He had prepared a list of dependable notables headed by the merchant Józef Kusztelan to succeed his outgoing committee, and was sure his list would win at an orderly meeting. But the populists had prepared a counter-list, headed by the physician Tomasz Drobnik, and Dobrowolski felt sure that they would disrupt orderly civic life until their list were accepted. He therefore called for a third meeting for 16 August, but took certain precautions to exclude as many enemies as possible. First, he timed the meeting to take place during working hours, thereby excluding many workers. Second, he charged an admission fee of 20 pfennigs, ostensibly to cover the committee's debts but likely devised to keep out the poor who he knew would support the populists. Finally he asked that the police check the identity papers of participants, to prove their age and their residence.(152) These measures were extreme but Dobrowolski found support in the Kuryer and the Goniec, which had advocated an admission fee in late May to "keep out the troublemakers".(153)

The measures were successful - only 500 Poles turned up for the 16 August meeting, with populists and Dobrowolski's supporters evenly balanced. Nevertheless, the meeting was characterized by the same disorder and emotional outbursts as the two earliers ones. Szymański and Offierski protested vehemently against the exclusion of so many of their supporters and charged that having the police on hand checking documents, constituted a national insult. When a vote was taken on the two rival lists pandemonium broke out and according to the police report it was impossible to determine who had won.(154) Dobrowolski turned to the jurors, who with one exception stated that his list had won. Taking no chances he wrote the minutes of this meeting into the committee files himself; he did not want any vague wording to lead to future quarrels.(155) The Dziennik described the 16 August meeting as "The Victory of Law and Order!" "The population of Poznań showed that they are not interested in secessionists and anarchists a la Szymański."(156) The strict controls imposed by Dobrowolski were "intended to keep out outsiders and minors". The Kuryer praised Dobrowolski's handling of the crisis and regretted only that the "admission fee was too low. It allowed many German socialists to enter... The new committee is clearly legal."(157) The Wielkopolanin defended the 20 pfennig charge as a way to offset the debts created by the Poznań run-off election, which had cost the committee 880 Mk.(158)

The populist press did not recognize the legitimacy of the meeting. In the Orędownik Szymański wrote, "We call them secessionists!... Dobrowolski chaired the meeting ineffectively. He applauded the chaos begun by the Wielkopolanin crowd and did nothing to stop their excesses. At the critical moment of the vote he left the hall. The hall divided into two but the meeting broke up without a decision. (the juror) Mniszewski said that the populist list had the majority, Jeżewski and Skrzydlewski said the court party had it. (Father Antoni) Stychel was undecided."(159) In his editorial comment the next day (19 August) Szymański wrote, "The court party has divided Polish society. It had to use the police, extrance fees and tax cards to hold back the will of the people. The court party, seeing that it was in the minority, chose a committee arbitrarily, against the wishes and will of the majority of the voters."(160) The Postęp also did not recognize the legality of the Kusztelan committee. On 19 August the Postęp wrote, "To our great surprise the court papers are saying that at Wednesday's meeting the court committee was elected. This is the height of shamelessness and lies! Usurpers!"(161)

Thus, the foundations for the Populist Party, "partya ludowa", were formed. Szymański, Knapowski and their supporters decided the 16 August meeting had not chosen a legitimate successor to the Dobrowolski committee. What had begun as a one-man crusade to destroy the gentry's stranglehold on political power had now evolved into the nucleus of a powerful middle-class challenge. The gentry, however, still had many weapons at its disposal. In his capacity as secretary of the Central Committee Dobrowolski confirmed the validity of the Kusztelan committee, writing him a formal letter to that effect signed by the chairman, Żółtowski, and its treasurer, Cegielski. The challenge had been accepted.

6.4 The Press War at its Height August-October, 1893

The summer months of 1893 in Poznan were marked by an ever-widening rift in the fabric of national solidarity in the Polish community. Vigorously challenged by the populists, the gentry powerbrokers forgot their own differences and closed ranks behind legitimacy and tradition. The Dziennik, Kuryer and Wielkopolanin recognized a common threat and combined their resources to destroy it. On the other side of the barrier, Szymański and Knapowski, viewed the populist movement as the force of the future: egalitarianism, urbanization, commerce and a folkish version of democracy. The gentry "Dworusy" were the dishonest and foolish representatives of all that was negative in the Polish past: rhetorical bravura, oppression of other social groups, laziness, greed, and a stranglehold on social and political power. Perhaps the only "objective" newspaper at this point was the Goniec, which, for all its overblown nationalist rhetoric, saw clearly both the faults of the populists and the inevitability of a gradual democratization of the Polish political apparatus. The Goniec shrewdly observed on 22 July, "Dass die Polen von der Regierung etwas erhalten werden, unterliegt keinem Zweifel. Dies wird jedoch nicht das Verdienst der Abgeordneten, sondern eine Folge unserer erwachenden Kraft und Selbstaendigkeit sein."(163)

The verbal extremes which the populist and the gentry press resorted to in combating each other represented a dark hour in Polish history. The vindictiveness exhibited by both sides knew no paralell in Galicia or the Congress Kingdom, where similar processes of urbanization and democratization were taking place. The charge of "treason" was made so often in editorials as to become virtually meaningless. Ludwig Bernhard wrote in 1907 that the degree of conflict was exaggerated in the press and that most Polish residents took a middle road, "Zwischen beiden aber, also zwischen Hofpartei und Volkspartei, stand die Majoritaet der politisch Denkenden abwartend, misstrauisch und doch bemueht, die Gunst des Augenblickes zu benuetzen."(164) The police were more sensitive to the importance of the quarrel. In mid-June, 1893, an analysis noted, "In die

Einigkeit der polnischen Buerger ist ein tiefer Riss hineingekommen und Anhaenger und Gegner der Militaervorlage oder wie sie in der die Spaltung betreibenden radikalen Presse genannt werden, die Hofpartei und die Buergerpartei, befehden sich auf das erbittertste. Dr. Szymański ist es, welcher schon seit mehr denn Jahresfrist den Funken geschuert hat, der jetzt zur hellen Flamme gewachsen ist und den Wahlkampf hier zu einem ungemein heftigen gemach hat."(165)

Given the wide degree of agreement on major issues affecting the Poles in Prussia, one is hard put to answer the question of why the strife was so bitter. A major reason was the intractable personality of Szymański and his unshakable belief in the inevitable victory of the middle class. Szymański's role in the 1893 crisis was paramount; his stubborn convictions, persistant activity and sheer audacity were the driving force behind the the populist movement. Another reason was undoubtedly personal antagonisms. The Dobrowolski-Szymański feud had been going on for over 20 years; Szymański had launched lawsuits against the Kuryer for defamation; and the demagogic Knapowski was out to prove that he constituted a political force in the Polish community. Finally, an important reason was the constellation of opinionated and overbearing editors; each editor appeared convinced that only he was politically mature and responsible; all rivals had "no idea about politics" and could not possibly have anything to contribute. The idea of pluralism in political affairs and alternative, competing political philosophies had not yet made significant inroads into the Polish community in Prussia.

The level of verbal abuse found in the gentry press towards the populist challenge and secession escalated as the movement became stronger. In early February the Kuryer referred to the Orędownik's supporters as "partya Schwalbe'go" claiming that they were indirectly supporting the work of repressive German officials.(166) In mid-April the Kuryer urged all reasonable Poles to "throw the troublemakers into the rubbish bin"(167), and at the end of May repeated an oft-made accusation that, "Szymański's behaviour is creating the way for the expansion of socialism in Poznań... helping along the road of subversion."(168) A favourite tactic was to point to articles in the German press which praised the Orędownik's challenge, thus insinuating that the challenge furthered Germanization.(169) The Wielkopolanin's favourite tactic was to depict the populist leaders as anti-Catholic. On 5 August it made an emotional appeal to its readers, "Poles! We call out to you, beware! Poles, keep close to us! Do not believe him!(Szymański) This (the populist challenge) has nothing to do with politics!"(170) Increasingly, the Wielkopolanin's chief critic became the Postęp, partly because Szymański felt it below his dignity to respond and partly because Knapowski's journalistic talents were better suited to confront its insults. On 23 June, for example the Postęp wrote, "The Wielkopolanin has a clear case of diarrhoea - of the brain".(171) The Kuryer and Wielkopolanin soon took note of the new critic and spared it no degree of verbal abuse. In a sharply worded editorial of 1 August the Kuryer wrote, "The Postęp is just as bad as the Orędownik. It is more radical than the Gazeta Robotnicza. It claims that our deputies fell into a 'Jewish trap' when they voted for the Army Bill... The Postęp has become more radical in its destructive work than its mentor the Orędownik. It learned its trade from the Orędownik but does not measure up to it in intelligence."(172)

The assault on the priest Skrzydlewski at the conclusion of the tumultuous political assembly in Poznań on 27 July gave the gentry press a great propaganda tool to use against the Orędownik and Postęp. On 29 July, the Orędownik condemned the act but repeated its belief that, "Priests should not abuse their clerical authority."(173) On 3 August, Szymański defended himself against charges that he "hated the Church". "The court party papers are exploiting Catholicism for their cause. The Wielkopolanin charges that Szymański hates the Church - this is a dirty slander and a lie!"(174) In order to dispel suspicions of hostility towards the Catholic faith, Szymański and his followers called a "populist-Polish Catholic" rally for 8 August. According to the Orędownik and Postep as many as 2000 "industrialists, craftsmen and workers - the Polish people" attended. The rally passed a resolution condemning the assault on Skrzydlewski and received a telegram from the populist priest in Galicia, Stojałowski, who was active at the time organizing Galician peasants into a political force.(175)

The response of the gentry press to the rally was predictable. The Kuryer called it a "Rally of Lies!" "It was neither Catholic nor Polish (but) anarchistic. It was the partly conscious, partly unconscious work of socialists." (176) The Wielkopolanin wrote, "This was a act of deception! A new deception by the Orędownik and Postęp behind which these two anti-Catholic papers are hiding...It is an insult to the Polish Catholics and their religious feelings... Shameless and hypocritical! We condemn it most strongly."(177) As soon as the rally was announced the Dziennik wrote, "This is a continuation of their sinful work...no one from the clergy will attend, no one who respects law and order will attend."(178) After the rally the Dziennik ridiculed the speech given by Knapowski, "(His) speech was characterized by a total lack of political insight, an ignorance of elementary principles of logic and so many historical falsehoods that the few intelligentsia who attended were dumbfounded."(179)

In addition to conflicts with the Catholic clergy, the populists engaged in an unnecessary and futile conflict with Maksymilian Jackowski. Jackowski, patron of Poznania's rural societies, called the supporters of the Orędownik and Postęp in Inowrocław "zbijobrucy" (loafers and riff-raff) at a meeting of the societies on 13 August, 1893, and the populist press promised to take its revenge.(180) The Postep charged that Jackowski was transforming the rural societies into "fortresses of the gentry-courtiers in the countryside", which earned it a resolution of condemnation from the societies.(181) Szymański, in an article of 6 September wrote, "Pan Jackowski is agitating against the Orędownik and Postęp with all the power of the rural societies... His whole agitation only discloses his deep ignorance of of our social conditions. (He) is attacking the Postęp because it is the only one-mark per quarter populist paper."(182) The climax of the quarrel between Jackowski and Knapowski of the Postęp came in January, 1894, when the two competed to become chairman of the committee to celebrate the centenary of the Kościuszko Uprising, which Jackowski won.(183) Insulting the respected 'King of Polish peasants' proved to be a tactical error which undoubtedly reduced populist appeal among Poznania's rural poor.

A new phase of the newspaper war took place when the creation of the Populist Party formalized the opposition. They held a rally on 18 August and formed a secessionist committee for Poznań, with Drobnik as chairman and Offierski as treasurer.(184) "Now the comedy is over", wrote the Orędownik in triumph, "the Kusztelan committee is illegal because of the illegal measures taken by Dobrowolski". The new committee duplicated all the work of the gentry political apparatus and in the upcoming Landtag elections fielded secession candidates. All attempts to reconcile the two feuding committees failed until 1901 when Bernard Chrzanowski emerged as the first National Democratic member to sit in the Reichstag. In an act of desparation, Dobrowolski sent out a secret circular to all local committees forbidding any dealings with the populist committee, which exceeded his authority and was to cause him deep embarrassment in 1894 when the circular was disclosed.(185) Frustrated at the growth in populist strength, the gentry press initiated a boycott of the populist newspapers.(186) "Not a broken pfennig for the secessionists!" raged the Wielkopolanin on 29 August, "Close your doors to them!"(187) The Postęp derided the initiative as futile, "these 'dworacy' are not our opponents, but simple ruffians who are planning our destruction and triumphantly claiming in their press that our last hour is at hand."(188) On 13 September the Postęp wrote, "The lengths to which the Wielkopolanin is descending in its glowering lies and servility exceeds the bounds of imagination... It is not enough to call us anarchists, socialists, devils, firebrands etc. Now they are searching for a new description to insult the whole populist movement. In the eyes of the Wielkopolanin, dear readers, you are today - heretics!"(189)

It was perhaps inevitable that the escalating verbal violence would thrust the populist newspapers into a damaging conflict with Archbishop Stablewski. Szymański was angry at the way the Catholic Church was using its influence to support the gentry political apparatus through homilies and semi-official declarations. Thus, on 26 August the Orędownik wrote in an article entitled "The Clergy in the Mould of the Court Party", "There is a feeling that the clergy is siding with the court party to dominate our society. The people are beginning to look with disdain upon priests who speak out against the national opposition."(190) Szymański had enough political sense to recognize the need to avoid a confrontation. "An open quarrel between the clergy and the Populist party would be a death blow to the latter. A majority of our population will not stand beside those opposed to the clergy."(191) Nevertheless, in a provocative article of 27 August entitled "Let There Be Light!" the Orędownik insinuated that the Archbishop was directly behind the anti-populist movement. "Let the Kuryer tell us once and for all if its new-Polish or new-Prussian politics and the Archbishop-countryman is one and the same... Let us know clearly if it is the voice of the Archbishop-countryman or is it just pretending to be?"(192) The article further went on to claim that Kantecki of the Kuryer, and Łebiński of the Wielkopolanin had "protectors among the clergy". A few days later the Orędownik hinted darkly that the Archbishop had forced the Reichstag deputies to vote for the Army Bill.(193)

The response of the gentry press was immediate and fierce. They now had what they wanted; Szymański had slurred the sacrosanct personage of the Polish Primate and spiritual overlord. The Kuryer screamed, "The thrust against our Archbishop exceeds every imaginable evil...The Orędownik exceeds the Gazeta Robotnicza by far in its passionate hatred towards everyone who does not participate in its sinful and subversive work."(194) On 6 September the Wielkopolanin wrote in sinister tones, "Our Archbishop has been insulted. You serpents of discord, you dark spirit. Now we shall not let you free, ignoble Orędownik until we have condemned you."(195) The Dziennik called the populist newspapers a "National Cancer". "The article (in the Orędownik T.K.) is un-Polish. It is directly opposed to the Polish national tradition. This article was written by a born Pole but by a Pole who has lost all his national instincts and his heart, not to mention his political responsibility, in an atmosphere of anarchy."(196)

Szymański tried to retreat gracefully in follow-up articles, and on 6 September wrote, "The Orędownik criticizes those priests who demonstratively supported the court party during the last rallies and used their religious influence to direct the political sentiments of the voters... This is not an attack upon the clergy nor even a call for the clergy to withdraw from political affairs."(197) On 7 September, it denied that it had assaulted the Archbishop, and denied that it was undermining the Archbishop's authority or rebelling against it.(198) However, on 8 September, the Gniezno-Poznań Capitula issued an official rebuff to the Orędownik, stating that the Archbishop had felt personally insulted by Szymański's statements and warning the populist press to improve their behaviour.(199) For many weeks afterwards the gentry papers published letters from local priests and rural societies condemning the populist press and sympathizing with the 'offended' Archbishop. One such resolution warned that any cleric who joined the forces of the Orędownik or Postęp would face grave penalties. "We will cut him off from us like a rotten or poisonous wart."(200)

Sensing that he had again gone too far in challenging the Church, Szymański called for another "Catholic Populist" rally on 14 September at Kempf Hall in Poznań. The impassioned Szymański claimed 1500 populists attended; the more dispassionate Prussian police observer put the crowd at 600.(201) The rally, chaired by Offierski, passed two resolutions, 1) "We stand solidly behind the Church" and 2) "We express our deep respect, obedience, love and allegience to Archbishop Stablewski".(202) The rally further went on to dispute a recent pamphlet written by Mielżyński and printed in the Kuryer, "Ein Wort zu ernster Stunde an die deutschen Mitbuerger von einem polnischen Buerger". The pamphlet urged Germans to recognize the loyalty of Poles in Prussia and continue along the road of reconciliation, hinting darkly that if more concessions were not forthcoming Poles could fall into socialism or anarchy.(203) It was praised by the Kuryer which claimed it had "made a sensation in the German press and has silenced the German voices of alarm in the east".(204) The Dziennik, which had earlier voiced scepticism at Mielżyński's declaration of loyalty in the Herrenhaus in 1890, called it a "voice of reason". "Chauvinist passion blinds the German press, and it does not see that continual repression of the Polish people is paralyzing the reconciliation efforts of the Reichstag Party and is awakening among the mass of uncritical Poles pessimism, distrust and partisan emotions, aiding the work of firebrands and demagogues."(205)

The Goniec criticized the pamphlet as too obsequious and subservient. "We who have had all promises to us broken, should get down on our knees? This is too much."(206). At the populist rally on 14 September it was reviled in a speech by the Orędownik's junior editor Siemianowski. "No one has to date dared to insult the Polish people and grind them into the mud as the author of this pamphlet has done. It is a denunciation of the Polish people to the Prussian government."(207) Earlier, the Orędownik had interpreted the pamphlet as a desperate appeal to the government to keep the court party in power. "No one has ever made such a statement about the Polish people. There is no word in the Polish language to adequately describe this campaign launched by the gentlemen of the court party."(208) The populist rally of 14 September was accordingly ridiculed by the gentry press. The Wielkopolanin described the participants as the "Society of Poznań Troublemakers".(209)

German public opinion was not ignorant of the Polish rival groups nor was the importance of the outcome lost on the Prussian government. Chancellor Caprivi was well aware that continued Polish support of his Reichstag policies depended on the predominance of the aristocratic faction and he cited the power struggle in a memorandum to Kultusminister Bosse urging a limited concession in language teaching to win Polish support for the Romanian trade treaty.(210) Many German newspapers interpreted the secession as another example of the resistance among the Poles to reconciliation. Heinrich Geffecken wrote in 1907, "Erst das Jahr 1893 brachte dann die Spaltung in die sogenannte 'Hofpartei' und in die von der polnischen Presse gestuetzte demokratische Richtung, welch letzterer die bis dahin den Polen gewaehrten Zugestaendnisse nicht genuegten."(211)

6.5 The Prussian Landtag Election of October 1893

The first real competition for the allegiance of the Polish voters in Poznan between the established gentry leadership and the Populist party was the Prussian Landtag election of 30 October, 1893. Szymański's candidacy in the 15 June, 1893, Reichstag election constituted a protest vote and even his supporters viewed it as an undesireable secession movement. By the October election, however, the populists had a municipal committee, propaganda organs, and an electoral organization. Although their greatest strength lay in Poznan, other urban areas in the province featured powerful populist groups, in particular Bromberg where the maverick Czarliński held the Reichstag seat, and Inowrocław, the district of the unpopular Kościelski. Unlike the Reichstag election, where voting was based on universal male suffrage, the Prussian Landtag elections were based on the three class system, which heavily favoured the wealthier German minority. Thus the Poles, who constituted about 5% of the population of the Reich, held 4% of the Reichstag seats (19 of 397); but in Prussia, where they comprised 10% of the population, they possessed only 3% of the seats (15 of 433). In Poznań, the Reichstag seat was invariably held by a Pole, while in the Prussian Landtag it was always held by a German. In this respect the introduction of a new political party in Poznań did not constitute a threat to the Polish position, since it was a foregone conclusion that no Pole could win. Much of the conflict arose not over the candidates, but over the choices for delegates to attend the provincial congress in Poznań on 25 October.

Szymański had called on the Populist Party to field candidates for the upcoming Landtag elections as early as 4 September, claiming that it was better to lose the election than have the court party win it.(212) He justified the move in a major policy article of 29 September. "The court party committee is self-appointed. It has been recognized by the Central Committee, but this does not concern us. It was recognized on the basis of the minutes of the 16 August Bazar meeting. Who wrote up these minutes? Pan Dobrowolski. Who recognized them in the Central Committee? Once again, Pan Dobrowolski. Together with his pal, Pan Cegielski, Pan Dobrowolski writes up his own minutes and then certifies them! That meeting was illegal!"(213)

The populists in Poznań were given a big lift by pre-election rallies in Inowrocław, where on 27 September a huge crowd of 2000 voiced criticisms of the political leadership and challenged the candidates put forward by the local committee.(214) Led by Józef Grossman and Józef Czapla, the populists succeeded in overturning the committee's choices, and in a follow-up meeting of 8 October forced through a more moderate list of candidates. (215) Szymański called the Inowrocław episode "a great event that will constitute a milestone in the populist movement."(216) In Bromberg Polish politics during the fierce summer of 1893 were highlighted by the campaign to exonerate Czarliński for his abstention on the Army Bill vote. A counter-committee arose, headed by the lawyer Moczyński, who had been removed from the list of candidates for the Reichstag election.

Commenting on a rally of the Bromberg populists on 15 August the Kuryer ridiculed the assembly as: "150 true Polish voters, 300 villagers not from Bromberg, 150-200 socialists, and 100 people too young to vote".(217) The official Bromberg committee, under the leadership of baron Chłapowski, found its support eroding, and was again challenged by a populist rally on 12 October. (218) Chłapowski submitted the resignation of his whole committee to Dobrowolski on 17 October, and the populists quickly held a rally that commended Czarliński's leadership and unanimously nominated him to run in the Landtag election.(219) Czarliński, the incumbent chairman of the Landtag Party, was also nominated in Brodnica and Lubaw, and his popularity reflected public approval of his repudiation of loyalist politics. Moczyński was selected to represent Bromberg at the upcoming provincial congress in Poznań on 25 October.

The populists were also successful in making their presence felt in several smaller towns. In Jarocin, the police were forced to break up a rally on 16 October, after a close vote between the committee's candidate Jaździewski and the populist Offierski threatened to lead to violence. The committee chairman, Sadowski, in a letter to Dobrowolski of 24 October, blamed the supporters of the Orędownik for the police intervention, but admitted that at least a third of the assembled voiced approval of the populist candidate.(220) "Glory to Jarocin!" wrote the Orędownik on 18 October, while the Kuryer wrote that the meeting was "terrorized by the supporters of the Orędownik and Postęp, who had come specifically to break up the meeting." (221) A second rally on 23 October attracted about 1000 voters, a remarkable number in a town of less than 10,000 inhabitants that shows the degree of politicization evident within Poznania's Polish community. It was addressed by the loyalist deputy Dziembowski, who said, "The new Polish politics is gradually but steadily winning converts (among Germans T.K.)...We must be patient, as it is not easy to change the tide of German public opinion formed so long by the Iron Chancellor and the National Liberals."(222) Yet tumult threatened again when it came to a vote, and the committee chairman decreed his list of candidates to be the winner before the police could intervene.(223)

The populists immediately wrote a protest letter to Dobrowolski declaring, "The committee declared its list had won, when in fact the reverse was the case." The letter called for a third rally, but time did not permit one to be held and Dobrowolski was disposed to recognize the chairman's statement.(224) In Mogilno, around 800 voters renominated Stanisław Rożanski as the Landtag candidate but also appointed Stark to attend the provincial congress. The Orędownik wrote triumphantly, "Contrary to their expectations, the court party suffered a total defeat".(225) More orderly meetings were held in Śmiegel, where Cegielski was obliged to fend off a populist challenge from the teacher Kutzner(226), in Strzelno, where 400 voters confirmed the candidacy of the deputy Józef Grabski(227) and in Września, Stablewski's former riding, where Dr. Jan Żółtowski was easily renominated.(228)

In Poznań, the election campaign began on 29 September. Jażdżewski had the unpleasant task of defending the Army Bill vote to a crowd of 600-800 voters in Lambert Hall. He stated, "As you are aware, the Polish Party voted for the Army Bill without any compensation in the hope that, seeing our good will, the government would extend its hand to us... Our Party has done everything possible to facilitate the position of the Prussian government. We chose to accept material hardships and a grave moral burden. I think that if the Ministry (Education T.K.) continues to follow its present policy then the Emperor will remember our loyal behaviour at a critical time for the state and give us what the Ministry will not. If this concept fails, then we shall have to organize ourselves differently, but no one will be able to say that the Poles do not know how to fulfil their obligations."(229) Jażdżewski was nominated to run in Poznań and confirmed by acclamation.

The populist papers, which had earlier defended Jażdzewski during his courageous stand against Kościelski and Stablewski in 1891, now derided his speech. The Orędownik had first called on its supporters to boycott the meeting, but admitted that about 150 populists had attended.(230) Knapowski wrote on 4 October, "The Polish Party and the politicians behind it... are resorting even to terrorism to intimidate opposition deputies (i.e. Jażdżewski T.K.) along a treacherous and slippery road leading to the collapse of the national spirit and the humiliation of the Polish name in all Europe. Let the minority leave the Party who have come to power through the terrorism of a corrupt press."(231) On 3 October the Orędownik called on keeping priests out of the Party and noted about Jażdżewski's speech, "Everyone is repeating the same theme - that in Berlin the deputies received nothing and have nothing."(232) The Goniec condemned the divisive work of the Orędownik and Postęp, writing on 16 October, "(They) have broken with the Polish people forever. We regret the hypnotic effect he (Szymański) has upon his followers... He is misusing the people's name to further his own ambitions."(233)

The Goniec urged the formation of a "Polish party of the middle", in which both loyalists and radical populists would be excluded.(234) This middle party was to be the National Democrats, and their first newspaper would be the Goniec under Karol Rzepecki.

In response to the Lambert Hall meeting sponsored by the Kusztelan committee the populist committee held a "people's rally" on 16 October in Kempf Hall. About 350 populists attended to hear rousing speeches by Szymański and Knapowski ridiculing the court party, and put forward Offierski to run in Poznań.(235) Both parties worked feverishly to get out the vote on election day, appointing agitation committees, "mężowie zaufania" (trusted citizens designated to instruct Poles how and where to vote) and engaging in spirited verbal attacks upon each other. In a clever move the Kusztelan committee described itself as the "national party", to offset the derogatory "dworusy" levelled at it by the populists. The Kuryer exhibited a less energetic anti-populist campaign than heretofore, perhaps as a result of the illness of its long-term editor and former chairman of the Central Committee Antoni Kantecki.

On 25 October, 5 days before election day, a provincial congress met at the Bazar in Poznań to confirm the list of candidates and settle outstanding business. For the first time, populist delegates were present, from Bromberg (Moczyński) Srem (Celichowski) Inowrocław (Czapla) and Mogilno (Stark). The first item on the agenda was the confirmation of the candidates, and here a good deal of diverse opinion was evident. Thus Jażdżewski, who had announced the Polish vote on the Army Bill in the Reichstag, was approved by a vote of only 23-15; the populist favourite, Czarliński, was approved by only 24-14; Cegielski, a key loyalist, was approved by 26-13.(236) These votes are significant because previous congresses had unamimously confirmed candidates selected by local committees, and points to a growing pluralism in political thought. Secondly, the congress was asked to approve of another term for members of the Central Committee. Chairman Żółtowski, was unanimously approved, but the treasurer, Cegielski barely won on the first ballot and the secretary, Dobrowolski, was confirmed only after a run-off vote against the physician Heliodor Święcicki.(237)

A lively debate arose over the third point on the agenda, the Poznań secession. The populist delegates questioned the legitimacy of Poznań's Kusztelan committee, pointing to the "illegal" conditions imposed by Dobrowolski on the 16 August meeting. Dobrowolski denied calling in the police and vigorously defended the legitimacy of the 16 August meeting. After a sharp debate a vote was taken and the congress agreed to recognise the Kusztelan committee by a vote of 27-11.(238) Once again, Dobrowolski had emerged victorious, but at a cost to his personal integrity.

The General Assembly then called for "attempts to be made to end the Poznań secession", and ended with an election manifesto entitled, "In the Spirit of Unity and Agreement". "Our strength is our solidarity, (we must vote) like one man".(239) It had lasted six hours and exhausted everyone; nevertheless it failed to reconcile the rival parties. The Kusztelan committee interpreted the conclusions as a call to to isolate the populists. The populists felt the Assembly had authorized the dissolution of both camps and called for the establishment of a compromise third force.(240) When Dobrowolski failed to comply, the Postęp launched a stinging attack against him. "The Central Committee has insulted the Polish people in not recognizing the populist committee! The blame for this lies with Dobrowolski. We shall never deliver the fate of Polish society under Prussian rule into the hands of those politicians who deliberated in the Bazar yesterday."(241) In last-minute articles Szymański tried to win over to the populists some of the undecided vote. He was well aware of the strong hold that tradition had over the lower classes and knew the impact of slogans like 'national solidarity'. On 29 October the Orędownik wrote, "That we are running our own candidates is the fault of the Central Committee, which had treated the Populist party unfairly... It is more of a protest vote against the Central Committee."(242) And so once again the Poles went into an important election with two rival oraganizations.

The results of the Landtag election of 1893 well illustrate the socio-economic realities in the province of Poznania through the medium of the Prussian three-class voting system. In the countryside, because so many German farmers were leaving for a better livlihood in the western provinces (the Ostflucht) the Poles picked up two seats in the Landtag, increasing their strength from 15 to 17 seats (in combination with West Prussia).(243) Yet in all the province's larger cities the Polish candidates lost, because although they constituted a majority in many towns their financial resources were far behind that of Germans. The results in Poznań are instructive. Of 254 'Wahlmaenner' (electors) only 68 were Poles, (of whom 9 went to the Populist party) despite the fact that the city was over 50% Polish. The Jewish community, according to the calculations of the Kuryer named 83 electors (32%), although their percentage of the population was only about 8.6%.(244) The Kuryer lamented that the Poles had lost 17 electors since 1888, and resented the growing financial power of the Jews. The gentry press was angry that in critical districts populist voters abstained rather than grant the "dworusy" a victory. The Dziennik wrote that the secessionists had "committed a national crime in breaking national solidarity. In their rage they deliberately abstained in run-off votes and thus aided the Germans to defeat Polish candidates."(245) The Goniec claimed wrongly that the "unbegrenzte Stolz und Neid des Sezessionsfuehrers" had prevented a Polish victory in Poznań, and characteristically called their behaviour an "act of treason".(246) The Kuryer threatened to publish a list of everyone who had voted for the Populists. Szymański called this a denunciation of the Polish people and wrote, "Because of its professional lying and slander the Kuryer is today the most repulsive paper in the Duchy. Lay people will not touch it, and many priests want nothing to do with it."(247)

The final 'Wahlmann' totals in Poznań were: Progressives (Jaeckel)- 115, Conservatives (Nathusius)- 81, National Polish Party (Jażdżewski) - 59 and Populist Party (Offierski)- 9. As no candidate possessed a majority a second election was needed. Polish sympathies clearly lay with the Conservative Nathusius. He had been a fair-minded Landrat in Oborniki during the Kulturkampf and as police chief of Poznań constituted a "spirit of toleration and kindness."(248) No doubt behind the scenes negotiations between the Poles and Conservatives in Poznan took place between the first vote on 31 October and the run-off on 6 November. However no deal was made and in the run-off the Poles abstained, allowing the more aggressive candidate, Jaeckel to become the deputy for Poznan.(249) The inability of Poles and German Conservatives to work together at even such an elementary level constituted yet another blow at the much-heralded "Christian alliance". The views of the Goniec of 10 September perhaps best summed up the view of an increasingly large number of disillusioned Poles, "Wir wollen geduldig 100 Jahre, ja noch laenger warten. Der 'neue Kurs' wird wechseln und vielleicht erleben auch wir das noch, was jeder rechte Pole mit ganzer Seele ersehnt... Die Mehrheit der Polen wollen die Kapitulation und den Grabstein des 'neuen Kurses'".(251)

NOTES FOR CHAPTER SIX

1. Hammann, Der neue Kurs..., p. 43.

2. Schulthess'...,1893, p. 1.

3. Komierowski, Koło polskie w Berlinie..., p. 174.

4. "Pan Kościelski a Germania" Dziennik Poznański, 22.2.1893, no. 43

5. Ibid. See also the edition of 17.2.1893, no. 39.

6. Ibid., 21.3.1893, no. 66.

7. Ibid., 29.3.1893, no. 72.

8. Ibid., 2.4.1893, no. 76.

9. Ibid., 30.4.1893, no. 99.

10. Ibid., 5.5.1893, no. 103.

11. PP-Posen, file no. 4806a , Goniec Wielkopolski, 25.3.1893, no. 70

12. Postęp, 29.10. 1892, no. 249.

13. Ibid., 30.10.1892, no. 250.

14. Ibid., 17.2.1893, no. 39.

15. Ibid., 20.4.1893, no. 90.

16. Ibid., 3.5.1893, no. 101.

17. Orędownik, 1.2.1893, no. 26.

18. Ibid., 11.2.1893, no. 34.

19. Ibid., 4.2.1893, no. 28.

20. Ibid., 8.2.1893, no. 31.

21. Ibid., 11.2.1893, no. 34.

22. Ibid., 4.5.1893, no. 102.

23. Ibid., 7.5.1893, no. 105.

24. Ibid., 21.3.1893, no. 66.

25. Ibid., 29.4.1893, no. 98.

26. Kuryer Poznański, 24.1.1893, no. 19.

27. Ibid., 25.2.1893, no.

28. Ibid., 25.3.1893, no. 70.

29. Ibid., 20.4.1893, no. 90.

30. Ibid., 16.4.1893, no. 87.

31. Ibid., 4.5.1893, no. 102.

32. Ibid., 7.5.1893, no. 105.

33. Ibid., 21.3.1893, no. 66.

34. Ibid., 27.4.1893, no. 96.

35. Ibid., 7.5.1893, no. 105.

36. Ibid., 21.5.1893, no. 115.

37. Ibid., 6.7.1893, no. 151.

38. Ibid., 30.7.1893, no. 172.

39. Dziennik Poznański, 21.10.1893, no. 241.

40. Ibid., 18.10.1893, no. 238; 24.10.1893, no. 243.

41. Postęp, 29.6.1893, no. 146.

42. Ibid., 18.7.1893, no. 161.

43. Ibid., 22.8.1893, no. 190.

44. Orędownik, 27.4.1893, no. 96.

45. Ibid., 22.8.1893, no. 190. The historian of the Centrum Party, Karl Bachem, regretted the Polish-German Catholic rift, and noted in his history, "Das Verhaeltnis des Zentrums zur Fraktion der Polen konnte von deren jetziger Wendung nicht unberuehrt bleiben und gewann niemals mehr den freundschaftlichen Charakter, welchen es frueher besessen hatte." Karl Bachem, Vorgeschichte, Geschichte und Politik der deutschen Zentrumspartei (Koeln, 1929 nachdruck von 1967) vol. 5, p. 303.

46. Roman Komierowski in the Reichstag, 5 May, 1893. "Ich erklaere nun, meine Herren, im Namen der polnischen Fraktion, dass wir fuer diesen Antrag mit allen unseren Stimmen eintreten werden...wir bewilligen, weil wir den Konflikt mit der preussischen Regierung nicht auf den Konflikt mit der deutschen Regierung uebertragen wollen, weil wir diesen Konflikt den wir mit der preussischen Regierung haben, dem Gesamtinteresse vorlaufig unterstellen." Berichte Rtg., 1893, vol. 4, pp. 2192-2194.

47. Dziennik Poznański, 10.5.1893, no. 106.

48. Ibid., 17.5.1893, no. 111.

49. Postęp, 11.5.1893, no. 107.

50. Orędownik, 17.5.1893, no. 111.

51. Wielkopolanin, 10.5.1893, no. 106.

52. Kuryer Poznański, 10.5.1893, no. 106.

53. Ibid., 14.5.1893, no. 109.

54. Dziennik Poznański, 16.5.1893, no. 110.

55. Kuryer Poznański, 17.5.1893, no. 111.

56. "Akta PKW", Ms. no. 867, "Powiat Kościan", 21.5.1893, card no. 1.

57. Ibid., Ms. no. 771, "Powiat Września", 24.5.1893.

58. Ibid., Ms. no. 888, "Powiat Wągrowiec", 28.5.1893; Ms. 890 "Powiat Inowrocław", 28.5.1893, card no. 7.

59. Ibid., Ms. no. 892, "Powiat Gniezno", 23.5.1893, card no. 2; Ms. no. 877, "Powiat Pleszew", 28.5.1893; Ms. no. 868, "Powiat Leszno", 25.5.1893, card no. 3; Ms. 863, "Powiat Opalenic", 23.5.1893, card no. 7.

60. Dziennik Poznański, 17.5.1893, no. 111; 18.5.1893, no. 112.

61. Kuryer Poznański, 16.5.1893, no. 110.

62. Wielkopolanin, 17.5.1893, no. 111.

63. Orędownik, 17.5.1893, no. 111.

64. Dziennik Poznański, 20.5.1893, no. 114.

65. Kuryer Poznański, 20.5.1893, no. 114.

66. Wielkopolanin, 21.5.1893, no. 115.

67. Orędownik, 20.5.1893, no. 114.

68. Ibid., 21.5.1893, no. 115.

69. Postęp, 20.5.1893, no. 114.

70. PP-Posen, file no. 4806a, p. 237. Goniec Wielkopolski, 20.5.1893, no. 114.

71. The "Akta PKW" manuscript for Poznań (854) does not contain a copy of the text of the resolution, but it was adoptęd by the voters of Września and is cited from ms. no. 871, "Powiat Września", 24.5.1893.

72. Dziennik Poznański, 19.5.1893, no. 113.

73. Orędownik, 24.5.1893, no. 110.

74. Ibid.

75. Kuryer Poznański, 24.5.1893, no. 116.

76. Dziennik Poznański, 24.5.1893, no. 116.

77. Wielkopolanin, 24.5.1893, no. 116.

78. Dziennik Poznański, 25.5.1893, no. 117.

79. Kuryer Poznański, 25.5.1893, no. 117.

80. PP-Posen, file no. 4806a, p. 241. Goniec Wielkopolski, 24.5.1893, no. 116.

81. Postęp, 25.5.1893, no. 117.

82. Orędownik, 25.5.1893, no. 117.

83. Ibid., 28.5.1893, no. 120.

84. Dziennik Poznański, 27.5.1893, no. 119; Kuryer Poznański, 27.5.1893, no. 119.

85. Orędownik, 30.5.1893, no. 121.

86. The text of the appeal and the signatures are found in Kuryer Poznański, 30.5.1893, no. 121, and the Dziennik Poznański of the same date.

87. "Akta PKW", Ms. no. 894 II "Organizacja i działalność Komitetu Prowincyonalnego Wyborczego", 30.5.1893.

88. Ibid., Ms. no. 882, "Miasto Bydgoszcz", 1.6.1893; Dziennik Poznański, 3.6.1893, no. 124.

89. Ibid., Ms. no. 882, "Miasto Bydgoszcz", 31.5.1893, 1.6.1893; Orędownik, 4.6.1893, no. 125.

90. PP-Posen, file no. 4806a, p. 259. Goniec Wielkopolski, 3.6.1893, no. 124.

91. Dziennik Poznański, 6.6.1893, no. 126; 8.6.1893, no. 128; Kuryer Poznański, 9.6.1893, no. 129.

92. Orędownik, 9.6.1893, no. 129.

93. Dziennik Poznański, 31.5.1893, no. 122; 3.6.1893, no. 144; Orędownik, 6.6.1893, no. 126.

94. Dziennik Poznański, 9.6.1893, no. 129.

95. Ibid; Orędownik, 9.6.1893, no. 129.

96. Postęp, 31.5.1893, no. 122.

97. Kuryer Poznański, 13.6.1893, no. 132.

98. Dziennik Poznański, 11.6.1893, no. 131.

99. Ibid., 7.6.1893, no. 127; Kuryer Poznański, 11.6.1893, no. 131.

100. Kuryer Poznański, 16.6.1893, no. 135.

101. Postęp, 10.6.1893, no. 130.

102. Orędownik, 7.6.1893, no. 127; 17.6.1893, no. 136.

103. Ritter, Das deutsche Kaiserreich..., pp. 366-367.

104. Ibid., Rzepecki, Pobudka Wyborcza..., p. 23.

105. Fritz Specht, Die Reichstagswahlen 1867-1897 (Berlin, 1898), Provinz Posen pp. 149-157, Provinz Westpreussen pp. 114-121.

106. Ibid., Provinz Posen, p. 150; Dziennik Poznański, 18.6.1893, no. 137.

107. Kuryer Poznański, 17.6.1893, no. 136.

108. Dziennik Poznański, 21.6.1893, no. 139.

109. Orędownik, 22.6.1893, no. 140.

110. Ibid., 25.6.1893, no. 143.

111. Wielkopolanin, 29.6.1893, no. 146.

112. PP-Posen, file no. 4806a, p. 270. Goniec Wielkopolski, 24.6.1893, no. 142.

113. Nevertheless, the "Goniec Resolution" was sent to the Reichstag Party on the eve of the second crucial vote on the bill. It read in part, "Die ueberwiegende Mehrheit der polnischen Gesellschaft sei der Meinung, dass man einer Regierung, die den Polen Alles entzogen habe, was Ihnen im Jahre 1815 zugesichert worden sei, weder einen Groschen noch einen Tropfen Blut mehr bewilligen duerfe." PP-Posen, file no. 4806a, p. 281. Goniec Wielkopolski, 4.7.1893, no. 149.

114. Dziennik Poznański, 2.7.1893, no. 148.

115. Ibid., 7.7.1893, no. 152.

116. Orędownik, 27.6.1893, no. 144.

117. Postęp, 8.7.1893, no. 153.

118. Kuryer Poznański, 1.7.1893, no. 147.

119. Trzeciakowski, Polityka polskich klas..., p. 84.

120. Ibid., p. 71.

121. Mueller, Nationalpolnische Presse..., p. 71. "Danach war es ein Privatbrief Caprivis, in welchem er Stablewski erklaerte, 'er (Caprivi) gestehe persoenlich zu, dass den Polen Unrecht geschehe'. Stablewski liess nun das Schreiben durch einen besonderen Boten nach Berlin senden und einem Mitglied der polnischen Reichstagspartei mitten waehrend einer Fraktionssitzung einhandigen. Der Erfolg war, dass man in der Sitzung beschloss, fuer die Militaervorlage zu stimmen." See also Korth, Die preussische Schulpolitik..., p. 50; Galos, "Tragizm Ugody...", p. 241.

122. Ludwik Jaździewski in the Reichstag, 8 July, 1893. "Wir Polen werden fuer die Vorlage der verbundeten Regierungen eintreten... Ich sollte meinen, dass, wenn wir in einer durchweg loyalen Weise auftreten und unsere schweren Bedenken zurueckhalten, wir auch auf Seiten der massgebenden Regierungskreise eine loyale und entgegenkommende Haltung zu erwarten haben, und ich hoffe, dass wir sie finden werden. Finden wir sie nicht, so kann uns von keiner Seite ein Vorwurf treffen; wir haben dann nur bewiesen, dass wir es verstehen, unsere Schuldigkeit, wo es darauf ankommt, zu thun, und werden es nicht zu vertreten haben, wenn ebenso die pflichtmaessige Schuldigkeit und Gerechtigkeit von anderer Seite uns gegenueber nicht erfullt worden ist." Berichte Rtg., 1893, vol. 1, pp. 53-54.

123. Komierowski, Koło polskie w Berlinie..., p. 256.

124. Dziennik Poznański, 11.7.1893, no. 155.

125. Orędownik, 11.7.1893, no. 155.

126. Ibid., 12.7.1893, no. 156.

127. PP-Posen, file no. 4806a, p. 283. Goniec Wielkopolski, 5.7.1893, no. 150.

128. Ibid., 30.8.1893, no. 197.

129. Ibid., file no. 4806b, Goniec Wielkopolski, 30.12.1893, no. 296.

130. Postęp, 12.7.1893, no. 156.

131. Ibid., 15.7.1893, no. 159.

132. Kuryer Poznański, 11.7.1893, no. 155.

133. Wielkopolanin, 21.7.1893, no. 164.

134. PP-Posen, file no. 4806a, p. 298.

135. Dziennik Poznański, 21.7.1893, no. 164.

136. Orędownik, 20.7.1893, no. 163.

137. Ibid., 21.7.1893, no. 164.

138. Ibid., 22.7.1893, no. 165.

139. Postęp, 21.7.1893, no. 164.

140. Kuryer Poznański, 20.7.1893, no. 163. To Czarlinski's defence sprang the populist papers. See Orędownik, 22.7.1893, no. 165, "Behind Pan Czarliński stand the people, and the Poznań deputy Pan Cegielski should have followed his example. The Postęp had a long-term fondness for Czarliński, and wrote on 27.10.1892, no. 247, "Pan Czarliński is the foremost spokesman for craftsmanship, and craftsmen place their faith in him."

141. Kuryer Poznański, 4.8.1893, no. 176; Dziennik Poznański of the same date; Orędownik, 6.8.1893, no. 178.

142. Dziennik Poznański, 27.7.1893, no. 169.

143. Ibid., 29.7.1893, no. 171.

144. PP-Posen, file no. 4806a, p. 298.

145. Orędownik, 29.7.1893, no. 171.

146. Postęp, 29.7.1893, no. 171.

147. Kuryer Poznański, 2.8.1893, no. 174.

148. Wielkopolanin, 1.8.1893, no. 173.

149. Dziennik Poznański, 29.7.1893, no. 171.

150. Ibid., 30.7.1893, no. 172.

151. Kuryer Poznański, 29.7.1893, no. 171.

152. Orędownik, 13.8.1893, no. 184; Dziennik Poznański, 13.8.1893, no. 184; Kuryer Poznański, 13.8.1893, no. 184.

153. PP-Posen, file no. 4806a, Goniec Wielkopolski, 26.5.1893, no. 118.

154. Ibid., p. 307.

155. "Akta PKW", Ms. no. 854 "Akta miasta Poznania" Bazar, 16.8.1893.

156. Dziennik Poznański, 18.8.1893, no. 187.

157. Kuryer Poznański, 18.8.1893, no. 187.

158. Wielkopolanin, 18.8.1893, no. 187.

159. Orędownik, 18.8.1893, no. 187.

160. Ibid., 19.8.1893, no. 188.

161. Postęp, 19.8.1893, no. 188.

162. "Akta PKW", Ms. no. 854. Letter from Central Committee to Józef Kusztelan of 11.9.1893.

163. PP-Posen, file no. 4806a, p. 290. Goniec Wielkopolski, 22.7.1893, no. 165.

164. Bernhard, Das polnische Gemeinwesen..., p. 141.

165. PP-Posen, file no. 4806a, p. 237.

166. Kuryer Poznański, 24.2.1893, no. 45.

167. Ibid., 11.4.1893, no. 82.

168. Ibid., 21.5.1893, no. 115.

169. Ibid., 6.6.1893, no. 126.

170. Wielkopolanin, 5.8.1893, no. 177.

171. Postęp, 23.6.1893, no. 141.

172. Kuryer Poznański, 1.8.1893, no. 173.

173. Orędownik, 29.7.1893, no. 121.

174. Ibid., 3.8.1893, no. 175.

175. Ibid., 10.8.1893, no. 181; Postęp, 10.8.1893, no. 181.

176. Kuryer Poznański, 15.8.1893, no. 185.

177. Wielkopolanin, 12.8.1893, no. 183.

178. Dziennik Poznański, 9.8.1893, no. 180.

179. Ibid., 10.8.1893, no. 181.

180. Jakóbczyk, Patron Jackowski..., p. 263.

181. Dziennik Poznański, 31.8.1893, no. 198.

182. Orędownik, 6.9.1893, no. 203.

183. Jakóbczyk, Patron Jackowski..., pp. 266-267; Karwowski, Historya Wielkiego Księstwa..., vol. 3, p. 29.

184. Orędownik, 20.8.1893, no. 189.

185. For a copy of the secret circular, dated 18.9.1893, see Przegląd Poznański 23.9.1894, no. 26.

186. PP-Posen, file no. 4806a, p. 354.

187. Wielkopolanin, 29.8.1893, no. 196.

188. Postęp, 13.8.1893, no. 184.

189. Ibid., 13.9.1893, no. 208.

190. Orędownik, 26.8.1893, no. 194.

191. Ibid.

192. Ibid., 27.8.1893, no. 195.

193. Ibid., 1.9.1893, no. 199.

194. Kuryer Poznański, 29.8.1893, no. 196.

195. Wielkopolanin, 30.8.1893, no. 197.

196. Dziennik Poznański, 30.8.1893, no. 197.

197. Orędownik, 6.9.1893, no. 203.

198. Ibid., 7.9.1893, no. 204.

199. Mueller, Nationalpolnische Presse..., p. 59; Karwowski, Historya Wielkiego Księstwa..., vol. 3. p. 30; Dziennik Poznański, 8.9.1893, no. 205.

200. Kuryer Poznański, 8.9.1893, no. 205.

201. Orędownik, 16.9.1893, no. 211; PP-Posen, file no. 4806a, p. 354.

202. Orędownik, 16.9.1893, no. 211.

203. Kuryer Poznański, 3.9.1893, no.

204. Ibid., 7.9.1893, no. 204.

205. Dziennik Poznański, 8.9.1893, no. 205

206. PP-Posen, file no. 4806a, p. 341. Goniec Wielkopolski, 10.9.1893, no. 206.

207. Postęp, 19.9.1893, no. 213.

208. Orędownik, 8.9.1893, no. 205.

209. Wielkopolanin, 16.9.1893. For a description of the rally in the other gentry papers, see Dziennik Poznański, 16.9.1893, no. 211, and Kuryer Poznański, 21.9.1893, no. 215.

210. Caprivi in a memorandum of 18.11.1893, "Die Motive, die ich fuer die Ansicht des Herrn Kultusministers unserer inneren Politik entnehme, sind darauf zurueckzufuehren, dass meines Erachtens die preussischen Polen in einer Spaltung begriffen sind, die in der Presse und bei den Wahlen bereits zum Ausdruck kam. Der polnische Mittelstand tritt in Opposition zu den polnischen Aristokraten. Diese Trennung zu verschaerfen, liegt in Interesse der Regierung. Dass was mir fuer unsere Auswartige Politik ausnuetzen koennen, ist der aristokratische Theil der Polen..." DZA Merseburg, Ministerium des Innern, Geheime Registratur I, Akta betr. die Einfuehrung eines fakultativen polnischen Lese- und Schreibunterrichts fuer die Volksschulen in Provinz Posen, Rep. 77, Tit. 50, no. 21, Adh. 5, pp. 103-108. Cited in Trzeciakowski, Polityka polskich klas..., p. 59.

211. Heinrich Geffecken, Preussen, Deutschland und die Polen seit dem Untergang des Polnischen Reiches (Berlin, 1907), p. 118.

212. Kuryer Poznański, 6.9.1893, no. 203

213. Orędownik, 22.9.1893, no. 222.

214. Kuryer Poznański, 28.9.1893, no. 221; 30.9.1893, no. 223.

215. Ibid., 11.10.1893, no. 232.

216. Orędownik, 30.9.1893, no. 223.

217. Kuryer Poznański, 17.8.1893, no. 186.

218. Orędownik, 14.10.1893, no. 235.

219. Ibid., 21.10.1893, no. 241; Dziennik Poznański, 19.10.1893, no. 239.

220. "Akta PKW" Ms. no. 872, "Powiat Jarocin" letter from chairman Sadowski to Dobrowolski, 24.10.1893.

221. Orędownik, 18.10.1893, no. 238; Kuryer Poznański, 21.10.1893, no. 241.

222. Kuryer Poznański, 25.10.1893, no. 244.

223. "Akta PKW" Ms. no. 872, "Powiat Jarocin", 23.10.1893.

224. Ibid., letter to Dobrowolski of 23.10.1893.

225. Orędownik, 10.10.1893, no. 231. For the account of the Kuryer Poznański, 11.10.1893, no. 232.

226. "Akta PKW", Ms. no. 866, "Powiat Śmigiel", card no. 2, 15.10.1893.

227. Kuryer Poznański, 17.10.1893, no. 237.

228. "Akta PKW", Ms. no. 871, "Powiat Września", card no. 4, 16.10.1893.

229. Dziennik Poznański, 1.10.1893, no. 224; Kuryer Poznański, 1.10.1893, no. 224.

230. Orędownik, 30.9.1893, no. 223.

231. Postęp, 4.10.1893, no. 226.

232. Orędownik, 3.10.1893, no. 225.

233. PP-Posen, file no. 4806a, p. 356. Goniec Wielkopolski, 16.10.1893, no. 211.

234. Kuryer Poznański, 7.10.1893, no. 227.

235. PP-Posen, file no. 4806a, p. 393; Dziennik Poznański, 20.10.1893, no. 240; Orędownik, 20.10.1893, no. 240.

236. "Akta PKW", Mş. no. 894, "Organizacja i działalność Komitetu Prowincjonalnego Wyborczego", vol. 2, Bazar meeting of 25.10.1893.

237. Ibid.; Orędownik, 27.10.1893, no. 246.

238. PP-Posen, file no. 4806a, p. 403.

239. "Akta PKW", Ms. no. 894, "Organizacja..." vol. 2, Bazar meeting of 25.10.1893. "Moczyński, while recognizing the delegate Leitgeber, (delegate from the Kusztelan committee T.K.), criticized the former Committee's behaviour and the circumstances around which the new committee was selected (showing of tax-cards, 20 pfennig entrance fee). This is why he agrees with Dr. Celichowski that the new (Kusztelan T.K.) committee is illegal, and that both committees should dissolved and new elections held that would reflect the true wishes of the voters."

240. Dziennik Poznański, 29.10.1893.

241. Postęp, 27.10.1893, no. 246.

242. Orędownik, 31.10.1893, no. 249.

243. Schulthess'..., (1893), p. 147.

244. Kuryer Poznański, 3.11.1893, no. 251.

245. Dziennik Poznański, 3.11.1893, no. 251.

246. PP-Posen, file no. 4806a, p. 423. Goniec Wielkopolski, 5.11.1893, no. 253.

247. Orędownik, 8.11.1893, no. 255.

248. Dziennik Poznański, 4.11.1893, no. 252; Kuryer Poznański, 3.11.1893, no. 251.

249. Dziennik Poznański, 8.11.1893, no. 255.

250. PP-Posen, file no. 4806a, p. 341. Goniec Wielkopolski, 10.9.1893, no. 206.

Chapter Seven: The Collapse of Loyalism.

7.1 The Trade Treaties: The Poznanian Powerbrokers Divided

In late 1893 the domestic rift in Poznań was overshadowed by the growing controversy over the upcoming votes in the Reichstag on the Romanian and Russian trade treaties. The question of Caprivi's trade policies has been extensively explored elsewhere(1); however it would be useful in the present study to briefly outline the position of the major parties and statesmen to appreciate the difficult position of the Polish deputies. Chancellor Caprivi had planned a series of trade treaties with all of Germany's major trading partners as a way to encourage German exports of manufactures and lower prices on imports of raw materials and foodstuffs. But by the end of 1893, however, Caprivi had incurred many enemies and could not be sure of the passage of the Romanian treaty, and in particular the all-important treaty with Russia. Once again, as in the Army Bill vote of July 1893 the Centrum Party allowed its deputies to vote according to their consciences, and every vote counted. Thus, the 19 Polish votes had a special relevance.

The sentiments of the Polish landowners were decidedly against the treaties from the outset. A considerable amount of support existed for co-operation with German landowners to defeat the treaties and improve the state of rural life in Prussia's eastern provinces. Yet the Poles were in the same quandary as with the Army Bill. If they voted against Caprivi they placed their chances of acquiring language and land concessions in jeopardy; if they voted for, they would undermine their own economic standing and enrage the Conservatives. A vote for would also ruin the prospects of the "grand coalition" of Christian parties, which had suffered in 1893 when the Catholic Centrum and Conservative parties had split over the Army Bill. Having supported the Chancellor on every bill in the Reichstag for three years, the Polish aristocrats were torn between their economic interests and their pro-government strategy. By late 1893 the situation was complicated further by the visible erosion of Caprivi's position.

The mixed emotions evident within the Polish Reichstag Party were illustrated only two weeks before the vote on the Romanian treaty by Dziembowski.(2) The Dziennik admitted the divided opinions when it wrote of the speech, "Our deputy Dziembowski criticized the Bund der Landwirte for its position on the Polish question, and this we wholeheartedly commend. We are strongly convinced that our Party, while conscious of the interests of our agriculture and the effects of the treaties, will not allow itself to be a party to Graf Caprivi's downfall and will not pave the way for the return to power of Bismarck or whoever would follow his policies." (3) The decision to support the Romanian trade treaty was likely made after it was announced on 30 November, 1893, that Kultusminister Bosse would re-introduce the formal teaching of Polish in the public schools of Poznania in some way by Easter of 1894.(4) On the day of the vote Radziwill stated that the Poles would support the treaty but at the same time voiced his concern over its consequences on agriculture in the Prussian east.(5)

Because of the Polish vote the treaty with Romania passed by 189-165. (6) The left was delighted by the Polish vote, but the Conservatives were furious. On 15 December the Conservative Party leader, von Kanitz-Podangen, accused the Poles of selling their votes for a concession on language rights.(7) The Dziennik triumphantly wrote of "Graf Caprivi's Parliamentary Victory" (8), and denounced the "Hammerstein Crusade" of the Kreuzzeitung against the Poles. "The government does not attach any importance to the banal and superficial arguments of this Conservative organ."(9)

The Romanian treaty was only a prelude to a far more important and controversial one with Russia. Germany's trade with Russia had been declining since the early 1880s and featured a deficit in 1891 of over 400 million Mk.(10) Furthermore, both countries were engaging in a "tariff war" which severely damaged Russian agriculture and prevented German manufactured goods from entering Russia. Determined to improve relations with Russia after the Franco-Russian military convention of late 1892, Caprivi entered into serious negotiations over a trade treaty in October, 1893, and by December both sides had reached an agreement that abolished tariffs on 393 items and reduced tariffs on others.(11) The cost to Germany was lower tariffs on Russian cereals, which threatened to flood the Reich and ruin many landowners. It was so clearly a sacrifice of the interests of the rural sector to the interests of the urban and commercial sectors that Conservatives called Caprivi a "traitor to his class"(12), and vowed to topple his government. Chancellor Caprivi viewed passage of the bill as of vital importance to the maintenance of good relations between Germany and Russia.(13) He was being criticized by the Bismarckfronde for upsetting the fundamentals of the German-Russian friendship, and the treay helped offset some of the more severe censure. Kaiser Wilhelm II also voiced support for the treaty with Russia.(14)

As early as March, 1893, the Polish landowners had begun their agitation against the Russian treaty. On 3 March, the Goniec predicted that the Polish Party would vote for the bill and warned of a dangerous split between Poles in Prussia and Austria, as the treaty would be a blow to the interests of Galician landowners.(15) In mid-March, Żółtowski, president of the Centralne Towarzystwo Gospodarcze drew up a petition against the bill and sent it to the deputies in Berlin. His example was followed by landowners in other parts of Poznania.(16) Surprised at the vote on the Romanian treaty, the Żółtowski family (Stanisław and Marceli) joined with Adam Czartoryski at a meeting of 21 December, 1893, and sent another petition to the deputies. (17) In a mood of angry frustration further petitions came from the provinces. One such petition from the "Towarzystwo Rolnicze" (Farmers' Society) of Września-Gniezno dated 6 February, stated, "In all fairness, supporting this trade treaty would be a great blow to us. This treaty would improve German-Russian relations, and anyone with a rudimentary knowledge of history knows how the Poles will fare at the hands of this friendship."(18) The deputies were at a loss. Follow the economic instincts of their provinces and vote against the bill, or vote for it and keep Caprivi in office?

The press began to show serious interest in the Russian treaty at the beginning of 1894. The Dziennik argued strongly against it. It sympathized with Chancellor Caprivi and hoped that he would carry on even if the treaty were rejected, but it felt Caprivi's much-heralded Neue Kurs had not given the Poles enough to warrant yet another sacrifice in the public interest. On 18 January, it wrote, "We are fully loyal citizens of Prussia and Germany. But this does not mean that are obliged to nod our heads and agree with every government proposition. No! As loyal citizens we shall judge every bill under consideration objectively, accordidng to its contents."(19) The Dziennik adopted much the same reasoning that it had used in the question of the Army Bills of 1890 and 1893- that the Polish Party should reject any bill that conflicted with the economic or political interests of the community. On 16 February, the Dziennik wrote, "We cannot be supporters of the trade treaty. We are convinced that our deputies will be influenced in their vote on the treaty exclusively by the needs of our community."(20)

The Goniec ridiculed the other gentry newspapers over the treaty, "Weil weder der Dziennik noch der Kuryer bisher wussten welcher Ansicht die Mehrheit der Aktionaere beider Blaetter sei"(21), and deplored the fact that Polish votes were saving the Reich at crucial moments, comparing it with King Jan III Sobieski's relief of Vienna in 1683 for which no reward was received. "It would be better to be in captivity", it concluded on 12 January.(22)

Both populist newspapers argued for the acceptence of the trade treaty with Russia because it promised lower food prices for the impoverished townspeople. The Postęp of 14 January, 1894, wrote, "Our small businesses and townspeople that do not base their livlihood on agriculture cannot but be in favour of the treaty."(23) It linked the treaty to the continuing social diversification of Polish society and the growth of the middle class. On 13 February, it wrote, "Our powerful landlords, just like German landlords, are against the treaties and have even threatened our deputies with a vote of no-confidence should they support them. Yet, for Polish trade, industry and craftsmanship, and for the broad masses of our people, the trade treaty can bring tremendous benefits. We demand that our deputies vote for the Russian treaty, not because the government wants it but because it is beneficial to our society."(24)

Szymański fully appreciated the dilemma of the landed classes. On 5 January, the Orędownik wrote that "The deputies are between the hammer and the anvil... There is no escape from their loyalty pledge... If the treaty does not pass, then Caprivi must resign and new elections must be called. With 19 votes the Poles can once again carry the day. Our landowners are claiming that the bill will ruin the urban classes, but is this true? Not at all. The landowners have convinced only themselves of this."(25) On 13 February the Orędownik printed a sympathetic "voice from the city" and disclosed the views of the urban population. "The (Russian) trade treaty is very important for Germany and for German industry. The government is correct in attaching so much importance to it. This is a matter of great importance to Poles living in the eastern provinces, because, although we have no great industries here, we can also benefit from lower food prices. In addition a greater consumption of foodstuffs will lead to a gradual rise in our standard of living and a recovery of prices for agricultural goods."(26)

The Kuryer was also in favour of the Russian treaty, though not because of economic reasons. It was imperative that Chancellor Caprivi survive, and further imperative that the Polish Party in the Reichstag form a reliable source of strength for him. Any perspective replacement for Caprivi was bound to be more hostile to a Polish-German reconciliation.

In forming its strategy the Kuryer was forced to do without the services of Antoni Kantecki, who had died on 17 November, 1893.(27) Throughout 1894 it suffered from the erosion of faith in the Neue Kurs and was clearly put on the defensive. It was still a gentry organ, and throughout 1893 it had urged a greater state effort tc improve rural conditions in Germany; it initially manifested a great interest in co-operation with the Bund der Landwirte. As late as 14 January 1894, the Kuryer wrote, "Last year we voiced our rejection of the trade treaties several times... Today we say no to the treaty as unhelpful to the Polish community. A majority of our landowners are against it. Still, we should not exert any pressure on the Party. If the landowners want to send a petition to the Party in this matter, all right, but make it short. The fate of reconciliation does not depend on this vote. The Party should take the opinions of the farmers into account."(28) Before long, however, the Kuryer took a different view. On 23 January it reported that, "the landowners are changing their minds" and argued that agriculture would benefit if tariffs on Russian imports were the same as that on Austrian.(29) In contrast to the Dziennik, which stressed the dissatisfaction of Polish landowners in Galicia, the Kuryer wrote that voting for the treaty would be a great advantage to the hard-pressed Poles under Russian rule.(30)

This is an interesting argument; earlier the Kuryer had been criticized by the anti-loyalist papers for its needless sabre-rattling that could only worsen the lot of Poles in the Russian Empire. Now the Kuryer was emerging as the champion of Polish landowners in Russia, as the true "Polish patriot" that was able to consider the welfare of Poles in all three partitioned zones. Yet its most convincing argument was simple and all too visibly true: if Caprivi fell, all hopes of dismantling Bismarck's anti-Polish laws would fade. On 2 February the Kuryer wrote, "High duties (on foodstuffs from Russia T.K.) have not helped us... The agitation of the Bund der Landwirte is to get rid of Caprivi, which we do not want. They are using duties and the treaty as an excuse." (31)

The degree to which Poznania's landowners were alarmed at the upcoming vote is evidenced in yet another petition sent to the Reichstag deputies in mid-February, 1894. A group of 24 leading Polish landowners, meeting in Poznań under the leadership of Stanisław Żółtowski, voted 14-10 to advise the Party to vote against the treaty.(32) Later, Żółtowski wrote an open letter to the gentry newspapers appealing to all landowners to support the petition. "It is the duty of every farmer to defend his threatened interests, not only to uphold his own material standards, but also the needs of our whole society... Above all, our political actions should strive to strengthen our financial position. We must speak out in a most determined manner against any bills detrimental to our national interests, and in particular the bill now under consideration in the parliament."(33) Żółtowski went on to warn that the treaty would affect animal husbandry as well as cereals and facilitate the work of the detested Ansiedlungskommission, ruining many landowners and forcing them to sell their property. The Kuryer printed Żółtowski's letter but voiced its disagreement, and printed other letters from "farmers" sympathetic to the treaty.(34)

One factor that may have influenced the deputies in Berlin to support Caprivi once again was the formal reconciliation between Bismarck and Wilhelm II in January 1894, evidenced in Bismarck's triumphant visit to Berlin.(35) With Bismarck now back in the royal favour, the Polish deputies had reason to fear even the slightest suspicion of opposition on their part. The Polish press described the reconciliation between the former chancellor and the Emperor with dismay but were quick to point out that it did not signal Bismarck's return to power. The Kuryer saw it as only a "gesture to an old man before his death."(36) The Dziennik theorized that the Emperor was trying to convince Bismarck to speak out in favour of the Russian treaty. "This may tone down the violent attacks of the (agrarian) opposition. We think it will have political repercussions."(37)

Another factor that may have worked to the advantage of the loyalists was the statement by General von Gossler in the Prussian Landtag in early February that Polish recruits could stay in their home provinces during their compulsory army service.(38) The statement evoked a storm of protest in the Kartell press, especially the Kreuzzeitung, which warned of the formation of a national Polish army.(39) The Dziennik, never convinced of the sincerity of the Kreuzzeitung in regard to the Polish question, shouted back that "The attack upon Polish recruits is an attack upon Wilhelm II. The Kreuzzeitung should change its motto of 'God and country'."(40) Taken by surprise by the violent reaction of the German press to his statements, General Gossler retreated and said that the decision was only an experiment. (41) Finally, only 5% of Poznan's soldiers were to be Polish, hardly a concession at all.(42)

The debate among the Reichstag deputies was undoubtedly heated. In December, 1894, Czarliński told a crowd in Bromberg that he had argued against the treaty but that the internal debate had been "vigorous". (43) Several deputies protested and wanted to break the principle of Party solidarity, but the bloc principle prevailed. Kościelski, in his last Reichstag speech, hinted at the way the Poles would vote on 1 March,(44) but the final decision was announced by Radziwiłł on 10 March. Radziwiłł acknowledged the tremendous opposition of Polish landowners to the bill but concluded that there was not enough evidence to reject the treaty on economic grounds.(45)

The Russian treaty was the last manifestation of Polish loyalty made to the Prussian government and to German public. The internal debate had exhausted the Poles' patience and led to the resignation of Kościelski on 9 March, the day before the vote. Dziembowski and Teodor Kalkstein abstained on article I of the treaty (46), but, unlike Czarliński the year before, they escaped censure. The Dziennik was disappointed at the Party's vote, and wrote, "We do not want to analyze the decisions of our deputies. Their posture on the Army Bill and the trade treaties has gone so far (against our economic interests T.K.) that only the hope of obtaining an equitable response from the government in the areas of our national needs can still the outrage that has grown from our material losses."(47)

Later on in the year the Dziennik wrote, "With the trade treaties we have lost all our independence and resistance to foreign effects upon our domestic markets. The principal fault, one that cannot be forgiven, of our present trade policy, is to make us absolutely dependent upon the fortunes and will of our neighbours."(48) The Dziennik was obviously voicing the the views of the majority of the landed gentry. Harry Rosenthal has written, "The vote for the trade treaties show that the deputies were more Pole than landowner... This cost them dearly."(49) The failure to secure any significant concession for the vote on the Russian treaty led directly to the demise of the loyalist faction.

The Polish vote furthermore provoked an irreversible break with the Conservatives. Hanne-Lore Land has written, "Die Kreuzzeitung bemuehte sich bis

1892, aus taktischen Gruenden den Versoehnungskurs der Caprivi-Zeit zu verteidigen: sie warnte die Konservativen davor, die ohnehin wegen des Gegensatzes in der Wirtschaftspolitik vorhandenen Spannungen zur Regierung durch eine unduldsame Haltung in der Polenfrage zu vergroessern. Ab 1893 setzte sich jedoch der Ruf zur Rueckkehr eines scharfen Ostmarkenkurses im Sinne Bismarcks immer mehr durch."(50) Already angry at the Centrum Party for its 'betrayal' of the conservative cause, the Conservative break with the Poles signalled the end to the grand alliance of all 'Christian parties'. The old Bismarck coalition of National Liberals, Conservatives and Free Conservatives reconstituted itself and all hopes of making any gains in the Kartell-dominated Prussian Abgeordnetenhaus faded.

In a last attempt at a Polish Conservative co-operation in the Landtag that may have yet changed the course of the relations, Czarliński appealed to the Conservative deputies to allow unlimited freedom of movement of Poles into Prussia's Polish provinces.(51) The appeal fell on deaf ears. No Conservative deputy rose to support Czarliński, and Ministerpraesident Graf zu Eulenburg rejected the proposal of unlimited immigration.(52) Indeed the tone of the speeches made in the Landtag by Conservative deputies grew visibly sharper during 1894, one that was to characterize the Prussian Junkers until the outbreak of the First World War. Hermann von Dewitz voiced the convictions of many Conservatives when he wrote, "Die Unabhaengigkeits- und Einheitsbestrebungen des Grosspolentums sind eine ernste Gefahr fuer das deutsche Vaterland".(53)

The vote for the Russian trade treaty was so out of character for the landowners who dominated Polish political life that virtually no one in Germany could believe in the sincerity of their loyal proclamations. It seemed all too obvious that Chancellor Caprivi was 'buying' their votes with concessions, 'do et des', trading away the interests of Germans in the east for short-term Polish support in the Reichstag. An undesireable side-effect of Polish loyalty was the alienation of virtually all segments of German public opinion, giving credence to Bismarck's vocal charges of Polish intrigue and deception.

7.2 The March, 1894 Language Bill: Concession or Insult?

The edict of April 1891, permitting the teaching of the Polish language on a private basis, had satisfied no one. The National Liberals and the Bismarckpresse had denounced it as a sellout of the German interest while the Poles felt it was only the introductory step to the formal return of the Polish language into the school curriculum. Throughout 1892 and 1893 the Polish press complained of financial difficulties in keeping the private lessons going. From 1 September, 1891, to 1 December, 1893, the private lessons in Poznań had cost the community 10,759 Mk., while only 9559 Mk. had been raised over this period, showing a deficit of 1200 Mk.(54).

When the news was disclosed at the end of November 1893 that Bosse was planning to re-introduce the Polish language into the school system at Easter, 1894 the Polish press regarded this as a step in the right direction. Stories in the German press that Bosse had decided to annul private lessons because they led to agitation and constituted a political demonstration were strongly rebuffed. In the words of the Dziennik, "If the minister has decided to finally grant us a degree of justice... it is because he has been convinced by the appeals of our deputies and our ecclesiastical authorities of the shortcomings of the Graf Zedlitz ruling. That "concession" has been too expensive. It is also unjust, because having paid all our taxes there is no reason why we should have to pay extra for these lessons."(55) The Kuryer felt the decision vindicated its resolute loyalism. "The shrieks and pathetic declamations (of the irreconcilables T.K.) no longer make any impression on anyone one. Thus we can hope that the government will not abandon the road it is on and our deputies in Berlin will not be led away from loyalty by the loud shouts of our chauvinists. An honest loyalty towards the Prussian government is our only salvation."(56)

In fact, Kultusminister Bosse was doing all in his power to avoid any more concessions on the Polish question. Throughout 1893, Chancellor Caprivi had been in need of Polish votes on important Reichstag legislation and advised Bosse to grant some sort of concession. Archbishop Stablewski also wrote numerous appeals. On 22 May, 1893, Bosse wrote to the Chancellor that he was obliged to reject Stablewski's pleas because, "Die Folge davon wuerde ein Rueckgang der bisher von der Staatsregierung befolgten Sprachenpolitik auf der ganzen Linie sein. ... wuerde alle deutschen Elemente in den genannten Provinzen (Poznania and West Prussia T.K.) tief verletzen. Er wuerde in allen nationalgesinnten deutschen Kreisen dieser Provinzen Bestuerzung und Verwirrung erregen, und der Staatsregierung als Schwaeche angerechnet werden."(57) Chancellor Caprivi's reasoning was clearly pragmatic; he needed Polish votes on the Army Bill and the trade treaties.(58) Von Wilamowitz-Moellendorf also favoured a re-introduction of Polish lessons as a minimum concession to the Polish community.(59)

The ruling was ordered by the Cabinet on 26 February, 1894, and it was officially published on 16 March. (60) Nevertheless, its contents leaked out to the German press at the end of February, and was quickly reprinted in the Polish press. The decree abolished private lessons, and permitted one to two hours per week for Polish children for only two years, provided they already had a sufficient command of German. It further made no provision for lessons in West Prussia or Upper Silesia. Significantly, Bosse used the occasion to link private, uncontrolled lessons to "Great Polish national agitation". He stated in the Landtag that he had discovered long ago that private Polish lessons were getting out of control and that his decision was in no way a "payment" for Polish votes in the Reichstag.(61) Predictably, the German press felt it was a "weitgehendes Entgegenkommen gegen unberechtigte polnische Ansprueche".(62) The Poles were stunned at its severe limitations and the press reaction was explosive. In a mood of desperation Archbishop Stablewski wrote to Chancellor Caprivi on 3 March begging him to intecede with the Emperor to extend the length of lessons to at least four years. His intervention was in vain.(63)

While the German press took aim at Bosse and what was regarded as Caprivi's "soft" Polish policy, the Polish press turned on its own politicians. "Der Bankrott der Herren Versoehnler!" screamed the headline of the Goniec on 6 March. "Minister Bosse is not interested in dealing with beggars, like Pan Kościelski and his crowd. One can get rights only if one deserves them, fights for them, and wins the respect (of the Germans T.K.)"(64) A month later the Goniec wrote, not without some satisfaction, "Der verhaengnisvolle Erlass ist ein neuer Beweis dafuer, dass die Regierung uns keine wirklichen Zugestaendnisse machen will."(65) The outrage of the populist press knew no bounds. The

Orędownik called it a "defeat of the Polish nation", (66) and denied it was a concession at all. The bankruptcy of the gentry was plain for all to see. Four years of blind pro-government votes had led to two hours of lessons per week for only two years, and this only for Polish children whose command of German was strong enough so as not to "suffer". In an article of 4 March, 1894, entitled "The Alleged Concession", the Orędownik wrote, "Whoever among us appreciated the good intentions of Kościelski and Komierowski and the rest of the court party, that they would bring back the Polish language lessons taken from us six years ago through a meek submission in Berlin, now see clearly and are bitterly disappointed."(67) The strongest words were reserved for the Kuryer, which was doing its best to defend the 'concession'. "The Kuryer writes that private lessons were getting us nowhere. But is this progress?... (The Kuryer) does not want to admit that Bosse's act has destroyed the last vestiges of its loyalist program."(68)

The Postęp called the Bosse edict "a new anti-Polish piece of legislation that means to turn back to the 'old course'". "Even the Prussophiles among us are forced to admit that the Easter concession is a fiasco. Our villager and worker knew better what to expect from the Prussian government than those bright deputies, because the Polish people never for a moment entertained any false hopes... There is no one stupid enough among our lower classes who would tie our national future to the 'concessions' of the German government."(69) On 9 March the Postęp called on all the deputies in the Reichstag Party to resign, charging that, "Our deputies, consciously or unconsciously, have deceived themselves and our society. All their hopes have turned into ashes. We, the Polish people and the opposition, could not convince the deputies of their folly. It has taken the government itself to do that."(70)

Only the Kuryer welcomed Bosse's Easter decree. Unwilling to admit that it had been wrong the Kuryer could only feebly hope that Bosse would soon come u with more. On 6 March it wrote, "We see we still have a long way to go to win over the good will of all Germans so that all our children can benefit from the teaching of Polish... We are hurt that the decree does not apply in West Prussia."(71) While not very happy over the limitations of the Bosse decree, the Kuryer insisted that the ruling did represent a concession, as it annulled the decree of 1887 formally forbidding the teaching of Polish and it took away the financial burden of private lessons. On 4 April, it wrote, "Whoever understands politics and the way things happen only shows his own immaturity by engaging now in recriminations, childish sophistries and pretentious injury."(72) In its defence the Kuryer wrote on 31 May, "Whoever thinks reasonably will admit that Bosse's edict is a concession. This is not to say that we are enthusiastic over the ruling and we regret that it does not meet all our needs. Yet, we cannot deny that we have now only 40 districts in the whole Duchy where Polish is taught privately... We must take advantage of this ruling and not get involved in phraseology and shouting at each other."(73)

The Dziennik's patience with the Polish loyalists had declined noticeably after the vote on the trade treaties. It attacked the Kuryer for its timidity and denied that the Bosse ruling constituted a concession. On 10 June, 1894 it called the ruling a "sham concession", and went on, "Bosse's edict has not satisfied those who voted for the Army Bill and the trade treaties. All the old arguments against us have been repeated by the minister in the Landtag sessions on the budget. We see his edict in a wider context, and cannot agree that this is a concession. Bosse will not withdraw from the present schooling system and this is a great injustice to us."(74) On 2 September the Dziennik wrote on this same theme, "We were promised certain concessions in the language issue, not because of our national aspirations and needs, but because of proper religious instruction for our children. Yet that which has been granted is so insignificant, and so at the mercy of school inspectors and the authorities that it is in danger of fading away like fog. The price of this edict is the taking away of our private lessons."(75) The populists delighted in the quarrel between the two chief gentry papers and sided with the Dziennik.(76)

An interesting feature of the March 1894 Bosse ruling is the way both the government and the Poles tried to avoid all hints of a "deal". They were hard pressed by the National Liberals, Free Conservatives and Conservatives to prove that Bosse's ruling was not 'payment' for votes in the Reichstag. As early as mid-February Landtag deputies were warning the government that the Poles were angling for such a payment.(77) Pressed by the strong questioning of critical deputies in the Landtag, Minister Bosse was obliged to defend his ruling by citing the need to control Polish language lessons and prevent the spread of Polish national agitation.(78) The Dziennik reacted to this speech with bitterness. "He is treating us like naughty schoolchildren, not like fellow-citizens. The decree is a great disappointment; it is almost nothing. Minister Bosse thinks it is generous and says no more will come. On our part, we can only state that we shall not be satisfied with this trifle."(79) The Dziennik was distressed that so many Germans were alarmed at the ruling, and regretted the changing mood in Germany towards greater nationalism and indeed chauvinism.(80) Throughout the spring of 1894, Polish deputies in the Landtag were obliged to refute charges of intrigue and deception in order to win concessions from the Prussian government.(81)

The language teaching edict is important in understanding the final demise of Polish loyalism in Prussia. The view of the Polish press was that after painful votes in the Reichstag that had severely tested the fabric of national solidarity a real concession was their just due; a total re-introduction of the Polish language at all levels and in all schools of Poznania and West Prussia. Instead, they were given only two hours a week for two years, and only in Poznania. Furthermore, Bosse had definitively stated that this was the last 'concession' towards the Poles under his administration and had brought up charges of Polish national agitation once again. The failure of loyalism was evident for all to see. The Postęp of 16 March, 1894 wrote, "It is time for us to wake up! The 'dworska' politics is completely bankrupt. Not even we thought the defeat of our national cause could have been so total."(82)

7.3 Józef Kościelski's Departure - Loyalists Without a Leader

Two key moments in 1894 deliniate the era of reconciliation in Polish-German affairs from the new phase of heightened antagonism that followed: Kościelski's resignation from the Reichstag on 10 March, and the speech by Wilhelm II in Thorn on 22 September. Kościelski's resignation resulted from a revolt of the

Reichstag deputies against his domination of the Party. Only five days after Bosse had told the Landtag deputies that no more concessions could be expected, the Reichstag Party was called upon to approve funds for two German armoured naval vessels. In a hastily-called meeting just before the vote, Kościelski informed the other deputies that he had promised Polish support for the vessels. Led by Jażdżewski and Czarliński, however, the deputies present balked and voted to abstain as a sign of their displeasure with the limitations of Bosse's decree.(83) They had had enough of positive support for the Caprivi administration in the Reichstag and no progress on Polish questions in the Landtag. Kościelski was out-voted on the naval credits issue only because most of the loyalists failed to show up for the pre-vote caucus.(84) The principle of block voting in the Reichstag obliged him to abstain when the crucial votes were taken on 9 March. The "Ersatz Preussen" managed to pass 134-94, but the funds for the "Ersatz Leipzig" were rejected 95-117.(85) Had Kościelski been able to marshal the Poles behind the "Ersatz Leipzig", it would have passed. This was the first time that the Polish Reichstag Party had rejected a government bill under Chancellor Caprivi. The leader of the loyalists had suffered a severe loss of face and felt compelled to resign on 10 March, 1894.(86)

Kościelski's departure had a great effect upon the deteriorating Polish-German relationship. His tremendous wealth and his high standing in the Polish community had kept the Reichstag Party solidly behind Caprivi for four full years despite some very stormy moments and highly unpopular votes. He also boasted a "special relationship" with the Kaiser and was well-known in Berlin's fashionable salons.(87) If any Pole could use his personal influence to further the issues of vital concern for the Polish community it was Kościelski. His loss signalled to many Germans that a new mood had overtaken the Polish deputies, and that they would now return to the ranks of the opposition. To dispel such suspicions Radziwiłł was obliged to stress that the principle of Polish loyalty remained untouched despite Kościelski's resignation in a Reichstag speech of 16 March.(88)

The Reichstag statement convinced no German who glanced at the pages of the Polish press in Poznań. Apart from the Kuryer, all other papers breathed a sigh of relief that the loyalist leader had gone and called for a more resolute position in the Reichstag. The happiest of all was the Goniec, which had consistently opposed Kościelski's leadership of the Party. On 13 March the Goniec wrote, "Endlich! Kujawien verdammt ihn, denn es hat sich ueberzeugt, dass die schoenen Worte und Versprechungen des polnisch-sprechenden Preussen es nicht nur getauescht, sondern auch seinen Patriotismus verletzt hat... Wir sehen eine grosses Nichts. Das Gefuehl der grossen Taeuschung koennen selbst die besten Freunde des von Kościelskis nicht verbergen."(89) The populist newspapers were similarly relieved. The Oredownik charged that Koscielski had tried to shape Polish politics around his private contacts to ministers and the court in Berlin. "The atmosphere in which the Reichstag Party now finds itself contradicts both the Vienna accords, by which we were incorporated into Prussia, and the Prussian constitution... No one more than he has caused the collapse of national solidarity in Poznań. Our deputies will be responsible for even graver faults if they continue to harbour his theories in their hearts."(90)

The Postęp expressed its hope that now the Party would return to a healthy, balanced program in the Reichstag. "We must cleanse the Kujawy from the stain on its honour that Pan Kościelski has brought upon it," it wrote on 14 April.(91) The Dziennik, in a forgiving mood, wrote on 13 March, "We did not agree with deputy Kościelski at times, and fought against him at other times, but as we know him quite well we admit that he was and is a faithful servant of the public good (the Polish public good T.K.). He always had the good of the nation in his heart."(92)

The Kuryer was quick to stress that the resignation had nothing to do with the failure of loyalism and hinted that Kościelski might be re-elected. "It was not caused by any crucial political issue that would signal any sort of split within the Polish Party... Kościelski is making a sort of sacrificial lamb out of himself. Perhaps the voters will renominate this admired deputy. Just about all of German public opinion considers him their greatest enemy."(93) The Kuryer had utterly failed to recognize the shift in public opinion in both the Polish and German communities and refused to the very last to concede that loyalism had failed miserably.

Kościelski's resignation was the first opportunity for the newly-established Przegląd Poznański (first edition 1 April, 1894) to take part in Polish political life. The Przegląd took a stand firmly opposed to blind loyalism. "The fanaticism of Pan Kościelski inspired the tone of his radical loyalism, which went so far that it often obscured the difference between 'we' and 'they'... None of our deputies has lost his sense of moderation like Kościelski."(94)

Just how unpopular Kościelski had become is seen in the campaign to choose his replacement, which dominated Polish public affairs from April to mid-May, 1894. On 29 March he defended his policies and listed the motives for his resignation as ill-health and the need to look after his estates to a silent crowd in Inowrocław. According to the Kuryer, he was politely received. "Pan Kościelski complained that deputies had to spend too much time in Berlin and could not attend to matters at home. He hopes that now unity and agreement will return to the Party. He stated he held a different view of Germany and Prussia from the other deputies, and he feels that the government will draw closer to the Poles."(95)

The Orędownik saw the rally in another light. "The chairman of the Mogilno committee, Józef Stark, demanded to know who had asked Kościelski to speak. The chairman of the Inowrocław committee, Stanisław Łyskowski, said he had, and an argument broke out whether Kościelski should be allowed to speak at all. Finally it was agreed he should be given the chance to explain himself. In a short, curt speech Kościelski praised his political ideals to the heavens, and sobbed how he had sacrificed everything, even his health, to get us concessions in Berlin. He hinted that he would be ready again to sit in Berlin if called upon by his constituents He also said that there is no consensus in the Party at the moment."(96) An embarrassing moment for the ex-deputy was the failure to vote him a formal note of thanks for his ten years service in the Reichstag. The Kuryer complained that rowdy populists had caused such an uproar when the vote was made that police represenatives had to break up the meeting, while the Orędownik claimed that the pro-Kościelski group had called the police in to break up the rally lest their favourite be denied the formal thanks that was customary.(97)

A fiercely-fought campaign evolved out of the efforts to find a replacement for Kościelski. The Populist Party, particularly strong in Inowrocław and Mogilno, promoted Czapla's candidacy, the veterinarian who had been Kościelski's strongest critic during 1893-1894, while the gentry put forward the candidacy of Father Piotr Wawrzyniak, the popular priest who had been supported by the populists in 1892 to replace Stablewski in the Landtag district of Wrześnía. For the first time the Polish community was subjected to the experience of a modern political campaign, with a credible alternative to the gentry's candidate. Both camps held pre-election rallies, both disposed of their own newspapers, and both showed a fierce determination to win. The Kuryer and the Dziennik were decidedly behind Wawrzyniak, though they differed on their description of him. The Dziennik praised the priest's qualifications and wrote, "We know he will not vote for every government bill."(98) On 18 April it was forced to state that "he is not the candidate of Kościelski" promoting his candidacy by dissociating him from the former loyalist deputy.(99)

The Kuryer favoured Wawrzyniak because "he is a candidate worthy of Kościelski".(100) Evidently, the Kuryer felt that the former leader's prestige would help his successor, while the Dziennik felt it would lessen his chances. The populist press was squarely behind Czapla. "Long live Pan Czapla, the first Populist deputy from Wielkopolska!" heralded the Postęp of 14 April 1894. The Orędownik felt that only Czapla's nomination would send the correct signal to the deputies in Berlin. "The politics of Pan Kościelski placed us at the mercy of the Prussian government."(101) The Goniec kept away from a clear endorsement of Czapla but wrote, "In allen drei Kreisen herrscht eine solche Erbitterung und Wuth gegen Kościelski." Any candidate was acceptable so long as he furthered an "extrem-oppositionellen Standpunkt gegenueber den Anschauungen des Kościelski". (102)

The first round in the campaign rallies fell to Father Wawrzyniak. On 15 April the voters of Strzelno, under the leadership of the committee chairman Father Kittel, nominated Wawrzyniak in a fairly quiet session.(103) Supporters of Wawrzyniak described their favourite as a strong-willed candidate. "He will not be told what to do. He is not a 'Kościelski candidate', and no one from the Party has appointed him."(104) But that same day in Inowrocław the populists were successful in preventing Wawrzyniak's nomination, unleashing such an uproar that the police were forced to intervene. Anywhere from 1200 participants (the Kuryer's estimate) to 2000 (the Dziennik) showed up. Populists claimed that the court party had tried to push through Wawrzyniak's nomination without listening to the views of his critics; the committee chairman and the gentry newspapers claimed that Czapla's advocates, seeing that their candidate had no chance in a fair vote against Wawrzyniak, initiated the disorder that brought on the police intervention.(105) The Przegląd Poznański, in a major article entitled, "From the War Front", took the side of the Populist Party and criticized the Dziennik for condoning the actions of chairman Łyskowski.(106)

In Mogilno, where Józef Stark dominated the local committee, the candidacy of Czapla prevailed at a rally on 21 April.(107) This time the gentry supporters protested that the rally was illegal and another meeting was called for 28 April. According to the minutes of this second meeting, "The committee proposed the following list of candidates: Józef Czapla, veterinarian, Moczyński, lawyer, and Józef Grosman, banker. A second list of Father Wawrzyniak, Józef Grabski (landowner) and Dr. Józef Krzymiński (physician) was introduced. A show of hands failed to determine which list had the majority. Chairman Stark asked the room to divide into two. At that point a tremendous uproar ensued, with impassioned voters preventing people from reaching their side of the hall, thus making it impossible to take a count. Finally fistfights broke out. After three calls for calm, the chairman was forced to terminate proceedings."(108) Stark decided to recognize the earlier selection of Czapla. The gentry's supporters held a counter-rally immediately following the official one and nominated Wawrzyniak, notifying Dobrowolski of their decision.(109) Another secession was threatening to disrupt Polish solidarity.

Dobrowolski was well-disposed to the feelings of the Wawrzyniak partisans in Mogilno. The Dziennik's description of the 28 April rally was clearly designed to discredit Stark and the populist committee in Mogilno. "Because of the timidity of the national party, power was seized by ambitious and unscrupulous men. About 800 were present... The committee presented a list of Czapla, Moczyński and Józef Grosman. More than three quarters of the assembled were against Czapla's nomination. Stark then broke up the meeting. The national party was properly enraged. Father Wawrzyniak was nominated at a second meeting but only after Stark and the committee members had left the hall."(110) The Kuryer also joined in the condemnation of Stark. "Chairman Stark cheated to allow in voters through the back door after proceedings had started... An uproar threatened. Stark called for a recess when he saw that the citizens were acclaiming Father Wawrzyniak. Only 15 citizens of Mogilno supported Stark."(111) Criticism of Stark was so strong that he had to defend his management of the 28 April meeting in an open letter to the Orędownik. "I broke up the meeting because of the growing resentment against the clergy and because of fistfights. ... I had to call it off to prevent bloodshed."(112) The Orędownik defended Stark and claimed that the rally had to be terminated because, "Priests agitating for the court party and Wawrzyniak continuously interrupted proceedings. The meeting had to be terminated by Chairman Stark and no vote was taken."(113)

Dobrowolski was alarmed at the signs of secession and attended the second rally in Inowrocław on 29 April, 1894, himself, hoping to avoid a repetition of developments in Poznań. A solution appeared near after Czapla announced he was no longer a candidate, citing his "concerns over the clergy", but the populists immediately nominated Moczyński. Dobrowolski worked closely together with Łyskowski to force through Wawrzyniak's nomination but encountered fierce resistance. At the rally Dobrowolski wanted to speak but "because of the general disorder, he could not continue."(114) A vote was taken and, "The list headed by Father Wawrzyniak seemed to be the winner, if one could decide from the tumultuous voices all raised at once. The general tumult made it difficult to determine who was for, and who against. Chairman Łyskowski declared Wawrzyniak the winner."(115) Predictably the Inowrocław populists compiled a letter of protest and sent it to the Central Committee. "The honourable Central Committee should consider that if it does not take our just demands into account, then the blame for breaking up national solidarity and disrupting society falls on those who insist on disregarding the spirit of the times and crush the general will."(116) Dobrowolski had no reservations with regard to who had won. The Dziennik of 1 May wrote, "About 1200 attended, of whom 5/6 acclaimed Wawrzyniak... The national party has won in both Mogilno and Inowrocław!"(117) But other members of the Central Committee were not so sure. Confronted by indecisive votes, protest letters, and threats of secession, they rejected the candidacies of both Father Wawrzyniak and Moczyński, and chose Krzymiński, who had appeared on both lists of candidates at the Inowrocław meeting of 29 April.(118) The Kuryer was dissatisfied with Krzymiński and felt that the Central Committee should have stayed with Wawrzyniak, but the Dziennik and the Orędownik were happy that a secession had been avoided. To explain the decision Chairman Żołtowski wrote an open letter to the Kuryer. (119) With the approval of the Central Committee, Krzymiński won the election on 16 May easily, polling 10,612 votes against 3414 for all German candidates combined.(120)

Although Krzymiński was not the first choice of the populists in Inowroclaw, his candidacy represented a great step forward for the Polish middle class in its growing political power. It was another sign that the gentry was slowly losing its monopoly of political power. The unpopularity of Kościelski and the policy of blind loyalism was speeding up the process of modernization and democratization and the gentry apparatus could no longer count on unconditional obedience. The Orędownik of 24 May wrote, "This is a manifestation of the people's disgust with the present policies of the Party. For the first time the Polish Reichstag Party has been dealt a severe blow... The residents of the Kujawy have given an example to the whole Polish people how to remove from the Polish Party all those who pursue the politics of the 'dworusy'.(121)

7.4 The Events of September, 1894 in Berlin, Varzin, Lwów and Thorn

The events of September 1894 dispelled all remaining illusions of a permanent Polish-German reconciliation. The tide had definitely turned against Caprivi and against reconciliation. Public opinion was becoming more nationalistic and the ruling classes were able to manipulate these aspirations to maintain their solid control of the Army and the bureaucracy. Similarly, the Kaiser, who had shown such a keen desire for labour legislation and internal reforms in 1890, had switched his concerns to a more assertive German Weltpolitik. Germany under Wilhelm II was entering a stage of grandoise expansion abroad but stagnation in the process of democratization at home.

The Polish community had barely got over the struggle to nominate a successor to Kościelski when they were faced by a series of hard blows. The first of these was a rally of the Alldeutsche Verband in Berlin on 9 September.(122) The principal speaker at the rally, Alfred Hugenberg, had recently been appointed "Assessor" of the Ansiedlungskommission in Poznań and was surprised at the way its work was being contradicted by the Generalkommission set up in Bromberg as part of the Rentengutsgesetz. Hugenberg wrote a two-part essay entitled "Der preussische Staat als Polonisator" and had it printed in "Die Alldeutsche Blaetter".(123) This newspaper had a circulation of over 10,000, more than all Polish newspapers put together except for the Wielkopolanin. At the Berlin congress Hugenberg denounced the "soft" Polish policy of Chancellor Caprivi and introduced a ten-point program directed at combating the decline of the German element in the East. (124)

The immediate effect of Hugenberg's essay was to draw public attention to the activities of the Generalkommission in Bromberg. The Polish press, which had hitherto ignored the Generalkommission altogether, now rose to defend the Rentengutsgesetz and the Bromberg Generalkommission. Polish newspapers reprinted articles from the German press which praised the constructive work of the Commission and cited at length statements from employees defending their work.

(125) The Wielkopolanin of 23 August noted that twice as many Poles as Germans had taken advantage of the Rentengutsgesetz, "The Rentengutsgesetz has been conceived differently from the Ansiedlungsgesetz... In the first, Poles are rightly treated as equals with Germans."(126) The Dziennik, which had hardly mentioned the passage of the Rentengutsgesetz earlier, now offered its readers statistics on how beneficial the legislation was. "We do not belong to the critics of the Rentengutsgesetz. It was a solid move to avoid impoverishment (in the eastern provinces T.K.) Our deputies supported the bill... It has been successful because it lacks a political character. The Ansiedlungskommission is unjust, and hence it has failed."(127) In regard to the Berlin rally itself, the Dziennik wrote that it was undoubtedly, "The most perfidious example of brutal chauvinism... (They) have made a call for a return to the old system. But the old system had shown itself to be bankrupt... A return to the old system would violate the general sense of justice and a better understanding of the interests of the state in Germany. The small changes in the 'Polenpolitik' have not been motivated by a 'weak' government, or by any special sympathy for Poles, but by an appreciation of what lies in the interests of the state."(128) The Polish newspapers ridiculed the suggestion that the Prussian state was acting as "Polonisator".(129)

The news that German residents of Poznania were planning a "Huldigungsfahrt" to Bismarck was first announced on 5 June by the Posener Tageblatt.(130) These journeys of homage played a large role in the development of the "cult of Bismarck; those who came to hear the elder statesman were lead German society during the first decades of the next century. It was thought about 1000 would make the journey, but no one was prepared for the crowd of 2400 that finally showed up in Varzin.(131) The orgainzers of the journey were bitterly disappointed that Oberpraesident Wilamowitz-Moellendorf and General Richard von Seeckt, the senior military commander in Poznania, refused to allow a military detachment to escort the visitors, and quickly pointed to this as another example of the "soft" policy towards the Poles.(132) In the event Bismarck had little new to offer his admirers; he gave a half-hour speech that recapitulated his principal convictions regarding the Polish question.(133) A week later, Bismarck addressed another crowd of 1400-1500 admirers from West Prussia.(134) The effect of these two speeches was well described by Ernst Huber, "Gleichwohl wirkten Bismarcks Reden als ein maechtiger Antrieb der jetzt in Deutschland mit voller Kraft einsetzenden anti-polnischen Propaganda".(135) Within six weeks prominent German residents of both provinces formed the Verein zur Forderung des Deutschtums in den Ostmarken.

To the Poles, Bismarck's speeches contained nothing new and nothing out of character. The Goniec called upon Poles to commemorate one of their own heroes on the day Germans travelled to Varzin, and described the speech as, "eine Enttaeuschung. Enttaeuscht waren namentlich diejenigen, welche von dem eisernen Kanzler irgendwelche wichtigen Andeutungen in der Polenfrage zu hoeren hofften... unser grosser Feind ist nur noch eine in Trummer gefallene Ruine aus der Zeit des Kulturkampfes und des antipolnischen Feldzuges."(136) The Orędownik was upset that the former chancellor had not noticed the growing power of the middle class. "Bismarck does not understand the new conditions at all...the Prussian government will no longer have any difficulty from the Polish gentry, but it will have difficulty from the Polish people".(137)

The Dziennik of 8 September charged that the purpose of the journey to Varzin was to have Bismarck launch a civil war against the Poles. "We understand entirely the respect and praise given to great leaders and statesmen. But every cult requires pure and noble inspiration and intentions. Those from Poznania who are making the pilgrimage to Varzin are not going to thank Bismarck for the 'bellum Gallicum', but are looking for a 'bellum civile', turning one part of the population against the other. The voice of the dying man in Varzin, or the voice from his grave, is needed to proclaim the slogan of civil war, for which no no civil courage is necessary."(138) The Dziennik criticized Bismarck's strong comments on Caprivi's Polish policy and denied that the Poles represented any opposition in Prussia. "In any case the profanity of 'Polish opposition' against Prussian rule is utterly groundless. The Polish people do not oppose but only demand their just rights and equality."(139) The Varzin journey was "anti-government as well as anti-Polish", declared the Dziennik on 20 September.(140)

The Kuryer began its denunciation of the planned Varzin visit as early as mid-July. It warned that the show of admiration for Bismarck was a provocation. "They (the organizers T.K.) want to provoke us to words of rage and angry counter-demonstrations, thus discrediting us in the eyes of those who want to grant us justice. (These chauvinists) want to disturb our peace and force us to assume the politics of passion."(141) The Kuryer wrote that attacking the Neue Kurs was the same as attacking the Emperor himself, and assessed Bismarck's speech of 16 September as "colourless". "Those expecting an anti-Polish explosion were disappointed. Bismarck is too old and cannot think of anything new to say on this theme."(142)

On the same day as the Varzin speech to the Poznania Germans a group of Poznania Poles was in Lwów as delegates to the "Wystawa Krajowa", a huge national exhibition put together by Poles in all three partitioned zones to display their material achievements and national unity. The exhibition was also an excellent example of the post-1863 mood of the Poles. The violent and futile insurrections of the period 1792 to 1863 had given way to an assertive Positivism, in which concentration was placed upon material betterment for the people and deliberation about a reborn Poland was left to Providence. On the evening of 17 September, at a gala dinner given by the mayor of Lwów, Mochnacki, emotional speeches were made to commemorate the occasion. Carried away by the patriotic mood, Kościelski made a speech without thinking through its reception in Germany. He proclaimed the indivisibility of the Polish nation in the face of territorial divisions and compared the partitions of the 18th century to a knife cutting through the heart of the nation. "The whole nation is one organism and one unit. It has one heart and one thought We can be divided materially, but never in our thoughts."(143) The reaction to this speech in Germany was disastrous. Germans of all persuasions were alarmed at what was uniformily felt to be a manifestation of Polish national agitation. Raschdau felt vindicated by the Lwow speech. "Wir (Raschdau and Miquel T.K.) erorterten hierbei die Vorgaenge auf dem Nationalfeste zu Lemberg... Die in Lemberg gehaltenen Reden beweisen, wie sehr die politischen Bestrebungen der Polen infolge der Caprivischen Politik an Kraft gewonnen hatten. Miquel fand die Warnungen, die Fuerst Bismarck von Varzin aus in jenen Tagen an die Deutschen richtete, sehr zeitgemaess, zumal sie, vielleicht ein Satz ausgenommen, massvoll gehalten seien."(144)

The Polish newspapers were understandably proud of the Lwów exhibition and followed its progress closely since the first organizational moves were made in 1892. The Dziennik wrote that the day of the exhibition's opening should constitute a national holiday. "This is one of the most brilliant achievements of partitioned Poland... It is a quiet protest against the brutality brought upon our Fatherland a century ago."(145) The Goniec wrote, "The Lwów exhibition is a moral victory of Poland over the three partitioning powers."(146) Kościelski's speech was duly reported by the gentry papers without editorial comment, but it received some criticism from his sworn enemies. The Goniec described his speech as "misch-masch". "Derselbe, welcher mit vollen Handen Geld fuer preussische Bajonetten und 'Seeulanen' hergibt, welcher uns von der parlamentarischen Rednerbuehne herab 'Preussen polnischer Zunge' nennt, derselbe Herr Kościelski erklaert in Lemberg, dass die Polen einen einzigen unzertrennlichen Organismus bilden!"(147) The Orędownik complained of the "talkative Pan Kościelski" who had managed to discredit both loyalty and opposition through his speech.(148)

Yet the Polish newspapers were completely taken aback only four days later when Wilhelm II made his critical remarks of their behaviour at Thorn. The Emperor said, "Es ist zu meiner Kenntnis gekommen, dass leider die polnischen Mitbuerger hierselbst sich nicht so verhalten, wie man es erwarten und wuenschen sollte. Sie moegen es sich gesagt sein lassen, dass sie nur dann auf meine Gnade und Teilnahme in demselben Masse wie die Deutschen rechnen duerfen, wenn sie sich unbedingt als preussische Untertaenen fuehlen. Ich hoffe, dass die Thorner polnischen Mitbuerger sich entsprechend dem, was ich in Koenigsberg gesagt habe, verhalten werden; denn nur dann, wenn wir alle mann an mann geschlossen wie eine Phalanx zusammenstehen, ist es moeglich, den Kampf mit dem Umsturz siegreich zu Ende zu fuehren."(149) Furthermore, the Emperor was overheard to say unofficially "Was Ich heute gesagt habe, mag wohl beachtet werden. Ich kann auch sehr unangenehm werden."(150) The Polish and Centrum press were adamant that the Emperor did not utter these words, and breathed a sigh of relief when the Reichsanzeiger published the speech but left out the sharp warning to the Poles.(151)

The Thorn speech constituted a deep blow and destroyed whatever hopes the loyalists may have had in the supportive views of the Emperor. Since 1890 the loyalists had assumed that the Kaiser's silence on the nationality question in the Prussian east indicated support for Polish ambitions; it was a forelorn belief in the "good Emperor" who only needed to be informed of the evil deeds of "unjust ministers". It had been felt that the few concessions obtained in 1891 were primarily due to the Kaiser's goodwill. Now the Emperor had finally taken a stand on the Polish question, and his statement seemed to repudiate Chancellor Caprivi's reconciliation course. A number of German newspapers welcomed the speech, and in the words of Richard Tims, "chose to view the parallel remarks at Varzin and Thorn as evidence that the Kaiser and Bismarck were drawing still closer and that Caprivi's days were numbered."(152) Graf Waldersee wrote in his memoirs, "Der Kaiser hat sich in Thorn sehr deutlich ausgesprochen, die Freundschaft mit Kościelski wird nun wohl ein Ende haben."(153) Hans Herzfeld, Miquel's biographer, wrote, "Zugleich mit dem Sturze Caprivis verkundete dann die Thorner Rede des Kaisers vom Herbst 1894 den bevorstehenden Wechsel der Polenpolitik."(154)

The Polish newspapers were stunned by the speech but failed to draw the conclusion that Wilhelm II was reacting to Kościelski's remarks in Lwów.(155) Instead, they chose to interpret his remarks literally, and wondered what the Poles in Thorn could have done to anger the monarch. The Kuryer, which only a week earlier had welcomed Wilhelm II's vigorous speech in Konigsberg condemning the 'Umsturzparteien',(156) asked why the Emperor had signalled out the Polish community in Thorn for special criticism. In its first editorial on the speech of 25 September, the Kuryer wrote, "Probably only (Gustav von) Gossler knows why Wilhelm II made such a statement about us. We are encouraged, however, that the Emperor only demands of us that we behave as fully loyal Prussian subjects. No one can say that we do not feel ourselves to be full Prussian subjects."(157) Two days later it admitted, "A few impassioned newspapers have drawn the conclusion that the Thorn speech had signalled a change of course towards the Poles. This is not at all true."(158) The Kuryer described as "perfidious" statements in the German press warning the bureaucracy in Poznania and West Prussia to heed the Emperor's change of course. The only answer to the Thorn speech was to declare once again Polish loyalty.(159)

The Dziennik was equally puzzled by the Thorn speech. "We know of nothing in Thorn that may have formed a pretext for the Emperor's remarks. Like other citizens we carry the obligations of citizenship and should be given the same rights."(160) On 26 September the Dziennik added, "We do not admit to any guilt in this affair. In our struggle to defend our holiest national interests we have never exceeded the bounds of legality. In a spirit of innocence and conviction of the rectitude of our cause we do not fear the chauvinist storm."(161) The reason for the Emperor's remarks was eventually traced to Varzin. "We have not done anything wrong", it protested on 27 September, "The accusation (in Thorn T.K.) was rather general and is probably due to officials from the old course... We do not have to be reminded of the need to fight against insurrectionary elements. Bismarck is trying to convince Wilhelm II that the Polish gentry constitutes a subversive party. But we outlasted him when he was in power, and we can outlast him now."(162)

The Wielkopolanin described the Thorn speech in a calm manner. On 26 September it wrote, "The Kaiser demands that 1) we consider ourselves full Prussian subjects, and 2) that we form a strong front against subversion. But he does not demand that the Poles in Thorn renounce their nationality, their language or their special status. He promises the Thorn Poles that they can count on his grace on an equal level with Germans if they obey him unequivocally. Hence, we are ready to follow our Emperor to the battlefield against subversion and anarchy. We have the unshakeable belief that we shall be granted his justice on an equal following as our German fellow-citizens... We should place our faith in our generous monarch."(163) The Wielkopolanin rejected the notion that the Emperor was addressing Kościelski's remarks made in Lwów on 17 September and denounced stories in the German press which described the Poles as being part of the subversive movement in Prussia. "Is it possible to remain calm when faced with this hate campaign?", it concluded on 27 September.(164)

The Goniec, never reconciled to the acceptance of the partitions, was overjoyed at the remarks signalling the end to the politics of reconciliation. In the words of the police, the Goniec of 25 September, "schreibt triumphierend", that , "Der Konig von Preussen erklaert selbst, und unmittelbar nach der Lemberger Koemodie des Herrn Kościelskis, dass die unter preussischem Szepter lebenden Polen sich germanisieren mussten, wenn sie der koeniglichen Gnade theilhaftig werden wollen."(165) The essence of the Emperor's statement was, "We can only achieve equality by giving up our nationality... This is a brutal blow to our 'Stanczyks' and also a lesson to them: do not lie to your countrymen, and do not lie to your monarch."(166) On 28 September the Goniec noted the loud response the Thorn speech had aroused in the German press. "Die ganze deutsche Presse von den angesehensten Organen an bis zu den kleinsten Winkelblaettern, triumphiert ueber die Rede des Kaisers, die Freunde Bismarcks freuen sich darueber, dass der Kaiser gewissermassen die Worte des ehemligen Reichskanzlers bestaetigt."(167)

In a similar tone the Przegląd Poznański signalled that the speech represented the final defeat for the Polish loyalists. "'Public opinion against us, but the Emperor with us' - this was the sweet music of the loyalists, suppressing the warnings of the opposition. Among our emotional masses the loyalist leaders aroused a deep faith in the monarch's grace. Wilhelm II, however, remained silent like a sphinx. He never made a single public statement about the Poles. Now, his threat and condemnation has come as a surprise to us, deceived as we were by the fairy tales from Berlin... A great part of our society looked to the throne with the trust of a child, expecting a kind word of hope and joy, any manifestation of his sympathy. It was the first time that the German Emperor spoke to us directly, and it was a painful blow."(168) The Orędownik felt that the blame lay with Gossler and made no reference to the speech by Kościelski in Lwów.(169) The Postęp wrote of the "universal surprise at why the Kaiser is dissatisfied with the Poles in Thorn. He is probably not very well informed. This is likely the fault of Gossler. The Poles in Thorn have done all they could to prove their loyalty."(170)

The shock of the events of September, 1894 coming as they did one after another with increasingly vocal anti-Polish overtones placed the German-Polish reconciliation on the edge of collapse. Alarmed, Archbishop Stablewski, the key loyalist spokesman following the resignation of Kościelski from the German Reichstag, granted a rare interview to the Berlin Boersen-Kourier on 26 September in which he pleaded for the continuation of a Polish- German understanding.(171) Unfortunately, by late 1894 few Poles or Germans were willing to listen to the message of reconciliation.

7.5 The Failure to Resolve the Poznań Secession

Despite the gathering clouds on the horizon the Polish community could not forget its internal differences and form a united defense of Polish interests By late 1894, despite increasing signs of German hostility, the call of "national solidarity" no longer brought all Poles together; it was now derided by the populists as a slogan for preserving an anachronistic gentry domination. An example of the escalating rivalry between Polish groups was the struggle to nominate a chairman to commemorate the centenary of the Kościuszko Uprising of 1794. At a packed meeting of 20 February, the populists called for the appointment of Knapowski, but the gentry was able to force through the candidacy of the peasant leader Jackowski.(172) Throughout the year the two rival municipal committees called separate rallies and condemned the other's activities. A populist rally of 13 March attracted 400 supporters to the Kempf Hall in which Bosse's language bill described in the Landtag on 1 March was attacked.(173)

The Przegląd Poznański examined the secession crisis in a major article on 27 May and concluded, "What political differences exist do not result from radically different principles, but above all from parliamentary tactics, forms and levels of loyalty. The populist faction exhibits a more sober version of loyalty; the politics of the court party have been demoralizing."(174) Later on the Przegląd noted that the press war had exaggerated the situation. "One would think we are all divided into Prussophiles and chauvinists," it wrote on 12 August, "but this is only a legend. The populists lack a popular leader. They need a leader like the Irishman Parnell."(175)

Yet it was the Przegląd which added fuel to the fire on 23 September, 1894, when it published Dobrowolski's 'secret' circular of 18 September, 1893. The circular called upon the various local committees to do everything possible to combat the "intrigues of the secessionists and subversives and allow all those who desire law and order to take their full part in the political process."(176) It appears likely that Rabski, a former employee of the Dziennik, might have convinced one of Dobrowolski's disgruntled employees to obtain a copy of the circular. In the Przegląd, Rabski condemned Dobrowolski's taking sides in the secession crisis. "It appears that the Central Committee regards any opposition as subversion and secession. It was the Central Commitee which was behind the campaign to exclude the populists in 1893."(177) The populists were enraged by the circular; Knapowski wrote on 27 September, "From this document it is apparent that the court party can keep itself in power only through shameless terrorism and duplicity."(178)

The secret circular became a major theme at an assembly of the Central Committee and delegates from local committees held at the Bazar in Poznań on 23 October, 1894. The ostensible reason for the meeting was to establish a new set of voting regulations, and this was duly drawn up with a populist demand satisfied that the highest authority in the province should be the General Assembly and not the Central Committee.(179) Yet the two chief themes were the secret circular of September, 1893, and what to do about the Poznań secession. Populist delegates Moczyński, Czapla and Kutzner grilled Dobrowolski on the legality of the circular. It was a violation of the electoral regulations for the Central Committee to intervene, publicly or secretly, in the affairs of local committees.

Dobrowolski answered the charges with the standard calls for law and order. "Franciszek Dobrowolski declares that the Central Committee had no intention of taking the side of either group. He felt it was his duty to write secretly to the local committees asking for their aid in incorporating all elements of Polish society who respect unity and agreement and at the same time reject the condemnation of national solidarity."(180) The assembly did not dispute this statement directly, but criticized Dobrowolski sharply when the Poznań secession came up for discussion. The populists demanded the resignation of the Kusztelan 'national' committee; Dobrowolski stressed the legality of the Kusztelan committee that had already been confirmed by the Central Committee in 1893. Yet the other members of the Central Committee decided to placate the populist opposition and agreed, over Dobrowolski's objections, to accept Kutzner's resolution: "The General Assembly asks that the existing Poznań committee (the Kusztelan committee T.K.) call an electoral rally and, in the interests of ending the secession, resign its office." This resolution was hotly debated and only passed by a vote of 17-15. (181)

The press accounts of the 23 October General Assembly were surprisingly accurate in view of the many divergent descriptions of political events in the past. The Dziennik and Kuryer rightly regarded it as a defeat for the gentry and offered a short but accurate account.(182) The Goniec expressed its satisfaction with Dobrowolski's censure. "In general we are satisfied. Dobrowolski had to defend himself due to his secret circular... This could have developed into a vote of no-confidence. The majority of the delegates were angered by the manner and tone of the circular... Dobrowolski and the shareholders at the Dziennik Poznański were against the disbanding of both Poznań committees and forming a new one."(183) The Przegląd in an insightful commentary described the Assembly as a "public legalization of the opposition group." The editorial went on, "In the matter of the circular a general condemnation was made of those who, like the Reichstag Party are always ready with a witchhunt and bonfire for dissenters. The... issue of the Poznań secession also was a triumph of political objectivity... Dobrowolski carried on a perfidious polemic against the apostles of harmony and agreement."(184) The tone of the Orędownik and the Postęp was similar.(185)

Two days after the meeting the Kusztelan committee duly announced its resignation and called a rally in the Lambert Hall for 27 October. Dobrowolski perhaps underestimated the appeal of the populists and saw only the menace of Szymański's demagogy. The Dziennik campaigned hard to bring out the voters on Kusztelan's behalf. "Instead of partisan polemics the so-called 'Populist committee' should resign. Unfortunately it is clear that personal ambitions, and- let us be frank- vanity, have been victorious. The slogan of today's meeting must be: mutual understanding, mutual concessions and above all the recognition of our public cause."(186) The Postęp, whose aggressive tone was beginning to exceed that of the Orędownik, prepared its readers for the 27 October meeting by listing a number of 'crimes' committed by the Kusztelan committee, including lying on the part of Dobrowolski. "The 'dworska' committee should have resigned long ago. Simple honesty and justice demanded this. It should not have held the office it obtained through brutality and illegality."(187)

The rally of 27 October, 1894, that was intended to select a compromise committee ended, as so often in the past, in police intervention because proceedings got out of hand. According to the secret police report the 1200 Poles present were divided almost equally into the two camps. Three lists of candidates were presented: a "national", a populist and a compromise list drawn up by the Goniec, not the last time this future National Democratic paper counselled unity while not giving up its central theme of national independence. When a vote was attempted such a tremendous uproar developed that the police had to intervene. However, Knapowski, who had been appointed chairman decided that the populist list had received the majority and declared it the winner as the police were clearing the building.(188)

What was supposed to end the secession in Poznań only prolonged it and deepened the mutual hostility. Significantly, the moderates, represented by the Goniec and the Przegląd, protested Knapowski's handling of the meeting and declared his decision invalid. Rabski, the Przegląd's editor, was a juror during the meeting and was prevented from speaking by Knapowski. Insulted, he wrote a protest letter signed by five other jurors declaring the populist 'victory' invalid. The Goniec charged that the rally failed because of "the plebeian boot of Pan Knapowski". "Nothing helped, not the moderation of Pan Rabski or others... the tribune of the people has crossed the road to what is commonly refered to as dictatorship... Knapowski calls his committee legal. The Goniec Wielkopolski will not recognize it... The populist movement has lost the sympathy of those who had, up to Saturday's meeting, been receptive to it."(189)

The Kuryer refused to recognize Knapowski's decision, charging that he had displayed "partisan absolutism". "The meeting was disbanded before a final decision had been made."(190) For the Dziennik, the meeting was only "one more scandal" which vindicated its opposition to the resignation of the Kusztelan committee. "It did not want to resign," wrote the Dziennik on 30 October, "but it acceded to the will of the General Assembly in the search for unity and calm... In the interests of peace Knapowski was appointed chairman and he named the jurors. Franciszek Dobrowolski protested but was shouted down."(191) The Wielkopolanin offered the opinion that, "The whole spectacle was an example of the most repulsive terror practised by the secessionists."(192)

The Postęp and, less enthusiastically, the Orędownik, declared the populist committee the legal representative in Poznań. "Justice has finally be done!", exclaimed the Postęp on 30 October. "1500 people attended...The populist list of candidates for a new municipal committee was approved by a majority. The police intervention took place only after the vote."(193) Both papers published the minutes of the meeting, written by the populist Mniszewski, on 3 November to prove its legality.(194) Mniszewski was proclaimed chairman and Szymański's promising young protege, Siemianowski, secretary. The final episode in the was the letter from the Central Committee of 6 November, 1894, proclaiming its results invalid and reverting to the Kusztelan 'national' committee as Poznań's legal representative. "Disagreements and rivalry only strengthen the arm of our opponents. We ask the citizens of our capital city Poznań to show that Poles can forget personal objections and rival political views and walk in unison and in solidarity against our opponents." (195) Needless to say, the populists refused to accept this judgment and continued to recognize the Mniszewski committee. Just how detrimental this was to the Polish community in general can be seen from the results of municipal council elections of 22 November, 1894 in Poznań. Of 2448 voters, 1095 voted for the Kusztelan committee's party, 307 for the populists, and 1046 for the German candidates.(196) What might have been an unquestionable Polish victory over the German candidates was less significant due to the secession.

The deep social and political cleavage within the Polish community in Poznania was to plague Polish politics for another decade before both conservative landowners and urban populists were overcome by the National Democratic movement. The secession in Poznań lasted until the 1903 Reichstag election, when the National Democrat Bernard Chrzanowski won the support of both sides.(197)

7.6 Caprivi's Resignation and the End of the Era of Reconciliation.

Only a day before the disputed 27 October Polish rally at Lambert Hall in Poznań, Chancellor Caprivi resigned and was succeeded by Furst Hohenlohe. While his resignation had been foreseen by many insightful observers, its occurrence following the rejection of the first Umsturzvorlage in the Reichstag on 12 October surprised many Poles and gave them cause for alarm. On 11 October the Kuryer complained that the anti-Polish press was leading a crusade of the Emperor and Bismarck against Caprivi, the Poles and the socialists,(198) and expressed joy at Caprivi's parliamentary victory. "The attacks upon Graf Caprivi have failed. Despite all the articles in the press Graf Caprivi's position is strong and he is supported by Wilhelm II. It is a victory for the chancellor, but he cannot let down his defences. The Kartell forces will continue to try and undermine him."(199) The Kuryer chose not to accept the view that the "new era" in Prussian policy towards the Poles was definitely over; this would have discredited it completely after its four years of consistent pro-government editorials. Instead it wrote, "Graf Caprivi's code of knightly conduct dictated resignation. Those hoping for a return to the old course will be disappointed. In politics continuity does not and cannot exist. He has left the political scene too soon, but his political programs will remain and disrupt the former, repulsive tradition."(200)

No other Polish newspaper entertained any hopes in a Polish-German reconciliation following Caprivi's resignation. The Dziennik reminded its readers that Caprivi had made no real attempt to dismantle Bismarck's 'old course', but was uncharacteristically moved by his departure. On 28 October it wrote, "This news has touched us all very deeply. Despite the terrible press attacks upon him, inspired from well-known sources, Graf Caprivi enjoyed universal recognition as a noble man and statesman... It will be difficult to replace this endearing person. He had a clear and honest program... With deep regret we have accepted the news of his resignation, not because we obtained any special rights under his rule, but rather because he did not repress us or harass us."(201) On 30 October the Dziennik compared Caprivi's Polish policy favourably with Bismarck's sharp anti-Polish legislation and concluded, "What we found especially positive and praiseworthy in the differences between the old and new course was the honesty and the law-abiding behaviour (of Graf Caprivi). He never resorted to disreputable machinations, to brutal extra-legal methods which under the cloak of reasons of state violated the law and the notion of justice."(202) Similarly, the Wielkopolanin regretted Caprivi's departure. On 31 October it wrote, "He was a decided opponent of all extra-legal decrees... He enjoyed the trust and sympathy of all those who feel justice should be based on the rights of individuals and nations, and not on the wishes of chauvinists." (203)

The populist press viewed Caprivi's resignation as yet another defeat for the gentry loyalists. On 28 October the Postep reported, "The dismissal of Graf Caprivi is a setback for the policies of our court party. They had placed so much trust (in him). One should never surrender to illusions but look at political affairs with a cool, objective eye. Graf Caprivi was a noble and just man, and his dismissal signifies nothing good for the Polish community."(204) The Orędownik, which had appreciated Caprivi's honest intentions from the outset but had rejected the idea of a permanent Polish-German reconciliation from mid-1892, called the resignation a "truncheon blow to the head" to the court party.(205) The Goniec was the only newspaper to pass over the resignation without much regret. "The root of all our evils," it wrote assertively on 27 October, "is the false current of reconciliation, which Poles do not want and which Germans hate. We shall not win ourselves the goodwill of Germans by acting like Pharisees; indeed we shall never win (it) just like France will never forgive the Germans for the injustice shown them... Every true patriot will appreciate this."(206) What awaited the Poles under Fuerst Hohenlohe constituted no mystery for the Goniec; on 4 October it confidently predicted, "Now we shall see the 'newest' course, something similar to Bismarck's truncheon."(207) It was a sad but accurate preview of the last phase in the German-Polish relationship before World War One.

NOTES TO CHAPTER SEVEN

1. For a detailed study of the passage of Chancellor Caprivi's trade policies see, Georg Gothein, "Die Wirkung des Handelsvertrages", in: Volkswirtschaftliche Zeitfragen, vol. XVII (1896); Hans-Christian Sievers, Die Innenpolitik des Reichskanzlers Caprivi (Kiel, 1953) 2 vols.; Horst Oehlmann, Studien zur Innenpolitik des Reichskanzlers Leo von Caprivi (Freiburg, 1953); and the most recent studies by Peter Leibengurth, Modernisierungskrisis des Kaiserreichs an der Schwelle zum wilhelmischen Imperialismus: politische Probleme der Aera Caprivi 1890-1894 (Koeln, 1975) and Rolf Weitowitz, Deutsche Politik unter Reichskanzler Leo von Caprivi 1890-1894 (Duesseldorf, 1978).

2. Zygmunt Dziembowski in the Reichstag on 25 November, 1893. "In der Hauptsache verfolgen wir dasselbe Ziel, (as the Bund der Landwirte T.K.) unser landwirtschaftliches Programm ist im Grunde genommen auch Ihr Programm, unser Endziel ist der Schutz und die Wohlfahrt der Landwirtschaft - dasselbe haben Sie auch in Ihr Programm aufgenommen. Aber, wenn auch unsere Endziele gleich sind, so sind doch die Wege, die wir verfolgen, andere; und sobald Ihre politische Aktion schon den Boden des rein Agrarischen verlasst, sind wir nicht in der Lage, mit Ihnen zusammen zu gehen". Berichte Abg.H., 1893, vol. 1, p. 86.

3. Dziennik Poznański, 28.11.1893, no. 271.

4. Ibid., 2.12.1893, no. 275; Kuryer Poznański, 2.12.1893, no. 275; Orędownik, 2.12.1895, no. 275.

5. Ferdynand Radziwiłł in the Reichstag on 13 December, 1893. Berichte, Rtg., 1893, vol. 1, p. 433.

6. Radziwill, Briefe..., p. 78; Orędownik, 15.12. 1893, no. 285; Nichols, Germany after Bismarck..., pp. 292-298.

7. Von Kanitz-Podangen in the Reichstag on 15 December, 1893. Berichte Rtg. 1893, vol. 1, p. 488.

8. Dziennik Poznański, 19.12.1893, no. 288.

9. Ibid., 21.12.1893, no. 290. See also the Kuryer Poznański of 17.12.1893, no. 287.

10. Gothein, "Die Wirkung des Handelsvertrages"... p. 28. The declining German Russian trade volume is seen in the following table:

	Imports (000 Mk.)	Exports (000 Mk.)
1890	541,887	206,457
1891	580,396	262,605
1892	383,400	239,500
1893	353,400	184,600
1894	543,900	194,800
1895	568,400	220,900

Statistisches Jahrbuch..., 1892, p. 65; 1893, p. 65; 1894; p. 93; 1895, p. 123; 1896, p. 121; 1897, p. 129.

11. Weitowitz, Deutsche Politik und Handelspolitik..., pp. 304-305.

12. Balfour, The Kaiser and his Times..., p. 171.

13. Chancellor Caprivi in the Reichstag on 27 February, 1894. "Wenn wir nun die Hand, die Russland uns jetzt geboten hat, zurueckweisen, wird dann nicht Russland dem Panslawismus erst recht verfallen? Wenn Sie diesen Vertrag ablehnen, meine Herren, den ich fuer einen starken, kraeftigen, neuen Draht halte, dann wird nicht nur der neue Draht nicht gelegt, sondern Sie zerschneiden dann auch die alten Draehte - und Sie tragen die Verantwortung dafuer und nicht die Regierung!" Berichte Rtg., 1894, vol. 2, p. 1451.

14. Waldersee, Denkwuerdigkeiten..., vol. 2, p. 306 quotes Wilhelm II at a dinner party on 9 February, 1894: "Ich habe keine Lust, wegen hundert dumme Junker mit Russland Krieg zu fuehren!". Waldersee continued in his memoirs, "Dann hat er (the Kaiser T.K.) behauptet, der Zar naehme eine Ablehnung persoenlich sehr uebel, das russische Volk, das kein Verstaendnis fuer parlamentarisches Wesen habe, werde ueberzeugt sein, dass er, der Kaiser Wilhelm, doch eigentlich Gegner des Vertrages sei. Auf die russischen Truppenansammlungen an unseren Grenzen hinweisend, erklaerte e schliesslich, bei Ablehnung des Vertrages wuerden wir sicherlich in laengstens drei Monaten Krieg haben, er wuerde dann das rechte Weichselufer preisgeben usw."

15. PP-Posen, file no. 4806a, p. 113, Goniec Wielkopolski, 4.3.1893, no. 52.

16. Kuryer Poznański, 17.3.1893, no. 63; Dziennik Poznański, 10.1.1894, no. 6.

17. Orędownik, 4.1.1894, no. 2.

18. Dziennik Poznański, 8.2.1894, no. 30.

19. Ibid., 18.1.1894, no. 13. See also the issue of 6.1.1894, no. 4.

20. Ibid., 16.2.1894, no. 37.

21. PP-Posen, file no. 4806b, Goniec Wielkopolski, 10.1.1894, no. 6.

22. Ibid., 12.1.1894, no. 8.

23. Postęp, 14.1.1894, no. 10.

24. Ibid., 13.2.1894, no. 34.

25. Orędownik, 5.1.1894, no. 3.

26. Ibid., 13.2.1894, no. 34.

27. Karwowski, Historya Wielkiego Księstwa..., vol. 3, p. 39.

28. Kuryer Poznański, 14.1.1894, no. 10.

29. Ibid., 23.1.1894, no. 19.

30. Ibid., 2.2.1894, no. 26.

31. Ibid.

32. Orędownik, 15.2.1894, no. 36.

33. Ibid., 18.2.1894, no. 39; Dziennik Poznański, 16.2.1894, no. 37.

34. Kuryer Poznański, 18.2.1894, no. 39.

35. Radziwiłł, Briefe..., pp. 82-83; Nichols, Germany after Bismarck..., p. 301; Komierowski, Koło polskie w Berlinie..., p. 261.

36. Kuryer Poznański, 23.1.1894, no. 19.

37. Dziennik Poznański, 30.1.1894, no. 23.

38. Ibid., 23.2.1894, no. 43; Raschdau, Unter Bismarck und Caprivi..., p. 288.

39. Kuryer Poznański, 16.2.1894, no. 37. The fury felt by the Conservative Party is well illustrated in a letter from its leader, Wilhelm von Kardorff, to his wife of 17.2.1894. "Um die Polen fuer die russischen Vertraege zu kaufen, hat man ihnen geradezu die wahnwitzige Konzession gemacht, die polnischen Rekruten, die bis jetzt unter die deutschen Regimenter verteilt wurden, nur im V. Armeekorps (i.e. Poznań T.K.) zu lassen. Sie brauchen also kuenftig nur ihre Offiziere totzuschiessen, um eine polnische Nationalarmee zu haben, die bei einem franzoesischen Kriege uns in den Ruecken faellt." Wilhelm von Kardorff. Ein nationaler Parlamentarier im Zeitalter Bismarcks und Wilhelm II. 1828-1907. Ed. Siegfried von Kardorff, (Berlin, 1936), p. 291.

40. Dziennik Poznański, 17.2.1894, no. 38.

41. Ibid., 23.2.1894, no. 43.

42. Orędownik, 14.8.1894, no. 184.

43. Goniec Wielkopolski, 14.12.1894, no. 284.

44. Józef Kościelski in the Reichstag on 1 March, 1894. Berichte Rtg., 1894, vol. 2, pp. 1518-1521.

45. Ferdynand Radziwiłł in the Reichstag on 10 March, 1894. "Meine Herren, die Meinungen ueber die Folgen dieses Vertrages fuer die Landwirthschaft in unseren Wahlkreisen sind sehr getheilt. Ich moechte sagen: mit groesserer Energie ist uns aus unseren Wahlkreisen die Ansicht entgegentreten, dass unter keinen Umstaenden diesem Vertrage zuzustimmen sei, dass er den Ruin der heimischen Landwirthschaft inaugurieren wuerde." Berichte Rtg., 1894, vol. 3, p. 1743

46. Ibid., p. 1751.

47. Dziennik Poznański, 23.3.1894, no. 66.

48. Ibid., 19.7.1894, no. 162.

49. Harry K. Rosenthal, "Nation or Class: the Bund der Landwirte and the Poles" Australian Journal of Politics and History 19 (1973), p. 203.

50. Land, Die Konservativen und die preussische Polenpolitik..., p. 46.

51. Leon Czarliński in the Abgeordnetenhaus on 17 February, 1894. Berichte Abg. H., 1894, vol. 1, p. 552.

52. Ibid., p. 554.

53. Hermann von Dewitz, Von Bismarck bis Bethmann. Innerpolitische Rueckblicke eines Konservativen (Berlin, 1918), p. 84.

54. Wielkopolanin, 28.12.1893, no. 294.

55. Dziennik Poznański, 7.12.1893, no. 279.

56. Kuryer Poznański, 5.1.1894, no. 3.

57. Gatz, Akten zur preussischen Kirchenpolitik..., p. 158.

58. Raschdau, Unter Bismarck und Caprivi..., p. 289.

59. Herzfeld, Johannes von Miquel...vol. 2, pp. 496-497.

60. Schulthess'... (1894), p. 98; Korth, Die preussische Schulpolitik..., p. 50.

61. Dr. Robert Bosse in the Abgeordnetenhaus on 1 March, 1894. "...die Verfügung meines Herrn Amtsvorgaengers, des Grafen von Zedlitz, vom 11. April 1891, durch welche gestattet wurde, dass unsere Lehrer in den Schullokalen polnischen Privatunterricht ertheilen. Ich habe im vorigen Jahre und ich glaube schon im Jahre 1892 hier nach meiner Reise in Posen anerkannt, dass dies der schwache Punkt in unserer Schulverwaltung ist, den ich dort empfunden habe." Berichte Abg. H., 1894, vol. 2, p. 781. For the evaluation of the decree in the Polish community, see Komierowski, Koło polskie w Berlinie..., p. 262, and Karwowski, Historya Wielkiego Księstwa..., vol. 3, p. 41.

62. Schulthess'...,(1894), p. 98.

63. Trzeciakowski, Polityka polskich klas..., p. 133.

64. PP-Posen, file no. 4806b, Goniec Wielkopolski, 6.3.1894, no. 52.

65. Ibid., 3.4.1894, no. 75.

66. Orędownik, 3.3.1894, no. 50.

67. Ibid., 4.3.1894, no. 51.

68. Ibid., 7.3.1894, no. 53.

69. Postęp, 6.3.1894, no. 52.

70. Ibid., 9.3.1894, no. 55.

71. Kuryer Poznański, 6.3.1894, no. 52.

72. Ibid., 4.4.1894, no. 76.

73. Ibid., 31.5.1894, no. 121.

74. Dziennik Poznański, 10.6.1894, no. 130.

75. Ibid., 2.9.1894, no. 200. In fact, the edict effectively strangled the teaching of Polish altogether, and ceased in practise in 1896. See Maria and Lech Trzeciakowski, W Dziewiętnastowiecznym Poznaniu..., p. 303

76. Orędownik, 12.6.1894, no. 131.

77. Dr. Krause (Koenigsberg) in the Abgeordnetenhaus on 17 February, 1894. "Von Anspielungen, dass die Herren etwas Besonderes erstreben, bin ich fern, aber allerdings will ich durchaus nicht verschweigen, dass mir das hervorheben dessen, dass die Regierung keine Veranlassung hatte, mit den Polen unzufrieden zu sein, nicht gefiel; denn sowohl die Mitbuerger polnischer Zunge wie wir sollten lediglich nach sachlichen Gesichtspunkten Entschliessungen fassen, und wenn wir sie fassen, haben wir keinen Anspruch auf Anerkennung der Staatsregierung, und noch viel weniger darauf, dass die Staatsregierung ihrerseits in irgend einer Weise entgegenkommt." Berichte Abg. H., 1894, vol. 1, p. 559.

78. Dr. Robert Bosse in the Abgeordnetenhaus, Ibid., vol. 2, pp. 781-782.

79. Dziennik Poznański, 4.3.1894, no. 51.

80. Ibid., 3.4.1894, no. 75.

81. For example, Marcelli Motty in the Abgeordnetenhaus on 25 April, 1894. "Meine Herren, durch unsere Stimmen ist die Militaervorlage durchgebracht worden, und wir sind dabei von dem Grundsatz ausgegangen: si vis pacem, para bellum; wir haben den russischen Handelsvertrag durchbringen helfen, weil man drohte - und die Drohung mag wohl auch in gewisser Beziehung gerechtfertigt gewesen sein -;dass wenn der Vertrag nicht angenommen wird, wir vor einem moeglichen Kriege mit unserem oestlichen Nachbar stehen. - Und weil wir eben keinen Krieg wollten, deshalb haben wir fuer den russischen Handelsvertrag gestimmt, und die Folge ist, dab mit unserer Beihuelfe Europa ein zehnjahriger Friede gesichert ist, was schon seit langer Zeit nicht der Fall war." Berichte Abg. H., 1894, vol. 3, p. 1785.

82. Postęp, 16.3.1894, no. 61.

83. Bernhard, Das polnische Gemeinwesen..., p. 149; Karwowski, Historya Wielkiego Księstwa..., vol. 3, p. 41-42.

84. Orędownik, 16.3.1894, no. 61; Dziennik Poznański, 13.3.1894, no. 58.

85. On the "Ersatz Preussen" vote, see Berichte Rtg., 1894, vol. 3, pp. 1704-1705. For the "Ersatz Leipzig" vote, Ibid., pp. 1710-1711.

86. The resignation was announced in the Reichstag on 10 March. Ibid., vol. 3, p. 1731.

87. Ryszard Kołodziejczyk, Jan Bloch 1836-1902 (Warsaw, 1983), p. 282, pp. 288-289. Bloch, a wealthy Warsaw banker, was Kościelski's father-in-law.

88. Ferdynand Radziwiłł in the Reichstag on 16 March, 1894. "Nun, meine Herren, fuehlen wir um so mehr die Verpflichtung, uns mit den Aeusserungen unseres frueheren Mitgliedes solidarisch zu erklaeren... Wir bedauern, dass wir dieses Mitglied nicht mehr unter uns haben; aber den sanguinischen Konsequenzen, welche Freund und Feind an diese Mandatsniederlegung geknuepft haben, denen, glaube ich, wird die weitere Entwicklung nicht entsprechen." Berichte Rtg., 1894, vol. 3, p. 1904.

89. PP-Posen, file no. 4806b, Goniec Wielkopolski, 13.3.1894, no. 58.

90. Orędownik, 20.3.1894, no. 64.

91. Postęp, 14.3.1894, no. 59.

92. Dziennik Poznański, 13.3.1894, no. 58.

93. Kuryer Poznański, 13.3.1894, no. 58.

94. Przegląd Poznański, 8.4.1894, no. 2.

95. Kuryer Poznański, 1.4.1894, no. 74.

96. Orędownik, 3.4.1894, no. 75.

97. Ibid.

98. Dziennik Poznański, 15.4.1894, no. 86.

99. Ibid., 18.4.1894, no. 88.

100. Kuryer Poznański, 14.4.1894, no. 85.

101. Orędownik, 10.4.1894, no. 81.

102. PP-Posen, file no. 4806b, Goniec Wielkopolski, 10.4.1894, no. 81.

103. Akta PKW, Ms.no. 891, "Powiat Strzelno", meeting of 15.4.1894, card no. 4.

104. Dziennik Poznański, 17.4.1894, no. 87.

105. Orędownik, 19.4.1894, no. 89; Kuryer Poznański, 18.4.1894, no. 88; Dziennik Poznański, 17.4.1894, no. 87.

106. Przeglad Poznański, 22.4.1894, no. 4.

107. Orędownik, 25.4.1894, no. 94.

108. Akta PKW, Ms. no. 889, "Powiat Mogilno", meeting of 28.4.1894, card no. 8.

109. Protest letter to Dobrowolski dated 28.4.1894. Ibid., card no. 10.

110. Dziennik Poznański, 1.5.1894, no. 99.

111. Kuryer Poznański, 1.5.1894, no. 99.

112. Orędownik, 5.5.1894, no. 102.

113. Ibid., 1.5.1894, no. 99.

114. Akta PKW, Ms. no. 890, "Powiat Inowrocław", meeting of 29.4.1894. card no. 10.

115. Ibid.

116. Resolution approved on 3 May, 1894 and sent to Dobrowolski, Ibid., card no. 11.

117. Dziennik Poznański, 1.5.1894, no. 99.

118. Ibid., 8.5.1894, no. 104; Orędownik, 6.5.1894, no. 103; Kuryer Poznański, 8.5.1894, no. 104.

119. Kuryer Poznański, 12.5.1894, no. 107.

120. Schulthess'..., (1894), p. 120; Kuryer Poznański, 23.5.1894, no. 115.

121. Orędownik, 24.5.1894, no. 116.

122. Hartwig, "Der Alldeutsche Verband und Polen"..., p. 252.

123. Alldeutsche Blaetter, no. 16, no. 34, 1894.

124. Land, Die Konservativen und die preussische Polenpolitik..., pp. 37-38; Bużek, Historya polityki narodowościowej..., p. 231; Kuryer Poznański, 13.9.1894, no. 208; Baier, Der deutsche Osten..., p. 23.

125. Dziennik Poznański, 5.9.1894, no. 202, reprinted a letter from the Commission employee Stobbe to the Gesellige.

126. Wielkopolanin, 23.8.1894, no. 191.

127. Dziennik Poznański, 19.8.1894, no. 188.

128. Ibid., 31.8.1894, no. 198.

129. Kuryer Poznański, 3.9.1894, no. 200; Dziennik Poznański, 28.8.1894, no. 195

130. Fuerst Bismarck nach seiner Entlassung, ed. Penzler..., vol. 5, p. 300.

131. Ibid., p. 312; Guenzel, Die nationale Arbeit..., p. 10; Wiegand, Die antideutsche Propaganda..., p. 9.

132. Dziennik Poznański, 23.9.1894, no. 217; Fritz Grause, Deutsch-slawische Schicksalsgemeinschaft (Wuerzburg, 1967), p. 237.

133. Bismarck, GW., vol. 13, pp. 538-543.

134. Ibid., pp. 543-549.

135. Ernst Huber, Deutsche Verfassungsgeschichte seit 1789 (Stuttgart, Berlin, 1969), vol. 4, 498. Earlier the scholar Johannes Guttzeit described the impact of the two speeches in a similar manner. "In der deutschen Bevoelkerung war die polengegnerische Stimmung fast verschwunden; aber zwei Reden Bismarcks genuegten, den Hass von neuen zu schueren, die Gegensaetze zu verschaerfen und die unter Caprivi festgelegte gegenseitige Verstaendigung auf neue Jahrzehnte hinaus zu vereiteln." Johannes Guttzeit, Geschichte der deutschen Polenentrechtung (Danzig, 1927), p. 100.

136. PP-Posen, file no. 4806b, Goniec Wielkopolski, 19.9.1894, no. 213. Fuerst Bismarck nach seiner Entlassung, ed. Penzler..., vol. 5, pp. 302-303.

137. Orędownik, 21.9.1894, no. 215.

138. Dziennik Poznański, 8.9.1894, no. 205.

139. Ibid., 19.9.1894, no. 213.

140. Ibid., 20.9.1894,no. 214.

141. Kuryer Poznański, 13.7.1894, no. 157.

142. Ibid., 18.9.1894, no. 212; 20.9.1894, no. 214.

143. Schulthess'...(1894), p. X; Dziennik Poznański, 20.9.1894, no. 214.

144. Raschdau, Unter Bismarck und Caprivi..., p. 355. Von Miquel's discouragement with the Poles has been described by his biographer Hans Herzfeld, "Das Zwischenspiel der Caprivizeit ist an ihm nicht ohne Eindruck voruebergegangen. Trotzdem hat er die 1894 beginnende Rueckkehr zur Bismarckischen Politik persoenlich durchgesetzt." Herzfeld, Johannes von Miquel..., vol. 2 p. 493. See also Waldersee, Denkwuerdigkeiten...vol. 2, p. 323; Holstein to Hohenlohe on 20.9.1894 in: Holstein und Hohenlohe, ed. Rogge..., p. 404. For the views of later historians, see Deutschland und Polen, ed. Brackmann..., p. 237; Schinkel, Polen, Preussen, und Deutschland..., p. 201; Massow, Die deutsche innere Politik..., p. 184; Werner Frauendienst, "Preussisches Staatsbewusstsein und polnischer Nationalismus in: Das oestliche Deutschland (Wuerzburg, 1959), (Goettinger Arbeitskreis) p. 356; Wiegand, Die anti-deutsche Propaganda..., p. 7. Land, Die Konservativen und die preussische Polenpolitik..., p. 39 writes, "Die Lemberger Rede Koscielskis von 17.9.1894 wurde als verhuelltle Kampfansage gegen die preussische Regierung aufgefasst und besiegelte endgueltig den Bruch mit dem Versoehnungskurs."

145. Dziennik Poznański, 5.6.1894, no. 125.

146. Goniec Wielkopolski, 18.10.1894, no. 238.

147. PP-Posen, file no. 4806b, Goniec Wielkopolski, 20.9.1894, no. 214.

148. Orędownik, 28.9.1894, no. 221.

149. Das persoenliche Regiment. Reden, Aeusserungen Wilhelms II. (Muenchen, 1907), pp. 105-106.

150. Schulthess'..., (1894), p. 152.

151. Wielkopolanin, 29.9.1894, no. 222.

152. Richard W. Tims, Germanizing Prussian Poland (New York, 1941), p. 28.

153. Waldersee, Denkwuerdigkeiten..., vol. 2, p. 323.

154. Herzfeld, Johannes von Miquel..., vol. 2, p. 497.

155. Kuryer Poznański, 26.9.1894, no. 219; Dziennik Poznański, 7.10.1894, no. 229. Future observers and German comtemporaries made the link between Koscielski's speech and the Kaiser's Thorn remarks right away. See Laubert, Die preussische Polenpolitik..., p. 140; Karwowski, Historya Wielkiego Księstwa..., vol. 3, p. 44; Buzek, Historya polityki narodowościowej..., p. 215.

156. Kuryer Poznański, 14.9.1894, no. 209.

157. Ibid., 25.9.1894, no. 218.

158. Ibid., 27.9.1894, no. 220.

159. Ibid., 28.9.1894, no. 221.

160. Dziennik Poznański, 25.9.1894, no. 218.

161. Ibid., 26.9.1894, no. 219.

162. Ibid., 27.9.1894, no. 220.

163. Wielkopolanin, 26.9.1894, no. 219.

164. Ibid., 27.9.1894, no. 220.

165. PP-Posen, file no. 4806b, Goniec Wielkopolski, 25.9.1894, no. 218.

166. Ibid.

167. Ibid., 28.9.1894, no. 221.

168. Przegląd Poznański, 30.9.1894, no. 27.

169. Orędownik, 26.9.1894, no. 219; 30.9.1894, no. 223.

170. Postęp, 25.9.1894, no. 218.

171. Schulthess'..., (1894), pp. 158-160 carries the interview. It was in reply to an article in the Koelnische Zeitung of 20.9.1894, entitled "Polnischer Hochmut und deutsche Demut".

172. Postęp, 22.2.1894, no. 42; Dziennik Poznański, 22.2.1894, no. 42; Karwowski Historya Wielkiego Księstwa..., vol. 3, p. 49.

173. PP-Posen, file no. 4806b, Betr. die im Kempf'schen Saale abgehaltene Volksversammlung, 13.3.1894. Postęp, 15.3.1894, no. 60.

174. Przegląd Poznański, 27.5.1894, no. 9.

175. Ibid., 12.8.1894, no. 20.

176. Ibid., 23.9.1894, no. 26 prints the secret circular in full.

177. Ibid.

178. Postęp, 27.9.1894, no. 220. See also Orędownik, 25.9.1894, no. 218.

179. The new regulations agreed upon were printed by the Dziennik Poznański under the title, "Regulamin Wyborczy i instrukcya dla Komitetów powiatowych Wielkiego Księstwa Poznańskiego uchwalone 23.10.1894".

180. Akta PKW, Ms. no. 894, "Organizacja i Działalność Komitetu Prowincyonalnego Wyborczego", vol. 2, meeting of 23.10.1894.

181. Ibid.

182. Dziennik Poznański, 25.10.1894, no. 244.

183. Goniec Wielkopolski, 25.10.1894, no. 244.

184. Przegląd Poznański, 28.10.1894, no. 31.

185. Postęp, 25.10.1894, no. 244.

186. Dziennik Poznański, 28.10.1894, no. 247.

187. Postęp, 26.10.1894, no. 245.

188. PP-Posen, file no. 4806b, p. 341.

189. Goniec Wielkopolski, 30.10.1894, no. 248. The Przegląd Poznański group resigned from the "victorious" populist committee in a body: Bernard Chrzanowski, Bolesław Krysiewicz, Władysław Rabski, Stanisław Brzeski and Wincenty Stefański. See Wielkopolanin, 3.11.1894, no. 251.

190. Kuryer Poznański, 30.10.1894, no. 248.

191. Dziennik Poznański, 30.10.1894, no. 248.

192. Wielkopolanin, 30.10.1894, no. 248.

193. Postęp, 30.10.1894, no. 248.

194. Orędownik, 3.11.1894, no. 251.

195. Goniec Wielkopolski, 8.11.1894, no. 255; Dziennik Poznański, 8.11.1894, no. 255; Kuryer Poznański, 8.11.1894, no. 255.

196. Orędownik, 24.11.1894, no. 268; Dziennik Poznański, 24.11.1894, no. 268.

197. Karol Rzepecki, Pobudka Wyborcza (Poznań, 1907), p. 66.

198. Kuryer Poznański, 11.10.1894, no. 232.

199. Ibid., 13.10.1894, no. 233.

200. Ibid., 28.10.1894, no. 247.

201. Dziennik Poznański, 28.10.1894, no. 247.

202. Ibid., 30.10.1894, no. 248.

203. Wielkopolanin, 31.10.1894, no. 249. Roman Komierowski best summarized the warm feelings of the Poles to Chancellor Caprivi, "I doubt if at any time the highest political official in Prussia showed us as much friendliness as Graf Caprivi. This friendliness did not stem from any special affection toward us but rather from his feeling of humanity, respect and adherence to Christian principles. These convictions were diametrically opposed to those of his predecessor." Komierowski, Koło polskie w Berlinie..., p. 208.

204. Postęp, 28.10.1894, no. 247.

205. Orędownik, 15.11.1894, no. 261; Postęp, 16.11.1894, no. 262.

206. Goniec Wielkopolski, 27.10.1894, no. 246.

207. Ibid., 4.10.1894, no. 226.

CONCLUSIONS.

At the outset of this study, it was stressed that an examination of the Polish press was valuable from two viewpoints: the internal development of Polish society under Prussian rule, and the wider Polish-German relationship undergoing its last period of reconciliation before World War One. The conclusions must also be grouped with these two viewpoints in mind.

There appears no doubt that the newspapers were an instrumental part of the unprecedented domestic strife experienced by the Poles during the Caprivi era. In fact, it would be very difficult to appreciate the domestic scene in Poznań and the province of Poznania without considering the press. While the growth of newspapers had a great impact on the formation of public opinion within all European nations in the last decades before World War One, in Prussian Poland, their importance seemed to take on an added dimension. The clearest evidence of this is the role of journalists and editors in local Polish politics. Of the six editors-in-chief active during the Caprivi years (excluding Wladysław Rabski of the Przegląd Poznański, who arrived on the scene almost at end of the period), four were members of Poznan's Polish municipal committee from 1888-1893: Franciszek Dobrowolski as chairman, Maksymilian Kantecki as secretary until 1890, Stanisław Knapowski from 1891, and Ludwik Rzepecki. A fifth, Roman Szymański, was the acknowledged leader of the populist opposition. Two newspapermen, Dobrowolski and A. Kantecki, were members of the seven-man Central Committee, the supreme political authority for Poles in Poznania. Later on, Stefan Cegielski, one of the Dziennik Poznański's executives, became vice-president of the Central Committee responsible for Polish politics for the German Reich. Furthermore, shareholders of the leading newspapers, like the Kwileckis and Józef Mielżyński of the Dziennik, and the Chłapowskis of the Kuryer Poznański, were also deputies in the Reichstag or Prussian Landtag, and other wealthy deputies like Józef Kościelski and Ferdynand Radziwiłł very likely made donations to the newspapers to keep them solvent. In a word, the press lords and the powerbrokers were largely the same group of people.

Thanks to the general laxity of Prussian bureaucracy, in particular the press monitors, during the Caprivi years, the Polish press was able to reveal emotions and beliefs that had long been suppressed under Bismarck's chancellorship. The extreme degree of uniformity and convention that characterized the Polish press was broken in a number of ways. It is thus possible to obtain a clearer view of the many social and political conflicts affecting the Polish community. Self-censorship relaxed for a time, though it must be stressed that an "objective" standard or reporting in a modern sense was still a long way off.

In a way, the outbreak of fierce polemic among groups in Polish society which the Caprivi era witnessed was inevitable. The pattern of social and political hegemony exercised by the gentry was anachronistic and collapsing all over Europe in the 19th century with different degrees of speed and extent. Because of the evident need for 'national solidarity', i.e the the need to close ranks against Germanization and the conform to the political and social views of the powerbrokers, the Polish gentry had been able to maintain their monopoly far longer than their economic power warranted. Already their financial weakness had become evident in their inability to withstand the early efforts of the Colonization Commission and raise enough capital to make the Bank Ziemski effective. The failure of the Polish loyalist initiative sponsored by the wealthiest of the gentry provided a great stimulus to the breakdown of their domination of social and political life. The subsequent growth of party politics and occasionally fierce debate , which many contemporaries decried as weakening the national resistance against Germanization, proved instead to be a godsend. It politicized the middle class, which now, led by National Democratic Party, picked up the national banner that the gentry could no longer carry. The wave of the future belonged not to the gentry's hallowed tradition of insurrection, but to modern, material forces: capital, industry, urbanization, professionals and skilled workmen. The Caprivi interlude acted as a catalyst to bring about the political changes that economic forces were demanding. Within a decade after the failure of loyalism, the hegemony of the gentry was definitely broken in Prussian Poland. More and more middle-class professionals: physicians, lawyers, journalists and businessmen were elected to the parliaments in Berlin. The National Democratic Party took control of the press and the many economic and social organizations that were now to constitute the great barriers to Germanization. Many of the old arguments and alliances forged by the gentry collapsed: the alliance with the Centrum was broken over the Upper Silesian question and a more modern, nationalistic conception of 'Poland' was developed which rejected the strict legalism of the Vienna Treaties. By the 1903 Reichstag election the National Democratic movement had, in effect, conquered Prussian Polish politics.

The importance of the Polish press during the 1890-1894 period in hastening the decline of the gentry and the emergence of poltical pluralism cannot be underestimated. It was a newspaperman, Roman Szymański, who issued the challenge to the gentry hegemony, and newspapermen who formed the nucleus of the Populist Party, the forerunner of the National Democrats. Political groups revolved around newspapers; even the Prussian police spoke of the "Orędownikgruppe". They formed the public opinion that finally forced the loyalists out of control of the Reichstag Party and accelerated the disintegration of the gentry hegemony.

With respect to the wider issue of the Polish-German relationship during the Caprivi era, the role of the newspapers is harder to measure. Leading loyalists like Kościelski, Komierowski and Archbishop Stablewski later stated that irreconcilable Polish press sentiment had undermined the reconciliation process as much as the heated attacks of the Bismarckpresse. Indeed, apart from the Kuryer Poznański, no Polish paper was wholeheartedly behind the loyalist initiative. The majority of papers were sceptical at the outset and outright hostile after 1892. A study of the Polish press tends to support the pessimistic views of Lech Trzeciakowski and Harry K. Rosenthal that Polish loyalism was built on very slim foundations and was predestined to collapse given the long list of difficulties Chancellor Caprivi had to face on many issues. The Polish press demanded results: they saw the Poles as the injured party who had a just claim against the Prussian state to dismantle the whole network of anti-Polish laws enacted since the accession to office of Bismarck. What the German press regarded as significant, indeed even dangerous, concessions on the part of the Prussian government, such as the appointment of Stablewski and the language teaching legislation, were regarded as unimportant cosmetic changes that avoided the key issue : the end to all discriminatory legislation in the eastern provinces.

Unfortunately, the press does not answer many questions which continue to intrigue the historian. A key question is why the Polish landowners who dominated the Reichstag Party decided upon a policy of blind loyalism under Caprivi. Was it in fact, as Szymański claimed, only the last desparate manoeuvre of a bankrupt political force clinging frantically to power through any possible means? Or was it part of a well-thought out plan to improve Polish life in Prussia through a Galician-style loyalty to Crown and State? Were the Poles acting all on their own, or did the deputies have clear evidence that Chancellor Caprivi intended to overhaul the Polish policy? Further, why did they carry on their support long after it became clear that their favourite could do no more for them in the hostile Prussian Landtag? Those who knew the answers: Kościelski, Stablewski and perhaps a few other loyalist deputies, gave no information on this to the newspapers, leaving all to openly speculate on what went on behind the scenes.

The same applies to the question of the Polish factor in the event of a war against Russia. There is sufficient evidence in other sources to indicate that key Poles were in contact with German and Austrian military men with various projects of a resurrected Poland in mind, projects that came to nought when German-Russian relations improved after the trade treaty of late 1893. Yet one would look in vain for even the slightest mention of this, even editorially, in the Polish press.

Finally, the question of the Polish press as a factor in the growing Polish-German antagonism that dominated the relationship during the last two decades needs to be addressed. Newspapers, whether intentionally or not, did create an image of the German in the popular mind that was important to the overall relationship. What image, then, did the Polish press portray? Was the German the natural enemy who had to be fought at all costs, or was an amicable co-existence possible in the Prussian East provided Germanization ceased?

The answer is ambiguous. On the one hand, the mainstream papers (i.e. apart from the Goniec Wielkopolski) repeatedly stated that there were "good" Germans, who disapproved of anti-Polish legislation and were in favour of recognizing the special status of Poles as specified in the 1815 Treaties of Vienna. To this group belonged German Catholics with Ludwig Windthorst at their head, though relations with the Centrum Party visibly deteriorated after Windthorst's death, and publicists like Hans Delbrueck who felt the German element in the East would be best served by the neutrality of the Prussian government. The "bad" Germans were the "chauvinists", the Bismarckfronde and the merciless machine-like Prussian bureaucrats. Given a complete reversal of Germanization, the papers argued, peaceful co-existence was not only possible but a certainty.

On the other hand, a careful perusal of the Polish press offers some disturbing evidence that challenges this view. In particular after 1892, the Polish press made the distinction between "good" and "bad" Germans less frequently, and at every anti-Polish article in the Bismarckpresse threw up their hands in frustration at the seemingly insurmountable German antagonism. This was particularly true in regard to the pilgrimages of the West Prussian and Poznania Germans to Varzin to hear Bismarck in 1894; the huge number of those present seemed to confirm the view that the German was at heart fearful of the Pole and committed to maintaining his second-class status. Throughout the period one finds references that seem out of place in what was supposed to be an era of reconciliation. For example, Polish newspapers would admonish women who read German light novels for relaxation, insisting that this was a form of 'unwitting Germanization; Polish novels should be read instead. One can well wonder whether national antagonisms could be reduced by this sort of cultural isolation. One article even warned parents of blind children not to send their afflicted offspring to special German homes for the blind, although there were no equivalent Polish homes! Polish newspapers were as vexed at cases of mixed marriages as German nationalists, and spared no level of criticism for a parent who willingly allowed his child to be Germanized.

A full reconciliation between the two nationalities was impossible so long as Poznania and West Prussia remained a disputed area between Prussian and Polish territorial claims. What the Poles considered their 'just national rights' was interpreted by the Prussian state as 'Grosspolnische nationale Agitation'. One of the two nationalities would have to be content to live without these areas. During the partitioned era the Poles never gave up their claims to incorporate them into a future Polish state; in the Weimar Republic era Germany never recognized their loss. Reconciliation in our own times appears only possible if territorial disputes no longer act as an obstacle.

BIBLIOGRAPHY

I. Unpublished Primary Source Materials

1. Biblioteka Raczyńskich w Poznaniu. Oddzial Rękopisów.

1a. Akta Komitetu Prowincjonalnego Wyborczego na Wielkie Księstwo Poznańskie.
Manuscript no:
784 I, 784 II - Papiery po przewodniczacym PCKW Ks. Piotra Wawrzyniaka
854 - Powiat Poznań miasto
855 - " Poznań Zachodni
856 - " Poznań Wschodni
859 - " Miedzyrzecz
863 - " Grodzisk
866 - " Śmigiel
867 - " Kościan
868 - " Leszno
869 - " Srem
871 - " Września
882 - " Bydgoszcz miasto
888 - " Wągrowiec
889 - " Mogilno
890 - " Inowrocław
891 - " Strzelno
892 - " Gniezno
894 I, 894 II, Organizacja i dzialalność Komitetu Prowincjonalnego Wyborczego
939 - Książka protokołów Komitetu Prowincjonalnego Wyborczego 1896-1922

1b. Manuscript no. 1375 Bernard Chrzanowski, "Wspomnienia"

1c. Manuscript no. 1636 Korespondencja Henryka Szumana

1d. Manuscript no. 1527 J. Kusztelan "Ks. Piotr Wawrzyniak"

2. Archiwum Państwowe Miasta Poznania i Województwa Poznańskiego.

2a. Polizeipraesidium zu Posen.
File no. 2789 - Acta betr. die polnische Agitation im Kreise Gnesen 1887-1904
" 3496 - Personalbogen der Agitatoren Erfasst von der Ueberwachungsstelle Posen 1890-1918
" 3515 - Personal Akten betr. Stephan Cegielski
" 3525 - " Leo von Czarliński
" 3571 - " Roman von Komierowski
" 3599 - " Arthur von Lossow

" 3660 - " Fuerst Ferdynand Radziwiłł
" 3682 - " Karl Rzepecki
" 3696 - " Jozef Siemianowski
" 3740 - " Dr. Roman Szymański (Szymanski Fonds Posen)
" 4194 - Aufsicht von oeffentlichen Gesellschaften
" 4759 - Ueberwachung und Beschlagnahme 1864-1891
" 4772 - Zeitungsberichte 1886-1894
" 4786 - Berichte polnischer Blaettern in der Provinz Posen ueber Kirchen- und Schulangelegenheiten 1890
" 4804- Uebersetzungen aus polnischen Blaetter ueber allgemeine politische Angelegenheiten 1890-1891
" 4805 - " 1891-1896
" 4806a - Gesamtueberblick ueber die polnische Tagesliteratur 1893
" 4806b - Gesamtueberblick " " " 1894
" 4869 - Sammlungen von Subskriptionen
" 4876 - Haltung der polnischen Presse gegenueber der kaiserlichen Russischen Regierung
" 4877 - Acta betr. die polnische Tagespresse, ihre Haltung und Verbreitung
" 4912 - Acta betr. den Kuryer Poznanski 1871-1894
" 4914 - Acta betr. das polnisch-ultramontane Tageblatt Goniec Wielkopolski. Bestrafungen der Redakteure 1877-1907
" 5096 - Acta betr. den Reichstag 1866-1890
" 5116 - Buergermeister, Landtagsabgeordnete und Stadtverordnete, Wahlen 1884-1913
" 5117 - Kommissions Acten des Oberbuergermeister Witting als Wahlkommissarius fuer die Wahl des Abgeordneten der Stadt Posen, 7 November, 1893

2b. Oberpraesidium zu Posen
File no. 6135 - Verhalten und die Parteistellung der katholischen Geistlichen bei den Reichstags- und Kammerwahlen 1887-1903
" 6138 - Diejenigen katholischen Geistlichen, welche durch patriotisches Verhalten den nationalen Agitationen gegenueber sich hervorgetan haben 1860-1896

3. Biblioteka PAN w Korniku. Oddział rękopisów.
3a. Manuscript no. 1456/1457 - Protokoły posiedzień Koła Polskiego w Berlinie.

II. Published Primary Sources

1. Memoirs, Documents, Letters.

Akten zur preussischen Kirchenpolitik in den Bistuemern Gnesen-Posen, Kulm und Ermland 1885-1914, ed. Erwin Gatz (Mainz, 1977).

Ballhausen, Lucius von, Bismarckerinnerungen (Stuttgart, 1920).

Bismarck, Otto von, Die gesammelten Werke (Berlin, 1922-1930), 15 vols.

Blum, Hans, Das deutsche Reich zur Zeit Bismarcks (Leipzig, 1893).

Bockh, Richard, "Die Verschiebung der Sprachverhaeltnisse in Posen und Westpreussen", in: Preussische Jahrbuecher 77 (1894)

Briefwechsel zwischen dem Chef des Generalstabes Grafen Waldersee und dem Militaerattache in Petersburg Grafen Yorck von Wartenburg 1885-1894, ed. Heinrich O. Meisner, in: Historisch-Politisches Archiv 1 (1930).

Crispi, Francesco, Die Memoiren Francesco Crispi's. Erinnerungen und Dokumente. ed. T. Palamenghi-Crispi, (Berlin, 1912).

Darf Caprivi Bleiben? von einem alten Politiker, (Berlin, 1892).

Delbrueck, Hans, "Die Polenfrage", in: Preussiche Jahrbuecher 78 (1894).

Dewitz, Hermann von, Von Bismarck bis Bethmann. Innerpolitische Rueckblicke eines Konservativen (Berlin, 1918).

Dmowski, Roman, Myśli nowoczesnego Polaka (Lwów, 1907, reprints from articles in the 'Przegląd Wszechpolski' in 1903)

____ Polityka Polska i odbudowanie państwa (Warszawa, 1926).

____ Upadek myśli konserwatywnej w Polsce (Warszawa, 1914).

Ebmeyer, Major von, "Aus den Erinnerungen des Majors v. Ebmeyer, Persoenlichen Adjutanten des zweiten Kanzlers. Caprivis Entlassung." in: Deutsche Revue 47 (1922).

Eulenburg, Philipp zu, Aus 50 Jahren (Berlin, 1923).

Fechenbach-Laudenbach, Reichsfreiherrn, Die Kaiserlichen Erlasse vom 4.2.1890 (Frankfurt/Main, 1890).

Fuerst Bismarck 1890-1898, ed. Hermann Hofmann, (Stuttgart, 1913), 3 vols.

Fuerst Bismarck nach seiner Entlassung, ed. Johannes Penzler, (Leipzig, 1897), 7 vols.

Grosse Politik der Europaeischen Kabinette 1871-1914, ed. Johannes Lepsius, A. Mendelssohn-Bartholdy, Friedrich Thimme, (Berlin, 1922)

Hammann, Otto, Der Neue Kurs (Berlin, 1918).

Harden, Maximilian, "Erzbischof v. Stablewski ueber die Polenfrage", in: Die Zukunft 1 (1892).

____ Kopfe. Portrats, Briefe und Dokuments, ed. Hans-Juergen Froehlich, (Hamburg, 1963).

Hatzfeldt, Paul Graf von, Botschafter Paul Graf von Hatzfeldt. Nachgelassene Papiere 1838-1901, ed. Gerhard Ebel, (Boppard am Rhein, 1976), 2 vols.

Hohenlohe-Schillingfuerst, Chlodwig Fuerst zu, Denkwuerdigkeiten der Reichskanzlerzeit (Stuttgart, 1931), 3 vols.

Holstein und Hohenlohe, ed. Helmut Rogge, (Stuttgart, 1957).

The Holstein Papers, ed. Norman Rich and M.H. Fisher, (Cambridge, 1955), 2 vols.

Hutten-Czapski, Bogdan Graf von, Sechzig Jahre Politik und Gesellschaft (Berlin, 1936), 2 vols.

Wilhelm von Kardorff. Ein nationaler Parlamentarier im Zeitalter Bismarcks und Wilhelms II. 1828-1907. Ed. Siegfried von Kardorff, (Berlin, 1936).

Komierowski, Roman, Koło polskie w Berlinie 1875-1900 (Poznan, 1906).

Kościelski, Józef, "Prussia and the Poles", in: The National Review 43 (1904).

Lerchenfeld-Koefering, Hugo Graf von, Erinnerungen und Denkwuerdigkeiten 1843-1925 (Berlin, 1935).

Letters of the Empress Frederick, ed. Sir Frederick Ponsonby, (London, 1928).

Moltke, Helmuth Graf von, Die deutschen Aufmarschplaene 1871-1890, ed. a.D.v. Schmerfeld, (Berlin, 1929).

Monts, Anton Graf von, Politische Aufsaetze (Berlin, 1916).

Der Polenring, ed. Fritz Wagner, (Berlin, 1899).

Polenspiegel. Die Umtriebe der Polen nach ihrer eigenen Presse, ed. Fritz Wagner, Fritz Vosberg, (Berlin, 1908).

Polenstimmen. Eine Sammlung von Aeusserungen der polnischen Presse, ed. Fritz Wagner, Fritz Vosberg, (Berlin, 1902).

Poschinger, Heinrich von, Fuerst Bismarck. Neue Tischgespraeche und Interviews (Stuttgart, vol. 1, 1895; vol. 2, 1899).

Puttkamer (Robert von), Staatsminister von Puttkamer. Ein Stueck preussischer Vergangenheit 1828-1900, ed. Alfred von Puttkamer, (Leipzig, 1928).

Radziwiłł, Marie, Briefe vom deutschen Kaiserhof 1889-1915 (Berlin, 1936).

Raschdau, Ludwig, "Ostmarkenfrage", in: Deutsche Revue 33 1908).

____ Unter Bismarck und Caprivi. Erinnerungen eines deutschen Diplomaten aus den Jahren 1885-1894 (Berlin, 1939).

Reden, Aeusserungen Wilhelms II. Das persoenliche Regiment (Muenchen, 1907).

Reden des Grafen von Caprivi im Deutschen Reichstage, Preussischen Landtage und bei besonderen Anlaessen 1883-1893, ed. Rudolf Arndt, (Berlin, 1894).

Reichsgesetzblatt, Berlin (1874)

Rosinski, Adolf, Fuerst Bismarcks Kampf gegen den Grafen Caprivi (Berlin, 1897).

Schlieffen, Alfred von, Briefe, ed. Eberhard Kessel (Goettingen, 1958).

Schneidewin, Max, "Briefe des Reichskanzlers von Caprivi", in: Deutsche Revue 47 (1922).

Schulte, von, "Erinnerungen an Graf Caprivi", in: Deutsche Revue 24 (1899).

Schulthess' Europaeischer Gesichtskalender, 1888-1894, ed. Hans Delbrueck, (Nordlingen, 1889-1895).

Schweinitz, Hans Lothar von, Briefwechsel des Botschafters General von Schweinitz (Berlin, 1928).

____ Denkwuerdigkeiten des Botschafters General von Schweinitz (Berlin, 1927), 2 vols.

Sering, Max, Die innere Kolonisation im oestlichen Deutschland (Leipzig, 1893).

Statistik, Preussische, ed. Koeniglichen statistischen Bureau in Berlin, vol. 20. Das gesammte Volksschulen im preussischen Staate im Jahre 1891.

Statistisches Jahrbuch fuer das Deutsche Reich, ed. Kaiserlichen Statistischen Amt, 1890-1895, vols. 11-16.

Stenographische Berichte ueber die Verhandlungen des Preussischen Hauses des Abgeordneten. 1890-1894

Stenographische Berichte ueber die Verhandlungen des Preussischen Herrenhauses 1890-1894

Stenographische Berichte ueber die Verhandlungen des Reichstages. 1890-1894

Sułkowski, Antoni, "Vorschlaege ueber eine friedliche Loesung der Ostmarkenfrage, in: Deutsche Revue 33 (1908)

Szuman, Henryk, Wspomnienia berlińskie i poznańskie z r. 1848 (Warszawa, 1899).

Tiedemann, Christoph von, Erinnerungen an den Fuerst Bismarck (Leipzig, 1898).

Tiedemann, Christoph von, Erinnerungen an den Fuerst Bismarck (Leipzig, 1898).

Wagner, Georg, Der Polenkoller (Leipzig, 1899).

Waldersee, Alfred Graf von, Denkwuerdigkeiten des Alfred Grafen von Waldersee ed. Heinrich O. Meisner, (1922, Nachdruck von 1967, Osnabrueck) 3 vols.

Wedel, Carl Graf von, Zwischen Kaiser und Kanzler. Aufzeichnungen des General-adjutanten Carl Grafen von Wedel aus den Jahren 1890-1894, ed. Erhard Graf von Wedel, (Leipzig, 1943).

Wielkopolska, wybór źródeł 1851-1914, ed. Witold Jakóbczyk, (Wrocław, 1954).

Kaiser Wilhem II. Ereignisse und Gestalten aus den Jahren 1878-1918 (Leipzig, Berlin, 1922).

Wybór tekstów do dziejów kultury Wielkopolski (Poznań, 1962).

2. Newspapers

Dziennik Poznański	1888-1894
Goniec Wielkopolski	1894
Kuryer Poznański	1890-1894
Orędownik	1888-1894
Postęp	1890-1894
Przegląd Poznański	1894
Wielkopolanin	1888-1894

III. Secondary sources

Altkemper, Johann, Deutschtum und Polentum in politisch-konfessioneller Bedeutung (Leipzig, 1910).

Altreicher, Helmut, Konstitutionalismus und Imperialismus. Der Reichstag und die deutsch-russischen Beziehungen (Frankfurt/Main, 1977).

Bachem, Karl, Vorgeschichte, Geschichte und Politik der deutschen Zentrums-partei (Koeln, 1967, Nachdruck von 1929), 9 vols.

Bade, Klaus, "Kulturkampf auf dem Arbeitsmarkt. Bismarcks Polenpolitik 1885-1890", in: Innenpolitische Probleme des Bismarck-Reiches, ed. Otto Pflanze, (Muenchen-Wien, 1983).

Baier, Roland, Der deutsche Osten als soziale Frage (Koeln, 1980).

Balfour, Michael, The Kaiser and his Times (London, 1964).

Banaszak, Marian, Na okazanie drogi. Poświęcona pokoleniu Księdza Piotra Wawrzyniaka (Poznań, 1975).

Becker, Otto, Das französisch-russische Buendnis (Berlin, 1925).

Behrendt, Johannes, Die polnische Frage und das oesterreichisch-deutsche Buendnis 1885-1887 (Berlin, 1927).

Benyskiewicz, Joachim, Posłowie polscy w Berlinie w latach 1866-1890 (Zielona Góra, 1976).

Bergstrasser, Ludwig, Geschichte der politischen Parteien in Deutschland (7th edition, Muenchen, 1952).

Bernatt, Stanislaus von, Die deutsche politische Tagespresse Polens (Poznan, 1926).

Bernhard, Ludwig, Das polnische Gemeinwesen im preussischen Staat. Die Polenfrage (Leipzig, 1907).

Biskup, Marian, ed. Wybitni ludzie dawnego Torunia (Warszawa, 1982).

Blanke, Richard, "An Era of Reconciliation in German-Polish Relations 1890-1894", in: Slavic Review 36 (1977).

____ "The Development of Loyalism in Prussian Poland 1886-1890", in: Slavonic and East European Review 52 (1974).

____ Prussian Poland in the German Empire 1871-1900 (New York, 1981).

Boguslawski, Albert von, 85 Jahre preussische Regierungspolitik in Posen und Westpreussen von 1815 bis 1900 (Berlin, 1901).

Boras, Zygmunt, and Trzeciakowski, Lech, W dawnym Poznaniu (Poznań, 1969).

Born, Karl Erich, Staat und Sozialpolitik seit Bismarcks Sturz 1890-1914 (Wiesbaden, 1957).

Brackmann, Albert, ed. Deutschland und Polen (Berlin, 1933).

Broszat, Martin, Zweihundert Jahre deutsche Polenpolitik (Muenchen, 1963).

Buzek, Józef, Historya polityki narodowościowej rządu pruskiego wobec Polaków od traktatów wiedeńskich do ustaw wyjątkowych z r. 1908 (Lwów, 1909)

Canis, Konrad, Bismarck und Waldersee (Berlin-Ost, 1980).

Chojnacki, Władysław, "Niemieckie tłumaczenia z prasy polskiej", in: Przegląd Zachodni 14 (1958).

Cieślak, Tadeusz, Z dziejów prasy polskiej na Pomorzu gdańskim w okresie zaboru pruskiego (Gdańsk, 1964).

____ "Gazeta Grudziądzka 1894-1918. Fenomen wydawniczy", in: Studia i materiały do dziejów Wielkopolski i Pomorza 3 (1957).

____ "Główne problemy historii politycznej ziem pomorskich w latach 1870-1914", in: Studia i materiały do dziejów Wielkopolski i Pomorza 2 (1956).

____ "Prasa polska na Pomorzu w II połowie XIX wieku i początkach XX wieku", in: Szkice z dziejów Pomorza (Warszawa, 1961), vol. 3.

Craig, Gordon, The Politics of the Prussian Army (Oxford, 1955).

Crankshaw, Edward, Bismarck (London, 1981).

Czartoryski, Zygmunt, Ueber die anti-polnische Politik der preussischen Regierung aus Anlass des Enteignungsgesetzes (Krakow, 1911).

Danilczuk, Bolesław, Dzialalność SPD i PPS zaboru pruskiego w Poznańskim w latach 1891-1914 (Toruń, 1962).

Deuerlein, Ernst, Deutsche Kanzler. Von Bismarck bis Hitler (Muenchen, 1968).

____ ed. Der Reichstag: Aufsaetze, Protokolle und Darstellungen 1871-1933 (Frankfurt/Main, 1963).

Dulczewski, Zygmunt, "Prasa ludowa w W. Ks. Poznańskim w okresie Wiosny Ludów 1848-1850", in: Studia i materiały do dziejów Wielkopolski i Pomorza 2 (1956).

Eckardt, Julius von, Aus den Tagen von Bismarcks Kampf gegen Caprivi (Leipzig, 1920).

Eichhorn, Gunther, Geschichte des Zeitungswesen im deutschen Ostraum zwischen Frankfurt a.d.O. und Danzig, (Dresden, 1939).

Engelberg, Ernst, Bismarck: Urpreusse und Reichsgruender (Berlin-Ost, 1985).

Erzberger, Mathias, Der Kampf gegen den Katholizismus in der Ostmark. Material zur Beurteilung der Polenfrage durch die deutschen Katholiken (Berlin, 1908).

Evans, Richard J, ed. Society and Politics in Wilhelmine Germany (London, 1978).

Eyck, Erich, Bismarck. Leben und Werk (Zuerich, 1944), 3 vols.

Feldman, Józef, Bismarck a Polska (2nd. edition, Krakow, 1947).

____ Problem polsko-niemiecki w dziejach (Katowice, 1946).

Feldman, Wilhelm, Geschichte der politischen Ideen in Polen seit dessen Teilungen 1795-1914 (Muenchen, 1917).

Fischer-Frauendienst, Irene, Bismarcks Pressepolitik (Muenster, 1963).

Franke, Bernhard, Posen Residenzstadt (Posen, 1911).

Frankenberg, Richard, Die Nichterneuerung des deutsch-russischen Rueckversicherungsvertrages im Jahre 1890 (Berlin, 1927).

Franz, Georg, Kulturkampf (Muenchen, 1954).

Frauendienst, Werner, "Preussisches Staatsbewusstsein und polnischer Nationalismus 1815-1890", in: Das oestliche Deutschland, (Wuerzburg, 1959). Göttinger Arbeitskreis.

Gall, Lother, Bismarck. Der weisse Revolutionaer (Frankfurt/Main, 1980).

Galos, Adam, "Antypolska dzialalność policji pruskiej", in: Polska Niemcy Europa, ed. Antoni Czubiński (Poznań, 1977).

____ "Johannes Miquel a sprawy polskie", in: Studia z dziejów Polski, Niemiec i NRD, XVI-XX w. ed. Antoni Czubinski (Poznań, 1974).

____ "Klasy posiadające w Niemczech wobec sprawy polskiej 1894-1914", in: Przegląd Historyczny 45 (1954).

____ "Obraz Polaka w Niemczech w XIX w.", in: Śląski Kwartalnik Historyczny Sobótka 33 (1978).

____ "Tragizm ugody. Władze pruskie a arcybiskup Stablewski", in: Przegląd Zachodni 31 (1975).

Ganz, Hugo, Die preussische Polenpolitik (Frankfurt/Main, 1907).

Gause, Fritz, Deutsch-slawische Schicksalsgemeinschaft (Wuerzburg, 1967).

Geffecken, Heinrich, Preussen, Deutschland und die Polen seit dem Untergang des Polnischen Reiches (Berlin, 1907).

Geis, Robert, Der Sturz des Reichskanzlers Caprivi (Berlin, 1930).

Gey, Thomas, Die preussische Verwaltung des Regierungsbezirks Bromberg 1871-1920 (Koeln, 1976).

Giełżyński, Witold, Prasa warszawska 1661-1914 (Warszawa, 1962).

Glueck, Helmut, Die preussisch-polnische Sprachenpolitik (Hamburg, 1979).

Goebel, Heinz, Die Militaervorlage 1892-1893 (Leipzig, 1935).

Gothein, Georg, "Die preussische Polenpolitik", in: Patria. Buecher fuer Kultur und Freiheit, ed. Friedrich Naumann (Berlin, 1909).

____ "Reichskanzler Graf Caprivi", in: Fehler und Forderungen 5 (Muenchen, 1918).

____ "Die Wirkung des Handelsvertrages", in: Volkswirtschaftliche Zeitfragen Jahrgang 17 (1896).

Grot, Zdzisław, Dezydery Chłapowski 1788-1879 (Warszawa Poznań, 1983).

____ Hipolit Cegielski 1813-1868 (Poznań, 1980).

____ "Koło polskie w Berlinie", in: Wiek XIX. Festschrift Stefan Kieniewicz (Warszawa, 1967).

____ "Prezesi kół polskich w parlamentach niemieckich w latach 1867-1918", in: Rola Wielkopolski w dziejach narodu polskiego, ed. Stanisław Kubiak and Lech Trzeciakowski (Poznań, 1979).

Groth, Otto, Die Geschichte der deutschen Zeitungswissenschaft (Muenchen, 1948).

____ Die Zeitung (Berlin, Leipzig, Mannheim, 1929), 4 vols.

Grygier, Tadeusz, "Sprawa polska w Prusach Wschodnich w latach 1870-1900 w oświetleniu władz pruskich", in: Przegląd Zachodni 7 (1951).

Grzes, Bolesław, Kozłowski, Jerzy, Kramski, Aleksander, Niemcy w Poznańskiem wobec polityki germanizacyjnej 1815-1920 (Poznań, 1976).

____ "Rola naczelnych prezesów Poznańskiego w kształtowaniu i realizacji germanizacyjnej polityki rządu pruskiego w II połowie XIX w.", in: Studia z dziejów Polski, Niemiec i NRD, XVI-XX w., ed. Antoni Czubiński (Poznań, 1974).

____ "Teoretyczno-propagandowe aspekty dyskriminacji polaków Poznańskiego na przełomie XIX i XX wieku", in: Rola Wielkopolski w dziejach narodu polskiego, ed. Kubiak and Trzeciakowski, (Poznań, 1979).

Grzybowski, Konstanty, Historia państwa i prawa Polski. Tom IV, od uwłaszczenia do odrodzenia Państwa (Warszawa, 1982).

Guenzel, Walter, Die nationale Arbeit der polnischen Presse in Westpreussen und Posen zur Zeit der Kanzlerschaft Buelows 1900-1909 (Lodz, 1933).

Guttzeit, Johannes, Geschichte der deutschen Polen-Entrechtung (Danzig, 1927).

Hagan, William W., Germans, Poles and Jews. The Nationality Conflict in the Prussian East 1772-1914 (Chicago, 1980).

Hanus, Franciscus, Die preussische Vatikangesandtschaft 1747-1920 (Muenchen, 1953).

Hartung, Fritz, "Graf von Hutten-Czapski", in: Historische Zeitschrift 153 (1936).

Hartwig, Edgar, "Der Alldeutsche Verband und Polen", in: Wissenschaftliche Zeitschrift der Friedrich Schiller Universitaet Jena 19 (1970/1972).

Hayes, Carleton J.H., A Generation of Materialism 1871-1900 (New York, 1941).

Held, Walter, Caprivi und Bismarck (Leipzig, 1931).

Hemmerling, Zygmunt, Posłowie polscy w parlamencie Rzeszy Niemieckiej i w sejmie pruskim 1907-1914 (Warszawa, 1968).

Herr, E., Der Entscheidungskampf um den Boden der Ostmark (Muenchen, 1907).

____ Neue Bahnen der Polenpolitik (Berlin, 1903).

Herzfeld, Hans, Johannes von Miquel (Bielefeld, 1938), 2 vols.

Hink, Helma, Bismarcks Pressepolitik in der bulgarischen Krise und der Zusammenbruch seiner Regierungspresse 1885-1890 (Frankfurt/Main, 1977).

Huber, Ernst Rudolf, Deutsche Verfassungsgeschichte seit 1789 (Stuttgart Berlin Koeln, Mainz, 1969), vol. 4.

Husgen, Eduard, Ludwig Windthorst (Koeln, 1907).

Jaffe, Moritz, Die Stadt Posen unter preussischer Herrschaft (Leipzig, 1909).

Jakóbczyk, Witold, "Antypolski projekt Związku Wszechniemieckiego", in: Przegląd Zachodni 14 (1958).

____ "Z dziejów propagandy hakatystycznej 1896-1914", in: Studia i materiały do dziejów Wielkopolski i Pomorza 2 (1956).

____ ed. Dzieje Wielkopolski 1793-1918 (Poznań, 1973), vol. 2.

____ Patron Jackowski (Poznań, 1938).

____ Studia nad dziejami Wiekopolski w XIX w. Tom II 1850-1890 (Poznań, 1959).

____ ed. Wybitni Wielkopolanie XIX wieku (Poznań, vol. 1, 1959; vol. 2, 1969).

____ "Wielkopolska 1859-1918", in: Prasa Polska 1864-1918, ed. Jerzy Łojek, (Warszawa, 1976).

Jarkowski, Stanisław, Zbiory prasy w Polsce (Warszawa, 1932).

Kaminski, Lotte, Die Auseinandersetzung um die polnische Frage zur Zeit der Reichskanzlerschaft des Fuersten zu Hohenlohe-Schillingfuerst (Hamburg, 1938).

Karwowski, Stanisław, "Historya 'Dziennika Poznańskiego'", in: Książka jubileuszowa 'Dziennika Poznańskiego' 1859-1909 (Poznań, 1909).

____ Historya Wielkiego Księstwa Poznańskiego (Poznań, 1919), 3 vols.

Kiel, Diethelm, Die preussisch-deutsche Polenfrage der wilhelmischen Epoche vor 1914 unter besonderer Beruecksichtigung der Regierung Bethmann-Hollweg (Tuebingen, 1961).

Kieniewicz, Stefan, Historia Polski 1795-1918 (Warszawa, 1983), 6th edition.

Kissling, Johannes B., Geschichte des Kulturkampfes im Deutschen Reiche (Freiburg, 1911), 3 vols.

Koch, Friedrich, Bismarck ueber die Polen (Berlin, 1913).

Koehl, Robert Lewis, "Colonialism inside Germany 1886-1918", in: Journal of Modern History 25 (1953).

Kołodziejczyk, Ryszard, Jan Bloch 1836-1902 (Warszawa, 1983).

Korth, Rudolf, Die preussische Schulpolitik und die polnischen Schulstreiks (Wuerzburg, 1963).

Koszyk, Kurt, Deutsche Presse im 19. Jahrhundert (Berlin, 1966).

Kowal, Stefan, Społeczenstwo Wielkopolski i Pomorza nadwiślańskiego w latach 1871-1914 (Poznań, 1982).

Knoel, Paul, Geschichte der Provinz Posen (Kattowitz, 1911).

Krahl, Georg, Auf! Gegen die national polnische Wuehlarbeit (Heidelberg, 1901).

Krasuski, Jerzy, "Zagadnienie polskie w publicystyce Hansa Delbruecka 1887-1894", in: Przegląd Zachodni 14 (1958)

Krische, Paul, Die Provinz Posen (Strassfurt, 1907).

Kroeger, Karl-Heinz, Die Konservativen und die Politik Caprivis (Rostock, 1937).

Kruck, Alfred, Geschichte des Alldeutschen Verbandes 1890-1939 (Wiesbaden, 1954)

Krzyżanowski, Julian, Dzieje literatury polskiej (Warszawa, 1969).

Kucner, Alfred, "Polityka Koła Polskiego w Berlinie w erze Kanclerza Capriviego" in: Nauka i Sztuka 5 (1947).

Kuczynski, Juergen, Geschichte des Alltags des Deutschen Volkes. Studien 4 (1871-1918), (Berlin-Ost, 1982).

Kulczycki, John, "Social Change in the Polish National Movement in Prussia before World War One", in: Nationalities Papers 4 (1976).

Kumpf-Korfes, Sigrid, Bismarcks 'Draht nach Russland' (Ost-Berlin, 1968).

Lammich, Maria, Das deutsche Osteuropabild in der Zeit der Reichsgruendung (Boppard on Rhein, 1978).

Lange, Josef, Die Stellung der ueberregionalen katholischen deutschen Tagespresse zum Kulturkampf in Preussen 1871-1878 (Frankfurt/Main, 1974).

Lange, Karl, Bismarcks Sturz und die oeffentliche Meinung in Deutschland und im Auslande (Stuttgart, 1927).

Langer, William L., The Franco-Russian Alliance 1890-1894 (Cambridge, Mass., 1929).

Langhorne, Richard, The Collapse of the Concert of Europe 1890-1914 (New York, 1981).

Land, Hanne-Lore, Die Konservativen und die preussische Polenpolitik 1886-1912 (Berlin, 1963).

Laubert, Manfred, Die preussiche Polenpolitik (Berlin, 1920).

Leibenguth, Peter, Modernisierungskrisis des Kaiserreichs an der Schwelle zum wilhelmischen Imperialismus: politische Probleme der Aera Caprivi 1890-1894 (Koeln, 1975).

Loth, Wilfried, Katholiken im Kaiserreich (Duesseldorf, 1984).

Lotz, W., "Die Handelspolitik des deutschen Reiches unter Graf Caprivi und Fuerst Hohenlohe 1890-1900", in: Schriften des Vereins fur Sozialpolitik 92 (1901).

Luck, Kurt, Der Mythos vom Deutschen in der polnischen Volksueberlieferung und Literatur (Leipzig, 1938).

Łuczak, Czesław, Życie gospodarczo-spoleczne w Poznaniu 1815-1918 (Poznań, 1965).

Mai, Joachim, Die preussisch-deutsche Polenpolitik 1885-1887 (Berlin-Ost, 1962).

Manfrass, Klaus, Frankreich und die polnische Frage zur Zeit der franzoesisch-russischen Allianz 1891-1914 (Berlin, 1975).

Marczewski, Jerzy, Narodowa Demokracja w Poznańskiem 1900-1914 (Warszawa, 1967).

____ "Zmiany polityczne wśród polskiej burzuazji Poznańskiego 1900-1907", in: Studia i materiały do dziejow Wielkopolski i Pomorza 3 (1957).

Massow, Wilhelm von, Die deutsche innere Politik unter Kaiser Wilhelm II. (Stuttgart, Berlin, 1913).

____ Die Polen-Not im deutschen Osten (Berlin, 1903).

Meisner, Heinrich-Otto, "Der Reichskanzler Caprivi", in: Zeitschrift fuer die gesamte Staatswissenschaft 111 (1955).

Michel, Oskar, Handbuch deutscher Zeitungen (Berlin, 1917).

Mitscherlich, Waldermar, Die Ausbreitung der Polen in Preussen (Leipzig, 1913).

____ Der Einfluss der wirtschaftlichen Entwicklung auf den ostmarkischen Nationalstaatenkampf (Berlin, 1910).

Molik, Wiktor, "Dziennikarze polscy pod panowaniem pruskim 1890-1914", in: Inteligencja Polska XIX i XX w., ed. Ryszard Czepulis-Rastensis, (Warszawa, 1983), vol. 3.

____ Kształtowanie sie inteligencji polskej w W.K. Poznańskim 1841-1870 (Warszawa, 1979).

____ "Wokół 'Przeglądu Poznańskiego'. Próby politycznego usamodzielnienia się inteligencji polskiej w Poznańskiem w końcu XIX w.", in: Inteligencja Polska XIX i XX wieku, ed. Ryszard Czepulis-Rastensis, (Warszawa, 1981), vol. 1.

Morawski, Franciszek, Z zachodnich kresów (Kraków, 1906).

Mueller, Helmut, Die polnische Volksgruppe im Deutschen Reich, ihre Stellung in Verfassung und Verwaltung seit 1871 (Warschau, 1941).

Mueller, Leonhard, Nationalpolnische Presse, Katholizismus und katholischer Klerus (Breslau, 1931).

Muenstermann, Wilhelm, Die preussisch-deutsche Polenpolitik der Caprivizeit und die deutsche oeffentliche Meinung (Muenster, 1936).

Murzynowska, Krystyna, Polskie wychodźstwo zarobkowe w Zagłębiu Ruhry w latach 1880-1914 (Wrocław, 1972).

Muser, Gerhard, Statistische Untersuchung ueber die Zeitungen Deutschlands 1885-1914 (Leipzig, 1918).

Narkiewicz, Olga, The Green Flag. Polish Populist Politics 1867-1970 (London, 1976).

Neubach, Helmut, Die Ausweisungen von Polen und Juden aus Preussen 1885-1886 (Wiesbaden, 1967).

____ "Eduard von Hartmanns Bedeutung fuer die Entwicklung des deutsch-polnischen Verhaeltnisses", in: Zeitschrift fuer Ostforschung 13 (1964).

____ "Julius Dinder, der einzige deutsche Erzbischof von Gnesen-Posen", in: Jahrbuch Weichsel-Warthe 11 (1965).

Nichols, J. Alden, Germany After Bismarck. The Caprivi Era (Cambridge, Mass. 1958).

Nowakowski, Tadeusz, Die Radziwiłłs (Muenchen, 1966).

Nowy Korbut

Oehlmann, Horst, Studien zur Innenpolitik des Reichskanzlers Leo von Caprivi. Unpublished Ph.D. thesis, Freiburg, 1953.

Ohnesseit, Wilhelm, "Der Kampf um die Ostmark und der deutsche Ostmarkenverein", in: Preussische Jahrbuecher 213 (1928).

Oncken, Hermann, Das Deutsche Reich und die Vorgeschichte des Weltkrieges (Leipzig, 1933), 2 vols.

Pajewski, Janusz, "Niemcy a kwestia Polska 1871-1914", in: Studia Historica Slavo-Germanica 1 (1972).

____ ed. Die Hakatisten. Der Deutsche Ostmarkenverein 1894-1934 (Berlin-Ost, 1966).

Perdelwitz, Richard, Die Posener Polen von 1815-1914 (Schneidemuehl, 1936).

Pfeifer, Martha, Bismarcks Polenpolitik im Hinblick auf Russland. Unpublished Ph.D. thesis, Marburg, 1925.

Pfeiffer, Hans, Der polnische Adel und die preussiche Polenpolitik von 1863-1894 (Wuerzburg, 1939).

Pobóg-Malinowski, Władysław, Najnowsza historia polityczna Polski (London, 1963) vol. 1, 1864-1914.

Polski Słownik Biograficzny. Letters A-P. (Kraków).

Prause, Fritz, Die polnische Presse im Kampf gegen die deutsche Volksgruppe in Posen und Westpreussen (Wuerzburg-Auemuhle, 1940).

Puttkamer, Karl, Die Misserfolge in der Polenpolitik (Berlin, 1913).

Rakowski, Kazimierz, Dzieje W. Księstwa Poznańskiego w zarysie 1815-1900 (Kraków, 1904).

Recke, Walther, Die polnische Frage als Problem der europaeischen Politik (Berlin, 1927).

Rhode, Gotthold, Geschichte der Stadt Posen (Neuendettelsau, 1953).

Rich, Norman, Friedrich von Holstein (Cambridge, 1965).

Richter, Kurt, Der Kampf um den Schulgesetzentwurf des Grafen Zedlitz-Truetzschler vom Jahre 1892 (Halle, 1934).

Rieger, Isolde, Die wilhelmische Presse in Ueberblick 1888-1918 (Muenchen, 1957).

Ritter, Gerhard, ed. Das Deutsche Kaiserreich 1871-1914 (Goettingen, 1977).

Roehl, John C.G., "A Document of 1892 on Germany, Prussia and Poland", in: Historical Journal 7 (1964).

____ "The Disintegration of the Kartell and the Politics of Bismarck's Fall from Power 1887-1890", in: Historical Journal 9 (1966).

____ Germany Without Bismarck (Berkeley, 1967).

Rosen, Hans, Das deutsche Gut in Posen und Pommerellen (Rosbach, 1972).

Rosenthal, Harry K., "The Election of Archbishop Stablewski", in: Slavic Review 28 (1969).

____ German and Pole. National Conflict and Modern Myth (Gainsville, Florida, 1976).

____ "Germans and Poles in 1890. Possibilities for a New Course", in: East European Quarterly 5 (1971).

____ "Nation or Class: the Bund der Landwirte and the Poles", in: Australian Journal of Politics and History 19 (1973).

____ "The Problems of Caprivi's Polish Policy", in: European Studies Review 2 (1972).

____ "The Prussian View of the Pole. The Significance of the Year 1894", in: Polish Review 26 (1972).

____ "Rivalry between Notables and Townspeople in Prussian Poland. The First Round", in: Slavonic and East European Review 49 (1971).

Rothfels, Hans, Bismarck, der Osten und das Reich (Darmstadt, 1960).

Rzepecki, Karol, Historya ustawy wyborczej pruskiej (Poznań, 1913).

____ Naprzód czy wstecz? (Poznań, 1912).

____ Pobudka wyborcza (Poznań, 1907).

Schaefer, Jurgen W., Kanzlerbild und Kanzlermythos in der Zeit des Neuen Kurses (Paderborn, 1973).

Schieder, Theodor, Das deutsche Kaiserreich von 1871 als Nationalstaat (Köln, 1961).

Schinkel, Friedrich, Polen, Preussen und Deutschland (Breslau, 1931).

Schmidt-Volkmar, Erich, Der Kulturkampf in Deutschland (Goettingen, 1962).

Schmitz, H.J., Geschichte des Netze-Warthelandes insbesondere der Grenzmark Posen-Westpreussen (Leipzig, 1941).

Schultz, Fritz, Die politische Tagespresse Westpreussens (Deutsch Krone, 1913).

Schulze, Heinz, Die Presse im Urteil Bismarcks (Leipzig, 1930).

Schumacher, Bruno, Geschichte Ost- und Westpreussens (Wuerzburg, 1959). Goettinger Arbeitskreis

Sievers, Hans-Christian, Die Innenpolitik des Reichskanzlers Caprivi. Unpublished Ph.D. thesis, Kiel, 1953.

Sitarek, Henryk, Rola kredytu w rozwoju gospodarki Wielkopolski na przełomie XIX i XX wieku. Bank Związku Spółek Zarobkowych w Poznaniu 1885-1918 (Poznań, 1977).

Six, Franz, Die Presse in Polen (Berlin, 1938).

Spatz, M., Die Kampforganisationen Neu-Polens (Muenchen, 1910).

Specht, Fritz, Die Reichstagswahlen 1867-1897 (Berlin, 1898).

Stański, Mieczysław, Heliodor Święcicki 1854-1923 (Poznań, 1983).

Stribrny, Wolfgang, Bismarck und die deutsche Politik nach seiner Entlassung 1890-1898 (Paderborn, 1977).

Szenic, Stanisław, Za zachodnią miedzą. Polacy w życiu Niemiec XVIII i XIX wieku (Warszawa, 1973).

Szymańska, Maria, Bibliografia miasta Poznania (Poznań, 1960).

Thimme, Annelise, Hans Delbrueck als Kritiker der wilhelmischen Epoche (Duesseldorf, 1955).

Tims, Richard W., Germanizing Prussian Poland (New York, 1941).

Tirrell, Sarah Rebecca, German Agrarian Politics after Bismarck's Fall (New York, 1951).

Trzeciakowski, Maria and Lech, W dziewiętnastowiecznym Poznaniu (Poznań, 1982).

Trzeciakowski, Lech, "Geneza powołania Floriana Stablewskiego na stolicę arcybiskupią gnieźnieńsko-poznańską", in: Polska Niemcy Europa, ed. Antoni Czubiński, (Poznań, 1977).

____ "Kształtowanie się obrazu Niemca w polskiej opinii publicznej w okresie rozbiorów", in: Śląski Kwartalnik Historyczny Sobótka 33 (1978).

____ "Kształtowanie się nowoczesnego społeczeństwa miejskiego (1815-1919)", in: Dzieje Inowrocławia, ed. Marian Biskup, (Inowrocław, 1978).

____ Pod pruskim zaborem 1850-1914 (Warszawa, 1973).

____ Polityka polskich klas posiadających w Wielkopolsce w erze Capriviego 1890-1894 (Poznań, 1960).

____ "Polskie ugrupowania polityczne zaboru pruskiego wobec Niemiec 1871-1918", in: Dzieje Najnowsze 4 (1972).

____ "The Prussian State and the Catholic Church in Prussian Poland 1871-1914", in: Slavic Review 26 (1967).

____ "Roman Szymański 1840-1908", in: Wielkopolanie XIX wieku, ed. Witold Jakóbczyk, (Poznań, 1969), vol. 2.

____ "Roman Szymański. Poglądy i praktyka polityczna", in: Acta Universitatis Wratislaviensis 543 (1981).

____ Walka o polskość miast Poznańskiego na przełomie XIX i XX wieku (Poznań, 1964).

Tyszkiewicz, Teresa, Sobótka 1869-1871 (Poznań, 1961).

Vogel, Walter, Die Organisation der amtlichen Presse und Propagandapolitik des Deutschen Reiches (Berlin, 1941).

Vosberg, Fritz, "Die polnischen Organisationen", in: Ostland 1 (1912).

Warschauer, Adolf, Deutsche Kulturarbeit in der Ostmark (Berlin, 1926).

Wegener, Leo, Der wirtschaftliche Kampf der Deutschen mit den Polen um die Provinz Posen (Posen, 1903).

Weddern, Georg von, Das schlafende Heer der Polen (Berlin, 1912).

Wehler, Hans-Ulrich, "Bismarcks Imperialismus und spaete Russlandpolitik unter dem Primat der Innenpolitik", in: Das kaiserliche Deutschland, ed. Michael Stuermer, (Duesseldorf, 1970).

____ Das Deutsche Kaiserreich 1871-1918 (Goettingen, 1980), Deutsche Geschichte vol. 9.

____ Krisenherde des Kaiserreichs 1871-1918 (Goettingen, 1979), 2nd edition.

____ "Die Polenpolitik in Deutschen Kaiserreich 1871-1914", in: Politische Ideologien und nationalstaatliche Ordnung, Festschrift fuer Theodor Schieder ed., Kurt Kluxen and Wolfgang Mommsen, (Muenchen, 1968).

____ Sozialdemokratie und Nationalstaat (Wuerzburg, 1962).

Weitowitz, Rolf, Deutsche Politik und Handelspolitik unter Reichskanzler Leo von Caprivi 1890-1894 (Duesseldorf, 1978).

Wendel, Hermann, Die preussische Polenpolitik (Berlin, 1908).

Wendt, Hans, Bismarck und die polnische Frage (Halle, 1922).

Werdermann, Johann, Die Heeresreform unter Caprivi (Greifswald, 1928).

Wereszycki, Henryk, Koniec sojuszu trzech cesarzy (Warszawa, 1977).

Wetzel, Hans Wolfgang, Presseinnenpolitik im Bismarckreich 1874-1890. Das Problem der Repression oppositioneller Zeitungen (Bern, 1975).

Whittle, Tyler, Kaiser Wilhelm II. Eine Biographie (Muenchen, 1979).

Wiegand, Berthold, Die anti-deutsche Propaganda der Polen von 1890 bis 1914 (Danzig, 1940).

Wielkopolski Słownik Biograficzny (Warszawa, 1981).

Wierzchosławski, Szczepan, Polski ruch narodowy w Prusach Zachodnich w latach 1860-1914 (Wrocław, 1980).

Witting, Richard, Das Ostmarken-Problem (Berlin, 1907).

Wójciak, Jerzy, Walka polityczna w wyborach do parlamentu Rzeszy i sejmu pruskiego w Poznańskiem w latach 1898-1914 (Warszawa-Poznań, 1981).

Wrzesiński, Wojciech, "Niemcy w polskiej myśli politycznej", in: Polska i jej sąsiedzi, ed. Henryk Zieliński, (Wrocław, 1975).

____ "Oblicze polityczne 'Dziennika Poznańskiego' w latach 1859-1914", in: Na warsztatach historyków polskiej myśli politycznej, ed. Henryk Zieliński, (Wrocław, 1980), vol. 4.

Young, Harry F., Maximilian Harden. Censor Germaniae (The Hague, 1959).

Zaleski, Zygmunt, "Koniec niewoli (od r. 1890 do dni naszych)", in: Roczniki Historyczne 1 (1925).

Zechlin, Egmont, Staatsstreichsplaene Bismarcks und Wilhelm II. 1890-1894 (Berlin, 1929).

Zimmermann, Kaziemierz, Ks. Patron Wawrzyniak (Kraków, 1911).

Zitzlaff, Franz, and Vosberg, Fritz, Preussische Stadte im Gebiete des polnischen Nationalitaetenkampfes (Leipzig, 1909).

ZUSAMMENFASSUNG

Das Ziel der vorliegenden Untersuchung ist, das Verhalten der polnischen Minderheit in Preußen in der Ära des Reichskanzlers Leo (seit 1891 Graf) von Caprivi, also den Jahren von 1890 bis 1894, unter besonderer Berücksichtigung der "polnischen Frage" zu analysieren. Die polnischsprachigen Presseorgane dieser Zeit - sechs Tageszeitungen und seit 1894 eine Wochenzeitung - dienten der Arbeit aus folgenden Erwägungen als grundlegendes Quellenmaterial: 1. Sie wurden bis heute nicht von der Forschung systematisch ausgewertet, obgleich sich sowohl die polnische als auch die deutsche Forschung - hier sei nur auf Witold Jakóbczyk, Tadeusz Cieślak, Lech Trzeciakowski, Wiktor Molik sowie Berthold Wiegand, Fritz Prause, Leonhard Müller und Walter Günzel verweisen - intensiv mit der Bedeutung der polnischsprachigen Presse beschäftigt hat. Hier wurde jedoch ein anderer zeitlicher und thematischer Schwerpunkt gesetzt. Gemessen an den in vielen Darstellungen zur preußischen Polenpolitik bereits umfangreich aufgearbeiteten Archivalien gehört die polnischsprachige Presse bis heute zu dem am wenigsten beachteten, bearbeiteten und zitierten Quellenmaterials.

2. Die polnischsprachigen Presseorgane gewähren einen hervorragenden Einblick in die Entwicklung der polnischen Gesellschaft unter preußischer Herrschaft. Sie enthalten umfangreiche Informationen über Fragen des politischen, kulturellen, sozialen, wirtschaftlichen und nationalen Lebens, die die preußischen Archivmaterialen nicht abzudecken vermögen.

3. In Anbetracht der wenigen existierenden polnischsprachigen Quellen kommt diesen Zeitungen besondere Bedeutung zu, denn nur wenige Polen hielten sich in diesen Jahren Zeitschriften, die Auflagen der wenigen gedruckten Bücher war klein und schließlich blieben nur einige Briefe in Bibliotheken und Archiven

erhalten. Eine Analyse des polnischen Bevölkerungsteils in den letzten Jahrzehnten wäre ohne die zeitgenössische polnische Presse nahezu unmöglich.
4. Schließlich müssen die Zeitungen selbst als bedeutender politischer Faktor betrachtet werden, zumal sich ihre Herausgeber, Redakteure und Journalisten zum Großteil aktiv für die nationalen Belange der Polen engagierten. Unter diesem Gesichtspunkt erscheint das Urteil, daß die Geschichte der polnischen Presse in der Ära Caprivi auch ein Teil der Geschichte des politischen Lebens Polens sei, berechtigt.
Ihre Artikel und Beiträge müssen aber mit Sorgfalt und Vorsicht interpretiert werden. Sie wurden unter einer doppelten Zensur verfaßt, nämlich der offiziellen staatlichen, die alle Äußerungen gegen die Krone oder Staatsbedienstete unterdrückte, und der Selbstzensur, die gemäß den Richtlinien des Herausgebers versuchte, bestimmte gewünschte Eindrücke unter der Leserschaft sowie der deutschen und polnischen öffentlichen Meinung hervorzurufen. So waren alle Zeitungen bestimmten Interessengruppen der polnischen Gesellschaft zuzuordnen: der Dziennik Poznański fungierte als Organ der "nationalliberalen" Grundbesitzer, der Kuryer Poznanski als Organ der Ultramontanen und der katholischen Geistlichkeit, der Goniec Wielkopolski als Organ der unversöhnlichen Nationalisten, der Wielkopolanin, der dem Verleger des Dziennik gehörte, wandte sich an die städtischen und ländlichen Unterschichten, der Orędownik war das Sprachrohr des aufstrebenden mittelständischen Bürgertum, während der Postęp dem Antisemitismus des Kleinbürgertums entgegenkam.
Jede dieser Zeitungen beanspruchte für sich das Monopol der einzig wahren Berichterstattung, so daß sie sich untereinander genauso oft im Pressekrieg befanden wie mit der deutschsprachigen Presse. Die heutige positive Auffassung des Journalismus als eine freie und meinungsunabhängige Untersuchung aller

Fakten war der polnischen Presse des ausgehenden 19. Jahrhunderts gänzlich unbekannt. Nicht immer wurde eindeutig zwischen Faktizität und Meinung getrennt. Zu oft blieben unliebsame Ereignisse unerwähnt, oder die Meldung wurde den eigenen Bedürfnissen "angepaßt".

Nicht zuletzt auf Grund dieser Tatsachen wurden noch weitere Quellen herangezogen. Von besonderer Bedeutung waren hierbei die ungedruckten Materialien, nämlich die im Polnischen Staatsarchiv Poznań liegenden Polizeiberichte der Stadt, die Berichte des Polnischen Zentralen Wahlkomitees (Akta Komitetu Prowincjonalnego Wyborczego na Wielkie Księstwo Poznańskie), die sich in der Raczyński Bibliothek befinden, und schließlich die Berichte über die Versammlungen der Polnischen Partei vor den Debatten im Preußischem Landtag (Protokoły posiedzień Koła sejmowego).

Wichtig und wertvoll waren auch die gedruckt vorliegenden stenographischen Protokolle des Reichstages und des Preußischen Landtages, die die Polen als einziges nichtzensiertes politisches Forum nutzen konnten. Gerade die damalige "Polendebatten" erfreuten sich ungeteilter Aufmerksamkeit der polnischen Öffentlichkeit.

Der zeitliche Rahmen der vorliegenden Arbeit wurden aus mehreren Gründen gewählt. Zum einen, weil in der Ära Caprivi der letzte Versuch gemäßigter Deutscher und Polen unternommen wurde, den nationalen Konflikt zu beenden und einen "modus vivendi" für beide Bevölkerungsteile in den östlichen Provinzen Preußens zu finden, ohne die staatliche Integrität in Frage zu stellen. Vor und nach der Capriviära war das deutsch-polnische Verhältnis durch gegenseitiges Mißtrauen, ausgeprägte Animositäten und zum Teil sogar durch Haß bestimmt. Zwischen 1890 und 1894 versuchten einflußreiche deutsche und polnische Kreise, die gemeinsamen Beziehungen unter Abbau der negativen Faktoren zu verbessern. Diese Anstrengungen, die oft scharfe polemische

Angriffe - z.B in der Presse - nach sich zogen, stießen jedoch innerhalb der jeweiligen nationalen Gruppierungen auf Unverständnis und Ablehnung.
Zum anderen vollzog sich in diesen vier Jahren in der polnischen Gesellschaft ein grundlegender Strukturwandel, der die führende Rolle des Adels, welcher seit den Teilungen Polens die polnische Gesellschaft dominierend war, endgültig beendete. An seine Stelle trat die politisch und wirtschaftlich aufstrebende Mittelklasse. So vollzog sich in der Capriviära nicht nur - wenn auch langsam - ein stetiger Modernisierungsprozeß der polnischen Gesellschaft, der von einem erweiterten Nationalbewußtsein begleitet wurde, sondern auch eine - allerdings von den Zeitgenossen bedauerte - Entwicklung der Politisierung der Gesellschaft, die Gründung mehrerer Parteien und somit eines von parteipolitischen Erwägungen bestimmten Lebens.
Die Capriviära stellte die bis dahin politisch weitgehend einheitliche polnische Minderheit vor eine schwere innere Belasterungsprobe, bekämpften sich doch die Polen auf Gründ verschiedener parteipolitischer Ziele mit größerer Heftigkeit als die ihnen feindlich gesonnenen Deutschen.

II.

Die jeweilige Bedeutung der einzelnen Tageszeitungen kann z.T. an ihren Auflagen gemessen werden, die nach Angaben der Polizei für das Frühjahr 1890 folgende Größenordnungen erreichten: Dziennik Poznański 1600-1700 Exemplare, Kuryer Poznański 1000, Wielkopolanin 10000, Goniec Wielkopolski 1000, Orędownik, 750, Postęp 350. Die Zahlenangaben für den Wielkopolanin sind jedoch irreführend, weil die Auflagenhöhe - durch die kostenlose Verteilung von seiten der Großgrundbesitzer - nicht seinen wirklichen Marktanteil widerspiegelt. Das gilt auch für den Postęp, dessen Auflage nur in den ersten

Monaten seines Erscheinens so gering war. Sie wuchs dank seiner Popularität schnell an und erreichte 1902 eine Höhe von 5000 Exemplaren.
Die Organisationsformen der einzelnen Presseorgane differierte. Teilweise befanden sie sich im Privatbesitz. Stanisław Knapowski gehörte der Postęp, Ludwik Rzepecki der Goniec und Roman Szymański der Orędownik. Die anderen drei waren Kapitalgesellschaften. Unter den Teilhabern des Dziennik befanden sich mehrere bekannte polnische Großgrundbesitzer, wie z.B. die Potockis, die Mielżyńskis und die Kwileckis. Der Kuryer erhielt von seiten der Familie Chłapowski und von seiten der katholischen Kirche umfangreiche finanzielle Unterstützung. Der Einfluß der Kirche blieb aber nicht allein auf Zahlungen beschränkt; einige Geistliche arbeiteten auch als Redakteure mit. Der Wielkopolanin gehöhte denselben Besitzern wie der Dziennik, erhielt aber auch von dem Bankier Mieczysław Łyskowski, dessen Einfluß auch auf polnische Zeitungen Westpreußens nicht zu unterschätzen ist, finanzielle Unterstützung. Die notwendigen Finanzmittel zum Unterhalt der Zeitungen wurde aus dem Verkauf, durch Anzeigen und Spenden gedeckt.
Wer sich in der zweiten Hälfte des 19. Jahrhunderts entschloß, eine Karriere als Journalist in den polnischen Provinzen Preußens zu machen, tat dies nicht aus finanziellen Erwägungen, sondern auf Grund persönlicher Überzeugung. Die Besitzer des Orędownik, Goniec, und Postęp waren beispielsweise gezwungen, ihren Lebensunterkunft durch die Ausübung eines weiteren Berufs zu bestreiten. Besonders in Zeiten, in denen die polnischsprachige Presse um ihre Existenz kämpfte - und dies galt in erster Linie für die weitreichenden Repressionen während des Kulturkampfes -, erhielten sie von Sympathisanten aus Galizien und Russisch-Polen umfangreiche Geldspenden. Zu den Kosten für Herstellung und Vertrieb kamen noch Geldstrafen oder Verhaftungen, mit denen die Zeitungen im Rahmen der Zensur konfrontiert wurden. Die Strafen beliefen

sich durchschnittlich auf 500 Mark und drei Monate Gefängnis für den verantwortlichen Redakteur. Darüber hinaus wurde von den Zeitungen erwartet, daß sie ein Beispiel für die polnische Gemeinschaft setzen und sich für die gemeinsamen Ziele engagierten, wie z.B. die Schaffung polnischer Büchereien oder Bildungseinrichtungen, Hilfsmaßnahmen für die Opfer der Hungersnot in Galizien, die Überführung der sterblichen Überreste Adam Mickiewicz von Paris nach Krakau usw.

Die preußische Pressezensur überwachte die polnischen Tageszeitungen von dem Tag ihrer Gründung an. Mit der Expansion des polnsichen Pressewesens wandelten sich auch die Überwachungsmethoden. Die Zensoren übersetzten regelmäßig verschiedene Artikel der Zeitungen und schickten sie an die dafür zuständigen Behörden in Berlin. In Poznań sammelte und editierte der maßgebende Zensor der polnischen Presse in den 90er Jahren, Raimund Zacher, das übersetzte und nach Berlin gesandte Material. 1892 hatte die Materialfülle Dimensionen erreicht, die Zacher veranlaßten, die Berichte zu drucken. Unter dem Titel "Gesamtüberblick über die polnische Tagesliteratur" erschienen 150 Exemplare. Die einflußreichste der 6 Zeitungen war der Dziennik Poznański, der als offizielles Sprachrohr des Zentralen Wahlkomitees galt. Als Stimme der überwiegenden Mehrheit des Adels, versuchte der Dziennik deren Interessen wahrzunehmen und ihre Hegemonie im politischen und sozialern Bereich der polnischen Minderheit aufrechtzuerhalten. Seit 1871 leitete der aus dem russischen Teil Polens stammende und nach dem gescheiterten Aufstand von 1863 im preußischen Exil lebende Franciszek Dobrowolski den Dziennik. Als einer der einflußreichsten Politiker Poznańs wurde er zum Vorsitzenden des örtlichen polnischen Komitees und zum Sekretär des Zentralen Wahlkomitees gewählt. Als Anwalt des sozialen Konservatismus und der Herrschaft des Adels lehnte der Dziennik strikt den Ultramontanismus ab, vernachlässigte wirtschaftliche

Fragen, verwahrte sich gegen die Verschwörungen und 'Legenden' polnischer Intrigen zur Störung des Friedens in Europa und verwarf kategorisch die Idee eines unabhängigen polnischen Staates unter Verzicht auf die Provinzen Posen und Westpreußen. Der Dziennik stand in Oppositon zur Volksbewegung (ruch ludowy) und war zutieftst beunruhigt über das Vordringen der Sozialdemokratie. Gleichzeitig hielt der Dziennik eine umfassende antisozialistische Kampagne für unter seiner Würde. Die Position des Dziennik gegenüber Preußen und dem Deutschen Reich war streng legalistisch - die polnische Bevölkerung Preußens sei solange zufrieden und loyal, wie die Wiener Kongreßakte Beachtung fände.

Die politische Zielsetzung des Kuryer Poznański war der des Dziennik ähnlich. Seit den Tagen des Kulturkampfes nahmen sich beide der Verteidigung der polnischen Sache in Preußen an. Der Kuryer bekannte sich offen zu einer ultramontanen Einstellung. Er sprach sich für einen größeren Einfluß der katholischen Kirche auf das öffentliche Leben aus und sah die Lösung der umfangreichen sozialen Probleme, die die Industrialisierung und Urbanisierung mit sich brachten, in einer Verschmelzung des Modernisierungsprozesses mit der christlichen Religion. Als einzige unter den polnischen Tageszeitungen wagte der Kuryer die Probleme eines "falschen Liberalismus" sowie kapitalistische Denkweise mit der einzig wahren Alternative der traditionellen christlichen Moral und Lehre zu konfrontieren. In Übereinstimmung mit der Papstbulle "Rerum Novarum" befürwortete die Zeitung die Gründung christlicher Arbeiterorganisationen (Gewerkschaften, Bildungsvereine). Nach dem erfolgreichen Betrieben des preußischen Kultusministeriums, den Chefredakteur Antoni Kantecki abzusetzen, trat dessen jüngerer Bruder Maksymilian an seine Stelle. Er leitete die Zeitung bis zu seinem Tod im Jahre 1899. Durch seine Loyalität in der Capriviära diskreditiert, wurde das Erscheinen des Kuryer

1905 eingestellt.Der 1877 von Ludwik Rzepecki und Władysław Niegolewski gegründete Goniec Wielkopolski übernahm unter den polnischen Zeitungen die Funktion einer permanenten Opposition. Dabei bediente er sich aller möglichen Argumentationsmuster: angefangen mit denen der etablierten Presse, über die der Volksbewegung und der preußischen Regierung, bis hin zu denen der Sozialisten. Hauptziel des Goniec war die Schaffung eines unabhängigen polnischen Staates, der mit einem festen Programm der Verneinung einer deutsch-polnischen Annäherung und Kultivierung patriotischer Werte eines Tages das Übel der Teilungen Polens vergessen lasse. Er überwand die Vorurteile des grundbesitzenden Adels und erkannte die Notwendigkeit der Modernisierung der polnischen Gesellschaft. Dabei lehnte er die Volksbewegung nicht von vornherein ab.

Der Wielkopolanin mit einer Auflage von 10000 Exemplaren war 1883 mit der Intention gegründet worden, die städtischen und agrarischen Unterschichten vor dem extremen Nationalismus des Goniec und den kriegerischen antifeudalistischen Bestrebungen des Orędownik zu bewahren. Der Wielkopolanin war auf die Bedürfnisse eines nur gering gebildeten Leserkreises zugeschnitten und wurde durch den Adel, dessen Interessen er wahrnahm, finanziert. Die Zeitung setzte sich ein für Ehrfurcht vor Kirche und Adel, regelmäßige Teilnahme an religiösen und natonalen Feierlichkeiten, Verurteilung "unpolnischen" Verhaltens - wie z.B. Besuch sozialdemokratischer Veranstaltungen, Emigration oder Alkoholismus - und schließlich die Ablehnung aller spaltenden Einflüsse der Volksbewegung. Der Sprachstil war dem eines bäuerlichen Publikums angepaßt. Darüber hinaus enthielt der Wielkopolanin praktische Hinweise, wie z.B. Ernteerträge gesteigert werden konnten und wie neue Werkzeuge zu handhaben waren.

Die wahrscheinlich beeindruckendste Persönlichkeit in den Kreisen der

polnischen Presse Poznańs war der Herausgeber des Orędownik, der "Vater der polnischen Mittelklasse", Roman Szymański. Seit 1871 vertrat er unerschütterlich die Auffassung, daß die Herrschaft des Adels anachronistisch geworden und die Zeit für die Mittelklasse gekommen sei, die ihr im Leben des polnischen Bevölkerungsteils zustehende Position einzunehmen. Szymański war Herz und Seele des Orędownik, der bis zu seinem Tod 1908 in seinem Besitz blieb, auch wenn er seit 1906 eine nationaldemokratische Position vertrat.
In Übereinstimmung mit seinem mittelständischen Leserkreis sah der Orędownik die Quellen des Reichtums im Handel und in der Industrie, nicht mehr aber in der Landwirtschaft. Aus diesem Grund hielt er auch die Vormachtstellung des Adels für obsolet. Unbeirrbar setzte sich Szymański für seine neue Form der Verteidigung der polnischen Identität ein: wirtschaftliches Wachstum und finanzielle Solidarität sollten bei Verletzung der Wiener Kongreßakte an die Stelle des bisherigen erfolglosen, verbalen Protests treten. Darüber hinaus sprach er sich mit dem Argument, daß Geistliche nichts in der Politik zu suchen hätten, für eine strikte Trennung von Staat und Kirche aus. Dieser eindeutige Bruch mit der polnischen Tradition bereitete ihm in der Capriviära, als er die Volksbewegung gegen die Verdächtigungen des Antikatholizismus zu verteidigen hatte, manch schlaflose Nacht.
Die Berichterstattung des von Stanisław Knapowski gegründeten Postep konzentrierte sich auf ein einziges Gebiet, nämlich den Antisemitismus. Die Mehrheit der kleinen Dienstleistungsbetriebe Poznans war in jüdischem Besitz; außerdem verfügten die Juden über eine starke Vertretung im Stadtrat. Der Ärger und Neid der aufstrebenden polnischen Mittelklasse über die nicht zu übersehende Dominanz der Juden im lokalen Handel und Gewerbe waren die ausschlaggebenden Faktoren für das erhebliche Ansteigen der Auflage des Postęp. Knapowski war von die Notwendigkeit überzeugt, die polnische Minder-

heit vor der "jüdischen Gefahr" zu warnen. In zahlreichen Reden, die er bei seiner ausgedehnten Reisen durch die Provinz hielt, klagte er in immer neuen Varianten die vermeintlich von Juden begangenen Verbrechen an.

Abschließend sei noch auf den seit April 1894 wöchentlich erscheinenden Przegląd Poznański verwiesen. Diese Kulturjournal wurde von zahlreichen Intellektuellen wie z.B. dem talentierten jungen Rechtsanwalt Bernard Chrzanowski sowie den Ärzten Bolesław Krysiewicz und Tomasz Drobnik unter Leitung des Chefredakteurs Władysław Rabski geführt. Aber nicht durch ihre unbestreitbaren beruflichen Fähigkeiten, sondern vielmehr durch ihre Funktion als Träger der ersten nationaldemokratischen Bewegung im preußischen Teil Polens erwarben sie sich ihren Nachruhm. Unter Rabskis Führung erwies sich der Przeglad als scharfer Kritiker der politischen Organisation der Polen. Insgeheim unterstützte er die Volksbewegung. Auf Grund finanzieller Schwierigkeiten, die vor allem auf einen vom Adel initiierten Boykottaufruf gegen die Zeitschrit zurückzuführen waren, mußte das Erscheinen des Przeglad 1896 eingestellt werden.

III.

Die Anfänge einer loyalen Einstellung der Polen zu Preußen können bis zu dem Zeitpunkt zurückverfolgt werden, als ein Generationswechsel innerhalb der führenden aristokratischen und bürgerlichen Familien stattfand. Die Generation, die den Völkerfrühlung von 1848 und den zum Scheitern verurteilten Aufstand in Russisch-Polen im Januar 1863 miterlebt hatte, starb in den 80er Jahren aus. Ihre Söhne wurden hauptsächlich von den Grundsätzen des Positivismus beeinflußt, lehnten dementsprechend die Vorstellung von Konspiration und Aufstand ab und traten für eine größere Mitwirkung am

wirtschaftlichen und politischen Leben der jeweiligen Teilungsmacht ein.
Die entscheidende Zäsur für den Übergang von der unversöhnlichen Opposition zur Bereitschaft zu einer konstruktiven Loyalität kam 1884, als der Reichstagsabgeordnete und überzeugte Gegner eines Versöhnungskurses, Władysław Niegolewski, nicht wieder als Kandidat für die Reichstagswahlen im Bezirk Poznań nominiert wurde. An seine Stelle trat der Befürworter eines Versöhnungskurses, Stefan Cegielski.
Während der kurzen Herrschaft Friedrich III.. wurden die ersten Anzeichen dafür sichtbar, daß die Vertreter des Versöhnungskurses in der Mehrheit waren. Beide Flügel übersandten dem im Sterben liegenden Kaiser Loyalitätsadressen. Sie wurden erst Ende April 1888 beantwortet, und zwar nicht von Friedrich III., sondern von Bismarck in einer Art, die in polnischen Kreisen als grobe Beleidigung empfunden wurde. Hierunter litt die Position der Befürworter einer Annäherung ganz erheblich.
Erst zwei Jahre später, nach den Reichstagswahlen vom Februar 1890, bei denen die Kartell-Parteien schwere Einbußen erlitten, ergab sich für die Polen eine neue Möglichkeit, die durch die Entlassung Bismarcks im März noch weiteren Auftrieb erhielt. Drei Tage vor Bismarcks Entlassung hatten 16 polnische Politiker, die in Poznań zusammengekommen waren, den Entschluß gefaßt, Kooperationsbereitschaft mit der neuen Regierung zu zeigen. Eine Reihe von Faktoren begünstigten die Position der Anhänger der späteren Hofpartei (partya dworska). Wilhelm II. hatte sich zum Beginn seiner Regierung nicht nur gegen die Ausbeutung der Arbeit ausgesprochen, sondern auch Bismarck entlassen und gleichzeitig zu verstehen gegeben, daß er eine Verlängerung des Sozialistengesetzes, das die Polen entscheiden ablehnten, nicht beabsichtige. Auch eine Reihe deutschsprachiger Zeitungen forderte eine angemessenere Polenpolitik. Dieses galt im besonderen für die konservative Kreuzzeitung und die

fortschrittliche Freisinnige Zeitung. Hinzu kam, daß der neue Reichskanzler und preußische Ministerpräsident, Leo von Caprivi, seine Bereitschaft erklärt hatte, mit allen Parteien zum Wohl des Staates zusammenzuarbeiten und von der Politik des Kulturkampfes Abstand zu nehmen. Die Polen begrüßten ähnlich wie die übrigen Oppositionsparteien Caprivis Erklärung und hofften, daß sie für ein Deutschland stehe, das sich zum Parlamentarismus, zur Legalität und zur Verfassung bekenne.

Im Juni 1890 bot sich den Polen im Rahmen der Abstimmung über die Heeresvorlage die erste Möglichkeit, ihre veränderte Haltung zur Reichsregierung unter Beweis zu stellen. Bis zu diesem Zeitpunkt hatten die Polen konsequent gegen jede Vermehrung der deutschen Streitkräfte votiert. Dieses Mal jedoch rief die Heeresvorlage schwerwiegende Kontroversen in Poznań hervor. Lediglich der Kuryer befürwortete eine Annahme der Vorlage. Die übrigen Zeitungen vertraten die Ansicht, daß die Mehrausgaben die möglichen positive Auswirkungen - infolge der Annahme der Vorlage durch die Polen - mehr als aufwögen. Für den Kuryer hingegen bot die Annahme der Vorlage den nicht zu unterschätzenden Vorteil, die Aufmerksamkeit der Militärs - wie z.B. Caprivis auf die staatstragende Funktion der Polen zu lenken. Die Haltung der polnischen Reichstagsfraktion schien umso verständlicher, als auch das Zentrum - der parlamentarische Verbündete der Polen - die Vorlage billigte. Die Gegner der Vorlage wiesen darauf hin, daß die polnische Minderheit kaum in der Lage wäre, die erhöhten Steuern zur Finanzierung des Militäretats aufzubringen. Auch sei es die Aufgabe des neuen Reichskanzlers, als erster die Versöhnung mit den Polen anzustreben. Da nicht sie dem preußischen Staat Krieg erklärt hatten, sei es nicht ihre Aufgabe, von sich aus Frieden zu schließen.

Die polnische Reichstagsfraktion votierte schließlich für die Vorlage und erntete dafür den Beifall der deutschen, aber die schwere Kritik der eigenen

Presse.

Den Gegnern des neuen polnischen Kurses gab die Besetzung des Erzbistums von Gniezno-Poznan nach dem Tode des Erzbischofs Julius Dinder Ende Mai 1890 - während des Höhepunktes der Debatte über die Heeresvorlage - ein weiteres Argument in die Hand. Durch die schnelle Nominierung eines qualifizierten polnischen Geistlichen hätte Caprivi die Polen wahrscheinlich langfristig für sich vereinnahmen können. Aber unter dem Einfluß des Kultusministers Gustav von Goßler, verwarf Caprivi eine ihm von der Kirche vorgelegte, sechs Kandidaten umfassende Liste als unannehmbar, weil sie den staatlichen Interessen zuwiderlief. Mit der Ablehnung der Kandidaten wurde die Frage der Besetzung bis Ende 1891 vertagt.

Eines der größten Rätsel des deutsch-polnischen Annäherungsversuches war, daß die Polen nicht Willens bzw. nicht in der Lage waren, die ökonomischen Vorteile der Gesetzgebung in der Caprivi-Ära wahrzunehmen. Die Annahme der überaus wichtigen Rentengutsgesetze in den Jahren 1890 und 1891 gewährte den Polen die Möglichkeit, Kredite vom preußischen Staat zu erhalten und so die negativen Auswirkungen der Politik der Ansiedlungskommission auszugleichen. Die Rentengutsgesetze fanden jedoch in der polnischen Presse keine Beachtung. Die Vernachlässigung ökonomischer Belange mag zum einen auf die strenge Auslegung der sog. "polnischen nationalen Rechte" und zum anderen auf die Furcht der Polen zurückzuführen sein, durch positive Einschätzungen der Rentengutsgesetze zu einer Gesetzeänderung im deutschen Sinne beizutragen.

IV.

Der Höhepunkt der polnisch-deutschen Verständigung kam im Jahr 1891 mit einer Reihe von begrentzten, aber bedeutsamen Konzessionen. Der erste Schritt in in diese Richtung war die Entscheidung des Innenministers Ludwig Herrfurth, das Einreiseverbot von Saisonarbeitern aus Galizien und Russisch-Polen nach Preußen zu modifizieren. Während das Einreiseverbot die Regierungspläne einer Germanisierung der polnischen Provinzen eindeutig vorantrieb, führte es gleichzeitig zu kritischen Engpässen an billigen Arbeitskräften während der Erntezeit und zu schweren finanziellen Verlusten der Gutsbesitzer. Bismarck war darauf vorbereiten gewesen, dieses zu akzeptieren, und hatte dahingehend argumentiert, daß die Festigung der östlichen preußischen Grenzgebiete vorrangig wäre. Aber sein Nachfolger schien anderer Meinung zu sein. Ende 1890 gab Caprivi zahlreichen Petitionen von ostelbischen Gutsbesitzern nach, die sich über das Einreiseverbot beklagten und erließ eine Lockerung des Gesetzes.

Diese Entscheidung wurde von Poznańs Adelpresse begrüßt, obwohl die Zeitungen gleichzeitig darauf hinwiesen, daß nur eine Aufhebung des ungerechten Gesetzes von 1885 den chronischen Arbeitskräftemangel auf dem Lande zur Erntezeit beseitigen könne. Während der gesamten Kanzlerschaft Caprivis forderte die polnische Presse weitergehende Konzessionen in diesem Bereich, hatte damit aber keinen erfolg.

Der langerwartete Ministerwechsel in Berlin im März 1891 signalisierte für viele den Beginn des Aufgebens der Schul- und Sprachenpolitik Bismarcks gegenüber der polnischen Minderheit. Am 8. März wurde der Kultusminister Goßler entlassen und durch den Oberpräsidenten von Posen, Robert Graf von Zedlitz-Trützschler, ersetzt. Am 11. April 1891 gab Zedlitz-Trützschler eine Verordnung heraus, nach der der private Unterricht der polnischen Sprache in staatlichen Schulen, durchgeführt von staatlichen Lehrern, gestattet werden sollte, sofern die Kosten dafür von der polnischen Gemeinde getragen würden. Die ursprünglich enthusiastische Reaktion der polnischen Presse auf diese

Verordnung schlug um, als bekannt wurde, wieviel dieser Unterricht kosten würde. Obwohl die Zeitungen eine beispiellose Pressekampagne starteten, um Geld für diesen Zweck zu sammeln, stellte es bald heraus, daß eine geregelte Finanzierung dieses Unterrichts in allen Teilen der Provinz unmöglich war. Der Oredownik und der Postep begannen, das Edikt einfach als eine neue Steuer zu beschreiben, die der polnischen Gemeinde auferlegt wurde. Bald forderten alle Zeitungen eine vollständige Aufnahme der polnischen Sprache in die Lehrpläne der Schulen.

Ein Bereich, in dem die polnisch-deutsche Annäherung aussichtsreich war, aber nicht durchgesetzt wurde, war eine allgemeine Kampagne gegen die Sozialdemokratie. Prominente Polen und Deutsche waren sich in der Überzeugung einig, daß die Sozialdemokratie eine schwere Bedrohung der sozialen und wirtschaftlichen Stabilität im preußischen Osten darstellte, und bildeten im Juli 1891 einen gemeinsamen Ausschuß, um ihr entgegenzuwirken. Die Bildung dieses Ausschusses wurde von der polnischen Presse begrüßt, die sich in ihrer Ablehnung des Sozialismus einig war. Nichtsdestoweniger kam der Ausschuß in der Sache nicht weiter, da es die Polen ablehnten, nur Deutsch als Sitzungssprache anzuerkennen. Die Presse spielte in diesem Zusammenhang eine einflußreiche Rolle, da sie auf der Gleichberechtigung der polnischen Sprache neben dem Deutschen bestand.

Die Hofpartei erlebte ihren Höhepunkt im November 1891, als Florian Stablewski zum Erzbischof von Gniezno-Poznan und gemäß der Tradition gleichzeitig zum Primas von Polen ernannt wurde. Seine Ernennung war ein unbestreitbar Sieg für den Kuryer, der der Auffassung war, daß die Politik des Ausgleiches mit Preußen ihre Funktionstüchtigkeit unter Beweis gestellt habe und in Zukunft noch mehr Früchte trüge, wenn nur die Polen fest zu dem 1890 verabschiedeten Programm der Loyalisten ständen. Der Dziennik war sich der Tatsache bewüßt,

daß diese Ernennung weniger eine Konzession an die Polen war als vielmehr die Einsicht, daß die Ernennung eines Deutschen unklug und nicht durchführbar gewesen wäre. Der Orędownik kritisierte seit längerem Stablewskis antirussische Äußerungen, versprach aber dennoch, ihn zu akzeptieren.
Die Ernennung Stablewskis war der Höhepunkt der deutsch-polnischen Annäherung in der Capriviära. Es zeigte sich jedoch gleichzeitig, wie beschränkt die Kräfte, die diese Annäherung befürworteten, waren. Die Ernennung brachte die deutschen nationalistischen Kreise auf, stieß aber auch bei Gemäßigten wie z.B. dem deutschen Botschafter in Sankt Petersburg, von Schweinitz, auf Ablehnung und belastete zusätzlich das Verhältnis zu Rußland. Bei vielen Zeitgenossen erweckte Caprivi den Eindruck, er wolle den preußischen Polen eine führende Rolle in einem künftigen Konflikt mit Rußland zuweisen. Dieser Eindruck wurde durch die russisch-französische Annäherung (und deren späteren Vertrag) noch gestärkt.

V.

Die Aussichten für eine Verlängerung der deutsch-polnischen Versöhnungsbemühungen verschlechterten sich in dem als Übergangsperiode zu bezeichnenden Zeitraum von 1892 bis Fruhjahr 1893. Gleichzeitig belasteten mehrere Ereignisse das bilaterale Verhältnis nachhaltig. Als erstes Ereignis muß hier die Zurücknahme der Zedlitz-Trützschlerischen Schulreform im März 1892 genannt werden. Die Polen und das Zentrum hatten das Gesetz begrüßt, und jene hielten ihre Position selbst noch zu einem Zeitpunkt aufrecht, als Zedlitz-Trützschler spezifische Sprachrechte ausgeschlossen hatte.
Die Rücknahme des Schulgesetzes zog eine Kabinettsumbildung nach sich: Robert Bosse ersetzte Zedlitz-Trützschler als Kultusminister, Botho Graf zu

Eulenburg wurde an Caprivis Statt preußischer Ministerpräsident und in August des Jahres auch noch Ludwig Herrfurths Nachfolger als Innenminister. Sowohl Bosse als auch Eulenburg waren überzeugte Gegner weiterer Zugeständnisse an den polnischen Bevölkerungsteil. Aus diesem Grunde nahmen die polnischen Zeitungen ihre Ernennung mit Besorgnis entgegen. Die Vorwürfe gegen die "großpolnische Agitation" mehrten sich. Führende deutsche Politiker waren über das wachsende polnische Nationalbewüßtsein in Oberschlesien zunehmend beunruhigt. Dies kam Anfang 1893 in mehreren Debatten im Preußischen Landtag offen zum Vorschein.
Die vielleicht stärkste destruktivte Kraft in der polnisch-deutschen Verständigung während des Übergangsjahres war der entlassene Fürst Bismarck. Bismarck hielt eine loyale Einstellung der Polen für absolut ausgeschlossen. Für ihn waren die Polen Intriganten, die nur auf die Gelegenheit warteten, ihre frühere anarchistische Republik und "Adelstyrannei" wieder zu errichten. In meherern Interviews sowie in den Reden von Erfurt und Jena verurteilte Bismarck die Polenpolitik des Neuen Kurses nachdrücklich, weil sie die Erfolge der Germanisierungspolitik der vergangenen Jahre zunichte mache. Die polnischen Zeitungen waren über die erneuten Angriffe Bismarcks nicht überrascht. Betroffen waren sie jedoch über die große Resonanz, die Bismarck bei seinen öffentlichen Auftritten erzielte.
Der Dziennik, der ohnehin kein überzeugter Vertreter der Annäherung zwischen Polen und Deutschen war, zeigte sich erbittert über die scharfen antipolnischen Attacken der Bismarckpresse und kam zu dem Schluß, daß in der preußischen Polenpolitik der letzten Jahre kein grundlegender Wandel stattgefunden habe. Allein der Kuryer forderte die Fortsetzung einer loyalen Politik gegenüber Caprivi, weil die Tätigkeit als "Regierungspartei" mehr Erfolge verspreche als die in der Opposition.

Der wesentlichste Faktor, der zur Beschränkung der antipolnischen Ressentiments beitrug, war die drohende Gefahr eines Zweifrontenkrieges gegen Rußland und Frankreich. In diesen Zusammenhang gewannen die schon früher erwogenen Überlegungen des preußischen Generalstabes, die "polnische Karte" in einem kommenden Krieg zu nutzen, neuen Auftrieb. Durch die Bildung einer polnischen Armee unter deutschem oder österreichischem Kommando sollte nicht nur die russische Armee paralysiert, sondern auch gleichzeitig eine Insurrektion der Bevölkerung in Russisch-Polen hervorgerufen werden.
In diesem Kontext ist es notwendig, die Frage zu erörtern, inwieweit die preußischen Polen bereit waren, solche Überlegungen zu unterstützen. Die Aussagen hierzu sind mehrdeutig. Der polnischen Presse ist zu entnehmen, daß keiner einen Krieg gegen Rußland wünschte. Die Polen zogen es vielmehr vor, auf die "göttliche Gerechtigkeit", den Tag der allgemein Neugestaltung Europas auf demokratischer und nationaler Basis zu warten. Aktive Maßnahmen zur Entfesselung eines europäischen Krieges bzw. zur Erlangung der polnischen Unabhängigkeit wurden abgelehnt. Dieser Ansicht waren alle Zeitungen mit Ausnahme des Goniec. Aber auch dieser verwarf die Überlegung, sich mit einer der Teilungsmächte gegen eine andere zu verbünden. Allen sechs Zeitungen war die Überzeugung gemein, einen polnischen Staat in den Grenzen von 1772 unter Ausschluß der Provinzen Posen und Westpreußen abzulehnen.
Die Archivalien preußischer Ministerien sowie die Erinnerungen führender deutscher Staatsmänner zeichen jedoch ein anderes Bild. Ein Teil der polnischen Adels um Kościelski begrüßte demnach einen Krieg Österreich-Ungarns und des Deutschen Reiches gegen Rußland. Diese Überlegungen waren besonders unter den Magnaten und führenden Polen Galiziens und Russisch-Polens populär. Es ist bemerkenswert, daß die Presse diese Bestrebungen einflußreicher polnischer Kreise, die das Thema auf höchster Ebene mit deutschen Stellen

erörterten, nicht einmal annährend wiedergab.

VI.

Im Frühjahr 1893 hatte die Mehrheit der Polen ihren Glauben in die Politik eines "blinden" Loyalismus, der noch immer das Credo der Reichstagsfraktion war, verloren. Folgender Standpunkt trat dabei in den Vordergrund, nämlich Caprivis im Prinzip verständnisvolle Politik solange zu unterstützen, solange sie nicht zu Lasten der polnischen Bevölkerung ginge. Die mit der "Großen Heeresvorlage" von 1893 verbundenen steuerlichen Mehrbelastungen wurden von den Zeitungen Dziennik, Wielkopolanin, Goniec und Postęp als inakzeptabel empfunden. Szymański vom Orędownik befürwortete die Heeresvorlage, vermochte aber mit seiner höchst verworrenen Argumentation nicht einmal seine engsten Freunde und Anhänger zu überzeugen. Er schrieb, daß die Polen, unabhängig von der Annahme oder Ablehnung der Heeresvorlage, zum Leiden verurteilt seien. Durch eine Unterstützung der Vorlage bestünde hingegen die Möglichkeit, die Glaubwürdigkeit der Polen in den Augen der preußischen Regierung zu heben. Der Kuryer hatte im Gegensatz zum Jahr 1890 große Schwierigkeiten, seine Befürwortung der Vorlage zu begründen. Diese Vorlage erlangte nicht nur den Polen größe finanzielle Opfer ab, sondern wurde auch von der Zentrumspartei, die großen Einfluß auf die polnische Reichstagsfraktion ausübte, abgelehnt. Die polnische Reichstagsfraktion stimmte allen Bedenken zum Trotz für die Heeresvorlage. Dennoch erhielt Caprivi keine Mehrheit im Reichstag und schrieb für den 15. Juni 1893 Neuwahlen aus. Das Abstimmungsverhalten ihrer Reichstagsfraktion rief unter der polnischen Bevölkerung massiven Protest hervor. Vor allen in den größeren Städten wie Poznań, Bromberg und Inowrocław stießen die Mitglieder der Hofpartei auf große Schwierigkeiten, als Kandidaten für die Neuwahlen bestätigt zu werden.

Obgleich sich die Reichstagsfraktion der Tatsache bewußt sein mußte, daß die Mehrheit der Polen nicht mehr die Politik der Hofpartei unterstützte, votierte sie Anfang Juli erneut für die Vorlage und gab damit den Ausschlag zugunsten Caprivis. Die polnischsprachigen Zeitungen mit Ausnahme des Kuryer waren verstimmt über die klare Mißachtung der öffentlichen Meinung seitens der Reichstagsfraktion. Der Dziennik - eigentlich eine Stütze des Adels, brachte zwar ebenfalls sein Mißfallen zum Ausdruck, versicherte aber gleichzeitig, Ruf und Wurde der einzelnen Reichstagsdelegierten zu verteidigen. Der Goniec hingegen bezeichnete die Abgeordneten als Verräter und verglich ihr Verhalten mit dem der Magnaten während der Teilungen. Der Orędownik und der Postęp erklärten, daß dieses Abstimmungsverhalten Resultat des unentschlossenen und geteilten Adels sei, der seinen Einfluß auf die Politik verloren habe, und forderten den Mittelstand auf, an dessen Stelle zu treten. Der Postęp fügte noch hinzu, daß sich die Reichstagsfraktion "an die Juden verkauft" habe. Lediglich der Kuryer begrüßte das Abstimmungsverhalten und hoffte, daß die Regierung Zugeständnisse machen werde.

VII.

Nach der großen innerpolnischen Krise zwischen den Anhängern der Volksbewegung und des grundbesitzenden Adels verlagerte sich 1894 das Hauptgewicht der politischen Auseinandersetzungen nach Berlin.

Nach langen und kontroversen Debatten entschloß sich die polnische Reichstagsfraktion, Caprivi bei den Abstimmungen über die Handelsverträge mit Rumänien und Rußland, die den Interessen des polnischen grundbesitzenden Adels diametral zuwiderliefen, zu unterstützen. Anders als bei der Heeresvorlage war die öffentliche Meining in diesem Fall geteilt. Während der Kuryer und die Volkspresse überzeugte Verfechter der Verträge waren, lehnten sie der Dziennik und Goniec kategorisch ab. Der Dziennik vertrat die Auffassung, daß die überwiegend agrarisch strukturierte polnische Bevölkerung als Ganzes unter den Verträgen zu leiden hätte und daß es nicht im polnischen Interesse sein könne, ohne deutsche Gegenleistung weitere Opfer für ein stärkeres Deutschland zu erbringen. Der Kuryer argumentierte, daß Caprivi, unabhängig von den möglichen Folgen, unterstützt werden müsse. Die Volksblätter - als Sprachrohr der städtischen Bevölkerung - unterstützten die Verträge aus ähnlichen Grunden wie die deutschen Parteien, nämlich wegen der niedrigen Nahrungsmittelpreise und der Hebung des allgemeinen Lebensstandards in den Städten.

Trotz massiver Proteste von seiten polnischer Agrarier stimmte die polnische Reichstagsfraktion beiden Handelsverträgen zu. Es war das letzte Mal, daß sich der blinde Loyalismus durchzusetzen vermochte. Trotz der Sympathie, die Caprivi in polnischen Kreisen genoß, waren sie nicht länger bereit, eine Politik zu unterstützen, die ihren Interessen zuwiderlief.

Ein erstes Zeichen für diese neue Einstellung der Reichstagsfraktion war ihre Enthaltung bei der Abstimmung im März 1894 über den Bau zweier Panzerkreuzer. Kościelski gab aus Protest sein Mandat zurück. Führerlos geworden, brach die loyalistische Plattform der Reichstagsfraktion zusammen.

Im März kündigte der Kultusminister ein neues Gesetz zur Regelung der Sprachenfrage für polnische Kinder in den Volksschulen an. In den ersten beiden Schuljahren sollten wöchentlich zwei Stunden Polnisch gelehrt, der Privatunterricht aber verboten werden. Während diese Regelung deutscherseits als weiteres Zugeständnis verstanden wurde, empfanden die Polen sie als ungenügend und beleidigend. Bosses Verfügung wurde als zusätzliches Anzeichen des Scheiterns der Hofpartei interpretiert. Lediglich der Kuryer wagte es, die

Sprachenregelung als Konzession zu bezeichnen.
Drei Ereignisse im September 1894 besiegelten das Schicksal des Versöhnungskurses endgültig. Kościelski hielt in Lwów eine umstrittene Rede, in der die polnische Nation als unverletzliche Einheit bezeichnete - ein Terminus, den zahlreiche deutsche Journalisten als eine Verletzung der staatlichen Integrität Preußens verstanden. Während die Adelspresse die Rede ohne Kommentar abdruckte, kritisierten der Goniec und der Orędownik die inkonsistente Haltung Kościelskis, der ohne Schwierigkeiten vom preußischen zum polnischen Patriotismus übergegangen sei. Im selben Monat hielt Bismarck vor Deutschen aus den Provinzen Posen und Westpreußen, die sich auf sogenannten "Huldigungsfahrten" befanden, zwei Reden, in denen er seine alten Argumente gegen Caprivis Politik auflistete. Die polnischsprachige Presse reagierte betroffen auf diese Reden - nicht wegen ihres Inhalts, sondern vielmehr deswegen, weil es sich bei den Zuhörern um ihre unmittelbaren deutscher Nachbarn handelte. Ein Gutteil der Logik des Versöhnungskurses basierte auf der Überlegung, daß Deutsche und Polen friedlich miteinander leben könnten, gäbe es nicht die Einmischung des Preußischen Staates im Form der staatlich unterstützten Germanisierungsbestrebungen. Widerlegte aber nicht gerade die Anwesenheit zahlreicher glühender Verehrer bei dem ehemaligen Reichskanzler diese Überzeugung?
Am 22. September 1894 hielt Wilhelm II. eine Rede in Thorn, die mit der eindeutigen Warnung an die Polen endete, entweder preußische Staatsbürger zu werden oder sich den kaiserlichen Unwillen zuzuziehen. Es war für die öffentliche Meinung der preußischen Polen nicht einfach zu verstehen, warum der Kaiser mit ihrem Verhalten nicht zufrieden sei, hatten sie sich doch seit Bismarcks Entlassung als loyale Untertanen verhalten. Einen Monat später trat Caprivi von seinem Amt zurück. Damit hatte der letzte einflußreiche Politiker,

der Sympatien für die Polen hegte, die politische Bühne in Berlin verlassen. Viele Polen waren damit zufrieden, daß die von den Deutschen drohende Gefahr zu einem Zusammenschluß der gespalteten Teile der polnischen Gesellschaft geführt hatte. Viele betrachteten ein gespanntes deutsch-polnisches Verhältnis als "normalen" Zustand und lehnten deshalb weitere Versuche einer Versöhnung zwischen den beiden Nationalitäten als Belastung der Einheit des polnischen Bevölkerungsteiles ab.

VIII.

Aus der Betrachtung der polnischsprachigen Presse der Jahre 1890-1890 lassen sich zwei grundlegende Schlüsse ziehen. Der eine betrifft die Entwicklung der polnischen Gesellschaft unter preußischer Herrschaft, der andere den weiteren Kontext deutsch-polnischer Beziehungen in der Capriviära.

1. Es erweist sich als gesicherte Erkenntnis, daß die polnischsprachige Presse eine instrumentale Funktion bei der Gestaltung politischer Angelegenheiten des polnischen Bevölkerungsteils in Poznań und der ganzen Provinz Posen wahrnahm. Die politischen Strömungen richteten sich nicht nur nach den Zeitungen, sondern vielmehr wirkten auch ihre Redakteure und Herausgeber als maßgebliche Politiker an den Entscheidungen mit. Infolge der Lockerung den Zensurbestimmungen in der Capriviära ist es möglich, die sozialen und politischen Konflikt während des Versöhnungskurses genauer zu beleuchten. Die Auswertung der polnischen Presse gewährt Einblick in ein anachronistisches politisches System, nämlich die politische Hegemonie des grundbesitzenden Adels, dessen ökonomische Vormachtstellung durch die zunehmende Urbanisierung und Industrialisierung untergraben wurde. Der Anspruch des Adels als letzte Instanz politischer Entscheidung zu wirken, wurde durch die aufstrebende

städische Mittelschicht gefährdet. Die Beendigung des Versöhnungskurses der Capriviära fungierte als Katalysator einer Wiederherstellung der polnischen politischen Organisation. Die Presseorgane spielten beim Zerschlagen des Machtmonopols des Adels die entscheidende Rolle: sie diskreditierten die Führung des Adels, hinterfragten dessen Machtanspruch und politisierten den bürgerlichen Mittelstand. Innerhalb kurzer Zeit konnte die nationaldemokratische Partei die Früchte dieser Arbeit ernten.

2. In Bezug auf das Scheitern des Versöhnungskurses machten sowohl deutsche als auch polnische Politiker die polnischsprachigen Zeitungen verantwortlich, weil diese die Glaubwürdigkeit der Hofpartei angezweifelt habe. Mit Ausnahme des Kuryer war die Presse besonders nach 1892 kritisch bis feindschaftlich eingestellt. Die Presse forderte erkennbare Resultate und Fortschritte, z.B. die Aufhebung der von Bismarck verabschiedeten antipolnischen Gesetzgebung. Hätte Caprivi seine Überzeugung in aller Öffentlichkeit Ausdruck verliehen, die Germanisierungsbestrebungen aus der Bismarckzeit zu korrigieren, wären die Erfolgsaussichten der Hofpartei gut gewesen. Aber die Dichotomie seiner Politik sowie die heftigen Angriffe seiner Kritiker überzeugte die Polen, daß es auf deutscher Seite keinen äquivalenten Partner für eine Versöhnung gab. Welches Bild hatten die polnischen Zeitungen von den Deutschen in der Capriviära? Das Ergebnis ist nicht eindeutig. Es wurde zwischen sog. "guten" Deutschen , zu denen Hans Delbrück und der Führer des Zentrums Ludwig Windthorst, gehörten, und den "schlechten" Deutschen, der chauvinistischen Bismarck-Fronde und den gnadenlosen, unmenschlichen preußischen Beamten, unterschieden. Zum Ende der Capriviära dominierte die zweite Kategorie in der Berichterstattung der polnischen Presse. Vor allem die beiden Huldigungsfahrten Deutscher aus den Provinzen Posen und Westpreußen zu Bismarcks Aufenthaltsort in Varzin im September 1894 bestärkten die Polen in ihrer Einschätzung,

daß der "durchschnittliche" Deutsche mit den Ansichten Bismarcks sympathisierte und die Polen als Menschen zweiter Klasse behandelte. Der deutsch-polnische Antagonismus in Preußens östlichen Provinzen mußte solange ein ungelöstes Problem bleiben, wie die territorialen Ansprüche auf Posen und Westpreußen ungeklärt blieben. Eine der beiden Nationalitäten mußte zum territorialen Verzicht bereit sein. Seit den Teilungen Polens hatten die Polen ihren Anspruch auf diese Gebiete nie aufgegeben; in der Zeit der Weimarer Republik waren die Deutschen nicht bereit, den Verlust der Gebiete anzuerkennen. Eine vollständige deutsch-polnische Versöhnung erscheint erst möglich, wenn gegenseitige territoriale Forderungen kein Hindernis mehr bildeten.

I n d e x :

Z